The Politics of American Foreign Policy

The POLITICS *of* AMERICAN FOREIGN POLICY

How Ideology Divides Liberals and Conservatives over Foreign Affairs

PETER HAYS GRIES

STANFORD SECURITY STUDIES

An Imprint of Stanford University Press

Stanford, California

Stanford University Press
Stanford, California

Library of Congress Cataloging-in-Publication Data

Gries, Peter Hays—author.
  The politics of American foreign policy : how ideology divides liberals and conservatives
over foreign affairs / Peter Hays Gries.
        pages cm.
  Includes bibliographical references and index.
  ISBN 978-0-8047-8935-6 (cloth : alk. paper) —
  ISBN 978-0-8047-9088-8 (pbk. : alk. paper)
  1. United States—Foreign relations—Public opinion.   2. Liberals—United States—
Attitudes.   3. Conservatives—United States—Attitudes.   4. Ideology—United
States.   5. Public opinion—United States.   I. Title.

  E895.G75 2014
  327.73—dc23   2013043602

Typeset at Stanford University Press in 10/13 Minion

Special discounts for bulk quantities of Stanford Security Studies are available to
corporations, professional associations, and other organizations. For details and
discount information, contact the special sales department of Stanford University Press.
Tel: (650) 736-1782, Fax: (650) 736-1784

To my father, DAVID GRIES,
for his unwavering encouragement and support

CONTENTS

Figures and Tables   ix

Foreword, by David L. Boren: Partisanship and the
U.S. National Interest   xv

Introduction: Ideology and American Foreign Policy   1

PART I: CONCEPTS

1 Liberals, Conservatives, and Foreign Affairs   33

2 Beyond Red and Blue: Four Dimensions of American Ideology   49

3 The Moral Foundations of Ideology and International
   Attitudes   77

4 The Foreign Policy Orientations of Liberals and Conservatives:
   Internationalism, Realism/Idealism, and Nationalism   99

5 Partisan Elites and Global Attitudes: Ideology in Social
   Context   128

PART II: CASES

6 Latin America: Liberal and Conservative Moralities of
   Immigration and Foreign Aid   137

7 Europe: Socialist France, Mother England, Brother Germany,
   and the E.U. Antichrist   157

8 The Middle East: Christian Zionism, the Israel Lobby, and
   the Holy Land   183

9 East Asia: Red China, Free Asia, and the Yellow Peril 209

10 International Organizations and Treaties: Blue Helmets,
Black Helicopters, and Satanic Serpents 235

Conclusion: Ideology—Why Politics Does *Not* End at
the Water's Edge 263

Acknowledgments 273

Statistical Glossary 275

Notes 277

References 307

Index 325

FIGURES AND TABLES

FIGURES

0.1 Democrat William Jennings Bryan and the Anti-Imperialist League lament Republican president William McKinley's expansionist foreign policy, 1899   2

0.2 Uncle Sam convinces an American voter to support a patriotic McKinley against a treasonous Bryan, 1900   3

0.3 American feelings towards foreign countries and international organizations   6

0.4 The ideological gap: Liberals feel warmer towards foreign countries and international organizations than conservatives do   7

0.5 *"Remember the Maine! To hell with Spain!"* Militarist opinion pressures President McKinley into launching the Spanish-American War, 1898   23

0.6 Pacifist opinion delays the American entry into World War I, 1915   24

1.1 Liberalism vs. Dictatorship (Tyranny of the Right), 1917   34

1.2 Liberalism vs. Communism (Tyranny of the Left), 1968   35

1.3 The demographic correlates of ideology   36

1.4 Differential parental socialization into partisanship   39

1.5 Liberals support social welfare spending, while conservatives support defense spending   41

1.6 Liberals lament military spending at the expense of domestic social welfare programs, 1982 and 1969   42

1.7 The "halo effect" and the "affect heuristic": Conservatives desire a tougher policy towards North Korea than liberals do in large part because they feel cooler towards communist countries and hence North Korea   44

1.8   Group- and individual-level evidence that feelings are better
      predictors of foreign policy preferences towards fifteen foreign
      countries than their perceived military power is   46
1.9   The "affect heuristic" revisited   47
2.1   Does ideology shape American feelings about free trade between
      nations?   50
2.2   Economic conservatives and libertarians have long promoted
      free trade, 1901   51
2.3   Social conservatives view free trade and immigration as
      contaminating, 1892   52
2.4   The cultural, social, economic, and political dimensions of
      American ideology   54
2.5   Cultural ideology: Liberals decry Bush's Manichean foreign
      policy, 2003   57
2.6   The "Bible Belt": Southerners score the highest on biblical
      literalism   59
2.7   Social ideology I: Conservative fears of racial extinction, 1860s   62
2.8   Social ideology II: Liberal desires for racial equality, 1869   63
2.9   Economic ideology: Liberals object to income inequality at
      home and abroad, 1963   68
2.10 Democratic and Republican ideological profiles   73
2.11 Smoking is sin: "No tobacco use" signs posted outdoors on
      the campus of the University of Oklahoma, Norman, July 2012   75
3.1   The moral foundations of American ideology: Liberals care less
      than conservatives about purity, authority, and loyalty, but slightly
      more about injustice and suffering   80
3.2   Liberals and conservatives differ on cultural traditionalism   82
3.3   Cultural conservatives value *purity*, promoting paternalistic
      attitudes, 1899 and 1901   83
3.4   Liberals and conservatives differ on social dominance   84
3.5   Justice, compassion, and race relations in the USA, 1872   85
3.6   Liberals and conservatives differ on economic inequality   87
3.7   Liberals decry economic *injustice* and value *compassion* for the
      poor, both at home and abroad, 1962   89
3.8   Conservatives feel cooler towards the average foreign country
      than liberals do   91
3.9   Treason? A liberal view of war without honor, 1944   93
3.10 Liberals downplay national *loyalty*, highlight our common
      humanity, and display *compassion* for suffering foreigners,
      1968 and 1973   94

3.11 Conservatives prefer tougher overall foreign policies more than liberals do   95

3.12 Conservatives fear revolution, value *authority*, and desire tougher foreign policies, 1900   96

4.1 Unilateralism vs. multilateralism: A British view of American ambivalence towards the League of Nations, 1919   104

4.2 Diplomacy and international law, 1874   107

4.3 Military force: Peace through strength, 1875   108

4.4 Liberals are more supportive of humanitarian idealism   110

4.5 Humanitarian idealism: Liberal compassion confronts the Protestant ethic and opposition to family planning, 1981   111

4.6 Political idealism: The obligation to defend liberty abroad, 1895   113

4.7 Patriotism and nationalism in a land of immigrants, 1888   117

4.8 National narcissism: Imperial grandiosity and self-love, 1901   119

4.9 Although conservatives are both more patriotic and nationalistic than liberals are, only their greater nationalism accounts for their greater desire for tougher foreign policies   121

4.10 American foreign policy profiles   123

4.11 Republican foreign policy profiles   124

4.12 Democratic foreign policy profiles   125

4.13 Forceful idealists in the Democratic Party: Obama's foreign policy team watches the raid that killed Osama bin Laden, May 2, 2011   126

5.1 Americans raised in more-urban environments feel slightly warmer towards foreign countries than those raised in more-rural areas   132

5.2 As foreign travel, friends, and contacts increase, nationalism *increases* among cultural conservatives, but *decreases* among cultural liberals   133

6.1 Liberals tend to feel some compassion for Mexico and do not dislike it; conservatives tend to dislike Mexico and not feel sympathy towards it, 1901   138

6.2 Paternal and sisterly American visions of North-South race relations, 1901   141

6.3 The "Virginia idea": Immigration and labor, 1888   144

6.4 Among white Americans, differing liberal and conservative moralities of compassion and authority help account for their disagreement over Mexican border policy   145

6.5 On immigration, liberals value compassion and decry hypocrisy, 2005   146

6.6   A conservative morality of immigration: The challenge to authority and social order, 1891   148

6.7   Among whites, social, economic, and political ideologies all contribute to greater conservative opposition to aid for Haiti; cultural ideology does not   150

6.8   Liberals support foreign aid out of compassion, 2010   151

6.9   Liberals think that the United States should provide more foreign aid than conservatives do, 1963   153

7.1   Liberals respect and are not annoyed by France; conservatives are annoyed by France and do not respect it   160

7.2   "Socialist" France: Conservatives associate France with strong unions, strikes, and the social welfare state, which they decry at home as well, 2010   163

7.3   Midnight in Paris: Cultural traditionalism and attitudes towards high culture help account for the positive association between an open personality and warmth towards France   164

7.4   On France, liberals enjoy the fine arts, and are not as concerned about nudity and traditional values, 2005   165

7.5   Conservatives desire a tougher foreign policy towards France than liberals do   167

7.6   American responses to French Gaullism: Liberals laugh while conservatives bristle in anger? 1962   168

7.7   American Anglophobes and Anglophiles, 1895   171

7.8   Conservatives desire an even friendlier policy toward England than liberals do   172

7.9   German Americans: Traitors or patriots? 1900   176

7.10 German American Bund parade in New York City, October 30, 1939   177

7.11 Conflicted American feelings towards Germany: Cultural and economic ideologies offset each other   178

7.12 Conservatives feel much cooler towards the European Union than liberals do   181

8.1   Ideology polarizes American feelings towards Middle Eastern countries and peoples   185

8.2   Religious liberty and American compassion for the Jews, 1905   188

8.3   The socio-racial and biblical sources of conservative coolness towards Palestinians and Muslims, warmth towards Israel, and desires for a friendlier Israel policy   192

8.4   Among American Protestants, religiosity dramatically increases

warmth towards Israel, but only for those of Evangelical
denominations   194
8.5   David no more: A liberal view of Israel as Goliath, 1978   196
8.6   Biblical literalism and feelings towards Israel and the Palestinians
by American religious group   197
8.7   Secular liberals disregard cultural/religious differences, 2001   198
8.8   Israelis and Palestinians: A liberal view of moral equivalence, 1994   202
8.9   Middle East policy debated in the heartland: Oklahoma City
billboard, October 25, 2012   204
8.10 Greater nationalism and warmth towards Israel help account for
greater conservative than liberal desires for a tougher Iran policy   205
9.1   Bipartisan anti-Chinese prejudices, 1880   213
9.2   Japanese Americans interned at the Manzanar "War Relocation
Center," California, 1943   214
9.3   Conservatives desire a tougher China policy than liberals do   217
9.4   Conservatives feel cooler towards communist countries than
liberals do   218
9.5   Negative attitudes towards the Chinese people and government
act as separate pathways for four dimensions of American ideology
to shape China policy preferences   221
9.6   Chinese immigration: Conservatives value in-group *loyalty* and out-
group *obedience*, while liberals value *compassion*, 1870 and 1882   222
9.7   Libertarian fears of Oriental despotism, 1900   225
9.8   When knowledge is a double-edged sword: Contact with Chinese
increases knowledge about China, which *decreases* prejudice but
increases negativity towards the Chinese government   228
9.9   Conflicted American feelings towards Asian democracies:
Socio-racial and political ideologies counteract each other   231
10.1 President Theodore Roosevelt wins the 1906 Nobel Peace Prize for
brokering the 1905 Russo-Japanese Portsmouth Treaty, 1905   239
10.2 President Woodrow Wilson fails to win Senate ratification of the
Covenant of the League of Nations, which he helped craft at the
Paris Peace Conference, 1920   240
10.3 Cultural, social, economic, and political ideologies each uniquely
predict warmth towards the United Nations   242
10.4 Cultural conservatives feel cooler towards the United Nations than
cultural liberals do   243
10.5 Americans higher on social dominance feel cooler towards the
United Nations than those lower on it   250
10.6 The Nanny State: Libertarians feel cooler toward the United

Nations than communitarians do 255

10.7 Among liberals, greater education is associated with slightly greater *warmth* towards the United Nations; among conservatives, greater education is associated with greater *coolness* towards the United Nations 259

TABLES

5.1 World Knowledge Quiz: Five multiple choice questions and percentage correct 129

9.1 China Knowledge Quiz: Five multiple choice questions and percentage correct 227

Foreword: Partisanship and the U.S. National Interest

David L. Boren

Our dysfunctional political system is a national embarrassment.

Whether the issue is the budget, gun control, health care, or immigration, the executive and legislative branches are unable to work together to solve the nation's problems. Partisan posturing has pushed out bipartisanship and compromise. Cooperation between liberals and conservatives is becoming a quaint memory.

U.S. foreign policy is increasingly hamstrung by partisan politics as well. From Europe to the Middle East to China, Democrats and Republicans not only cannot agree; they are disinclined to work together to promote the national interest. Tom Brokaw's "Greatest Generation" was comprised of men and women who risked their lives to advance the national interest. Where is that spirit now? Senator Arthur Vandenberg, a conservative who was the champion of bipartisanship during World War II, laid the foundations for the Marshall Plan and a bipartisan foreign policy. Where are his successors today?

When I chaired the Senate Intelligence Committee in the 1980s and 1990s, I was able to work with my Republican colleagues on bipartisan solutions to our nation's security challenges. Intelligence Committee voting was usually unanimous. In fact, we never divided along strict party lines in any of our rare roll call votes.

Those days are long gone. Voting in most congressional committees today divides along partisan lines. The wise agreement that "politics should stop at the water's edge" has become a relic of the past.

David L. Boren is the president of the University of Oklahoma. He has also served Oklahoma as governor (1975–79) and U.S. senator (1979–94). He was the longest-serving chair of the Senate Intelligence Committee.

During my fifteen years in the Senate, I learned that partisan divisions over foreign policy have consequences. They complicate pursuit of the national interest. They distress our foreign allies and friends. They present to the world a distorted picture of America. At their most damaging, they turn friends into foes and make more difficult the task of advancing our national interest. When foreign policy becomes partisan, the national interest suffers.

In 2008, I wrote in *A Letter to America* that "partisanship clearly becomes destructive when partisan advantage is elevated above the national interest." Examples abound of partisan politics disrupting orderly governance. During the winter of 2012–13, the "fiscal cliff," sequestration, and the debt ceiling dominated political debate. Liberals and conservatives representing the extreme wings of their parties refused to compromise, allowing ideological purity to trump the national interest. During that same period, partisan disputes marred the confirmation hearings for President Obama's national security team. The incoming secretary of defense, former senator Chuck Hagel, received more "no" votes in the Senate than any previous candidate for that office, while confirmation of the new CIA director was held up for weeks by partisan wrangling.

For eleven years, some on the right in the Senate have blocked passage of the UN Convention on the Law of the Sea, despite support for passage from the business community, the military, and the public. More recently, a group of senators rejected the UN Convention on the Rights of Persons with Disabilities, even though the convention mirrored the much admired Americans with Disabilities Act of 1990, which passed the Senate with bipartisan support twenty-three years ago. In both cases, those in opposition held that the conventions ceded a piece of American sovereignty to the United Nations, an international body that conservatives love to hate.

The American people tolerate partisanship in foreign policy in part because they have little interest in foreign affairs—until something goes wrong. Nor do our citizens show much interest in American history. Despite the fact that we are a practical, problem-solving people, we are cynical towards government and doubtful that Washington will ever accomplish anything that directly affects us. Such cynicism is no surprise given that the picture that emerges in our media is of a people in decline, of special interest groups dominating politics, of vast sums of money lubricating our political system, of declining participation in civic organizations and activities.

But as I wrote in *A Letter to America*, "In all the ways that matter, we Americans have so many reasons to believe that our future can be even greater than our past." We prize a culture that is dynamic, pragmatic, and innovative. We prize our openness to change, which has long been America's default position. And we have surmounted obstacles in the past. In this instance, we can start by trying to understand why and how hyper-partisanship has come to dominate our political discourse.

In *The Politics of American Foreign Policy*, Peter Gries analyzes partisanship—affecting both domestic and foreign policy—and finds its origins in the deeply embedded ideologies that are changing our electoral landscape. Ideological self-sorting, aided by the gerrymandering that once again took place after the 2010 census, is dividing America into warring political camps. The majority of congressional districts have now become hyper-partisan—so red or blue that general elections are often mere formalities. Instead, a majority of the members of Congress face their stiffest competition in the primaries, where the 10 to 20 percent of eligible voters who do vote usually represent the extreme wings of their parties. "For the most part," Professor Gries writes, "politicians today are not elected by the median voters in their districts. Their job security, instead, depends upon a small minority within their parties." In these circumstances, candidates for office must cater to the ideological extremes, setting the stage for a partisan approach to governing and a bias against—even a fear of—compromise.

Professor Gries argues that while partisanship and ideology tend to go together, ideology is the more fundamental driver of political attitudes and behavior. *The Politics of American Foreign Policy* explores the nuances of American ideology, including its complex of values, beliefs, and motivations. While partisanship can be fluid, ideology appears more stable, frequently passed from generation to generation. For instance, the once solidly Democratic South is now the solidly Republican South. The partisan alignment has flipped, but the underlying ideologies have changed only marginally.

Since ideological positions are strongly held and change only slowly, does this mean that our dysfunctional political system will be with us for years to come? The very red and very blue congressional districts that dot the political landscape today are unlikely to change much—at least until the 2020 census, when redistricting and the gerrymandering that will inevitably follow it might partially reshape the electoral landscape, giving median voters a louder voice and reducing the clout of the extreme wings of both political parties.

For this to happen, the ideologies that undergird partisanship will have to change too. Internationalists in both parties must unite to oppose isolationists. Put another way, liberals and conservatives should try to move towards the middle, which is the only place where a bipartisan foreign policy can take root.

As I wrote in *A Letter to America*, "The history of our nation is one of almost unbroken progress. While there have been temporary ups and downs, each generation has been able to say that it has left America better in most ways than it found it." Despite our broken political system, I still believe that statement is correct. Our pragmatism, our determination, and our free and creative society will help us find ways to right the political ship and steer towards the goals we all share. As Peter Gries explains, the roots of hyper-partisanship have flourished in the extreme ideologies cultivated by the far left and far right of both our political parties. We understand the problem. The task for Americans now is to promote dialogue, cooperation, and compromise between liberals and conservatives, to bring our two great parties together in a joint effort to solve the problems facing us. We have done it in the past. We can do it now.

The Politics of American Foreign Policy

Introduction:
Ideology and American Foreign Policy

"Vietnam . . . cleaves us still. But . . . a new breeze is blowing, and the old bipartisanship must be made new again."[1]
— Republican President George H.W. Bush, 1989

"I do hope that the new Congress respects the time-honored tradition of leaving politics at the water's edge."[2]
— Democratic Secretary of State Hillary Rodham Clinton, 2010

Foreign policy has been a partisan issue ever since the United States of America won its independence. In his "Farewell Address," President George Washington counseled a foreign economic policy of free trade but a diplomatic policy of nonintervention: "Why, by interweaving our destiny with that of any part of Europe, entangle our peace and prosperity in the toils of European ambition, rivalship, interest, humor or caprice?"[3] Against Washington and the Hamiltonian Federalists, Thomas Jefferson and his Republicans cautioned against even economic internationalism. Instead, they advocated greater isolationism in jealous defense of America's hard won and fragile democracy at home.

And yet it was under the Republicans that the United States first fought against the Barbary pirates in Tripoli (1801–5) under Jefferson, and then declared war against Britain in 1812 under James Madison. After four days of heated debate, the House of Representatives voted 79 to 49 and the Senate 19 to 13 in favor of war, the first and closest vote to formally declare war in U.S. history. All thirty-nine of the Federalists in Congress voted against war.

Nearly a century later, American foreign policy was at the heart of the 1900 presidential contest between Republican president William McKinley and his Democratic challenger William Jennings Bryan. The United States had won Cuba from Spain during the 1898 Spanish-American War, and the Philippine-American War (1899–1902) was underway. McKinley and his vice presidential running mate, Theodore Roosevelt, a war hero, claimed that the United States had liberated Cuba from Spanish tyranny. Bryan countered that American rule over Cuba and the Philippines was no less cruel and imperialist than Spanish rule had been.

The debate over the U.S. annexation of Cuba, the Philippines, and Hawaii played out in the popular press as well. "We do not intend to free, but to sub-

Uncle Sam—*"Too late, my boys. I've already expanded."*

FIG. 0.1. Democrat William Jennings Bryan and the Anti-Imperialist League lament Republican president William McKinley's expansionist foreign policy, 1899.

Source: Clifford Berryman, *Washington Post*, September 14, 1899. Image courtesy of the National Archives. ARC 6010331.

jugate the people of the Philippines. We have gone there to conquer, not to redeem," Mark Twain argued in the *New York Herald*. "And so I am an anti-imperialist. I am opposed to having the eagle put its talons on any other land."[4] Twain later became vice president of the Anti-Imperialist League.

The debate over imperialism is captured visually in an editorial cartoon from an 1899 edition of the *Washington Post* (Figure 0.1). Clifford Berryman depicts President McKinley as a rotund Uncle Sam, contentedly smoking a cigar after having completed a three-course meal. An "Expansionist Menu" discarded on the floor describes the feast as one of "Hawaiian Soup," "Porto Rican Rum," and "Philippine Pudding." Bryan and a group of "anti-expansionists" watch from the door in dismay.

But McKinley had his popular supporters as well. Figure 0.2, from a 1900 issue of *Judge* magazine, depicts President McKinley in a patriotic light, raising the U.S. flag over the Philippines. "Old Glory" is already flying over Cuba and

TAKE YOUR CHOICE

"Do you want a man who, having raised the stars and stripes on our new possessions, will maintain them with dignity; or a man who will cut down 'Old Glory' and make us the laughing-stock of the world?"

FIG. 0.2. Uncle Sam convinces an American voter to support a patriotic McKinley against a treasonous Bryan, 1900.

Source: F. Victor Gillam, *Judge*, May 12, 1900. Image courtesy of the Library of Congress. LC-USZC4-5392.

Puerto Rico in the background. A treasonous Bryan, meanwhile, seeks to chop the flagpole down. Uncle Sam, back on American soil, convinces an American voter to support McKinley over Bryan in the 1900 presidential election: McKinley, Victor Gillam writes, will uphold American "dignity," while Bryan will "make us the laughing-stock of the world." McKinley won reelection in a landslide.

Pearl Harbor, in the words of Republican senator Arthur Vandenberg, "ended isolationism," and the first two decades of the Cold War are often remembered for having a bipartisan foreign policy. What bipartisanship there was, however, largely dissipated with the Vietnam War.[5] The 1972 presidential campaign witnessed liberals decrying Vietnam as "Nixon's War," while conservatives lambasted the Democratic challenger, George McGovern, as soft on defense and communism.[6] During the Watergate scandal the next year, a majority Democratic Congress passed the War Powers Resolution, overriding President Nixon's veto. The resolution required congressional approval of American military involvements overseas.

Over a quarter century later, during a January 2012 Republican presidential primary debate in South Carolina, the conservative audience became animated during an exchange between Newt Gingrich and Ron Paul over foreign policy. After Paul decried American militarism, Gingrich declared, "Andrew Jackson had a pretty clear-cut idea about America's enemies: Kill them." The audience exploded in cheers. Ron Paul responded on a more sober note: "Maybe we ought to consider a golden rule in foreign policy. Don't do to other nations what we don't want to have them do to us." The audience interrupted Paul with boos and jeers. But he was later applauded when he decried "warmongering" against Iran: "This country doesn't need another war. We need to quit the ones we're in. We need to save the money and bring our troops home."[7]

Secretary of State Hillary Clinton, meanwhile, was seeing her 2010 hopes for a bipartisan foreign policy, cited in the epigraph, dashed. Politics was not left at water's edge during her May 2012 push for the U.S. Senate to finally ratify the UN Convention on the Law of the Sea (UNCLOS), which she argued was necessary to protect U.S. security and advance American economic interests. She lamented that "I am well aware that this treaty does have determined . . . vociferous . . . opposition based in ideology and mythology, not in facts, evidence, or the consequences of our continuing failure to accede to the treaty."[8] Indeed, Republican senator Jim Inhofe of Oklahoma, in a letter cosigned by twenty-six of his Senate Republican colleagues, wrote to Democratic majority leader Harry Reid that "We are particularly concerned that United States sovereignty could be subjugated in many areas to a supranational government."[9] Despite the support of Big Oil and many business and security conservatives, thirty-four Republican senators successfully blocked UNCLOS ratification.

THE ENIGMA OF PARTISANSHIP IN AMERICAN FOREIGN POLICY

What best explains this persistent pattern of partisan discord over American foreign policy?

Foreign policy partisanship may sometimes be the product of clashing material interests, with American political parties representing distinct interest groups. For instance, the highly partisan debate over the War of 1812 was driven in part by opposing regional economic interests. Based in a New England whose economy was more dependent upon international trade, Federalists opposed a war against Britain; Republican "War Hawks," for their part, may have viewed war as an opportunity to annex Canadian territory from Britain. Similarly, as the Democratic Party came to represent Big Labor, and the Republican Party, Big Business, these opposed economic interests were later reflected in partisan disagreements over foreign policy issues like international trade.

Another explanation focuses on pure partisanship itself: politicians want their team to win the next election, so they attack both the domestic and foreign policies of their party rivals—regardless of substance or consequences. In October 2010, Senate minority leader Mitch McConnell (R–Kentucky) famously declared that "The single most important thing we want to achieve is for President Obama to be a one-term president." By refusing to cooperate with the president and causing gridlock, Republicans could later blame the Democrats for failing to accomplish anything. For instance, Republican opposition to UNCLOS in 2012 could be seen as part of a partisan strategy of obstructionism.

These arguments are not wrong. Conflicting interest groups do shape American foreign policy. And politicians do often act out of pure partisanship, motivated by the simple desire that one's own party wins and the other loses.

This book argues, however, that purely material explanations for foreign policy partisanship are incomplete, and that arguments based on partisan gamesmanship alone usually only touch the surface of the issue. Instead, partisanship over American domestic and foreign policy alike usually has its deeper roots in disparate American *ideologies*—widely shared and systematic beliefs about how the world does and should work. For instance, when thirty-four Republican senators voted against UNCLOS in 2012, they were expressing a deeply held conservative distrust of international institutions, one widely shared by the Republican primary voters who elected them. Based primarily upon an April 2011 survey of a representative national sample of one thousand American adults, this study argues that liberals and conservatives feel and think about foreign countries and American foreign policy in consistently different ways, and explores the psychological sources and foreign policy consequences of these ideological differences.

A number of recent books explore what Americans *should* think about the world. For instance, Charles Kupchan argues that America should stop seeking to export Western values and accommodate itself to working with the Chinese model of state capitalism.[10] Thomas Friedman and Michael Mandelbaum argue that Americans should view the rise of China and the other BRIC countries (Brazil, Russia, India) as a wakeup call to inspire national renewal.[11] By contrast, this book explores what Americans *actually* think about the world. More descriptive than prescriptive, it explores *what* and *how* American liberals and conservatives really feel and think about foreign countries and global affairs.

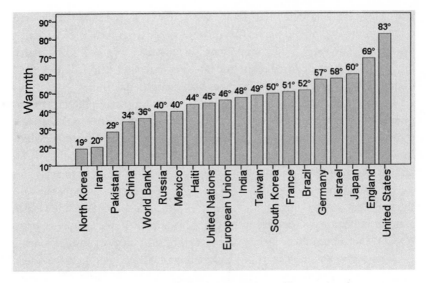

FIG. 0.3. American feelings towards foreign countries and international organizations.

Note: Temperatures are weighted mean scores for the full sample, in ascending order. *Data source:* OU Institute for US-China Issues, 2011.

Our survey asked all participants to rate a list of seventeen countries and three international organizations on a 0° ("very cold, unfavorable") to 100° ("very warm, favorable") feeling thermometer. Figure 0.3 displays the average score for each country and international organization for the full U.S. sample.[12] As might be expected, Americans felt the warmest towards the United States (83°) itself, followed by its closest allies, England (69°), Japan (60°), Israel (58°), and Germany (57°). They felt the coolest towards North Korea (19°) and Iran (20°), followed by Pakistan (29°) and China (34°).

These findings are consistent with other national surveys. Our sequence exactly replicates that of four-point "favorable" to "unfavorable" and "ally" to "enemy" assessments on nine of these same countries in a CNN telephone poll conducted in May 2011, less than a month after our own survey. England and Israel were CNN's top two (it did not include Japan), and Iran and North Korea tied at the bottom, as they did in our survey.[13] Our sequence also replicates that of a Chicago Council for Global Affairs Internet survey conducted less than a year earlier in June 2010.[14] Replication across independent samples using different survey methods increases confidence in the generalizability of findings from our survey.

Averages can be deceiving when they hide differences among significant

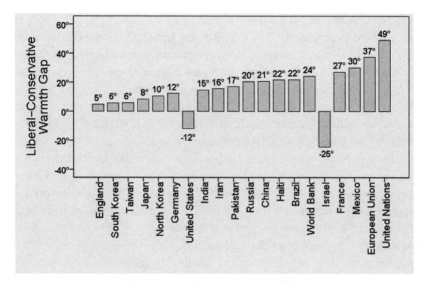

FIG. 0.4. The ideological gap: Liberals feel warmer towards foreign countries and international organizations than conservatives do, with the sole exceptions of Israel and the United States itself.

Note: Bars represent weighted mean scores for liberals minus conservatives, in ascending order.
Data source: OU Institute for US-China Issues, 2011.

subgroups within a population. Figure 0.4 displays the gap between liberal and conservative feelings for each country or international organization within our sample. Remarkably, there were statistically significant ideological differences on *all* seventeen countries and *all* three international organizations measured. These differences were small for England (5°), South Korea (6°), and Taiwan (6°), but large for Russia (20°), China (21°), Haiti (22°), Brazil (22°), the World Bank (24°), and Israel (–25°), and truly massive for the United Nations (49°), European Union (37°), Mexico (30°), and France (27°).[15] Note that other than the United States itself, Israel is the only country that conservatives feel more warmly towards than liberals do, topics we will take up in Chapters 4 and 9. Figure 0.4 thus reveals a consistent and substantial pattern of ideological differences in the international attitudes of the American people. This pattern of ideological differences, furthermore, is again replicated in other contemporaneous surveys, such as the 2010 Chicago Council survey,[16] and the U.S. data from the Pew Research Center's 2010 Global Attitudes Project.[17]

The predominant argument among public opinion researchers today, however, is that partisanship and ideology do *not* shape the international attitudes of the American people. The Chicago Council claimed in 2012 that "Democrats and Republicans are very similar in their views on foreign policy."[18] Political scientist Benjamin Page and pollster Andrew Kohut have similarly dismissed the influence of partisanship and ideology in separate 2006 books based upon earlier Chicago Council and Pew surveys, the two major sources of representative national survey data on the global views of the American people.[19] Writing in 2012 for *Foreign Affairs*, a group of younger political scientists went so far as to declare in their title that "American Foreign Policy Is Already Post-Partisan: Why Politics Does Stop at the Water's Edge."[20]

These public opinion scholars and pollsters have misinterpreted the existing survey data. For instance, to explore the impact of partisanship on foreign policy preferences, the Chicago Council first sorted all of its 2012 survey respondents by whether they lived in majority red or blue House districts. Statistical analysis, it reports, revealed that the two groups differed on "only four of the eighty-five" policy questions in its survey. It therefore concludes that the foreign policy views of Democrats and Republicans are "remarkably similar."[21]

Whether one lives in a red or blue House district, however, is an extremely indirect and poor proxy for partisanship. A majority of Americans are either Democrats or independents living in districts represented by a Republican, or Republicans or independents living in districts represented by a Democrat. Little wonder there were few differences between these two groups in their international attitudes.

The Chicago Council's decision to create an indirect proxy measure for partisanship is particularly galling given that its 2012 survey included a *direct* measure of partisanship: "*Generally speaking, do you usually think of yourself as a Republican, a Democrat, an independent, or what?*" Responses to this question allow for a straightforward comparison of the over 1,200 self-identified Democrats and Republicans in their 2012 sample, revealing substantial partisan differences over foreign affairs. For instance, the survey asked all respondents to assess whether nine possible "threats to the vital interests of the United States" were "critical," "important but not critical," or "not an important threat." Self-identified Democrats and Republicans differed on *all nine* items, an extremely large overall difference.[22] The survey also asked participants to assess whether they thought eleven listed "U.S. foreign policy goals" were "very," "somewhat," or "not" important. Democrats and Republicans differed on nine of the eleven goals.[23] This was again an extremely large overall partisan difference.[24]

To claim that partisanship does not shape American foreign policy preferences is a consequential mistake. What do foreign policy makers like Hillary Clinton think when they read assertions that American foreign policy is "post-partisan"? When political scientists and pollsters make claims that do not pass a reality check, they marginalize themselves from the policy world.

More importantly, because the United States is a democracy, the polarizing impact of ideology on the international attitudes of the American people shapes American foreign policy. Given that the United States is a superpower whose foreign policy will have a major impact on the prospects for war and peace in the twenty-first century, a better understanding of the polarizing role of ideology on its foreign policy is urgently needed.

BOOK OVERVIEW

This book proceeds in ten chapters. The first explores the nature of American ideology and its impact on American attitudes towards international affairs. It begins by suggesting that all Americans share a "big L" Liberalism that contributes to a cherishing of their individual freedoms and a wariness towards perceived foreign tyrannies. This helps explain why, on average, Americans feel the warmest towards fellow democracies like England and Japan, and the coolest towards authoritarian regimes like North Korea and Iran, as Figure 0.3 revealed.

Within the broad parameters of a shared Liberalism, however, American "small *l*" liberals and conservatives differ systematically and substantially, both psychologically and in their domestic and foreign policy preferences. Psychologically, liberal and conservative ideologies have their roots in differing motivational needs. Social psychologists have shown that conservatives consistently score higher than liberals on measures of epistemic needs for certainty, existential needs for security, and relational needs for solidarity. These psychological differences are the product of both nature and nurture, as parental and peer socialization shape gene expression. They are also associated with physiological differences. For instance, compared to liberals, conservatives possess both a stronger startle reflex, reflecting greater sensitivity to threat, and a larger right amygdala, a region of the brain directly involved in threat response.

Ideological differences have implications for both domestic and international attitudes. On the domestic front, the American culture wars are not a "myth," as prominent Stanford political scientist Morris Fiorina has claimed. There are consistent and substantial differences between liberals and conservatives on concrete policy issues like abortion and gay marriage. On international attitudes, with the sole exception of Israel mentioned above, liberals consistently feel warmer towards foreign countries than conservatives do. Ideology also shapes foreign policy preferences; conservatives usually desire tougher U.S. foreign policies than liberals do. The impact of ideology on foreign policy preferences, Chapter 1 further argues, is mediated by gut *feelings* towards foreign countries, which act as "affect heuristics" or mental shortcuts that help Americans assess a foreign country's intentions, thereby shaping their foreign policy preferences.

As we saw in the 2012 Republican presidential primary exchange between

Newt Gingrich and Ron Paul, not all conservatives share the same views on foreign affairs. The same can be said of Hillary Clinton and other liberals. There
are different kinds of liberals and conservatives. Chapter 2 explores the idea
that four dimensions of American ideology might differentially shape attitudes
towards foreign affairs. Specifically, American ideology is examined across
its cultural, social, economic, and political dimensions. Cultural liberals and
conservatives differ in their orientation towards traditional values, disagreeing
over such topics as sex, drugs, feminism, and homosexuality. Social ideology
is conceptualized as beliefs about the proper relations among social and racial groups; social conservatives hold a greater preference for social hierarchies,
while social liberals prefer a greater equality. Economic ideology is operationalized as orientations towards income redistribution, with liberals more in favor
and conservatives more opposed. Finally, political ideology is conceptualized as
one's position on the issue of individual rights versus the broader public good.
On average, conservatives tend towards the libertarian side, while liberals lean
more towards the communitarian, although we will see that Christian conservatives can be quite communitarian.

These four dimensions of American ideology can help us better understand
not just patterns of attitudes towards domestic issues like God, guns, and gays,
but also why different types of liberals and conservatives usually converge but
sometimes diverge in their international attitudes. For instance, the massive difference between liberals and conservatives in their feelings towards the United
Nations is in part due to these four dimensions of ideology converging in the
same direction. As we shall see in Chapter 10, cultural conservatives decry the
United Nations as an affront to God's rule; social conservatives remain wary of a
"colored U.N.," economic conservatives lament its role in North-South income
redistribution; and political conservatives (libertarians) condemn it as "World
Government." Meanwhile, cultural, social, economic, and political liberals share
more favorable—if distinct—attitudes towards the United Nations. This consistent pattern of ideological differences contributes to the massive overall gap
between liberal and conservative views of the United Nations. By contrast, as we
shall see in Chapters 2 and 7, on a few issues, like free trade among nations and
attitudes towards countries like Germany, different kinds of liberals and conservatives disagree amongst themselves, diluting the overall ideological divide.

Why do American ideologies shape international attitudes? Chapter 3 explores the idea that liberals and conservatives weigh five different moral values—fairness, compassion, loyalty, authority, and purity—in distinct ways, and
that these value differences help account for the impact of ideology on international attitudes. Liberals prize the "individualizing" values of *fairness* and *compassion* more than conservatives do, contributing to liberals' greater warmth

towards foreign countries in general, and especially towards the poor of the developing world. By contrast, conservatives esteem the "binding" moral values of *loyalty, authority,* and *purity* more than liberals do. For instance, greater loyalty to America contributes to a greater conservative coolness towards foreign countries. And the greater value that conservatives place on authority helps account for the greater average conservative than liberal desire for tougher foreign policies.

In Chapter 4 we turn to the broad foreign policy orientations of liberals and conservatives. Liberals are more "internationalist" than conservatives in three conceptually and empirically distinct ways: liberals are greater supporters of international engagement, multilateralism, and diplomacy, while conservatives are more likely to support isolationism, unilateralism, and the use of military force. We then explore three foreign policy "idealisms"—humanitarian, religious, and political—often juxtaposed against "realism." Ideology, it turns out, has the largest impact on the former: liberals are much more supportive of humanitarian interventions and foreign aid than are conservatives. Ideology also shapes nationalism, which moves beyond the love of country that is patriotism to a belief in American superiority over other countries. Conservatives, our data reveals, are both more patriotic and more nationalistic than American liberals are. This difference, furthermore, shapes the international attitudes and foreign policy preferences of liberals and conservatives.

The final section of Chapter 4 explores the interrelationships among these many foreign policy orientations, identifying distinct clusters of Democratic and Republican foreign policy preferences. For instance, Obama and the Clintons fit a "forceful idealist" Democratic foreign policy profile, supporting both multilateralism and the use of military force in the pursuit of humanitarian and other idealistic foreign policy goals. And while all Republicans are nationalists, two-thirds are "cautious idealists" supportive of idealism in U.S. foreign policy; the other third are hardcore "isolationist skeptics," realists highly skeptical of multilateralism. Our electoral system, however, has come to amplify the political influence of this vocal minority of Republican anti-internationalists.

The mainstream view in political science is that in the absence of much popular knowledge about the world, political elites and the media determine the international attitudes of the American people. Chapter 5 argues that while it is true that Americans are not very knowledgeable about the world, it is ideology more than the media or even partisanship that fills in the gaps, allowing Americans to maintain consistent—if consistently different—global views.

But ideology is not destiny. Our ideological predispositions *interact* with demographic variables like gender and race, and situational variables like media exposure, to shape our international attitudes. For instance, we will see that cultural ideology moderates the impact of foreign travel and international contacts on American nationalism. For cultural liberals, as international contacts increase, nationalism *decreases*. But for cultural conservatives, greater contact is associated with an *increase* in nationalism. In short, our international attitudes are the product of both psychological predispositions and environmental factors like the media.

The second part of the book applies the concepts developed in Part I to five empirical case studies. The first four address major geographic regions central to U.S. foreign policy. Chapter 6 looks south of the border, exploring how ideology shapes American attitudes towards Latin America and the Caribbean. On average, conservatives feel substantially cooler than liberals feel towards Mexico, Haiti, and Brazil; they also oppose aid to countries like Haiti more and desire a much tougher Mexican border policy than liberals do. This ideological divide, the chapter further argues, is driven by all four of the dimensions of American ideology that we measured in our 2011 survey. Libertarians and economic conservatives oppose foreign aid to places like Haiti out of a belief in the Protestant ethic of self-help and out of opposition to income redistribution. And cultural conservatives fear the impact of Mexican immigration on Christian values and America's WASP identity more than cultural liberals do. But it is social ideology that has the most pervasive influence on American attitudes towards Latin America. Relative to social liberals, greater social conservative desires for order and the maintenance of racial hierarchies cool their feelings towards the colored countries of Central America, South America, and the Caribbean.

Chapter 7 turns our attention east and across the Atlantic. Overall, our survey reveals that American views of the Old World are marked by a projection of domestic ideologies onto a European looking glass. Different kinds of American liberals and conservatives view different European countries in distinct ways. For instance, greater cultural conservatism is associated with desires for friendlier policies towards "Mother" England but with coolness towards secular France and Germany. Beliefs in prophesy even lead some on the religious right to view the European Union as the Antichrist. Economic conservatism is associated with warmth towards fiscally austere Germany but coolness towards "socialist" France. Economic liberals, by contrast, are more enamored of the French social welfare state. Greater conservative nationalism is associated with warmth towards a WASP England, but desires for tougher policies towards "Gaullist" France. To Americans of different ideological stripes, in short, Europe is decidedly not of a piece.

Chapter 8 explores how ideology polarizes American feelings and policy preferences towards the Middle East. Conservatives feel warmer than liberals towards Israel but cooler towards Iran, the Palestinians, and Muslims. The chapter argues that the same religious and culture wars that divide Americans on abortion, gay marriage, and prayer in public schools also divide them on Israel, Iran, and the Palestinians. Similarly, the same racial politics that divides Americans at home also divides liberals and conservatives in their feelings towards Arabs. Conservatives tend to view Arabs as threats, while liberals have a greater tendency to view their plight in the West Bank and Gaza as analogous to segregation or even apartheid, triggering liberal values of compassion and social justice. And the same nationalism that divides Americans on flag burning and defense spending also divides them on policy towards Iran. The role of the "Israel lobby" in the making of U.S. Middle East policy, the chapter argues, is best understood in the context of divided American public opinion towards the Middle East.

Chapter 9 turns to East Asia, with a focus on "Red China" and the divide between liberal Panda-huggers and conservative Dragon-slayers. While conservatives feel somewhat cooler towards the East Asian democracies than liberals do, they feel much cooler towards China. Greater average conservative prejudice does linger, shaping attitudes towards the "Yellow Peril" from all Asian countries. But communism is an even larger source of ideological differences on China. For cultural, economic, *and* political reasons, conservatives feel cooler than liberals do towards communist countries in general, and the Chinese government in particular. By contrast, conservatives' greater average libertarianism warms them towards Japan, Taiwan, and South Korea, mitigating the overall ideological divide on Asian democracies.

Ideology has the largest influence on American views of international organizations and treaties. Chapter 10 explores why liberals like the United Nations while conservatives dislike it. Cultural liberals and conservatives differ on the United Nations in large part because they differ over biblical literalism. Many premillennial dispensationalists, who believe that Christ will return before establishing his millennial kingdom, believe that the United Nations will join Satan's forces against Christ. Conservative Christians are also more likely than mainline Christians or nonreligious Americans to view the United Nations as a secular affront to God's rule on earth. Some cultural conservatives may also fear that interacting with pagans in the United Nations may dilute Christian purity. Although the effect size was small, racial thinking continues to divide Americans in their views of the "colored U.N." The impact of differences in economic ideology is larger; conservatives are more anxious than liberals that the United Nations seeks global income redistribution. Finally, greater anticommunism and jealousy of national sovereignty contribute to greater libertarian than communitarian paranoia about "blue helmets" and "black helicopters."

AN APPLIED POLITICAL PSYCHOLOGY OF PUBLIC OPINION AND AMERICAN FOREIGN POLICY

This book is an exercise in applied political psychology. As such, it differs from existing scholarship in five major ways.

Applied, not theory driven. First, mainstream political science and psychology are both largely deductive and theory driven. The goal is to derive and test hypotheses to develop better theory. In psychology, there are a few applied journals, but they are widely dismissed as second tier. "Applied political science," for its part, is largely an oxymoron, and is mostly confined to "area studies" journals, which are similarly disparaged.

Hypothesis testing, however, can lead to a variety of problems, such as when data that contradicts hypotheses is suppressed, or worse yet, when data is fabricated to support theory.[25] As a result, theories can be built upon very shaky empirical foundations. Theory-driven research is also often divorced from real-world issues, contributing to the vast chasm between the "ivory tower" and policy making.

This book is unapologetically "applied." It asks an empirical question: How does ideology shape American attitudes towards international affairs, and why? Rather than deductively testing hypotheses to build theory, it will *inductively* explore what existing and new survey data can teach us about public opinion and American foreign policy.

This book also seeks to be accessible to a broad audience. Although the statistical analysis of quantitative survey data is its primary methodology, statistical results are not presented in opaque regression tables of numbers, as is common in quantitative political science. Instead, this book presents its findings in figures that seek to be clear and visually engaging, such as bar, line, pie, and flow charts. It thus follows the example of Robert Putnam and David Campbell's *American Grace: How Religion Divides and Unites Us*, which also asks an applied empirical question and presents its survey findings visually, seeking to speak to a broad audience.

Like *American Grace*, this book also seeks to integrate quantitative and qualitative evidence. Statistical figures are complemented by political cartoons which are meant to illustrate the arguments and provide historical background. Although our survey was fielded in 2011, the ideological divisions over foreign affairs that it reveals have deep historical roots. Mixing figures of statistical data with editorial cartoons also makes a methodological point: the deep divide between qualitative and quantitative political science that plagues the discipline today is highly problematic. Statistical results, certainly, must be interpreted, and that process requires both historical knowledge and qualitative analysis. As much as possible, the historical background, the survey questions themselves, and the statistical results are presented as clearly as possible so that readers can judge my interpretations for themselves.

Foreign policy attitudes: bottom-up, not just top-down. Second, as political *psychology*, this book differs from the existing scholarship conceptually. Political science research on public opinion and foreign policy largely treats the American public as an empty vessel or bottle which political elites or the media fill with specific beliefs about foreign affairs. Scholarly debate largely centers upon whether the American people are passive bottles filled with whatever elites or the media feed them, or active bottles that engage in rational cost-benefit analysis of what they learn.

In the interwar and early postwar periods, Walter Lippmann, Gabriel Almond, and Phillip Converse disparaged the lack of structured or stable foreign policy attitudes among what they viewed as a largely uninterested and uninformed American public.[26] The "Almond-Lippmann consensus" on the public's "non-attitudes" was first empirically challenged in the 1970s.[27] By the 1980s, political scientists were arguing that the American public does indeed have structured and stable foreign policy attitudes.[28] Utilizing Chicago Council survey data, Eugene Wittkopf argued that the public's foreign policy beliefs were not only stable but structured around the two dimensions of "cooperative internationalism" and "militant internationalism."[29] Gathering their own surveys in their Foreign Policy Leadership Project, Ole Holsti and James Rosenau maintained that the same two dimensions structured elite foreign policy beliefs as well.[30]

Political scientists were divided, however, over where the public's foreign policy attitudes came from. One group has depicted the American public as responding rationally to objective news about wars and foreign affairs. In the early 1970s, John Mueller first argued that the American public responded sensibly to body-bag counts with reduced support for the Vietnam War.[31] Some scholars further developed this "casualty aversion" approach, while others made refinements, focusing instead on mission objectives or mission success.[32] The public, for these scholars, rationally responds to information about international events. Political scientists Christopher Gelpi, Peter Feaver, and Jason Reifler recently put this rationalist approach succinctly: "the public weighs the costs of a war against the expected benefits."[33]

Following the influential work of John Zaller on the impact of elite cues on public opinion more broadly, a second group of scholars has focused instead on the role that political elites and the media play in molding the public's international attitudes.[34] Some focus on elite partisan rhetoric as a direct source of public attitudes.[35] Adam Berinsky, for example, argues against the rationalist approach: "the public appears 'rational' only because it takes cues from elites" who mediate reality for them.[36] Others focus on the media's independent role. For instance, Matthew Baum and Tim Groeling have recently developed a "strategic bias theory" in which reporters, pursuing their own interests, add their own spin to both news events and elite cues.[37]

This book challenges the shared assumption of these two camps that because the American public is not very knowledgeable about international affairs, it must be an empty vessel that either partisan elites or the media fill with international attitudes. Instead, as political *psychology*, it will advance the idea that the American people already possess ideological predispositions that fill in the gaps left by a lack of much international knowledge. The American people are *not* empty vessels. Preexisting ideologies allow them to maintain consistent, if often consistently different, attitudes towards international affairs.

The book does not claim, however, that political elites and the media have *no* impact on individual attitudes. It suggests instead that the influence of ideological predispositions on the international attitudes of the American people is generally larger than the impact of situational variables like media exposure and cues from political elites. The bottle is already largely full of preexisting beliefs and values, so it will not be easily swayed. Chapter 5 will also explore, however, how the media and other situational factors *interact* with ideological predispositions to shape the international attitudes of the American people.

Bottom-up ideology, not just top-down partisanship. Third and more broadly, by focusing on ideology and not partisanship—the degree of attachment to or identification with a political party—this study differs from over fifty years of scholarship on American politics.

Following the publication of *The American Voter* in 1960, the "Michigan Model" of voting behavior, with its focus on partisanship, has dominated the study of American elections.[38] Ideology, by contrast, has been treated more skeptically if at all.[39] For instance, the thirty-eight-chapter 2010 edition of the authoritative and comprehensive *Oxford Handbook of American Elections and Political Behavior* does not even include entries for "ideology," "liberalism," or "conservatism" in its subject index, let alone chapters on them. The subject index entry for "party identification," by contrast, merits sixteen subheadings.[40] In 2012, political scientist Marc Hetherington even declared partisanship to be the "most important" variable shaping not just voting but "a person's political behaviors, positions on issues, or feelings about groups."[41]

Partisanship does not explain everything. Hetherington and other students of American politics have elevated partisanship too far at ideology's expense. While partisanship may do a better job than ideology in accounting for highly partisan attitude objects like Obama or "Obamacare," and overtly political behaviors like voting, the more psychologically fundamental ideology is usually the more powerful driver of our deeper sociopolitical attitudes and policy preferences. Partisanship is rooted in ideology, which is the real source of many seemingly partisan attitudes.

With the ongoing sorting of liberals into the Democratic Party and conservatives into the Republican Party, partisanship and ideology are increasingly intercorrelated. From 1972 to 2004, American National Election Surveys revealed a fourfold increase in their overlap, from 10 percent ($r = .32$) to 40 percent ($r = .63$).[42] In our 2011 survey, they overlapped a remarkable 53 percent ($r = .73$), perhaps reflecting further sorting over time or, more likely, more accurate survey measurement, to be discussed in the next section. Ideology and partisanship today, in short, appear to share as much as half of their variance.

When they are pitted against each other to explain domestic or international policy preferences, however, ideology is usually the stronger predictor. For instance, our survey included five questions tapping domestic policy preferences on (1) prayer in public schools, (2) the death penalty, (3) abortion, (4) gay marriage, and (5) gun control. A series of regression analyses revealed that on four of the five, ideology was by far the stronger predictor, with partisanship only approaching ideology in predicting positions on gun control.[43] When these five domestic policy issues were averaged together into a single "culture wars" scale, ideology accounted for 38 percent of its unique variance, while partisanship accounted for just 3 percent.[44] Similarly, only ideology and not partisanship predicted average feelings and foreign policy preferences towards the foreign countries discussed above (and listed in Figures 0.3 and 0.4).[45]

Ideology generally has a greater impact than partisanship on sociopolitical attitudes and policy preferences because it is more psychologically fundamental. William Jacoby describes partisanship as a "group influence" on individual behavior: political parties act as "sources of guidance" or "reference groups" shaping the individual.[46] Marc Hetherington agrees, suggesting that party identification is like "rooting for a sports team": "Once someone has decided that he roots for the Red Sox and not the Yankees, he does not usually change sides."[47]

Hetherington is right that we do not easily switch our team loyalties. But we can engage in what social psychologists call "social mobility" or "exit" from a particular social identity. When the Red Sox win, Boston sports fans can "bask in their reflected glory" (BIRG) by wearing their Red Sox caps.[48] But when they lose, fans can "cut off reflected failure" (CORF) by wearing their Celtics jerseys instead.[49] Similarly, when the Republican Party lost the presidential election in 2008, many conservative Americans likely "cut off reflected failure" by switching the focus of their political identification from the GOP to other political groups, like the Tea Party.

In short, while group identities like partisanship are powerful top-down drivers of our attitudes and behaviors, especially towards clearly partisan attitude objects like Obamacare, they are multiple and fluid. Our ideologies, by contrast, are deeper and more stable bottom-up drivers of our attitudes.[50] "The once solidly Democratic South is now the solidly Republican South," David Boren writes in the Foreword. "The partisan alignment has flipped, but the underlying ideologies have changed only marginally." American National Election Surveys data confirm Boren's argument: between 1972 and 2008, the U.S. South became more Republican but did not change ideologically.[51]

Chapters 1 through 3 will argue that our ideologies are multidimensional and complex, grounded in a deep web of motivations, beliefs, and values. So although they are highly intercorrelated, such that differences between liberals and conservatives are generally mirrored by differences between Democrats and Republicans, it is ideology and not partisanship that will be the focus of this book.

Measurement matters. Fourth, survey research in political science and psychology is marked by complementary strengths and weaknesses. Political science surveys are better at representative sampling than at measurement. Psychological surveys are the opposite, better at measurement than sampling. This book will adopt a combined *political psychology* approach to survey design, embracing the strengths of each discipline while seeking to avoid their weaknesses.

Improving both sampling and measurement is necessary to allow the full extent of the relationships among our variables to fully emerge. When psychologists limit themselves to university student samples, range restriction can reduce the size of the observed associations among variables. For example, because most university students are about the same age and education level, it is difficult to ascertain the true extent of any associations between age or education and any other variable using a student sample.

Political science surveys, for their part, often suffer from high measurement error, leading to type II errors, or false negatives. Public opinion surveys too often rely upon single questions with limited response options. While single, dichotomous questions are fine for some substantive opinions—"*Do you plan to vote for Barack Obama or Mitt Romney?*"—they are insufficient to capture more complex ideologies and (international) attitudes. Single-item measures can decrease the observed associations among variables as more error and less "true score" variation is captured and correlated.[52] Furthermore, binary response categories, such as forcing a choice between "engaging" and "containing" China, fail to capture the nuances of complex attitudes. They also limit the variation necessary to ensure that the full extent of the associations among variables can become apparent. In short, measures of low internal reliability and insufficient variability have often produced low or inconsistent associations between ideology and international attitudes in existing public opinion surveys, contributing to the many false negatives in existing scholarship.

Poor question wording also plagues many public opinion surveys, distorting our understanding of key concepts. For instance, for decades the American National Election Surveys (ANES) and the General Social Survey have measured ideology by asking respondents to place themselves on a seven-point scale from "extremely liberal" to "extremely conservative." To be "extreme" is not normatively desirable, however. This has pushed respondents away from the edges of the distribution. In 2010 ANES substituted "very" for "extreme," while also reporting the results from Knowledge Networks' public profile ideology question, which retained the "extreme" wording.[53] While only 7.4 percent of respondents were willing to describe themselves as "extremely" liberal or conservative, 18.4 percent of the *very same respondents* were willing to describe themselves as "very" liberal or conservative. "Extreme" even swelled the numbers of respondents choosing the neutral (4) position, from 30.9 percent to 38.1 percent, likely because of a negative exemplar effect: some people may associate "extremely liberal" and "extremely conservative" with people they find distasteful, like Bill Maher or Rush Limbaugh, so distance themselves from any ideology. In short, a poor choice of diction—"extremely"—has contributed to producing an artificially moderate picture of the American ideological landscape for decades.[54]

The way that ANES has measured partisanship, by contrast, suffers from the opposite problem, with a branching question format pushing respondents away from the center and towards the extremes of the distribution. Respondents are first asked if they think of themselves as a Republican, Democrat, independent, another party, or have no preference. If they choose one of the two major parties, they are then asked whether they would call themselves a "strong" or "not very strong" Republican or Democrat. Since being "strong" is the normatively preferable choice, partisans are pushed to the far edges of the scale. Meanwhile, those who choose independent, "another party," or "no preference" are further asked whether they think of themselves as "closer to" the Republican or Democratic Parties. Because people generally wish to please their interlocutors by providing new information,[55] this follow-up question pushes people away from their original neutral position into one of the partisan camps. For instance, in the 2010 ANES, over 42 percent of respondents chose independent, no preference, or another party in response to the first question. But after the second "closer to" question, less than 3 percent of respondents remained in the neutral position. Combined with the "strong" effect (a remarkable 32 percent of the 2010 ANES sample are in the 1 and 7 tails), which also pushed respondents away from the center of a normal bell curve, the derived PID variable suffers from a distribution so non-normal that it is of questionable value for statistical analysis.[56]

By combining the best of political science surveys (sampling) and psychological surveys (measurement), we hope to overcome these problems and provide a more accurate picture of the relationship between ideology and the international attitudes of the American people. For sampling, our Internet survey was fielded by the Palo Alto, California, survey research company YouGov. They used a "sample matching" methodology to generate a representative national sample, first matching respondents on gender, age, race, education, party identification, ideology, and political interest, and then weighing the final dataset to match the full U.S. general population on age, gender, race, education, and religion.[57]

For measurement, the majority of our variables were assessed with at least three questions, increasing the internal reliability of the underlying constructs. Question wording was refined over several years of pretests using large local and national convenience samples.[58] To minimize measurement error, we assessed the reliability of our constructs using Cronbach's alpha (α), which ranges from 0 to 1, where higher scores indicate greater internal consistency.[59] For instance, although we measured each survey participant's self-identified liberal-conservative ideology at two separate points in time, using completely different response scales and formats, together they formed a two-item scale of extremely high internal reliability, $\alpha = .93$.[60]

We chose to implement our survey on the Internet to decrease measurement error. First, completing a survey in the privacy of one's home on a personal computer reduces the self-presentation effects more likely in face-to-face and even telephone interviews. This is particularly important when surveys like ours touch on sensitive subjects like prejudice, where respondents are more likely to adjust their responses depending upon how they wish to be seen by others and even themselves. Second, the computer interface allows for easier use of rating scales affording more response options. These are much more difficult to use over the telephone or even in person than on the Internet. That is one reason why telephone surveys so often use "yes/no" or "support/oppose" questions, producing binary "variables" (which barely vary) of limited use for correlational research. The majority of our questions, by contrast, were measured on seven-point "strongly disagree" to "strongly agree" rating scales, although there were numerous eleven-point rating scales and even 101-point "placement rulers" in which respondents marked a position along an anchored but unnumbered ruler. Our goal was to create *variables that vary*—as much as possible. By using the Internet and boosting the variability of our variables, we were able to reduce measurement error and increase the likelihood that the true associations among our ideological and attitudinal variables would become apparent.

Finally, to our knowledge, our 2011 survey is the first to combine extensive questions about ideology with extensive questions about international attitudes within a single, national representative sample. To date, existing national surveys have largely explored one or the other. The General Social Survey and the American National Election Surveys have measured American ideology for decades, but rarely ask questions about international affairs. By contrast, the Chicago Council, Pew, and the Program on International Policy Attitudes have been asking questions about international affairs for years, but rarely ask many questions about ideology. By combining these two types of questions within a single survey, our dataset provides new leverage to explore how ideology shapes the international attitudes of the American people.

Size matters too. Fifth and finally, effect sizes—not significance tests—will be the focus of our statistical analysis. We thus follow a trend that began about a decade ago in the psychological sciences, and hope to help start a new trend in political science.

Political science remains, regrettably, a largely "sizeless" science, fixated on the "yes or no" *whether* question of statistical significance testing, rather than the more consequential real-world questions of *how much* or *who cares* (meaningfulness). "Statistical significance should be a tiny part of an inquiry concerned with the size and importance of relationships," Stephen Ziliak and Dierdre McCloskey rightly argue in *The Cult of Statistical Significance.* "Unhappily it has become the central and standard error of many sciences."[61] Jacob Cohen made the same criticism in the title of a 1994 article for *American Psychologist,* "The Earth Is Round ($p < .05$)."[62]

This book engages in inferential statistics, generalizing about the full U.S. population based upon representative samples of usually around one thousand Americans. To do so, a p (probability) value is calculated. Convention dictates that $p < .05$ is "statistically significant." This book adopts a tougher standard: if a p value is *not* reported, the reader should assume it to be less than .001. In other words, the likelihood that the observed relationship is actually due to chance is less than 1 in 1,000.

With a large enough sample size even tiny correlations can be statistically significant. Statistical significance testing, therefore, should only be the very first step of analysis. To interpret the *meaning* of our statistical findings, we must focus on the *size* of observed associations or differences. When dealing with continuous variables, this book treats zero-order correlations (Pearson's r) between variables and the partial coefficients (standardized β) from multiple regression analyses of .10 as small, .30 as medium, and .50 as large.[63] These numbers can be squared and multiplied by 100 to calculate the amount of shared variance (R^2) in percentage terms. In other words, in the social sciences sharing 1 percent of variance is considered small; 9 percent, medium; and 25 percent, large.

When comparing differences between subgroups within a population, such as men against women, or liberals against conservatives, we usually rely upon an effect size statistic called "partial eta squared," or η_p^2. Following statistical convention, a η_p^2 of .01 is considered small, .06 medium, and .14 large.[64] For instance, when we wrote above that the overall differences between Democrats and Republicans on the 2012 Chicago Council's "threats to the vital interests of the United States" rating scale and importance as "U.S. foreign policy goals" rating scale were both "extremely large," that choice of diction was deliberate, based upon effect size statistics (both $\eta_p^2 = .27$).

Readers are therefore encouraged to focus on the effect size statistics (r, β, R^2, η_p^2, etc.) reported in this book to interpret how *meaningful* (not merely statistically significant) differences or relationships are. They should bear in mind, however, that the causes of human behavior are usually multiple and complex, so the associations among psychological and attitudinal variables are usually much smaller than those found in the natural sciences, where the relationships among physical phenomena, such as the motion of the planets, are extremely regular and strong. Statistics are reported in the endnotes and online at SUP.org. Readers can also consult the Statistical Glossary at the back of the book as needed.

PUBLIC OPINION AND FOREIGN POLICY MAKING IN DEMOCRACIES

> "I have no hesitation in saying that in the control of society's foreign affairs, democratic governments do appear decidedly inferior to others."[65]
>
> —Alexis de Tocqueville, 1835

> "In the conduct of their foreign relations, democracies appear to me decidedly inferior to other governments."[66]
>
> —Democratic Secretary of State Dean Acheson, 1951

Does public opinion influence American foreign policy? And if so, does it matter if American opinion on international affairs is divided along ideological lines?

While popular opinion is certainly not the only factor shaping American foreign policy, the predominant argument today is that it is an important one. Since the United States is a democracy, and elected officials desire reelection, they usually make the foreign policy that the public wants. In a comprehensive review of this "electoral connection" argument, Duke political scientist John Aldrich concludes that "The potential impact of foreign policy views on electoral outcomes is the critical mechanism linking public attitudes to elite behavior."[67]

There is considerable empirical support for this "political responsiveness" view. In a longitudinal analysis of survey data, Benjamin Page and Robert Shapiro found that changes in public opinion on international events regularly *preceded* eventual changes in U.S. foreign policy.[68] Given that the most basic requirement of causality is that cause precedes effect, this is an important quantitative finding.

There is ample anecdotal evidence for the "electoral connection" as well. Politicians often say that they pay attention to public opinion when making foreign policy. For instance, President Bill Clinton's 1998 "National Security Strategy" declared that "The American people rightfully play a central role in how the United States wields its power abroad. The United States cannot long sustain a commitment without the support of the public."[69]

As the epigraphs from Alexis de Tocqueville and Dean Acheson reveal, pundits and policy makers alike have long lamented the impact of public opinion on foreign policy making in democracies. Authoritarian governments, by contrast, are seen as free of domestic constraints and thus at a diplomatic advantage over democracies.

Popular opinion in democracies is seen as compelling both aggression and nonaggression—against the will of leaders. "The *Maine*" and "Munich" frequently serve as shorthand for these twin arguments. Popular anger over

A SOLUTION TO THE MAINE EXPLOSION
"The court of inquiry made its report but could not fix the responsibility. This picture fixes the responsibility to the satisfaction of the American people."

FIG. 0.5. *"Remember the Maine! To hell with Spain!"* Militarist opinion pressures President McKinley into launching the Spanish-American War, 1898.

Source: F. S. Chance, Indianapolis, Indiana, 1898. Image courtesy of the Library of Congress. LC-USZ62-105376.

I HOPE WE KEEP OUT OF IT

FIG. 0.6. Pacifist opinion delays the American entry into World War I, 1915.

Source: John T. McCutcheon, *The Evening Mail*, September 6, 1915. Image courtesy of the Library of Congress. LC-USZ62-48224.

the February 1898 explosion and sinking of the *USS Maine* in Havana Harbor, resulting in the deaths of 166 American sailors, is often blamed for forcing President McKinley to launch the Spanish-American War, "a war which he did not want," according to historian Ernest May, "for a cause in which he did not believe."[70] American public opinion was already decrying the brutal Spanish response to the Cuban rebellion, and when the *Maine* exploded in Havana there was a major popular outcry. Although the U.S. government's official inquiry was inconclusive (it now seems likely that the explosion was an accident that had nothing to do with the Spanish), the American public remained indignant. The rallying cry in the popular press became, "Remember the *Maine*! To hell with Spain!" Figure 0.5 is a detail from an 1898 engraving depicting two men in Spanish clothing secretly plotting to blow up the *Maine* with a rigged underwater mine. A caption declares, "The court of inquiry made its report but could not fix the responsibility. This picture fixes the responsibility to the satisfaction of the American people." In April 1898 the U.S. Congress, responsive to public opinion, adopted a Joint Resolution for War with Spain.

"Munich" is shorthand for the danger of pacifist publics compelling democratic governments to adopt foreign policies of appeasement. Pacifist British and French publics are frequently blamed for Prime Ministers Chamberlain and Daladier's 1938 acquiescence to Hitler's annexation of Czechoslovakia. The belated U.S. entry into World War I is an earlier example of the impact of pacifist public opinion on foreign policy making. As visually depicted in Figure 0.6, in 1915 the American public watched the events unfolding across the Atlantic with great interest but, according to *The Evening Mail*'s John McCutcheon, with an overwhelmingly isolationist impulse of anti-interventionism: "I hope we keep out of it." As we shall see in Chapter 7, some Americans blamed German immigrants and spies for promoting a pacifism that kept the United States out of the Great War for too long.

A FOREIGN POLICY DISCONNECT?

A small group of scholars has contested the idea that political elites are responsive to public opinion, arguing that there is a "disconnect" plaguing American politics. Stanford's Morris Fiorina has made the broadest argument, claiming in his 2009 *Disconnect* that there has been a breakdown of representation, as political elites have become more polarized than the American people.[71] On foreign affairs, Steven Kull and I. M. Destler argued in their 1999 *Misreading the Public: The Myth of a New Isolationism* that the foreign policy elite had become more isolationist than the general public.[72] And in their 2006 *The Foreign Policy Disconnect*, Benjamin Page and Marshall Bouton used Chicago Council surveys to similarly argue that "U.S. foreign policy has often diverged markedly from what the public wants."[73]

Disconnect, Misreading the Public, and *The Foreign Policy Disconnect* should be commended for advocating a more "democratic" policy-making process in which elites are more responsive to the will of the American people. However, by treating "the public" as a "uniform whole," as Page and Bouton put it, these books misrepresent the nature of the "electoral connection" between voting and policy making.[74] For the most part, politicians today are no longer elected by the "median voters" in their districts.[75] Their job security, instead, depends upon a small minority within their own parties: primary voters. The logic of the electoral connection today is that elected politicians are responsive to the views of those who elect them: not "the public" as a uniform whole but a small group of the most liberal and conservative Americans who are motivated to vote in party primaries. Fiorina is right that "incumbents act strategically to preclude primary challenges."[76] While he may also be correct that elites are disconnected from the *average* American voter, that does not mean that they are disconnected from the primary voters who actually elect them. Instead, Emory's Alan Abramowitz is right that "Democratic and Republican candidates and officeholders are polarized precisely because they are highly responsive to their parties' electoral bases."[77] Whether the issue is domestic or international, the federal budget or a U.N. treaty, most politicians in Congress today have little incentive to compromise and every reason to cater to the views of primary voters. In short, it is not the average American's views on international affairs that influences the typical elected official, but those of the primary voters on the ideological extremes.

This is a new development. The vast majority of congressional districts today have become noncompetitive, solidly blue or red districts. Voters increasingly choose where to live based on their politics: liberals choose the two coasts and urban areas, while conservatives choose the heartland and suburban or rural areas. Americans cluster into communities of the like-minded.[78] This ideological self-sorting is exacerbated by gerrymandering, as the two parties manipulate district boundaries following each U.S. Census. Analyzing the fall 2012 elections, statistician Nate Silver estimates that just 8 percent of House districts today are competitive, while a remarkable 56 percent are "landslide districts" in which the presidential vote margin differed from the national result by over 20 percentage points. "Most members of the House now come from hyperpartisan districts where they face essentially no threat of losing their seat to the other party."[79] Deep blue and deep red are in; purple has become passé.

To keep their jobs, therefore, most U.S. politicians today no longer have to cater to the "median voter" in their districts, let alone voters from the other party. Instead, their main job is to curry favor with the primary voters most likely to remove them from office—the most conservative and liberal slices of the American public. U.S. congressmen understand this situation very well. "To avoid a party primary," as former Democratic congressman John Tanner from Tennessee put it, "these guys are gonna be responsive to the people that elected them . . . not their district or their country."[80] The views of "the median voter" are becoming irrelevant.

The same is true in the Senate. For instance, more than a Democratic challenger, most Republican senators today fear becoming the next Bob Bennett of Utah or Richard Lugar of Indiana, longtime Republican senators rejected in favor of Tea Party challengers during Republican primaries. Republican primary voters are a small group of very conservative people. For instance, approximately 10 percent of the Indiana population participated in its 2012 Republican primary. Richard Mourdock required the votes of just 6 percent of Indianans—the most conservative—to oust Lugar. The fear of being "primaried" can help explain why, as mentioned above, the vast majority of Republican senators voted against UNCLOS in 2012. As we will see in Chapter 10, Tea Party antipathy towards the United Nations is intense, and appears to outweigh other interest groups in the minds of most Republican senators when they vote on international treaties.

Blue states appear little different. Republicans have moved more to the right than Democrats have moved to the left. And political scientist Gary Jacobson has shown that compared to the average Democrat or Republican, it is Republican primary voters who are more ideologically extreme.[81] But senators from deep blue states have cause to fear being "primaried" as well. For instance, during his reelection bid in 2006, Joe Lieberman, who had served Connecticut in the U.S. Senate for almost two decades, lost the Democratic primary election to Ned Lamont. Left-wing groups like the National Organization for Women and MoveOn.org rallied against Lieberman, who was seen as too supportive of Bush administration policies such as the war in Iraq. Lamont won the Democratic primary with under 150,000 votes, less than 5 percent of the population of blue Connecticut.

The triumph of the ideological extremes may not be as true at the presidential level, where winning over independent voters still matters during general elections. But presidential primary campaigns are following the same trend. Moderate Republican Jon Huntsman, whose 2012 primary campaign never gained traction, later complained to the *New York Times Magazine* that people who "work for a living" don't turn out for primaries—"those who do turn out are professional activists."[82] Huntsman did not stand a chance in the Tea Party–dominated 2012 GOP primaries.

Public divisions over foreign policy issues can influence presidential general elections as well. Against the view that the public does not care about foreign policy—that campaigning on foreign policy is as silly as "Waltzing before a blind audience"—John Aldrich argued over two decades ago that during presidential races in which a foreign policy issue is salient, such as during Vietnam, foreign policy divides *do* shape voting behavior.[83] As we will see in Chapter 8, Middle East policy was a major issue in the 2012 elections. During the GOP primaries, Mitt Romney had tough talk for Iran, appealing to pro-Israel GOP primary voters. But after winning the GOP nomination, during the third presidential debate he tacked back to the center on Iran policy, fearing that Obama would successfully depict him as a warmonger.

IDEOLOGY, ELITES, AND U.S. FOREIGN POLICY

In democracies, therefore, ideology has an *indirect* impact on foreign policy via public opinion: self-interested politicians, attuned to the "electoral connection," are responsive to the views of those Americans—often primary voters on the ideological extremes—who elect them. But ideology also has a *direct* effect on foreign policy via foreign policy elites themselves. As Thomas Knecht succinctly put it, "politicians are Americans too." Politicians do not just *respond* to their constituents in a self-interested manner; they also *represent* them in the sense of sharing their attitudes and policy preferences.[84] Therefore, a better grasp of how ideology shapes international attitudes should help us understand not just American public opinion, but also the ways that American elites themselves view the world, framing and constraining the foreign policy options that they pursue.

For instance, President Woodrow Wilson was a devout Presbyterian, with many ministers on both sides of his family. As we shall see in Chapter 10, the idealism of his Fourteen Points and vision for a postwar League of Nations was not primarily the result of the lobbying of religious groups but because of his own progressive Christianity. Historian Andrew Preston puts it well:

> "Wilson . . . was so thoroughly steeped in mainline Protestant theology, so familiar with the premises of the Social Gospel, that it would have been surprising had his foreign policy resembled anything else. Wilsonianism was essentially an expression of Christian reformism, of the global application of progressive Christianity, not because of a conscious vision but simply because Wilson could not escape who he was."[85]

Wilsonianism cannot be understood apart from the Social Gospel, not because of public opinion or the lobbying of religious special interest groups, but because progressive Christianity was central to Wilson's very identity.

Similarly, George W. Bush's aggressive reaction to the September 11, 2001, terrorist attacks is difficult to understand apart from his personal belief system. Bush was a born-again Christian who believed in evil and the necessity to combat it with force. As conservative commentator George Will noted, Bush didn't "pander to the religious right" because "Bush *is* the religious right."[86]

President Barack Obama has also pursued a foreign policy that has very much reflected his own ideology. Like Wilson, Obama rejects absolutist political views, embracing the philosophical pragmatism of William James and John Dewey. For instance, Obama views the Constitution as a conversation. Obama's pragmatic view of democracy as deliberation, intellectual historian James Kloppenberg has thoughtfully argued, leads him to embrace compromise, not out of weakness but out of a conviction that in a pluralist society the common good can only emerge through the reconciliation of competing views.[87]

Yet Obama also recognizes that Christian love alone will not bring about social justice. As a Christian realist, he embraces a mantra he claims to have learned from Martin Luther King Jr.: "Love without power is mere sentimentality. Power without love is dangerous. Love plus power equals justice."[88] Obama's philosophic pragmatism and Christian realism very much inform his foreign policy decision making. "Make no mistake: Evil does exist in the world," Obama declared in his 2009 Nobel Peace Prize acceptance speech. "A non-violent movement could not have halted Hitler's armies. Negotiations cannot convince al Qaeda's leaders to lay down their arms. To say that force may sometimes be necessary is not a call to cynicism—it is a recognition of history; the imperfections of man and the limits of reason."[89] Like Reinhold Niebuhr, John Foster Dulles, and other progressive Christians before him, Obama's Christian realism did not abandon Christian love and the Social Gospel but adapted them to a hostile world.

More modest about American military dominance than his predecessor, Obama has nonetheless proven willing to deploy American power when humanitarian considerations demanded it. To prevent a massacre in Benghazi in 2011, Obama went beyond British and French calls for a no-fly zone over Libya to authorize U.S. military attacks on Muammar Gaddafi's advancing troops. "By virtually all accounts, the dominant influence on the Obama administration's foreign policy was the president himself," journalist James Mann writes in *The Obamians*. "It was Obama's own ideas . . . that have determined America's role in the world."[90]

Similar arguments could be made about all American foreign policy makers: the kind of Americans they are—their ideological profiles—shapes their foreign policy decision making. Political science has long disparaged the study of leaders in favor of the study of impersonal institutions and structural forces. If we are to "bring the statesman back" into the study of foreign policy, as Daniel Byman and Kenneth Pollack have rightly urged, this book contends that ideology must be central to that project.[91]

CONCEPTS

Part 1

1 Liberals, Conservatives, and Foreign Affairs

"BIG *I*" IDEOLOGY: AMERICAN LIBERALISM AGAINST FOREIGN TYRANNY

What are ideologies? Broadly, they are sets of widely held beliefs or theories about how the world works. Economist Thomas Sowell describes ideology as "an almost intuitive *sense* of what things are and how they work."[1] Like all theories, ideologies simplify. "Ideologies elucidate complex realities and reduce them to understandable and manageable terms," writes historian Michael Hunt.[2] Examples of "big *I*" ideologies that are the most ambitious in terms of the scope of the world that they explain are Liberalism, Communism, and Fascism.

"Big *L*" Liberalism seeks to maximize individual freedom. A comprehensive theory of the social world, it celebrates the individual across the major domains of human life: the democratic citizen (politics), the capitalist entrepreneur (economics), and the Protestant believer (religion) with his direct relationship with God.[3] Liberalism emerged during the English, American, and French Revolutions, when the "bourgeois" middle classes rebelled against the aristocracy. In *The Liberal Tradition in America*, Louis Hartz argued that because the colonies lacked a feudal past, American Liberalism was particularly consensual, lacking the divisive ideologies and class conflict of the Old World.[4]

"Big *L*" Liberalism sets the boundaries of the thinkable in American foreign policy. All Americans cherish their individual liberties, and will be suspicious of tyrannies of either the right or the left. In a 1917 edition of the *Washington Evening Star*, Clifford Berryman drew a direct link between World War I and the War of Independence (Figure 1.1). Entitled "Same Old Spirit of '76," the drawing depicts Uncle Sam, rifle in hand, proud to fight with our allies against the Central Powers. A flag reading "Liberty Forever" leaves no doubt about Uncle Sam's purpose: defending Liberty against Dictatorship.

SAME OLD SPIRIT OF '76

FIG. 1.1. Liberalism vs. Dictatorship (Tyranny of the Right), 1917.

Source: Clifford Berryman, *Washington Evening Star*, July 4, 1917. Image courtesy of the National Archives. ARC 6011256.

Fifty years later, Herbert Block (hereafter "Herblock") made a similar point in the *Washington Post*. In August 1968 the Soviet Union and her Warsaw Pact allies invaded Czechoslovakia, bringing an abrupt end to the Prague Spring. Over one hundred Czechs and Slovaks were killed. Herblock's drawing (Figure 1.2), sarcastically entitled "She Might Have Invaded Russia," depicts Soviet leader Leonid Brezhnev and a henchman holding smoking machine guns over the dead body of a young woman. Leaving no doubt about his ("big *L*") Liberal message, Herblock labels the woman "Freedom."

American Liberalism ensures that Americans will always be wary of tyrannies of any guise, whether fascisms and dictatorships of the right or communisms of the left. This sets broad constraints or parameters within which Americans understand the world. It is not surprising, therefore, that surveys have consistently revealed that Americans feel the coolest towards communist countries like North Korea and China and dictatorships like Iran, and the warmest towards fellow democracies like England, Japan, and Germany (see Figure 0.3).

This book, however, will focus on how the "small *i*" ideologies of American

SHE MIGHT HAVE INVADED RUSSIA

FIG. 1.2. Liberalism vs. Communism (Tyranny of the Left), 1968.
Source: A 1968 Herblock Cartoon, © The Herb Block Foundation.

liberals and conservatives contribute to *differences* in their worldviews. Within the overall constraints of a shared "big *L*" Liberalism, American liberals and conservatives maintain consistently different international attitudes and foreign policy preferences. As such, this book differs from a long line of largely historical scholarship emphasizing the influence of *shared* ideologies on American foreign policy. Against an earlier generation of historians like Charles Beard, who focused on conflicts between different groups of Americans, Richard Hofstadter argued in the early postwar period for a consensus view of American history: "Above and beyond temporary and local conflicts there has been a common ground, a unity of cultural and political tradition, upon which American civilization has stood. That culture has been intensely nationalistic and for the most part isolationist; it has been fiercely individualistic and capitalistic."[5]

Michael Hunt's pioneering 1987 *Ideology and U.S. Foreign Policy* followed in Hofstadter's "consensus history" tradition, arguing that three core ideas have persisted through the years, shaping U.S. foreign policy: nationalism, racism,

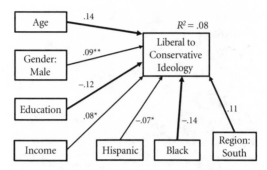

FIG. 1.3. The demographic correlates of ideology: Being older, male, wealthy, or from the South are associated with being more conservative; greater education or being Hispanic or black are associated with being more liberal.

Note: A regression analysis. * $p < .05$, ** $p < .01$, all other p's ≤ .001. Line thickness in this and all subsequent figures is proportionate to the size of the standardized coefficient. *Data source:* OU Institute for US-China Issues, 2011.

and a reactionary fear of revolution in defense of property. Subsequent historians have also followed in this "consensus history" tradition, arguing, for example, that a shared ideology of "manifest destiny" or the "warfare state" undergirds American imperialism and militarism.[6] Political scientist Michael Desch has also joined this tradition, arguing in his provocative "America's Liberal Illiberalism" that a "big *L*" Liberalism at home promotes illiberal foreign policies, such as the George W. Bush administration's pursuit of global hegemony.[7]

Hunt is right that inadequate attention has been placed upon the impact of ideology on American foreign policy.[8] Unlike Hunt's focus on shared ideologies, however, this book highlights the foreign policy consequences of ideological differences among Americans.

THE SOURCES OF IDEOLOGY:
THE MAKING OF LIBERALS AND CONSERVATIVES

How do Americans differ ideologically? Figure 1.3 displays how seven major demographic characteristics of the American people relate to ideology. In our 2011 survey, being older, male, wealthier, or from the South was correlated with being more conservative, while greater education or being Hispanic or black was associated with being more liberal. While their individual effects were small, each characteristic was statistically significant, together accounting for 8 percent of the variance in an American's liberal-conservative ideology.

This pattern is consistent with that found in the fall 2010 American National Election Surveys (ANES) data, providing further confirmation that our 2011 YouGov sample is representative of all Americans.[9] It is also consistent with previous scholarship on demographics and ideology in America. For instance, the gender gap in ideology first became evident in the 1970s as men became more conservative while women split into two groups, one group becoming more conservative and another more liberal.[10] Similarly, a long line of scholarship has explored how and why black Americans are more likely to self-identify as liberals.[11] Other scholars have repeatedly shown that greater income is associated with greater conservatism.[12] It is also noteworthy that while education and income level were strongly and *positively* correlated with each other in both our 2011 sample and the 2010 ANES sample (both at exactly $r = .45$), they correlated with ideology in the *opposite* directions: greater education was associated with being more liberal, while greater income correlated with being more conservative.

To ensure that the relationships between ideology and the other variables that we examine throughout this book are not the spurious products of these seven demographic variables, we include them as standard covariates or "control variables" in most of our statistical analyses. For instance, when we find in Chapter 4 that liberals enjoy soccer more than conservatives do ($\beta = -.15$), we can be confident that it's not just because Hispanics ($\beta = .13$) like soccer more than non-Hispanics and tend to be more liberal, or that older people, who tend to be more conservative, like soccer less ($\beta = -.09, p = .004$).

These demographic correlates of ideology, of course, only represent broad tendencies. So what makes some Americans liberals and others conservatives? Social psychologist John Jost has developed a complex functionalist account of the motivational underpinnings of ideology. Specifically, he argues that liberals and conservatives vary systematically in their (1) epistemic needs for *certainty*, (2) existential needs for *security*, and (3) relational needs for *solidarity*.[13] Specific psychological predispositions, in other words, lead certain types of people to be drawn to particular types of ideologies.

First, conservatives tend to be less tolerant of ambiguity than liberals, scoring higher on psychological scales measuring the Need for Closure, which taps desires for simplicity and *certainty*.[14] Interestingly, when liberals are put in situations where they are forced to think in more simple ways, such as when they are under cognitive load or even drunk, they tend to become more conservative.[15] Liberals also score higher on psychological measures such as the Need for Cognition, which taps the enjoyment of thinking.[16]

Of the "Big 5" personality traits or domains that psychologists use to describe personality, "openness to new experience" has been the most consistently and strongly associated with ideology: liberals are more open to new experiences while conservatives tend to be more conventional.[17] Liberal openness may be tied to their greater need for cognition, while greater conservative conventionalism may be tied to their greater need for closure and certainty. Borrowing from the Ten-Item Personality Inventory, we included two items, "*I see myself as open to new experiences, complex*" and "*I see myself as conventional, uncreative,*" in our survey.[18] After reverse-coding the latter, they were averaged together to create an "openness" scale, which correlated positively ($r = .22$) with liberal ideology, replicating earlier work. In a creative study, psychologist Dana Carney and her colleagues made inventories of bedrooms and office spaces, and found that liberals were more likely than conservatives to possess items related to openness, such as a greater number and variety of music CDs, books, maps, and art supplies.[19]

Second, a large body of scholarship has emerged in psychology demonstrating that conservatives are more fearful and sensitive to threat, attesting to greater existential needs for *security*. Some lab experiments have revealed that priming thoughts of death ("mortality salience") temporarily heightens conservatism.[20] Similarly, a natural or "real world" experiment revealed that survivors of the 9/11 terrorist attacks in New York experienced a "conservative shift" in the eighteen months following the event.[21]

Remarkably, the new field of political neuroscience has found that the brains of liberals and conservatives differ systematically in ways that reflect their differing needs for security.[22] For example, the volume of the right amygdala, which is directly involved in threat response, is larger in conservatives than in liberals.[23] There are also ideological differences in the physiological sensitivity to threat. Conservatives score higher than liberals on measures of skin conductance in response to threatening images (due to greater sweating caused by fear), and on eye blink responses to loud and unexpected bursts of sound.[24] Conservatives thus appear to be physiologically primed to be more fearful and sensitive to threat than liberals. To alleviate this sense of threat, conservatives turn to their in-group and cultural traditions for security.

Third and finally, Jost argues that conservatives possess greater relational needs for *solidarity*, belonging, and a shared reality with salient others than liberals do.[25] This is consistent with earlier work arguing that conservatives prefer group conformity more than liberals, who prefer autonomy and self-direction.[26] As we shall see in our discussion of moral values in Chapter 3, conservatives value *loyalty to the in-group* considerably more than liberals do, supporting Jost's argument that conservatives possess greater relational needs to belong.

These psychological predispositions interact with the social environment in producing liberals and conservatives. Our ideologies are the product of both nature and nurture. In their seminal 1981 *Generations and Politics*, Kent Jennings and Richard Niemi argued that ideological beliefs are transmitted from

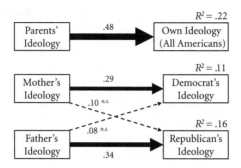

FIG. 1.4. Differential parental socialization into partisanship: Although parents together have a very large impact on the ideology of their children, mother's ideology dominates for Democrats, while father's ideology dominates for Republicans.

Note: Dashed lines here and in all subsequent figures are not statistically significant ($^{n.s.}$). R^2 (percent of variance explained) do not include seven standard demographics, not shown to reduce clutter. *Data source:* OU Institute for US-China Issues, 2011.

parents to their children.[27] Thirty years later, our survey supports their argument. We asked respondents to place not just themselves but also their mother and father on separate placement rulers anchored on the left and right by "very liberal" and "very conservative." We created a "parents' ideology" scale (α =.76) by averaging together the scores for both parents. Controlling for the standard demographics, parents' ideology alone accounted for a full 22 percent of the variance in a respondent's ideology. To what extent this large impact is due to genetics or to socialization is unclear.[28]

We also found that parental socialization patterns differed by party identification. When we pitted one parent's ideology against the other's to predict a respondent's ideology, we found diametrically opposite patterns for Democrats and Republicans. As displayed in Figure 1.4, for the average Democrat the mother's but not the father's ideology was associated with the respondent's ideology. For the average Republican it was exactly the opposite: the father's, not the mother's ideology correlated with the person's ideology. Cognitive linguist George Lakoff has argued, on the basis of qualitative discourse analysis, that liberal and conservative political discourse is notable for the underlying "nurturing parent" (read mother) and "strict father" metaphors respectively.[29] That our Democrats' ideology could be predicted only by their mother's ideology while our Republicans' ideology could be predicted only by their father's ideology lends quantitative support to Lakoff's argument.[30]

Liberal-conservative ideological differences seem to crystallize around two foundational sets of beliefs about human nature. Liberals tend to view human nature as basically good, and therefore maintain that mankind has the capacity to perfect the world through collective action. "Nothing can be more gentle than [man] in his primitive state," philosopher Jean-Jacques Rousseau declared in the eighteenth century. "Men are not naturally enemies." Thomas Sowell calls this the "unconstrained" vision of human nature; psychologist Steven Pinker calls it the "Utopian Vision."[31] It is the liberal vision of progressive Christianity. "Social Gospelers based their reform efforts on the conviction that people were not inherently evil or depraved but were conditioned by their surrounding environment," historian Andrew Preston writes. "Improve the environment, and you improve the person, which in turn would open the way to Christ."[32]

Conservatives, by contrast, view human nature as essentially flawed, and therefore view laws and traditions as essential safeguards against our inherent selfishness. Sowell calls this the "constrained" vision, which he traces back to Hobbes's *Leviathan*. It argues that man's natural state is not gentle, as Rousseau claimed, but "solitary, poore, nasty, brutish, and short."[33] Conservatives believe that "human nature . . . is relatively fixed and imperfect," writes political scientist Colin Dueck. They "believe that human self-interest renders perfectionist political visions not only unattainable but downright dangerous."[34] Pinker calls this the "Tragic Vision" of human nature.[35] With their focus on original sin, fundamentalist Christians generally dismiss human efforts at worldly improvement as futile, putting their faith instead in religious salvation.

These ideological differences over human nature manifest themselves in systematic differences in the willingness to trust others. Trusting liberals are more inclined towards cooperation; wary conservatives, by contrast, are predisposed towards competitive interpersonal and intergroup relations. Political scientist Brian Rathbun has convincingly tied these ideological differences in trust to elite partisanship over international organizations in twentieth-century America.[36] As we shall see in Chapters 4 and 10, Main Street liberals and conservatives are also dramatically divided over the possibility and desirability of multilateralism.

THE CONSEQUENCES OF IDEOLOGY: POLICY DIFFERENCES

Ideological differences thus have their origins in a combination of nature and nurture, as the social context (family, peers, the media) shapes gene expression. As individuals develop distinct personalities and motivational needs for certainty, security, and solidarity, they are naturally drawn to liberal or conservative ideologies.

But are there real-world policy consequences of these ideological differences?

Morris Fiorina argues that there are not. In his *Culture War? The Myth of a*

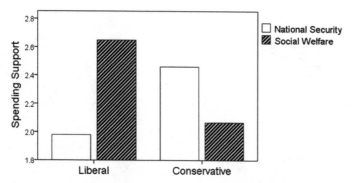

FIG. 1.5. Liberals support social welfare spending, while conservatives support defense spending.

Note: Social welfare ($\alpha = .73$): $F(1, 496) = 93.45, p < .001, \eta_p^2 = .16$; national security ($\alpha = .66$): $F(1, 496) = 106.04, p < .001, \eta_p^2 = .18$, both controlling for age, gender, education, income, and being from the South. *Data source:* Question 25, Chicago Council on Global Affairs, 2010.

Polarized America, which is now in its third edition, Fiorina claims that "The simple truth is that there is no culture war in the United States. . . . Elections are close, but voters are not deeply or bitterly divided." On domestic politics, he asserts that "there is little evidence that the country is polarized even on 'hot button' issues like abortion." On foreign policy, Fiorina claims that "Red and blue state voters have similar views on diplomacy vs. force in international affairs."[37]

The survey evidence suggests otherwise. On domestic politics, Alan Abramowitz is right that Americans are polarized in the culture wars.[38] In Chapter 2 we will see that Fiorina misrepresents existing General Social Survey data on abortion. Here we note that in comparing individuals by whether they live in red or blue states—a very poor proxy measure for ideology—Fiorina ends up committing a type II error, claiming that there are no ideological differences over foreign affairs when in fact there are.[39] As we shall see in Chapter 4, direct measures of ideology reveal that conservatives score much higher than liberals do on support for the use of military force.[40]

Ideology shapes spending priorities as well. Half of the respondents to the Chicago Council's 2010 survey were asked how much they supported spending on a list of federal programs. Comparing self-reported liberals and conservatives revealed very large differences (Figure 1.5). Liberals were much more supportive of spending on social welfare programs ("social security," "health care," and "aid to education") than conservatives, while conservatives were much more supportive of spending on national security programs ("defense spending," "homeland security," and "gathering intelligence infor-

SURVIVAL OF THE FATTEST   THE MINI-AND-MAXI ERA

FIG. 1.6. Liberals lament military spending at the expense of domestic social welfare programs, 1982 and 1969.

Sources: 1982 and 1969 Herblock Cartoons, © The Herb Block Foundation.

mation about other countries") than liberals. This is consistent with existing quantitative research using ANES survey data that found conservatives and Republicans to be more supportive of military spending than liberals and Democrats.[41] For most conservatives, security trumps even fiscal austerity. As Ronald Reagan put it: "Defense is not a budget issue. You spend what you need."[42]

Close observers of Beltway politics have also observed how ideology shapes spending priorities. Herblock, witness to many budget battles during his fifty-five years at the *Washington Post*, was repeatedly outraged by military spending at the expense of domestic social programs. Figure 1.6 displays two of his editorial cartoons on the subject. In 1969's "The Mini-and-Maxi Era," a warmly dressed and well-accessorized woman labeled "Military Spending" walks past a shabbily dressed woman freezing in the cold, labeled "Domestic Needs." In 1982's "Survival of the Fattest" the gender changes but not the theme: a rotund and warmly dressed man labeled "Pentagon Spending" looks on as several thin men, labeled "Domestic Programs," go literally belly up in the snow. Both cartoons reveal a liberal compassion for the dispossessed, which will be discussed further in Chapter 3.

HOW IDEOLOGY SHAPES FOREIGN POLICY PREFERENCES:
THE AFFECT HEURISTIC

How do liberal and conservative ideologies shape the foreign policy preferences of the American people?

This book contends that in the absence of much knowledge about the world, gut *feelings* towards foreign countries serve as a vital mediator between ideological predispositions on the one hand, and specific foreign policy preferences on the other. As such, it joins the recent revival of interest in emotion in both psychology and political science after a long period of its neglect during the behavioral revolution.

On average, Americans are not very knowledgeable about world politics. As we will see in Chapter 5, the average score on the five-item world knowledge quiz in our spring 2011 survey was 63 percent. Similarly, Pew's fall 2011 "news IQ" quiz included eight questions on world politics, for which the average score was 60 percent. Yet Americans respond to specific (and hence difficult) foreign policy questions like *"Should we strengthen international organizations?"* or *"Should we pursue a friendlier or tougher foreign policy towards Russia?"* in consistent, if often consistently different ways. If Americans are scoring a "D–" on world knowledge, how can they maintain such consistent foreign policy preferences?

Psychologist and Nobel laureate Daniel Kahneman suggests that we frequently answer complex questions by substituting simpler ones: "Heuristic questions provide an off-the-shelf answer to . . . difficult . . . target questions." As an example, Kahneman suggests that a difficult question like *"How should financial advisors who prey on the elderly be punished?"* is actually answered by substituting an easier question about feelings, *"How much anger do I feel when I think of financial predators?"*[43] Psychologist Paul Slovic calls this particular type of heuristic an "affect heuristic," a mental shortcut by which people let their gut likes and dislikes determine their beliefs and preferences.[44] Political scientists Henry Brady and Paul Sniderman similarly call this judgmental shortcut the "likability heuristic."[45]

Following Kahneman and Slovic, and Brady and Sniderman, this book suggests that when asked difficult foreign policy questions like *"Should the U.S. pursue a friendlier or tougher foreign policy towards North Korea?"* Americans resort to the simpler affect heuristic, *"How do I feel about North Korea?"* Our ideologies then become a major source of our gut feelings towards North Korea.

Furthermore, just as the "halo effect" has been shown to lead people to overgeneralize from limited initial information to broader judgments about other people's overall characters, we likely use similar mental shortcuts with foreign

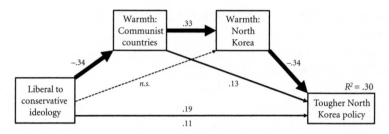

FIG. 1.7. The "halo effect" and the "affect heuristic": Conservatives desire a tougher policy towards North Korea than liberals do in large part because they feel cooler towards communist countries and hence North Korea.

Note: A serial mediation model. Both indirect paths running through "communist countries" were significant, but the one only via warmth towards North Korea was not. Indirect effect statistics are online at SUP.org. To reduce clutter, demographic covariates are not shown. In this and all subsequent mediation models, the standardized β coefficient above the line (.19) represents the direct relationship without the mediators; the β below the line (.11) is the coefficient after the mediators are included. Line thickness reflects the β coefficient *after* the mediators are included. *Data source:* OU Institute for US-China Issues, 2011.

countries, making guesses about unknown domains based upon what we do know.[46] For instance, respondents may not be able to locate North Korea on a map, but if they know that North Korea is a communist country, gut feelings about communism may exert a "halo effect" on their overall feelings towards North Korea, subsequently shaping their foreign policy preferences towards North Korea through the "affect heuristic."

Our survey data supports these ideas. In a serial mediation model (Figure 1.7) controlling for the standard demographics, feelings towards "communist countries" and "North Korea" accounted for over two-thirds of the direct relationship between ideology and North Korea policy preferences.[47] (Note the relative thickness of the arrows in the top indirect path compared to the thinness of the direct path below.) Mediation analyses are utilized to test whether one or more variables "transmit" variation from a predictor to a criterion variable, answering the *how* question of the mechanism(s) or pathway(s) through which two variables relate to one another.[48] Two of the three indirect pathways from ideology to North Korea policy preferences were statistically significant, with both running through broader feelings towards "communist countries." In other words, greater conservative than liberal coolness towards "communist countries" accounted for the bulk of conservatives' greater desire for a tougher North Korea policy. Halo effects and the affect heuristic thus both appear to be involved in a difficult judgment about a specific foreign policy preference.

The North Korea case is not unique. Of the fifteen countries that we measured feelings and foreign policy preferences towards, their mean correlation was $r = -.46$. Feelings thus accounted for a very substantial 21 percent ($-.46^2$) of the variation in policy preferences towards the average foreign country. This is very strong evidence that the affect heuristic plays a central role in allowing Americans to maintain consistent foreign policy preferences in the absence of much knowledge about foreign countries.

POWER AND AFFECT

The idea that gut feelings may shape our foreign policy preferences runs counter to mainstream international relations theory, which focuses on the role of relative power. Realist international relations theorists like Kenneth Waltz argue that states balance against military power.[49] Whether through internal balancing (arming themselves) or external balancing (developing alliances), states act on the basis of the objective distribution of power in the international system. Given that states are aggregates of individuals, from this realist perspective feelings towards foreign countries should be overwhelmed by rational assessments of relative military power in determining our individual foreign policy preferences.

The survey evidence suggests otherwise. In addition to the two rating scales measuring feelings and foreign policy preferences towards fifteen foreign countries, our survey also included a third rating scale assessing the perceived military power of those same fifteen countries. Three different statistical approaches to analyzing the resulting 4,500 data points (three variables for each of fifteen countries at one thousand respondents each) all point to the same conclusion: feelings towards foreign countries are much better predictors of foreign policy preferences than are assessments of their military strength.

Each dot in the two scatterplots at the top of Figure 1.8 represents mean scores for each of the fifteen countries for the full weighted sample. As the flat fit line on the left reveals, there was no relationship between mean judgments of the perceived military power of each of the fifteen foreign countries and the type of foreign policy desired towards them. Mean judgments of warmth towards each country, by contrast, were powerful predictors of foreign policy preferences, as the steep line to the right reveals: greater warmth was strongly associated with desires for friendlier foreign policies (a lower number on the y-axis). Respondents felt the coolest and desired the toughest foreign policies towards Iran and North Korea, while feeling the warmest and desiring the friendliest foreign policy towards England.

While this group-level data allows us to examine American views of each of fifteen foreign countries separately, it runs the risk of the "ecological fallacy"— making improper inferences about individuals based solely upon analyses of the groups to which they belong. The partial regression plots at the bottom

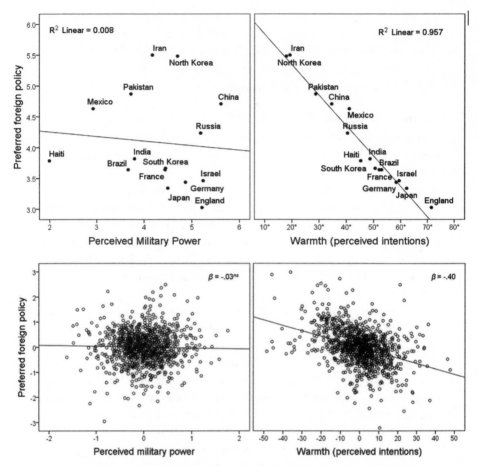

FIG. 1.8. Group- (top) and individual- (bottom) level evidence that feelings (right) are better predictors of foreign policy preferences towards fifteen foreign countries than their perceived military power (left) is.

Note: The two scatterplots at the top are of mean scores for each foreign country. The two at the bottom are partial regression plots for each individual, controlling for standard demographics. *Data source:* OU Institute for US-China Issues, 2011.

of Figure 1.8 therefore turn to an individual-level analysis of three scales of good internal reliability created by averaging the scores each participant gave for each of the fifteen countries on military power ($\alpha = .83$), warmth ($\alpha = .88$), and foreign policy preferences ($\alpha = .83$). Each dot in the two plots at the bottom represents an individual respondent's scores on two of the three scales. As can be seen from the flat plot line at left, perceived military power did not predict aggregate foreign policy preferences at the individual level. Warmth towards the fifteen foreign countries, however, substantially predicted an individual's foreign policy preferences towards them, as shown at bottom right.

Of course, we asked all three questions for only fifteen countries. While we tried to achieve a balance of friends and foes and countries from different continents, it could be argued that these results are influenced by a country selection bias. We therefore conducted individual regression analyses for each of the fifteen countries separately, with feelings, perceived military power, and the standard demographics predicting foreign policy preferences for each country. In every case, feelings were a stronger predictor of foreign policy preferences than were assessments of a country's military power (see regression table online at SUP.org). Indeed, the average coefficient for feelings was a substantial β = .42, while that for military power was statistically insignificant at just β = .05.

Together, these three statistical analyses provide strong support for the role of the "affect heuristic." Confronted with difficult questions about what foreign policy to adopt towards specific foreign countries we may not know much about, we instead substitute the easier question of how we *feel* about specific countries. Assessments of the military power of foreign countries, by contrast, have less impact on our foreign policy preferences towards them.

IDEOLOGY, AFFECT, AND FOREIGN POLICY PREFERENCES

Figure 1.9 reveals the powerful role that our gut feelings towards foreign countries play in mediating the relationship between our preexisting ideologies and our foreign policy preferences, accounting for over 80 percent of the direct relationship.[50] As the dashed arrow indicates, perceived power had no direct effect on foreign policy preferences.

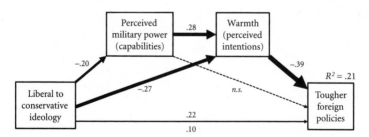

FIG. 1.9. The "affect heuristic" revisited: The impact of ideology and perceived power on overall foreign policy preferences is largely mediated through warmth towards foreign countries.

Note: A serial mediation model. Both indirect paths running through warmth were significant, but the one via military power only was not. Indirect effect statistics are online at SUP.org. *Data source:* OU Institute for US-China Issues, 2011.

Why would liberals and conservatives differ in their assessments of the objective military power of foreign countries ($\beta = -.20$, Figure 1.9 top left)? We do not perceive the world as it is, but instead actively construct our worlds. And our factual beliefs can be distorted by motivated reasoning. "If you are a hawk in your attitude toward other nations, you probably think they are relatively weak and likely to submit to your country's will," Daniel Kahneman suggests. "If you are a dove, you probably think they are strong and will not be easily coerced."[51] As we will see in Chapter 4, conservatives are more likely than liberals to be foreign policy hawks. Ideologically driven differences in hawkishness/dovishness appear to shape how militarily powerful we perceive foreign countries to be. Inclined more towards the use of military force, conservatives see a world that is weak and malleable; inclined more towards diplomacy, liberals see a stronger and less submissive world. In other words, although liberals and conservatives inhabit the same world with the same objective distribution of military power, their different psychological predispositions lead them to perceive very different distributions of military power. Perception is reality.

Perceived military power, Figure 1.9 also reveals, does not have a direct impact on foreign policy preferences. Instead, its effect is mediated through feelings towards foreign countries. This provides support for international relations theorist Stephen Walt's argument that states balance against threat (perceived malign intentions), and not against objective power itself.[52]

The most important lesson found in Figure 1.9, however, is that our feelings of warmth towards foreign countries, which act as gut intuitions about their intentions towards us, powerfully shape our foreign policy preferences ($\beta = -.39$). Those gut feelings, furthermore, are powerfully shaped by our preexisting ideologies ($\beta = -.27$). Affect mediates the impact of ideology on foreign policy preferences.

2 Beyond Red and Blue:
Four Dimensions of American Ideology

*"Free trade is no free lunch. . . . It . . . deepens the division between
rich and poor. . . . And American sovereignty is being eroded. . . .
We must start looking out for America first."*[1]
—Republican presidential candidate Patrick Buchanan, 1992, 1996

*"Prosperity comes not just from economic freedom at home, but also from the
freedom to trade abroad."*[2]
—Republican presidential candidate Ron Paul, 2008, 2012

Patrick Buchanan and Ron Paul are very different kinds of conservatives. Similarly, Dennis Kucinich and Hillary Clinton, both presidential primary candidates in 2008, are very different kinds of liberals. Are these differences among liberal and conservative political elites reflected on Main Street? Our survey data suggests that they are: Main Street liberals and conservatives are not all the same, and their differences matter for their international attitudes.

On the issue of free trade, a first glance at our survey data suggests that ideology does *not* shape American attitudes. We asked participants how they felt about "*free trade between nations.*" Their responses did not correlate with their liberal-conservative self-placement ($r = -.02$, $p = .49$), or whether they self-identified as Democrats or Republicans.[3]

We also, however, measured four distinct dimensions of American ideology with thirteen additional questions, and it turns out that three of the four were significant predictors of feelings about free trade. As Figure 2.1 reveals, while social conservatism ($\beta = -.10$) was associated with *negative* feelings towards free trade, both economic ($\beta = .11$) and political ($\beta = .09$) conservatism correlated with *positive* feelings towards free trade. These predictors appear to have canceled each other out at the aggregate level, so that there was no overall ideological or partisan difference.

The difference, instead, was between different *types* of liberals and conservatives. As the epigraphs reveal, different kinds of Republicans can hold very different attitudes towards free trade. Ron Paul is far from the first free-trade conservative. Louis Dalrymple's 1901 editorial cartoon in *Puck* magazine makes

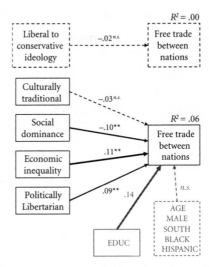

FIG. 2.1. Does ideology shape American feelings about free trade between nations? Only if disaggregated into its social, economic, and political dimensions, which offset one another

Note: Regression analyses. ** $p < .01$, "n.s." = not significant, all other *p*'s < .001. *Data source:* OU Institute for US-China Issues, 2011.

the argument for free trade visually (Figure 2.2). Uncle Sam, wearing an apron labeled "Trade Balance," proudly carries a tray brimming with American agricultural exports to a large table. Men representing the nations of the world are seated, all hungry for American products. England's John Bull sits prominently at the head of the table, holding a long list of American goods he desires. To reinforce the point, Dalrymple hangs a sign on the wall that reads, "Cafe Yankee. If you don't see what you want call for it." In this view, free trade is good for America and for Americans.

But not all conservatives agree. The protectionism that Pat Buchanan championed has roots in the old social Darwinist belief that the world is a competitive place in which trade is more often zero-sum than positive-sum. In this view, there are winners and losers in international trade, and the United States must fight to maintain its position of social dominance at the top of the international pecking order. Grant E. Hamilton's "Quarantined," from an 1892 *Judge* magazine, illustrates the debate over protectionism at that time (Figure 2.3). A laden boat approaches a pier, but a health officer declares, "No, gentlemen, you cannot land here; you have a bad attack of the free-trade plague, and it will take several years to fumigate you properly!" The news was Republican president Benjamin Harrison's executive order that, following a recent outbreak of

THE MOST POPULAR RESTAURANT IN THE WORLD

FIG. 2.2. Economic conservatives and libertarians have long promoted free trade, 1901.

Source: Louis Dalrymple, *Puck,* August 21, 1901. Image courtesy of the Library of Congress. LC-DIG-ppmsca-25557.

cholera brought by foreign ships entering New York Harbor, foreign vessels arriving at American ports were to be quarantined. But Hamilton's point is less about cholera than the "free-trade plague," a reference to the heated debate over protectionism that divided the political parties at the time. The sailors at the front of the boat include the Democratic presidential and vice presidential candidates Grover Cleveland and Adlai Stevenson I. Cleveland was a pro-business Democrat who supported free trade; Republican president Harrison was a protectionist who had presided over the passing of the 1890 McKinley Tariff, which raised average import duties to almost 50 percent. After winning his second (but nonconsecutive) term as president in 1892, Cleveland orchestrated the replacement of the McKinley Tariff with the much less onerous Wilson-Gorman Tariff of 1894.

Of course, liberals can and do disagree over free trade as well. For example, in 1993 organized labor and its Democratic Party supporters in Congress opposed the North American Free Trade Agreement (NAFTA), arguing that globalization harms American workers. The Clinton administration was able to secure NAFTA's passage in Congress only by relying upon the support of free-trade Republicans in both the House and Senate.

QUARANTINED

United States Health-Officer—*"No, gentlemen, you cannot land here; you have a bad attack of the free-trade plague, and it will take several years to fumigate you properly!"*

FIG. 2.3. Social conservatives view free trade and immigration as contaminating, 1892.

Source: Grant E. Hamilton, *Judge,* October 1, 1892. Image courtesy of the University of Oklahoma Libraries, Nichols Collection.

BEYOND LEFT AND RIGHT

Chapter 1 suggested that all Americans share a "big *L*" Liberalism that contributes to a jealousy of our individual freedoms against perceived foreign tyrannies. It then argued that within the broadly shared parameters of Liberalism, American "small *l*" liberals and conservatives differ systematically and substantially in their international attitudes and foreign policy preferences. These ideological differences, furthermore, are reflected in their gut feelings towards foreign countries, subsequently shaping their specific foreign policy preferences.

This chapter takes the argument a step further. Not all liberals and conservatives are alike, and different kinds of American liberals and conservatives hold systematically different foreign policy attitudes. Specifically, it contends that four dimensions of American ideology—cultural, social, economic, and political—have potentially disparate effects on international attitudes and foreign policy preferences. As in the case of free trade discussed above, the different dimensions of ideology will work occasionally against one another, *attenuating* the overall liberal-conservative divide. In most cases, however, these dimensions of ideology work together, *increasing* overall liberal-conservative differences. For instance, in Chapters 4 and 10 we will see that all four dimensions of ideology synergize when it comes to the United Nations, pitting powerful coalitions of different kinds of liberals against coalitions of disparate conservatives, resulting in massive differences on multilateralism at the aggregate liberal-conservative level.

The unidimensional view of ideology has a lengthy history. Christian symbolism in Europe has long associated the left with a preference for equality, and the right with the defense of social and religious hierarchies. During the French Revolution, defenders of the status quo sat on the right side of the National Assembly, and its opponents sat on the left. "Attachment to one's privileges and to the hierarchical order is on the right; the desire to bring order down is on the left," Jean Laponce writes. "The existing hierarchical structure . . . promotes security on the right, but oppresses on the left."[4]

The idea that there is a single dimension of ideology traveled to the New World, where it thrived. The diction changed, however. Although American political discourse today includes "left wing" and "right wing," the dominant language is of "liberals" and "conservatives." As noted in the Introduction, American national opinion polls have long used a single liberal-to-conservative self-placement question to measure ideology. John Jost finds it "difficult to think of another survey question in the entire social and behavioral sciences that is as useful and parsimonious as the liberalism-conservatism self-placement item."[5]

Jost is certainly right that the unidimensional ideology scale is an extremely valuable tool for understanding systematic variation in personality, attitudes, and policy preferences. A multidimensional approach to ideology also has its merits, however. On the basis of ANES survey data, political scientists Stanley Feldman and Chris Johnston argue that distinct cultural and economic dimensions of American ideology are not captured by the traditional unidimensional self-placement item. "Parsimony is a desirable goal in science," they argue. "However, this must be balanced against the need for an accurate description of social phenomena. A unidimensional model of ideology . . . does not do justice to the ways in which people actually organize their political beliefs."[6] Also working with ANES data, political scientists Shawn Treier and D. Sunshine Hillygus similarly argue that "the belief systems of the mass public are multidimensional." Many Americans, especially self-identified moderates and those who either refuse to answer the standard ideology question or respond "don't know," are "ideologically cross-pressured," holding liberal views on some issues and conservative views on others.[7]

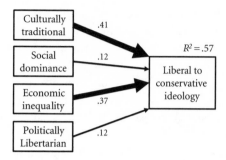

FIG. 2.4. The cultural, social, economic, and political dimensions of American ideology.

Note: A regression analysis. To reduce clutter, our seven demographic covariates, which account for 8 percent of the variance above, are not shown. Data source: OU Institute for US-China Issues, 2011.

These political scientists are right that while the unidimensional model is parsimonious, it fails to capture the full complexity of lived American ideologies. Indeed, this book contends that American ideology can usefully be understood across not just two dimensions but four: cultural, social, economic, and political. As displayed in Figure 2.4, each of these four dimensions contributes unique variance in a regression predicting the standard unidimensional measure of ideology, together accounting for about half of its variation.[8]

This analytic approach is consistent with commonsense understandings of the main issues that divide liberals and conservatives in America today. For instance, in a review of scholarship on postwar American conservatism, Kim Phillips-Fein argues that most historians believe that "its central concerns included anti-communism, a laissez-faire approach to economics, opposition to the civil rights movement, and commitment to traditional sexual norms."[9] In our terms, these refer precisely to the political, economic, social, and cultural dimensions of ideology, respectively. And liberal ideologies can be usefully understood to lie on the opposite end of each of these conservative positions. On politics, liberals tend to counter libertarian individualism and anti-communism with a greater communitarian concern for the public good. On economics, liberals favor more regulation of the market and redistribution of income than do conservatives. On social issues, liberals decry racism and support integration, affirmative action, and the civil rights movement. And on cultural issues, liberals oppose a return to traditional sexual and religious values in favor of a more modern and tolerant approach to morality.

While each of these four dimensions of ideology contributes unique variance to the unidimensional approach, it is also clear from Figure 2.4 that two dimensions, cultural and economic, do the majority of the work. This is empirically consistent with Feldman and Johnston's inductive analysis of the ANES survey data, which revealed two primary dimensions of American ideology, focusing on the culture wars and economics.[10] At a theoretic level, our data is also consistent with separate arguments made by psychologists John Jost and John Duckitt that the two major components of conservatism are resistance to change (in the form of traditional cultural values) and opposition to equality (which, in our sample, appears to be more about economic than social inequality).[11]

While cultural and economic ideologies seem to matter the most, we shall see that all four dimensions of ideology are useful for understanding the international attitudes of the American people. Socio-racial ideology will be important when we examine American attitudes towards nonwhite countries like those of Latin America, the Middle East, and East Asia, to be discussed in Chapters 6, 8, and 9. And political ideology (communitarianism/libertarianism) will have a big influence on attitudes towards communist countries and international organizations like the United Nations, to be explored in Chapters 9 and 10. We therefore introduce each dimension of ideology in turn.

CULTURAL IDEOLOGY: GOD, GAYS, AND . . . FOREIGN COUNTRIES?

"There is sin and evil in the world, and we're enjoined by Scripture and the Lord Jesus to oppose it with all our might. . . . Communis[ts] . . . are the focus of evil in the modern world."[12]
—Republican President Ronald Reagan, 1983

"North Korea is a regime arming with missiles and weapons of mass destruction, while starving its citizens. Iran aggressively pursues these weapons and exports terror, while an unelected few repress the Iranian people's hope for freedom. Iraq continues to flaunt its hostility toward America and to support terror. . . . States like these, and their terrorist allies, constitute an axis of evil, arming to threaten the peace of the world."[13]
—Republican President George W. Bush, 2002

William Jennings Bryan was the "perpetual candidate." He was the Democratic nominee for president in 1896, 1900, and 1908, losing all three elections. A devout Presbyterian, his faith informed his domestic and international politics. As noted in the Introduction, he stood and lost with the anti-imperialists in 1900 as President McKinley rode a wave of patriotic pride to reelection following the victorious Spanish–American War and the annexation of Cuba and the Philippines. A pacifist, Bryan later served as secretary of state for President Woodrow Wilson, but resigned in 1915 after Wilson took a tough stand on the German sinking of the British ocean liner *Lusitania*, which killed over one thousand people.

Bryan is better known, however, for his fundamentalist positions on domestic issues. His national campaigning helped Congress pass the Eighteenth Amendment to the U.S. Constitution in 1918, ushering in Prohibition. He later opposed the theory of evolution and social Darwinism, which he blamed for inciting the Germans to war. Bryan is perhaps best known for defeating Clarence Darrow in the Scopes Trial, in which the court upheld a Tennessee law prohibiting the teaching of evolution.

The fundamentalists lost the culture wars of the 1920s, however, as Prohibition was repealed and evolution entered school textbooks. They then retreated from the public sphere. Following the emergence of the sexual revolution, feminism, abortion, pornography, and gay rights in the 1960s and 1970s, however, they returned to political activism. Historian Daniel Williams argues that fundamentalists were reunited by a "belief that America was rapidly losing its Christian moorings and needed to repent . . . they were committed to the idea of a Christian nation with a Protestant-based moral code—and they turned to politics in order to realize that vision."[14] The earlier Protestant focus on opposing Catholics like Democrats Al Smith in 1924 and John F. Kennedy in 1960 was abandoned in favor of a broader agenda that would include Catholics, namely, protecting a Christian nation against the forces of secularism. By 1980 Evangelical Protestants had hitched their wagon to one candidate and one political party: Ronald Reagan and the Republicans. In his 1983 "Evil Empire" speech given to the National Association of Evangelicals, cited in the first epigraph, President Reagan equated the fight against communism and the Soviet Union with the fight against "evil."

The rhetoric of evil returned twenty years later when, following the September 11, 2001, terrorist attacks, President George W. Bush declared in his 2002 State of the Union address that North Korea, Iran, and Iraq, together with their terrorist allies, formed an "axis of evil." Unlike Reagan, Bush was a born-again Christian and a true believer. As noted in the Introduction, Bush didn't need to pander to the religious right, because he *was* the religious right.[15] Many liberals were alarmed. In a 2003 *New Yorker*, Lee Lorenz depicts the Devil's secretary reporting to his boss that he has sent cards to North Korea, Iran, and Iraq on the anniversary of the president's "Axis of Evil" speech (Figure 2.5). While poking fun of Bush, the cartoon also speaks to the discomfort that many liberals feel when religion shapes public policy.

The role of religion in American political life only appears to be increasing, as the culture wars thrive. In a December 2011 Iowa campaign ad run during the Republican presidential primaries, Texas governor Rick Perry declared, "I'm not ashamed to admit that I'm a Christian. But you don't need to be in the pew every Sunday to know that there's something wrong in this country when gays

"Oh, and I've taken the liberty of sending anniversary cards to the axis of evil."

FIG. 2.5. Cultural ideology: Liberals decry Bush's Manichean foreign policy, 2003.
Source: Lee Lorenz, *New Yorker,* February 3, 2003. Image courtesy of the Cartoon Bank.

can serve openly in the military, but our kids can't openly celebrate Christmas or pray in school. As president, I'll end Obama's war on religion."[16] Then, in the spring of 2012, liberals accused conservatives of waging a "war on women" by restricting access to contraception and abortion, opposing legislation that would mandate equal pay for women and end workplace discrimination, and opposing the Violence Against Women Act. In a fundraising e-mail, House Minority Leader Nancy Pelosi urged donations "to send a clear message that we will not tolerate or stand by while Republicans wage war on women's rights."[17]

Survey evidence suggests that Reagan, Bush, Perry, and Pelosi were *not* disconnected from the American public. As noted in Chapter 1, the survey data supports Alan Abramowitz and not Morris Fiorina: the culture wars are real. Americans are divided over cultural and religious values, and those differences shape their policy preferences. On the specific issue of the relationship between religiosity and abortion attitudes, which he depicts as a crucial case, Fiorina's assertion that "the churched and unchurched differ less on abortion than stereotypes suggest" is particularly galling. It is based upon his eyeball interpretation of General Social Survey (GSS) data on six specific conditions under which a woman should be allowed to have an abortion: "the difference . . . is

... about two circumstances—not exactly a religious war."[18] Remarkably, no statistical evidence is presented to support his interpretation; further, statistical analysis of the 2004 GSS data Fiorina presents actually reveals a *very large* difference between his "churched" and "unchurched" groups in their attitudes towards abortion.[19] Fiorina's argument, therefore, is contradicted by the very survey evidence he presents.

Other surveys also point to a culture war. On the basis of their 2006 Faith Matters Survey, Putnam and Campbell argue in *American Grace* that the most and least religious Americans differ substantially on issues like abortion and homosexuality.[20] Our own 2011 survey included three items that cohered well as a scale of religiosity ($\alpha = .86$):

- *Aside from weddings and funerals, how often do you attend religious services?*
- *Outside of attending religious services, how often do you pray?*
- *How important is religion in your life?*[21]

Following Putnam and Campbell, we defined the most and least religious Americans as the top and bottom quintiles on this scale.[22] Supporting their argument, in our survey the two groups disagreed *massively* on policy preferences towards abortion and gay marriage.[23] There were also massive differences between them on the issue of prayer in public schools, and moderate differences on gun control and the death penalty.[24]

Of course, frequency of religious *practice* is not the only way to measure religiosity. We also measured religious *beliefs* with a "biblical literalism" scale composed of five items that cohered very well ($\alpha = .89$):

- *The Bible is literally true, from Genesis to Revelation, from Adam and Eve to Armageddon.*
- *I have no doubt at all that God exists.*[25]
- *Whenever science and scripture conflict, science is right.* (reverse coded)
- *The basic cause of evil in this world is Satan, who is still constantly & ferociously fighting against God.*
- *God gave Palestine (today's Israel) to the Jewish people.*[26]

Biblical literalism, it turns out, is an even stronger predictor of policy preferences in the culture wars than religious practice is.[27]

Pew's Andrew Kohut maintains that "With the exception of policy towards Israel, religion has little bearing on how [the American people] think about international affairs."[28] The 2011 survey data paints the opposite picture: both religious beliefs (biblical literalism) and practices (religiosity) consistently and strongly correlate with attitudes towards international affairs. For instance,

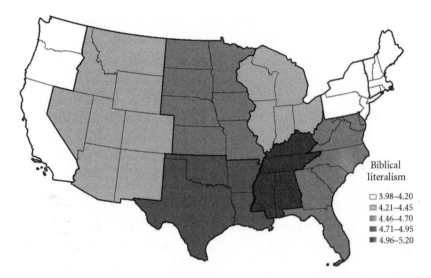

FIG. 2.6. The "Bible Belt": Southerners score the highest on biblical literalism.

Note: Map uses nine census divisions of the United States. $F(8, 1035) = 3.03$, $p = .002$, $\eta_p^2 = .023$, controlling for age, gender, education, income, race, and ethnicity. My thanks to May Yuan for her help with this map. *Data source:* OU Institute for US-China Issues, 2011.

biblical literalism alone accounts for 16 percent of the variation in Israel policy preferences, 13 percent of Mexican border policy preferences, and 13 percent of China policy preferences.[29] As we shall see in Chapters 6, 8, and 9, however, the direction of biblical literalism's impact varies, as greater biblical literalism is associated with desires for a *friendlier* Israel policy but *tougher* Mexico and China policies. And as we will see in Chapters 4 and 10, biblical literalism is also strongly associated with skepticism towards international treaties and opposition to multilateralism.[30] Similar patterns are found when substituting religiosity for biblical literalism.

There are statistically significant regional differences in biblical literalism. As shown in Figure 2.6, Southerners score the highest on biblical literalism, while Americans from the West coast and the Northeast score the lowest. These regional differences in biblical literalism are a major reason why we include region as a demographic covariate in most of the statistical analyses in this book. For instance, in a regression with the six other demographic covariates, Southerners are slightly less likely than other Americans ($\beta = -.06$, $p = .048$) to desire a tougher Israel policy. But when biblical literalism is added into the regression, the effect of being from the South drops to statistical insignificance ($\beta = -.01$, $p = .67$).

In this book, however, cultural ideology is conceptualized as broader than either religious practices or beliefs. The nonreligious can also subscribe to traditional cultural values. We draw three items from scales of what psychologist Robert Altemeyer calls "conventionalism," and John Duckitt calls "traditionalism"[31]:

- *There is absolutely nothing wrong with nudist camps.* (reverse coded)
- *This country will flourish if young people stop experimenting with drugs, alcohol, and sex, and focus on family values.*
- *There is nothing wrong with premarital sexual intercourse.* (reverse coded)

The resulting scale ($\alpha = .77$) is called "cultural traditionalism," with higher values indicating greater adherence to "traditional" values and lifestyles, and lower scores indicating a preference for "modern" or secular values and lifestyles. Cultural traditionalism, it turns out, is almost as powerful a predictor of culture war preferences as biblical literalism is.[32]

Cultural traditionalism influences foreign policy preferences as well. The topic of this book was inspired in part by the surprise discovery several years ago that policy preferences towards China could be predicted not just from positions on culture war issues like abortion, which can be linked to China's much publicized one-child policy, but even from attitudes towards gay marriage and prayer in public schools, which would seem to have nothing to do with China.[33] Remarkably, this book will show that cultural traditionalism predicts not just desires for friendlier policies towards Israel and tougher policies towards China, but also tougher policies towards Mexico and France. As we shall see in Chapter 6, Americans who score high on cultural traditionalism are more likely to view Mexico—a major source of illegal immigrants into the United States—as a threat to America's Christian values and WASP identity. And as we will see in Chapter 7, cultural traditionalism also divides Americans in their attitudes towards France: liberal Francophiles are drawn to French culture, while conservative Francophobes are repelled by its perceived "libertine" and secular ways.

SOCIAL IDEOLOGY: RACE AND AMERICAN FOREIGN POLICY

"Our country calls not for the life of ease but for the life of strenuous endeavor. The twentieth century looms before us big with the fate of many nations. If . . . we shrink from the hard contests where men must win at hazard of their lives and at the risk of all they hold dear, then the bolder and stronger peoples will pass us by, and win for themselves the domination of the world."[34]
—Republican Theodore Roosevelt, 1899

"Those who would have this nation enter upon a career of empire must consider not only the effect of imperialism on the Filipinos but they must also calculate its effects upon our own nation. We cannot repudiate the principle of self-government in the Philippines without weakening that principle here."[35]
—Democrat William Jennings Bryan, 1900

Theodore Roosevelt, war hero from his 1898 exploits with the Rough Riders in Cuba, was Republican president William McKinley's running mate in 1900. When McKinley was assassinated in 1901, Roosevelt became president at the age of forty-two, serving until 1909. His slogan "Speak softly and carry a big stick" captured a foreign policy that combined elements of both diplomacy and force. Roosevelt negotiated an end to the Russo-Japanese War in the 1905 Treaty of Portsmouth, earning himself a Nobel Peace Prize. But he also built the "Great White Fleet" of sixteen battleships and sent them on a circumnavigation of the globe in 1907–9 to parade American naval power.

Underlying Roosevelt's international activism was the dog-eat-dog view of international politics common at the turn of the century. The social Darwinist ideas that arrived in America in the late nineteenth century provided a rationale for Americans with imperial ambitions. As historian Richard Hofstadter writes, "Imperialists, calling upon Darwinism in defense of the subjugation of weaker races, could point to *The Origin of Species*, which had referred in its subtitle to *The Preservation of Favored Races in the Struggle for Life*. Darwin had been talking about pigeons, but the imperialists saw no reason why his theories should not apply to men."[36] In an excellent chapter on "The Hierarchy of Race," Michael Hunt similarly argues that "Darwinian notions served to reinforce pre-existing ideas of Anglo-Saxon superiority. . . . Lesser races, awed and grateful, could follow the lead of the Anglo-Saxon—or drop to the bottom of the heap to meet their fate, ultimate extinction."[37]

Hunt is right that racial thinking and racism have been a persistent theme in U.S. foreign policy. Where he emphasizes racism as a *commonality* among all Americans, however, this book follows Rogers Smith in emphasizing a very long tradition of *differences* among Americans over racial politics. "Inegalitarian ideologies," Smith writes, "have shaped . . . American politics just as deeply" as egalitarian ideals.[38] For instance, we saw in the Introduction that differences over race divided Americans even during the height of American imperial pride at the turn of the last century. Anti-expansionists like Mark Twain and William Jennings Bryan objected to the subjugation of other races, arguing that colored peoples like the Filipinos, for example, were endowed with an equal right to self-determination. McKinley and Roosevelt disagreed.

Immigration and slavery, of course, conspired to make race a contentious issue in American politics from its very beginnings. By the nineteenth century Americans were heatedly debating immigration and fought a civil war in part over slavery. One 1860s lithograph, entitled "The Great Fear of the Period: That Uncle Sam May Be Swallowed by Foreigners," depicts Uncle Sam being devoured from both ends at once, with an Irish man swallowing his head and a Chinese man eating from his feet (Figure 2.7). Irish and Chinese immigrants, of

FIG. 2.7. Social ideology I: Conservative fears of racial extinction, 1860s.
Source: 1860s lithograph courtesy of the Library of Congress. LC-DIG-pga-03047.

course, were busy laying America's transcontinental railroad system, displayed underfoot.

But this midnineteenth-century view of an Irish and Chinese racial menace did not go unchallenged. In an 1869 *Harper's Weekly,* Thomas Nast portrays "Uncle Sam's Thanksgiving Dinner" (Figure 2.8). The Civil War was over, and the Fourteenth Amendment had been ratified, granting equal rights and citizenship to all Americans. The peoples of the world, of every race, gather at the banquet table of "self-government" and "universal suffrage." Uncle Sam carves the turkey while Columbia sits between an African and a Chinese, engaging in polite conversation. It is a welcoming, multiracial vision of harmony and equality. Nast also makes his point explicitly, writing, "Come One, Come All" and "Free and Equal."

Americans continue, of course, to debate race today. Neither the Civil War nor the civil rights movement put an end to racism. Indeed, racial desegregation was a big part of what motivated the conservative backlash to the Great Society of the 1960s, contributing to Ronald Reagan's victory in 1980.

Much psychological research on racism today follows from the pioneering work of Jim Sidanius and Felicia Pratto on "social dominance orientation" (SDO), a generalized preference for social hierarchy and desire to dominate out-groups.[39] Following the separate work of psychologists John Jost, Mathew Kugler, and Arnold Ho, this book distinguishes between two facets of SDO—"group-based dominance" and "opposition to equality"—and utilizes the former.[40] Group-based dominance (SDO-D) is associated with greater perceived

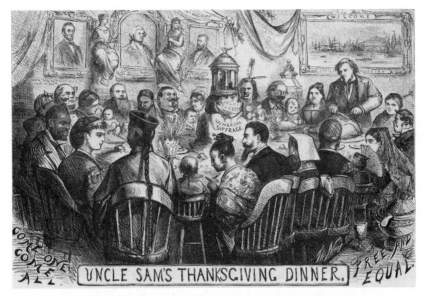

FIG. 2.8. Social ideology II: Liberal desires for racial equality, 1869.

Source: Thomas Nast, *Harper's Weekly*, November 20, 1869. Image courtesy of the Ohio State University Billy Ireland Cartoon Library and Museum.

intergroup competition, desires that "inferior" groups be actively subjugated, and "old fashioned" prejudice—the belief that some groups are inherently superior or more worthy than others.[41] As James Baldwin writes in *Nobody Knows My Name*, "The Negro tells us where the bottom is: *because he is there*, and *where he is*, beneath us, we know where the limits are and how far we must not fall."[42]

We measure the group dominance facet of SDO with three items:

- *Inferior groups should stay in their place.*
- *It's probably a BAD thing that certain groups are at the top and other groups are at the bottom.* (reverse coded)
- *Some groups of people are simply inferior to other groups.*

Note that none of these statements explicitly mentions race; "groups" is left ambiguous. Nonetheless, a large literature has overwhelmingly demonstrated that SDO consistently predicts prejudice against "colored" groups like Latinos, blacks, Asians, and Arabs, as well as opposition to social welfare and affirmative action policies.[43] Our 2011 survey data replicates these findings. In a series of multiple regressions pitting all four dimensions of American ideology against one another, and controlling for the standard demographics, social dominance was the strongest predictor of prejudice against "the Chinese people"[44] ($\beta = .21$), and coolness towards "Asians" ($\beta = -.15$) and "Muslims" ($\beta = -.21$).

On average, conservatives scored much higher on social dominance orientation than liberals did.[45] This finding supports Donald Kinder and Cindy Kam's argument, in *Us Against Them: Ethnocentric Foundations of American Opinion*, that "Americans who think of themselves as conservative are a bit more ethnocentric, on average, than are those who think of themselves as liberal."[46]

Our data also supports Sidanius and Pratto's speculation that "Whatever social dominance values one has developed about intergroup relations of one type (e.g., between races) are likely to be applied to intergroup relations of other types (e.g. between nations)."[47] Again pitting our four dimensions of American ideology against one another, and controlling for the standard demographics, social dominance orientation was the strongest predictor of warmth towards the nonwhite countries of Haiti ($\beta = -.20$), India ($\beta = -.14$), Taiwan ($\beta = -.11$), South Korea and Japan (both $\beta = -.10$, $p = .002$), but it did not predict feelings towards fellow Caucasian countries England ($p = .93$), Russia ($p = .62$), and Germany ($p = .32$). As we will see in our case study chapters on Latin America (Chapter 6), the Middle East (Chapter 8), East Asia (Chapter 9), and even the United Nations (Chapter 10), the international attitudes of the American people are not color-blind; they are tied to the same ideological divisions that animate racial politics at home.

ECONOMIC IDEOLOGY: INCOME REDISTRIBUTION AND THE SOCIALIST MENACE

"High inequality, which has turned us into a nation with a much weakened middle class, has a corrosive effect on social relations and politics, one that has become ever more apparent as America has moved deeper into a new Gilded Age."[48]

—Nobel Laureate Paul Krugman, 2007

"There is income inequality in America, there always has been, and hopefully there always will be."[49]

—Republican presidential candidate Rick Santorum, 2012

American liberals and conservatives are divided over inequality. "Liberals are not satisfied when only some people—members of an aristocratic class here, representatives of a business elite there—have the chance to determine how they will live," writes political scientist Alan Wolfe. "Any society that closes off opportunities for people to achieve their full human capacities, or allows persistent inequalities ... would not be a liberal one."[50] The conservative view is different. "There is no principle more basic in the conservative philosophy than that of the inherent and absolute incompatibility between liberty and equality," writes sociologist Robert Nisbet. "The abiding purpose of liberty is its protection of ... property. .... The inherent objective of equality, on the other hand, is that of ... redistribution."[51]

This disagreement has a long history. In an ambitious chapter of *Ideology and U.S. Foreign Policy* on the "Perils of Revolution," Michael Hunt argues that from the very founding, Americans have been united by a "political culture inimical to revolutionary upheaval and especially to the violation of property rights." He cites Alexis de Tocqueville, who claimed that "In no country in the world is love of property more active and more anxious than in the United States." This "dominant national attitude," Hunt maintains, has powerfully shaped American attitudes towards international affairs, from the French Revolution to the Mexican, Russian, and Chinese Revolutions.[52]

Our survey data proves Hunt right: attitudes towards property and its proper distribution do shape the international attitudes of the American people. It also, however, reveals that differences among Americans in their economic ideologies are associated with variation in their international attitudes. Indeed, although Hunt argues the "consensus history" view, his narrative often highlights disagreements. For instance, Hunt opens the "Perils of Revolution" with a thoughtful discussion of how the second and third U.S. presidents differed over the French Revolution. John Adams was a Federalist, wary of threats to property. Anxious about popular cries for economic leveling, he attacked the French Revolution for "chasing after the phantom of equality of persons and property." Thomas Jefferson, by contrast, was less alarmed by redistribution and more optimistic about the potential of revolution to bring liberty to France.[53]

Immigration and economic development in the nineteenth century only further polarized American views of foreign upheavals. Hunt notes that the 1871 Paris Commune "touched sensitive political nerves at home," as European immigrants had "swelled the ranks of labor . . . [and] had begun to challenge property rights and foment class conflict." Indeed, Hunt recognizes that both class and ethnicity later divided Americans over the early twentieth-century revolutions in Mexico, China, and Russia: "Revolutions . . . held few terrors for an American underclass. . . . On the other hand, the Adamsian [Federalist] view appealed most to the wealthy and socially prominent who identified culturally with England. They feared the radical potential of all revolutions and the implicit challenge they posed to . . . the sanctity of property at home."[54]

American debates over economic inequality only intensified with the 1890s Gilded Age of staggering income inequality, followed by the Great Depression and the New Deal of the 1930s. Economic disaster shattered the credibility of classical laissez-faire economics, and John Maynard Keynes provided a theoretical rationale for an active role for the state in the economy. Democratic president Franklin D. Roosevelt put it bluntly: "We have always known that heedless self-interest was bad morals; now we know that it is bad economics."[55] First during the New Deal and then during World War II, progressive income taxes, the expansion of unions, the 1935 Social Security Act, and massive government investment in infrastructure and the war effort combined to reduce the income gap between the rich and the working classes, producing what economic historians Claudia Goldin and Robert Margo have called the "Great Compression."[56]

After the war, "modern Republicans" like Dwight D. Eisenhower and his labor secretary Arthur Larson joined Democrats in embracing labor and an active role for the government in the economy. As Larson put it in *A Republican Looks at His Party*, "1896 was against labor; 1936 was against business; this administration is against neither, but is for both."[57] Rapid economic expansion in the 1950s and 1960s under conditions of relatively low income inequality, Paul Krugman argues, created the U.S. middle class.[58] This period culminated in Democratic president Lyndon B. Johnson's Great Society initiative, which included not only the Civil Rights Act of 1964 but also the 1965 creation of Medicare for the elderly and Medicaid for the poor.

The rise of modern conservatism and Ronald Reagan's election in 1980 is often attributed to "white backlash" against the sexual revolution, the civil rights movement, and the anti-Vietnam protests of the 1960s and 1970s. In other words, it is largely viewed in cultural and socio-racial terms. In *Invisible Hands*, however, historian Kim Phillips-Fein traces the *economic* origins of modern conservatism all the way back to the New Deal itself. Rejecting the "Keynesian consensus" from its very inception, wealthy businessmen fought labor unions, federal social welfare programs, and government regulation of the economy. Phillips-Fein cites Irénée du Pont of DuPont Chemicals, who wrote in 1935 that "the so called 'New Deal' advocated by the [Roosevelt] administration is nothing more or less than the Socialistic doctrine called by another name." Later, in the 1950s, wealthy businessmen disparaged "modern Republicans" like President Eisenhower as "collectivists," and sought to roll back the New Deal through the financing of new think tanks, radio stations, and magazines devoted to the struggle against labor unions and the welfare state.[59]

Although Republican senator Barry Goldwater lost the presidential election of 1964 to Lyndon B. Johnson in a landslide, his 1960 *The Conscience of a Conservative* became a bible for a generation of economic conservatives. Short and passionately written, it railed against the redistribution of income through taxation and social welfare services: "collectivists . . . have learned that socialism can be achieved through Welfarism quite as well as through Nationalization. They understand that private property can be confiscated as effectively by taxation as by appropriating it." Like Edmund Burke and the classical conservatives who preceded him, Goldwater grounded his defense of inequality in human nature: "We are all equal in the eyes of God but we are equal *in no other respect*.

Artificial devices [like the graduated income tax] for enforcing equality among unequal men must be rejected . . . [to] honor . . . the laws of nature."[60]

This conservative hostility towards economic equality is experiencing a revival. The rhetoric of class conflict heated up during the 2012 presidential contest. "We believe in free people and free enterprise, not redistribution," Mitt Romney stated in a September 18, 2012, interview with Fox News. "The right course for America is to create growth, create wealth, not to redistribute wealth."[61]

The last three decades of conservative ascendance has led, according to Paul Krugman, to a "Great Divergence," as income inequality has returned to levels not seen since the Gilded Age. The inflation of the Carter years discredited Keynesian economics, and Milton Friedman and other conservative economists advocated a return to laissez-faire. Taxes, government regulation of the economy, and social welfare spending came under renewed attack. As quoted in the epigraph, Krugman argues that we now live in a "second Gilded Age," where the rich get richer and the poor get poorer. Where Rick Santorum, also cited in the epigraph, embraces the new inequality as desirable, Krugman passionately opposes it: "I believe in a relatively equal society, supported by institutions that limit extremes of wealth and poverty. . . . That makes me a liberal, and I'm proud of it."[62]

Do these opposed liberal and conservative economic views shape the international attitudes of the American people? To find out, we developed a "support for income inequality" scale composed of three items that cohered very well[63]:

- *Differences between high and low incomes should remain as they are.*
- *The government should decrease income differences.* (reverse coded)
- *Class differences should be smaller than they are today.* (reverse coded)

On average, conservatives scored *vastly* higher on this support for income inequality scale than liberals did.[64] This is consistent with the U.S. data from the 2006 World Values Survey, implemented online by Knowledge Networks, in which self-identified Republicans ($N = 390$) scored much higher than Democrats ($N = 502$) on a ten-point scale from "*Incomes should be made more equal*" to "*We need larger income differences as incentives for individual effort.*"[65] A regression with our scale further revealed that support for income inequality was greatest among the wealthy ($\beta = .14$) and lowest among blacks ($\beta = -.15$). The elderly ($\beta = .08$) and men ($\beta = .06, p = .056$) were slightly more supportive of income inequality, while greater education was marginally associated with opposition to income inequality ($\beta = -.06, p = .08$).

Our support for income inequality scale, unsurprisingly, predicts coolness

"HIGH SIERRA"

FIG. 2.9. Economic ideology: Liberals object to income inequality at home and abroad, 1963.

Source: Chicago Sun-Times. Copyright Bill Mauldin, 1963. Courtesy of the Bill Mauldin Estate LLC.

towards communist and former communist countries like North Korea ($\beta = -.10$, $p = .005$), China ($\beta = -.10$, $p = .005$), and Russia ($\beta = -.09$, $p = .016$) in regressions controlling for the three other dimensions of ideology and the seven standard demographics. It also shapes feelings towards developing-world countries in Latin America. As we will see in Chapter 6, economic ideology ($\beta = -.18$) is the strongest predictor of feelings towards Mexico, followed by cultural ($\beta = -.14$) and socio-racial ($\beta = -.10$, $p = .002$) ideologies. Similarly, feelings towards Brazil are shaped by cultural ($\beta = -.18$) and economic ($\beta = -.14$) ideologies, but not by social or political ideologies.

Bill Mauldin captured how economic ideology shapes liberal views of the developing world in a 1963 editorial cartoon for the *Chicago Sun-Times* (Figure 2.9). Entitled "High Sierra," it uses a sombrero labeled "Latin America" to depict the mountain of income inequality that separates two aloof representatives of "the very rich," seated on the top of the mountain, from the countless "very poor," seemingly drowning far below. Compassion for the plight of the poor, we will see in Chapter 3, is a major reason why liberals tend to feel warmer towards developing-world countries than conservatives do.

Non-findings can often be as informative as findings. Pitted against the other three ideological dimensions, economic ideology is *not* associated with feelings towards European capitalist countries like Germany ($\beta = .003, p = .94$) and England ($\beta = -.06, p = .11$). But support for economic inequality does predict coolness towards both "Europeans" ($\beta = -.09, p = .015$) in general and France ($\beta = -.24$) in particular. As we will see in Chapter 7, while many conservatives view France coolly as a "socialist" European state, liberals like Eric Alterman view France and the European social welfare states warmly, as models of "what liberals want."[66] The economic conservatism of Margaret Thatcher and Angela Merkel may explain why Americans do not appear to view England and Germany as typically "European" social welfare states.

POLITICAL IDEOLOGY: COMMUNITARIANS, LIBERTARIANS, AND THE WORLD

> *"The Conservative's first concern will always be: Are we maximizing freedom?"*[67]
> —Republican presidential candidate Barry Goldwater, 1964

> *"Republicans celebrate the individual. But they forget the importance of community and generosity."*[68]
> —Democratic presidential candidate George McGovern, 1972

Former Texas congressman Ron Paul is not your typical Republican. We have already seen that he challenged Newt Gingrich's "warmongering" during a 2012 presidential primary debate, and that he disagrees with protectionists like Pat Buchanan over free trade. Paul first ran for president as a libertarian in 1988 and later ran twice as a Republican, in 2008 and 2012. With financial support from the billionaire Koch brothers, but also from abundant, small online donations, Paul was a very serious player in Republican politics.

The communitarian-libertarian divide represents a fourth and final, political dimension of American ideology. The core of libertarianism is the idea that individuals are sovereign and self-governing, and should be free to do anything they want as long as they don't aggress against others. From this perspective, taxation is theft and the government is basically a legalized mafia. Indeed, "anarchist libertarians" or "anarcho-capitalists," like Murray Rothbard, completely reject government, arguing that "Capitalism is the fullest expression of anarchism, and anarchism is the fullest expression of capitalism."[69] By contrast, Ron Paul and the majority of American libertarians today are "miniarchists," who acknowledge a limited role for a very small government in providing for common defense, police, and courts. The government, in this view, is little more than a "referee" between sovereign individuals, or a "night watchman" in their service.[70]

Libertarians often trace their ideology to classical liberals like John Locke, whose views on natural rights and the social contract are seen as celebrating individual liberty. Jacob Huebert declares that "Libertarians were the original liberals."[71] They also look to the U.S. Declaration of Independence, with its focus on the "inalienable rights" of the people, as "*in its essence* a libertarian document."[72]

But libertarianism today has its more proximate origins in the Cold War. Ayn Rand's novels *The Fountainhead* (1943) and *Atlas Shrugged* (1957), the "gateway drugs" for many Americans into libertarianism, are best understood in the context of the early Cold War conflation of communisms of the left and fascisms of the right. Rand, like "totalitarianism" theorists Hannah Arendt and Zbigniew Brzezinski, was an émigré from Europe.[73] "Rand's defense of individualism, celebration of capitalism, and controversial morality of selfishness . . . all sprang from her early life experiences in Communist Russia," historian Jennifer Burns writes in her biography, *Goddess of the Market: Ayn Rand and the American Right*. "Her indictment of altruism, social welfare, and service to others sprang from her belief that these ideals underlay Communism [and] Nazism."[74]

Libertarians today are often described as economic conservatives but cultural liberals, siding with the right in opposition to government regulations and social welfare programs, and with the left in opposing laws regulating private life, such as on homosexuality or drug use. On the basis of a very large convenience sample of 11,994 self-identified American libertarians, a group of social psychologists has recently demonstrated that, compared to liberals and conservatives, self-described libertarians do indeed value liberty more. Their intellectual style is more coolly cognitive, and they display more antisocial tendencies, scoring lower on interdependence and social relatedness.[75] The Cato Institute claimed that in 2010 about 14 percent of Americans were libertarians.[76]

A communitarian critique of radical libertarianism emerged in the 1970s and 1980s. "The defense of negative freedom, of civil rights and liberties, while ignoring massive injustice, poverty, and despair will be self-defeating," sociologist Robert Bellah wrote in his 1975 *The Broken Covenant*. "Negative freedom only defends the individual against incursions, whereas positive freedom actually creates the conditions for the full participation of all." Bellah passionately argued that the self-interest at the heart of American individualism had always been balanced by a Protestant republicanism, the "covenant" between God and man and among men themselves. In early New England political thought, "Calvinist 'individualism' only made sense within the collective context. Individual action outside the bounds of religious and moral norms was seen in Augustinian terms as the very archetype of sin."[77]

Michael Sandel then published *Liberalism and the Limits of Justice* in 1982, and Bellah's coauthored *Habits of the Heart: Individualism and Commitment in American Life* was released three years later.[78] Both books deplored the consequences of excessive individualism on American society. As communitarian Amitai Etzioni later argued, developments from the 1960s to the 1980s contributed to a "grand loss of commitment to the common good." In the 1960s, the left dismissed social obligations in favor of "finding themselves" and pursuing their innermost desires. Then in the 1980s, the right's "instrumental individualism added insult to injury as Reagan, like Thatcher, made a virtue out of watching out for oneself."[79]

In 2012, twenty years after *Liberalism and the Limits of Justice*, Sandel published *What Money Can't Buy: The Moral Limits of Markets*, decrying the emergence of a "market society" in America. "A market economy is a tool—a valuable and effective tool—for organizing productive activity," Sandel acknowledged. But "a market society is a way of life in which market values seep into every aspect of human endeavor. It's a place where social relations are made over in the image of the market." The commodification of the social realm, Sandel worries, has political implications: "Democracy does not require perfect equality, but it does require that citizens share in a common life. . . . For this is how we learn to negotiate and abide our differences, and how we come to care for the common good."[80]

In the fall of 2011 a video of Elizabeth Warren, a Democrat running for the U.S. Senate in Massachusetts, went viral on the Internet. Speaking at a campaign event, she argued passionately against the libertarian view of taxation: "There is nobody in this country who got rich on his own. NOBODY! You built a factory out there—good for you! But I want to be clear, you moved your goods to market on the roads *the rest of us* paid for. You hired workers—the rest of us paid to educate—you were safe in your factory because of police forces and fire forces that the rest of us paid for."[81] A former Harvard Law professor and advocate for the Consumer Financial Protection Bureau, Warren became a symbol of a growing communitarian opposition to radical antitax libertarianism.

But it is President Barack Obama who has harnessed communitarian rhetoric the most forcefully. "What makes America exceptional are the bonds that hold together the most diverse nation on earth. The belief that our destiny is shared; that this country only works when we accept certain obligations to one another and to future generations," he declared in his Chicago reelection victory speech in the early morning hours of November 7, 2012. "The freedom which so many Americans have fought for and died for comes with responsibilities as well as rights. And among those are love and charity and duty and patriotism. That's what makes America great."

Does this political dimension of American ideology shape the international attitudes of the American people? To find out, we created a four-item "communitarianism-libertarianism" scale:

- *American society has swung too far towards individual rights at the expense of social responsibilities.* (reverse coded)
- *Individual rights are more important than the good of the group.*
- *Individuals should be free to follow their own dreams in their own ways, without interference from government.*
- *Government must limit our individual freedoms so as to prevent unchecked selfishness, greed, and immorality.* (reverse coded)

Note that while the first pair of items set the individual against society, the second pair pit the individual against the government.[82]

There were no effects of age, education, income, region, or ethnicity on our communitarianism-libertarianism scale. But men were more libertarian than women ($\beta = .12$), who were more communitarian; and blacks were less libertarian ($\beta = -.12$) than nonblacks.

Political ideology, we will see, predicts a variety of international attitudes. Libertarianism is associated with greater opposition to humanitarian idealism in general (Chapter 4), and humanitarian aid for Haiti in particular (Chapter 6). In Chapter 9, on East Asia, we will see that libertarianism predicts coolness towards "red" countries like China and North Korea but warmth towards the "free" East Asian democracies of Japan, Taiwan, and South Korea. And we will see in Chapter 10 that libertarianism is a powerful predictor of feelings towards international organizations like the United Nations. Libertarians do not like the American government, let alone "world government."

AMERICAN IDEOLOGICAL PROFILES

How do these four dimensions of American ideology relate to one another?

The zero-order correlations among our four dimensions of ideology vary substantially. Economic ideology correlates strongly with both cultural ($r = .39$) and social ($r = .39$) ideology, and substantially with political ideology ($r = .29$). But libertarian ideology correlates only weakly with social dominance ($r = .09$, $p = .006$), and not at all with cultural traditionalism ($r = .01, p = .79$).

We can explore the ideological profiles of the American people using cluster analysis, a statistical technique that classifies individuals into groups on the basis of their scores on a set of variables—in this case our four ideological dimensions. Cluster members exhibit high levels of similarity on these variables within their cluster, and high levels of dissimilarity to those in other clusters.[83]

We first ran our four dimensions of ideology in a series of two-step clus-

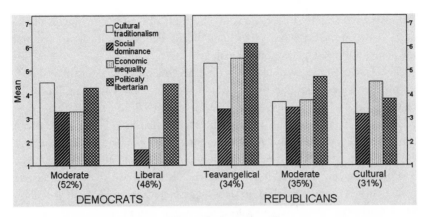

FIG. 2.10. Democratic and Republican ideological profiles.

Note: Two-step cluster analyses. The overall ideological differences between the two groups of Democrats and three groups of Republicans were both massive. Wilks' Lambda: $F(8, 598) = 180.06, p < .001, \eta_p^2 = .65$, and $F(4, 386) = 112.55, p < .001, \eta_p^2 = .61$, respectively. Both MANCOVA controlled for seven standard demographics. *Data source:* OU Institute for US-China Issues, 2011.

ter analyses on the full U.S. sample and found that a two-cluster solution fit the data best.[84] The first cluster was larger (61% of the full sample) and more conservative than the second cluster (39%) across all four dimensions, with massive differences on economic and cultural ideologies, a large difference on social dominance, and a small but statistically significant difference on political ideology.[85] Unsurprisingly, Americans are most divided on the culture wars and capitalism, and more Americans self-identify as conservative.

To explore the ideological profiles of Democrats and Republicans, we ran a series of cluster analyses on each subsample separately. Among self-identified Democrats, a two-cluster solution fit the data best.[86] As can be seen on the left side of Figure 2.10, the two clusters were of approximately equal size, with the second cluster substantially more liberal than the first on all but political ideology, for which the difference between the two groups was quite small.[87] The biggest difference between "liberal" and "moderate" Democrats was on social dominance, followed by cultural and economic ideologies.[88] The "liberal Democrats" in our survey appear to be the civil rights activists of old and the defenders of social welfare, homosexual rights, and women's rights of the present.

Among Republicans, a three-cluster solution fit the data best.[89] As can be seen on the right side of Figure 2.10, each cluster was approximately the same size, representing about a third of Republicans, or 10 percent of all Americans, each (29% of our sample were self-identified Republicans). There were no differences between the three groups on social dominance orientation; all three groups scored slightly under the scale midpoint of four.[90] The biggest differences between the three groups of Republicans were on political and cultural ideologies, followed by economic ideology.[91]

The first group of Republicans scored highest on both political and economic ideologies, and high on cultural ideology as well. Following journalist David Brody, I have labeled them "Teavangelicals." Brody argues that Evangelicals are "breaking bread" with the libertarian Tea Party: "Evangelicals can actually walk and chew gum at the same time. They can be a hundred percent engaged on the issues of life and traditional marriage and at the same time be a hundred percent engaged in fiscal matters. . . . Conservative evangelicals see fiscal issues as moral issues."[92] Our data suggests that there are about 31 million Americans who fit this "Teavangelical" Republican profile.

Not all Evangelical Christians appear to *want* to walk and chew gum at the same time, however. Our third cluster, which is equally large, scores the highest among the three groups on traditionalism, but the lowest on libertarianism. Where the Teavangelicals score extremely high on libertarianism ($M = 6.13$), these "cultural Republicans" are actually slightly communitarian ($M = 3.82$), a truly massive difference statistically.[93] Remarkably, Figure 2.10 suggests and statistical analysis demonstrates that cultural Republicans are *even more communitarian than the average Democrat.*[94] This may explain why, despite the presence of a large group of Teavangelicals, there was no overall zero-order correlation between political and cultural ideology. The cultural Republicans are perhaps best described as "pure" Christian conservatives, scoring the highest of the three Republican groups on biblical literalism and religiosity.[95]

These pure cultural Republicans may be those who, unlike the Teavangelicals, don't care to carry a copy of the Declaration of Independence along with their Bibles, and are willing to impose their values on other people if they think it best for the community. The photo in Figure 2.11 was taken on the campus of the University of Oklahoma, Norman, on July 14, 2012. In February of that year, Republican governor Mary Fallin signed an executive order prohibiting smoking on all state properties effective July 1. State law had already banned smoking in indoor workplaces, but she argued in her State of the State address that something further needed to be done.

Some Oklahomans protested on libertarian grounds, arguing that as long as smokers were outdoors in designated areas, there was no secondhand smoke danger to other people. The editorial board of the campus newspaper, *The Oklahoma Daily,* argued that "The state is playing the mother here, making decisions for citizens based on what Fallin thinks is best for them . . . the purpose of this ban is to coerce tobacco users to quit their habit."[96] The *Daily*'s liberal editorial board was taking a relatively libertarian position. As a member of the

FIG. 2.11. Smoking is sin: "No tobacco use" signs posted outdoors on the campus of the University of Oklahoma, Norman, July 2012.

Source: Photo courtesy of the author.

Christian right, Fallin took the more communitarian position. Not all conservatives are libertarians, and not all liberals are communitarians.

Harvard sociologist Theda Skocpol and Vanessa Williamson have described the Tea Party as a mix of religious and secular conservatives, the former being usually more outspoken and dominant than the latter. "Some Tea Partiers are social conservatives focused on moral and cultural issues ranging from pro-life concerns to worries about the impact of recent immigrants on the cultural coherence of American life," they concluded in 2012. "Others are much more secular minded libertarians, who stress individual choice on cultural matters and want the Tea Party as a whole to give absolute priority to fiscal issues." The cultural conservatives, they add, are more often from the South, while the secular libertarians tend to hail from the West and Northeast.[97]

Our 2011 survey included a one-hundred-degree feeling thermometer towards the "Tea Party." Our moderate (34°) and especially liberal (10°) Democrats felt downright frigid towards the Tea Party. By contrast, among our three groups of Republicans, Teavangelicals (86°) felt the warmest, followed by cultural (79°) and moderate (63°) Republicans.[98] This suggests that Teavangelicals, combining economic, political, and cultural conservatism, were the most likely Tea Party participants. Cultural Republicans likely felt slightly cooler towards the Tea Party because of their greater communitarianism.

While Paul Ryan and the libertarian right may have appeared ascendant in the Republican Party in 2012–13, not all Republicans appear comfortable with radical individualism. No major group of pure libertarians emerged from our Republican cluster analysis. Many on both the left and right have dismissed President George W. Bush's "compassionate conservatism" as a failure. But our 2011 data suggests that a deep communitarian strain remains within the Republican Party. "We are a nation of rugged individualists," Bush declared in his "The Duty of Hope" speech in 1999. "But we are also the country of the second chance, tied together by bonds of friendship and community and solidarity."[99] Remarkably, Barack Obama would run on a similarly communitarian plank in both 2008 and 2012.

AMERICAN IDEOLOGIES AND THE WORLD

This chapter has argued that not all liberals and conservatives are alike. Our 2011 representative sample of Americans varied meaningfully across cultural (traditional vs. modern values), socio-racial (group dominance vs. equality), economic (income inequality vs. redistribution), and political (libertarianism vs. communitarianism) dimensions of ideology. While each American varies across each of these four dimensions in a unique way, we identified distinct clusters of moderate and liberal Democrats, and Teavangelical, moderate, and cultural Republicans.

In the rest of this book we will explore how these four dimensions of ideology, and clusters of different kinds of Democrats and Republicans, differ in their international attitudes and foreign policy preferences. First, however, we turn to the moral underpinnings of these ideological divides.

3 The Moral Foundations of Ideology and International Attitudes

"Our society holds dear Judeo-Christian values that have stood the test of time: love your neighbor, give an honest day's work for an honest day's wages. Tell the truth and be honest. Don't cheat or steal. Respect others, respect their property and respect their opinions. And always remember: you are responsible for the decisions you make. And that is the hope for my generation's legacy: that we usher in the responsibility era. We can change today's culture from 'if it feels good, do it.'"[1]

—Governor (Republican–Texas) George W. Bush, April 6, 1998

"The Democratic Party has always stood for giving everyone an equal chance, despite the circumstances of their birth. My story is emblematic of that. I want to affirm those values."[2]

—Senator (Democrat–Illinois) Barack Obama, July 27, 2004

Why do the disparate ideologies of the American people polarize their international attitudes?

Terry Deibel of the National War College has suggested that during the Clinton administration, "The parties split over foreign policy because their core values on governance, the beliefs that make people become Democrats or Republicans, have foreign policy implications."[3] This chapter provides both conceptual and empirical support for Deibel's view: the same differences in moral values that divide liberals and conservatives on domestic policy also divide them on foreign policy. It first mines moral psychology to better understand the values that divide American liberals and conservatives. It then uses our survey data to demonstrate how value differences undergird liberal-conservative ideological divides. Finally, it shows how moral values mediate the relationship between ideology on the one hand, and both broad feelings towards foreign countries and generalized foreign policy preferences on the other.

THE MORAL VALUES OF LIBERALS AND CONSERVATIVES

Economists tend to view human beings as rational actors seeking to maximize their self-interest. *Homo economicus* is seen to weigh the costs and benefits of different options, coolly choosing the solution that maximizes benefits and minimizes costs. Originally developed in microeconomics, "rational choice" theory has now been widely applied in the social sciences.[4]

Psychologists generally disagree, arguing that *Homo sapiens*, like other mammals, evolved moral values beyond self-interest, allowing him to meet the challenges of collective social life. He cannot therefore be reduced to *Homo economicus*. Early developmental and moral psychologists like Jean Piaget and Lawrence Kohlberg focused on the moral value of *fairness*.[5] Carol Gilligan then argued for a separate "ethic of care," focusing on *compassion* for the suffering of others.[6]

These two moral values are consistent with work in sociobiology. Moralities of fairness/justice have their evolutionary roots in what Robert Trivers has called "reciprocal altruism," which requires that individuals closely monitor the fairness of the actions of others in their communities.[7] Similarly, in *The Selfish Gene* Richard Dawkins popularized the idea that moralities of compassion have their evolutionary origins in a "kin altruism" that promotes attention to the welfare of one's children and close family.[8]

Building on the work of anthropologist Richard Shweder, Jonathan Haidt and colleagues have recently argued that the study of moral psychology should not be limited to the two "individualizing" moralities of *fairness* and *compassion*.[9] Three additional moralities, they argue, work to "bind" individuals into communities. The morality of *loyalty* evolved to foster preferences for those who sacrifice for the good of the group, but also wariness towards traitors who might betray it. The morality of *authority* evolved to allow mankind to more easily cooperate within social hierarchies, reducing the need, common among primates, to resort to force to maintain status distinctions.[10] Finally, the morality of sanctity or *purity* has its origins in our physical nature as omnivores, who, like other primates, developed a keen sense of disgust to avoid disease. But purity has evolved to govern our social world as well, leading us to not just shun the "unclean" but also aspire to transcend the carnal world of the body in pursuit of sanctity and God.

Haidt and colleagues have further argued that liberals and conservatives rely upon different constellations of moral values. Based on a very large convenience dataset of survey responses gathered online at YourMorals.org, they found that while liberals tend to esteem the "individualizing" values of fairness and compassion more than conservatives, conservatives tend to prize the "binding" values of loyalty, authority, and purity more than liberals. Conservatives, they argue, value all five moral values roughly equally, whereas liberals only really value fairness and compassion. This survey finding, furthermore, was supported by a quantitative discourse analysis of sermons from liberal (Universalist-

Unitarian) and conservative (Southern Baptist) Christian churches. Sermons from the former tended to emphasize individualizing values, while sermons from the latter tended to emphasize binding values.[11]

Working independently in the field of cognitive linguistics, George Lakoff has similarly argued that "conservative and progressive modes of thought start from very different perspectives on what constitutes morality." He views *empathy* (read: compassion) and *authority* as the core of each morality. "Behind every progressive policy lies a single moral value," Lakoff argues. "Empathy, together with the responsibility and strength to act on that empathy." By contrast, "Conservative thought . . . begins with the notion that morality is obedience to an authority . . . who is inherently good, knows right from wrong, functions to protect us from evil in the world, and has both the right and duty to use force to command obedience and fight evil."[12]

Our 2011 survey included ten items borrowed from Haidt's moral foundations questionnaire. One five-item rating scale asked participants, "When you decide whether something is right or wrong, how relevant are the following to your moral judgments?"

- *Whether or not someone acted unfairly or was unjust.*
- *Whether or not someone was harmed or suffered.*
- *Whether or not someone was disloyal.*
- *Whether or not someone disrespected authority.*
- *Whether or not someone violated standards of purity and decency.*

A second five-item rating scale asked, "Do you agree or disagree with the following statements about moral values?"

- *When the government makes laws, it must ensure that everyone is treated fairly and with justice.*
- *Compassion for those who are suffering is the most crucial virtue.*
- *People should always be loyal and dutiful.*
- *Children need to obey authority.*
- *Chastity is an important and valuable virtue.*

For both rating scales, the sequence of items was randomized. Averaging each pair of items together allowed us to create individualized scores for each of the five moral foundations: fairness, compassion, loyalty, authority, and purity.

Although Haidt and his colleagues used a convenience sample in their research, our 2011 representative national sample almost exactly replicates their finding of ideological differences in moral value profiles.[13] The downward slopes of the top two lines in Figure 3.1 reveal that liberals score slightly higher than conservatives on the "individualizing" values of *fairness* and *compassion*.

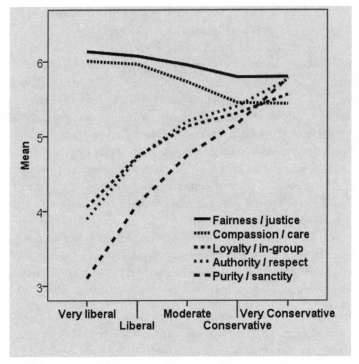

FIG. 3.1. The moral foundations of American ideology: Liberals care less than conservatives about purity, authority, and loyalty, but slightly more about injustice and suffering.

Note: Overall ideological differences were substantial, Wilks' Lambda: $F(20, 3443) = 22.40, p <$ .001, $\eta_p^2 = .10$, including seven standard demographic controls. *Data source:* OU Institute for US-China Issues, 2011.

The more dramatic upward slopes of the bottom three lines, however, reveal that conservatives score higher than liberals on the "binding" values of *loyalty, authority,* and especially *purity.*[14]

These survey findings suggest that liberals and conservatives are socialized into distinct moral communities that differ systematically in their judgments of which values matter in which situations. For instance, the popular response to the 2011 Penn State child sex abuse scandal was notable for how ideology polarized moral outrage. Liberals, *compassionate* towards the eight underage boys molested by assistant football coach Jerry Sandusky, called for a tough response. Conservatives, by contrast, were likely both *disgusted* by Sandusky's behavior and outraged by the *disloyalty* of the school's administration for firing head football coach Joe Paterno. Note the contrasting framing: conservatives highlight the Penn State in-group and advocate loyalty towards their coach, while liberals focus more on compassion towards defenseless minors—even if they are not Nittany Lions. Our moral values, Haidt and other psychologists have argued, are often involved in post-hoc moral reasoning that serves to justify preexisting intuitions after the fact.[15]

THE MORAL SUBSTRUCTURES OF THE DIMENSIONS OF AMERICAN IDEOLOGY

Can we extend Haidt's work, which treats ideology as unidimensional, to explore whether moral values can also help account for liberal-conservative differences on our four dimensions of American ideology? We ran four multiple mediation models to find out. As we shall see below, cultural, social, and economic ideologies all worked well.[16]

Establishing causal mediation is extremely difficult. First, it is nearly impossible to anticipate and measure all possible mediators of a relationship, so one cannot be fully confident that the mediators tested are the true drivers of an indirect relationship. Second, with correlational data like ours, one can never be sure of the exact causal sequence. For instance, it is always possible that the proposed mediator is actually the independent variable, and vice-versa. It may be best, therefore, to think of our mediation models as demonstrating syndromes—in this chapter, patterns of ideologies and moral values that go together—rather than as strong claims about which comes first. "Just as it took more than a century to discover why limes cure scurvy" (answer: vitamin C), political scientists Donald Green, Shang Ha, and John Bullock have written thoughtfully about the challenges of establishing mediation, "it may take decades to figure out the mechanisms that account for the causal relationships observed in social science."[17] Following Haidt's work, this chapter suggests that moral values are to many political judgments what vitamin C is to scurvy, but further research will be needed to demonstrate causation.[18]

Cultural traditionalism. As Figure 3.2 visually displays, two of the five moral foundations—purity and fairness—mediated the relationship between ideology and cultural traditionalism, together accounting for over 80 percent of the direct relationship.[19]

As the very thick arrows at the top of the figure reveal, purity was by far the stronger mediator. Conservatives tend towards greater cultural traditionalism than liberals do, in largest part because they value purity and sanctity more. Support for purity, it seems, contributes to support for a culture that is unsoiled by "dirty" activities like smoking, drug use, and sex. This finding is consistent with a remarkable experiment conducted by social psycholo-

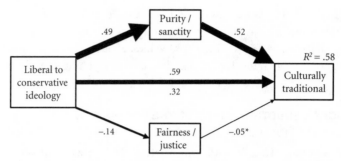

FIG. 3.2. Liberals and conservatives differ on cultural traditionalism in largest part because conservatives value *purity* much more than liberals do, but also because liberals value *fairness* more than conservatives do.

Note: A simultaneous mediation model. * $p < .05$, all other p's $< .001$. To reduce clutter, compassion, loyalty, and authority, which were not statistically significant mediators, and seven demographic covariates, are not shown. Male ($\beta = -.16$), age ($\beta = .09$), Hispanic ($\beta = .05$), and black ($\beta = .04$) were statistically significant at $p \leq .05$. Indirect effect statistics are online at SUP. org. *Data source:* OU Institute for US-China Issues, 2011.

gists Erik Helzer and David Pizarro, who found that simply asking research participants to sanitize their hands temporarily increased their self-reported conservatism.[20] More broadly, conservatives are more sensitive to disgust than liberals are, and are more likely to rely on this emotion in their moral judgments.[21]

Two editorial cartoons from the turn of the last century illustrate the centrality of purity to the Christian civilizing mission. The image to the left of Figure 3.3, a detail from an 1899 *Judge* magazine cover, depicts President McKinley scrubbing a dark-skinned baby. Entitled "The Filipino's First Bath," it suggests an American duty to purify America's new colony in the Philippines. Indeed, the scene brings to mind a baptism, with McKinley standing in a pool of water labeled "Civilization." America's paternalistic role is clear as McKinley reproaches the Filipino, "Oh, you dirty boy!"

A very similar message was conveyed in a *Literary Digest* cartoon just two years later (Figure 3.3, right). It depicts General Leonard Wood, a physician who was serving as military governor, scrubbing a black child representing Cuba. Wood's job is not easy: he is surrounded by "disinfectant," "lye," "corrosive sublimate," and "pure soap." Cuba is crying, but Wood is doing his paternalistic duty.

Today's culture wars focus on the sexual politics of homosexuality and abortion. Purity is at the center of the debate. Cultural traditionalists tend to depict sodomy as sin, and abstinence-only education as the best way to reduce heterosexual sex for purposes other than procreation. Robert Bellah traces this attitude all the way back to the Puritans, who were indeed puritanical: "The body and especially sex were dangerous because they had the power to pull

THE FILIPINO'S FIRST BATH
McKinley—*"Oh, you dirty boy!"*

*"If General Wood Is Unpopular in
Cuba, We Can Guess the Reason."*

FIG. 3.3. Cultural conservatives value *purity*, promoting paternalistic attitudes, 1899 and 1901.

Sources: Judge, June 10, 1899, and *Literary Digest,* March 30, 1901. Both images courtesy of the University of Oklahoma Libraries.

man away from his dependence on God and make him find his principle in himself. . . . Blinded by our lusts we fail to see the divine plan for our own salvation, and so, blinded, we go to our eternal doom."[22] Today's liberals, by contrast, are less concerned with chastity. They are more accepting of same-sex marriage and abortion, which they view as issues of fairness and justice, not purity.

Indeed, the bottom path of Figure 3.2 reveals that fairness also partially mediates the relationship between ideology and cultural traditionalism; liberals value fairness more, contributing to their greater opposition to cultural traditionalism. It may be that liberals are responding to the perceived injustice of the imposition of traditional values on oppressed groups like the colored peoples of America's past empire, or the homosexuals of America today. As noted above, our survey included a culture war item on gay marriage. Using it instead of cultural traditionalism as our dependent variable, we ran another multiple mediation model with a very similar result. The largest indirect pathway in opposition to gay marriage was through purity, and the largest indirect pathway in favor of gay marriage was through fairness.[23] Liberals appear to object to the injustice of a cultural traditionalism that imposes Christian values like purity onto minority groups like gays.

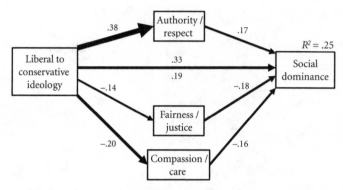

FIG. 3.4. Liberals and conservatives differ on social dominance, in part because conservatives value *authority* more than liberals do, but also because liberals value *fairness* and *compassion* more than conservatives do.

Note: A simultaneous mediation model. All p's < .001. Purity and loyalty, which were not statistically significant mediators, and seven demographic covariates are not shown. Education ($\beta = -.12$) and income ($\beta = .06$) were statistically significant at $p \leq .05$. Note that their signs point in the opposite directions, with greater education associated with desires for greater social group equality, and greater wealth associated with desires for greater dominance of subordinate groups. Indirect effect statistics are online at SUP.org. *Data source:* OU Institute for US-China Issues, 2011.

Social dominance. Why do American liberals and conservatives differ so much in their attitudes towards racial and gender hierarchies? The multiple mediation model displayed in Figure 3.4 reveals that conservatives are much more likely than liberals to value *authority*, contributing to a preference for the domination of subordinate social groups. Liberals, for their part, are more likely than conservatives to value *fairness* and *compassion*, leading them to oppose social dominance and support the equality of racial groups. Together, these moral values accounted for about 80 percent of ideology's influence on social dominance.[24]

Although the Union won the Civil War and slavery was abolished, suffrage, segregation, and the status of blacks in the South has remained an issue to this day. General Ulysses S. Grant, a Union war hero, won the presidency in 1868 with the campaign slogan "Let us have peace." Although he was an advocate for African American civil rights, his Republican Party split over the issue, with Horace Greeley's Liberal Republicans championing greater equality. Greeley ran against Grant in 1872. The center-spread from an 1872 edition of Frank Leslie's *Illustrated Newspaper* depicts Senator Charles Sumner as Moses leading African American slaves, as Israelites, across the Red Sea to freedom (Figure 3.5). The newspaper quotes Sumner: "Thus far, in constant efforts for the colored race, I have sincerely sought the good of all ... fulfilling the promises of the Declaration of Independence, making all equal in rights." Indeed, Sumner

THE MODERN MOSES TO HIS PEOPLE

"I have brought you out of the land of Slavery, out of the house of Bondage,
through the Red Sea of war to the Promised Land of equal rights for all."

FIG. 3.5. Justice, compassion, and race relations in the USA, 1872.

Source: Frank Leslie's *Illustrated Newspaper*, August 24, 1872. Image courtesy of Cornell University Library. 2214.PR0166.

advocated an amendment to the U.S. Constitution which would clearly state that "all people are equal before the law."

The engraving also depicts a cigar-smoking President Grant as the Egyptian Pharaoh. His top hat has blown off as he rides a chariot engulfed in the Red Sea (at center and top-left close-up). His troops are sinking around him. Speaking in favor of Liberal Republican Horace Greeley, depicted at the far right in glasses, Sumner belittles Grant's position on slavery: "President Grant, except as a soldier summoned by the terrible accident of war, never did anything against Slavery, nor has he at any time shown any sympathy for the colored race." A century later, the values of justice and compassion similarly motivate liberal champions of African American civil rights.

The same tension between the values of authority on the one hand, and fairness and compassion on the other, was on display when Michele Bachmann and four fellow Republican congresspeople sent a letter to the State Department on June 13, 2012. It accused Huma Abedin, aide to Secretary of State Hillary Clinton (and wife of disgraced congressman Anthony Weiner), of being "connected to Muslim Brotherhood operatives" and conspiring to infiltrate the U.S. government. They warned of a Muslim threat to American law and order.

Liberals decried the injustice and harm of Bachmann's "witch hunt" against Abedin. The *Daily Beast*'s Caitlin Dickson noted that Bachmann has a long history of attacks, not just against ethnic minorities but also against successful women, from Michelle Obama to Nancy Pelosi to Elena Kagan to Kirsten Gillibrand.[25] Social dominance orientation, psychologists have found, predicts not just racial prejudice but also sexism.[26] In May 2012 Bachmann joined House Republicans in blocking the Paycheck Fairness Act, which promotes equal pay for women; Senate Republicans then blocked it in June. The same moralities of authority, fairness, and compassion that divide many social liberals and conservatives over racism also divide them over sexism.

In November 2011, a video of Texas judge William Adams whipping his teenage daughter with a belt went viral on the Internet. The video, which pitted moralities of parental authority against moralities of compassion, was likely more shocking for liberals than conservatives. Our 2011 survey included two related items, "*Misbehaving children should be spanked*" and "*It's better to reward children's positive behaviors than to spank them for bad behavior.*" The latter was reverse-coded, and the two items were averaged together to create a "support for spanking" scale of good reliability ($\alpha = .70$). Ideology, it turned out, accounted for a full 14 percent of spanking attitudes; conservatives were more in favor of spanking than liberals were.[27] We then ran a serial mediation model to see if biblical literalism and the value of authority would help account for this ideological effect. They did. All three indirect paths were statistically significant, together accounting for nearly two-thirds of the relationship: conservatives endorse spanking more than liberals do, in part because of their greater biblical literalism, in part because they value authority more, and in part because greater biblical literalism is associated with valuing authority more.[28] This suggests that Judge Adams's behavior would be more acceptable in the Bible Belt than in coastal America. Indeed, in our survey, being male ($\beta = .11$), black ($\beta = .11$), or from the South ($\beta = .10$) predicted *support* for spanking, while only greater education ($\beta = -.17$) predicted *opposition* to spanking.

Economic inequality. Three of the five moral foundations—purity, fairness, and compassion—mediated the relationship between ideology and economic inequality, together accounting for over half of the direct relationship (Figure 3.6).[29]

Liberals often express compassion for the dispossessed. "Living in a community means being interconnected in myriad ways—including by empathy," Nicholas Kristof wrote in a fall 2012 *New York Times* column about health

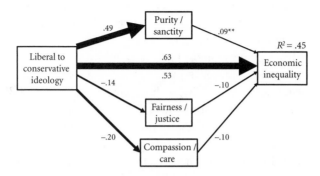

FIG. 3.6. Liberals and conservatives differ on economic inequality, in part because liberals value *fairness* and *compassion* more than conservatives do.

Note: A simultaneous mediation model. ** $p < .01$, all other p's $\leq .001$. Loyalty and authority, which were not statistically significant mediators, and seven demographic covariates, are not shown. Income ($\beta = .09$) and black ($\beta = -.07$) were statistically significant at $p < .01$. Indirect effect statistics are online at SUP.org. *Data source:* OU Institute for US-China Issues, 2011.

care.[30] "To feel undiminished by the deaths of those around us isn't heroic Ayn Rand individualism. It's sociopathic. Compassion isn't a sign of weakness, but of civilization."

Many Democratic politicians claim to share this liberal moral vision. "Above all, being a Democrat means having compassion for others. It means putting government to work to help the people who need it," writes George McGovern. "We are the party that believes we can't let the strong kick aside the weak."[31] In *The Audacity of Hope*, Barack Obama similarly ends up privileging empathy in his chapter on American values. "It is at the heart of my moral code, and it is how I understand the Golden Rule," Obama writes. "Not simply as a call to sympathy or charity, but as something more demanding, a call to stand in somebody else's shoes and see through their eyes." Indeed, Obama blames many of today's problems on a national "empathy deficit": "It's hard to imagine the CEO of a company giving himself a multimillion-dollar bonus while cutting health care coverage for his workers if he thought they were in some sense his equals."[32]

Many economic conservatives also claim to be empathetic towards the poor. "Everywhere in the world there are gross inequalities in income and wealth. They offend most of us," Milton and Rose Friedman write in *Free to Choose*. "Few can fail to be moved by the contrast between the luxury enjoyed by some and the grinding poverty suffered by others."[33] More recently, Republican president George W. Bush has promoted a "compassionate conservatism" of "tough love": "I think that it is far kinder to help people become independent than it is to trap them in a failed system. We must end dependency on government. . . . Any system that undermines the basic values of hard work, self-respect and personal responsibility is wrong."[34]

Our data lends greater support to the idea of "bleeding-heart liberals" than the idea of "compassionate conservatism." The social ills and human suffering associated with income inequality, such as poverty, violence, and diminished health care access, appear to bother liberals more than conservatives. This interpretation is consistent with research on ideological differences in self-reported happiness. Social psychologists Jaime Napier and John Jost have mined ANES and World Values Survey data to argue that "liberals may be less happy than conservatives because they are less ideologically prepared to rationalize (or explain away) the degree of inequality in society."[35] Conservatives are more likely to view the status quo as fair and legitimate, buffering them from the full psychological toll that inequality poses for liberals.[36] Michele Bachmann sleeps well at night; Bill Moyers does not.

Michelle Goldberg has even argued that for Christian nationalists like Newt Gingrich and George W. Bush, "compassionate conservatism" does not actually refer to compassion for the poor. Instead, it is really about a desire to return to the Gilded Age before the New Deal, when the poor had no social welfare safety net and thus no choice but to rely upon churches for charity. There, only those who repented, prayed, and accepted Christ would be given aid. Goldberg views "compassionate conservatism" as part of the Christian nationalist goal of "reconstructionism" or "dominionism": a complete restructuring of America into a Christian nation. It is a nation in which, Goldberg claims, non-Christians would have no place and receive little sympathy.[37]

The "bleeding hearts" that contribute to liberal compassion for the dispossessed at home also shape liberals' views of foreign countries. Herblock captures a liberal view of the developing world in a 1962 cartoon for the *Washington Post* (Figure 3.7). While a woman in a tattered dress works in a hut labeled "Extreme Poverty," outside a man labeled "Revolution" loads a gun. An onlooker points up a hill at a mansion labeled "Extreme Wealth" and is heard saying to his distressed companion, "—and his father lives up there." The cartoon reveals not only a liberal compassion for the poor but also a strong sense of injustice. Strong enough, it would seem, to condone violence. Liberals, after all, do not value authority as much as conservatives do; revolutions can be justified.

The values of compassion and justice, indeed, can be a combustible mix. It is when suffering is widely perceived as unjust that revolutions erupt. Barrington Moore writes in his thoughtful *Injustice: The Social Bases of Obedience and Revolt* that "Anger occurs when the rules of distributive justice are violated . . . when persons doing roughly the same kind of work see that their co-workers

"—and his father lives up there."

FIG. 3.7. Liberals decry economic *injustice* and value *compassion* for the poor, both at home and abroad, 1962.

Source: A 1962 Herblock Cartoon, © The Herb Block Foundation.

are receiving higher rewards."[38] Thomas Sowell perceptively notes that there is a connection between harm and injustice in liberal thinking about income inequality: "It [is] not merely that some have little and others have much. Cause and effect are involved: Some have little *because* others have much . . . the rich have *taken* from the poor."[39] As Herblock suggests in his cartoon, the poor have the *right* to revolt and take it back.

Finally, Figure 3.6 also reveals that some conservatives support the status quo of income inequality more than liberals do because, in part, they value purity more. One interpretation of this finding might be that conservatives are more fearful than liberals that the redistribution of income and the mixing of socioeconomic classes might lead to the "contamination" of their own bodies, values, and norms. Social psychologists have found that conservatives score higher than liberals on "contamination disgust," which may have evolved as part of a "behavioral immune system" to shield individuals from exposure to out-groups like the poor, who might be carriers of novel pathogens.[40] Some conservatives may find the very idea of redistributing wealth to out-groups such as the poor (whether at home or abroad) disgusting.

MORAL VALUES AND INTERNATIONAL ATTITUDES

Can these differing moral values help account for ideological differences in overall feelings towards foreign countries, and overall foreign policy preferences?

Feelings. In a multiple mediation model in which the five moral foundations mediated the relationship between ideology and our measure of average warmth towards fifteen foreign countries, only the indirect paths through loyalty and compassion were statistically significant (Figure 3.8). Together, however, they accounted for half of the direct relationship.[41] Overall, conservatives feel cooler towards foreign countries than liberals do, in part due to the greater value they place on loyalty and the lesser value they place upon compassion. In other words, liberals feel more favorably towards foreign countries than conservatives do, in part because they feel greater compassion towards the plight of foreigners and because they feel less loyalty to America as opposed to humankind as a whole.

This finding is consistent with the work of psychologist Ronnie Janoff-Bulman, who has argued that liberals and conservatives embrace *provide* and *protect* orientations, respectively. "Conservatives focus on protecting the group and emphasize social order," she writes, "whereas liberals focus on providing for the group and emphasize social justice."[42] Conservatives are thus motivated to *avoid*, preventing negative outcomes, while liberals are motivated to *approach*, advancing positive outcomes. Figure 3.8 suggests that liberals are motivated to approach other nations and provide for them out of compassion, while conservatives are motivated to avoid other nations to protect the U.S. in-group out of a more narrowly focused loyalty.[43]

All humans are loyal to their social groups. Two of the most basic findings in the social psychology of intergroup relations are that human beings (1) identify with social groups and (2) privilege them. First, social identity theory maintains that we associate ourselves with groups that, in effect, become part of our identities.[44] They become represented in the individual's self-concept—the group's concerns become the individual's concerns. Second, we see the groups we associate ourselves with as basically good. Indeed, the mere mention of in-group signifiers like "we," "us," and "our" is sufficient to generate positive affect.[45] "In-group positivity" leads us to favor our fellow in-group members

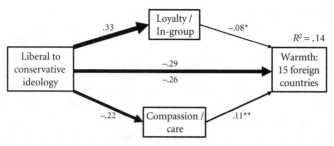

FIG. 3.8. Conservatives feel cooler towards the average foreign country than liberals do, in part due to the greater value they place on *loyalty* to the in-group, and in part due to the lesser value they place upon *compassion*.

Note: A simultaneous mediation model. * $p < .05$, ** $p < .01$, all other p's $\leq .001$. Purity, authority, and fairness, which were not statistically significant mediators, and seven demographic covariates are not shown. Education ($\beta = .11$), black ($\beta = .10$), and age ($\beta = -.07$) were statistically significant at $p < .01$. Indirect effect statistics are online at SUP.org. *Data source:* OU Institute for US-China Issues, 2011.

over out-group members, even when the individual has nothing to gain. For instance, social psychologists have found that we consistently favor in-groups over out-groups when making attributions, especially in ambiguous situations. Thus, if an in-group member does something good, we attribute it to his or her good disposition, reflecting well on our own character; however, if he or she does something bad, we write it off to the social situation beyond the person's control, thereby preserving our collective self-esteem.[46]

But what social groups are we loyal to? Do we vary in our loyalty to them? In the modern world, we are all defined to varying degrees by our national identities. In the Introduction we saw that while Americans on average feel warmer towards the United States itself (83°; see Figure 0.3) than towards any foreign country, conservatives on average feel 12° warmer towards the United States than liberals do (see Figure 0.4). This suggests that conservatives are more patriotic than conservatives. In the next chapter we will see that this is in fact the case. Greater patriotism and loyalty to the national group appear to be one reason why conservatives generally feel cooler towards foreign countries than liberals do.

Liberals, Figure 3.8 reveals, also feel more warmly towards foreign countries than conservatives do because they value compassion for the suffering of others more. "The Democratic Party's basic mission, its reason for being, is to help the disadvantaged in society, to relieve human suffering and uplift the downtrodden," Terry Deibel writes. "When it comes to foreign policy . . . Democrats cannot let go of morality. . . . Democratic idealists are explicit about wanting to . . . relieve foreign suffering."[47]

Greater compassion helps account for the greater liberal than conservative aversion to war. Although Franklin D. Roosevelt never served in uniform, as assistant secretary of the navy in the Wilson administration he visited the front lines in France. In 1936, he recalled the experience:

> I have seen war. I have seen war on land and sea. I have seen blood running from the wounded. I have seen men coughing out their gassed lungs. I have seen the dead in the mud. I have seen cities destroyed. I have seen 200 limping, exhausted men come out of line—the survivors of a regiment of 1,000 that went forward 48 hours before. I have seen children starving. I have seen the agony of mothers and wives. I hate war.[48]

These memories of World War I may have restrained Roosevelt from a quick entry into World War II.

Democratic president Barack Obama's foreign policy is also marked by the value he places upon compassion. "When you read the accounts of women being raped when they are out collecting firewood, when you read just horrendous accounts of entire villages being decimated and children being murdered," he said in a 2006 podcast on Darfur, "that just breaks your heart."[49]

Many conservatives today have little patience for such liberal compassion in foreign affairs. In the Introduction we saw Newt Gingrich draw a sharp line between America and other countries, reflecting a patriotism that privileges loyalty to country over compassion towards foreigners: "Andrew Jackson had a pretty clear-cut idea about America's enemies: Kill them." Similarly, in her *Treason: Liberal Treachery from the Cold War to the War on Terrorism,* Ann Coulter claims that "Whenever the nation is under attack, from within or without, liberals side with the enemy."[50] Sympathy for foreigners is disloyal.

There is a kernel of truth in Coulter's shrill and overblown critique: liberals do tend to be more sympathetic towards the downtrodden, even when they are America's enemies. Bill Mauldin, who was a GI in Europe during World War II, wrote, "Italy reminds a guy of a dog hit by an automobile because it ran out and tried to bite the tires. You can't just leave the critter there to die."[51] Even though the Italians were America's enemies and fought on the losing side of the war, Mauldin still had compassion for their plight in occupied Italy. Mauldin won a Pulitzer Prize for his wartime cartoons in *Stars and Stripes* depicting two grunts, Willie and Joe. His work is notable for a gallows humor that belittles the glory of war. The cartoon on the left of Figure 3.9 pokes fun at the cynicism that grunts developed on the front lines: "I need a couple guys what don't owe me no money for a little routine patrol." The cartoon on the right makes light of military honors: "Just gimme a couple aspirin. I already got a Purple Heart."

Mauldin was well aware that some conservatives viewed his work as treasonous. "My stuff has been loaded with politics from the beginning," he later

"I need a couple guys what don't owe   *"Just gimme a couple aspirin. I*
me no money for a little routine patrol."   *already got a Purple Heart."*

FIG. 3.9. Treason? A liberal view of war without honor, 1944.

Sources: *Stars and Stripes*, January 8, 1944, and July 14, 1944. Copyright by Bill Mauldin, (1945). Courtesy of the Bill Mauldin Estate LLC.

recalled. "One of the few men in the Army with the perspicacity to see what I was really up to was General George Patton. When he tried to put a stop to me ... accus[ing] me of being in the pay of the Germans ... somebody hollered 'Free Press' and I was allowed to go on inciting mutiny under the guise of simple soldier jokes."[52]

The *Washington Post*'s Herblock would view the war in Vietnam with a similarly liberal moral compass a quarter century later. The 1968 cartoon on the left of Figure 3.10 depicts civilians in South Vietnam fleeing the devastation wrought by U.S. aerial bombardment: "I don't know if either side is winning, but I know who's losing." From the perspective of conservatives like Ann Coulter, this is liberal disloyalty: siding with the Vietnamese against the American military. Herblock's 1973 cartoon on the right of Figure 3.10 also highlights compassion for the suffering of the Vietnamese people. It depicts a child crying amidst the devastation of a bombing. Several dead people, likely his family, surround him. Entitled "Peace with Horror," it mocks the idea that there can be an honorable end to a brutal war. For Herblock, like Mauldin, there is little honor in war. From the perspective of a liberal moral value system, war is suffering, even when its victims are not fellow Americans.

I don't know if either side is
winning, but I know who's losing

PEACE WITH HORROR

FIG. 3.10. Liberals downplay national *loyalty*, highlight our common humanity, and display *compassion* for suffering foreigners, 1968 and 1973.

Sources: 1968 and 1973 Herblock Cartoons, © The Herb Block Foundation.

Conservatives also care about morality in war and foreign affairs more broadly. In *The Expanding Circle*, moral philosopher Peter Singer argued that human empathy, which evolved so we would favor our kin, has gradually expanded from the family to the village to the nation, and even to all humanity as well as other animals.[53] It may be that liberals expand their circle of empathy more than conservatives do. When asked whether they agree or disagree with *"Compassion for those who are suffering is the most crucial virtue,"* conservatives scored lower than liberals, not because they are less compassionate towards fellow in-group members, like their families or fellow Americans, but because "those who are suffering" may have been too diffuse a group for them to identify with. Conservatives may direct their compassion and loyalty towards smaller in-groups. Similarly, when asked their views of *"People should always be loyal and dutiful,"* liberals may have scored lower than conservatives because they have a wider circle of living beings that they feel loyalty towards.

Social psychologist Sam McFarland's work on "Identification with all humanity" (IWAH) lends support for this view: his IWAH scale correlates *negatively* with both social dominance and right-wing authoritarianism, both of which correlate with greater conservatism; and *positively* with empathy.[54] In three additional student and adult samples, McFarland found that IWAH correlates with a unidimensional measure of liberal-conservative ideology as well.[55] So another way to interpret our mediation model (Figure 3.8) is that liberals feel warmer towards the average foreign country than conservatives do because their greater identification with all humanity (and lesser loyalty towards the narrower in-group "America") expands their circle of empathy beyond the U.S.A. more easily than happens for conservatives.

Foreign policy preferences. In another multiple mediation model in which the five moral foundations mediated between ideology and our measure of average foreign policy preferences towards fifteen countries, the two indirect paths via authority and harm were statistically significant.[56] But the correlation between harm and foreign policy ($\beta = -.07, p = .07$) was only marginally significant. So conservatives prefer tougher policies towards the average foreign country than liberals do for the most part because they value authority more than liberals do.

We learned earlier in this chapter that the moral value of authority is associated with desires for social dominance (see Figure 3.4). We therefore decided to explore a serial mediation model in which authority and social dominance acted as sequential mediators of the relationship between liberal-conservative ideology on the one hand, and average foreign policy preference on the other. All three indirect paths in the resulting model (Figure 3.11) were statistically significant, accounting for over two-thirds of the direct relationship.[57] On average, conservatives prefer tougher foreign policies more than liberals do, in part because they value authority more, in part because they desire to dominate other groups more, and in part because valuing authority more is associated

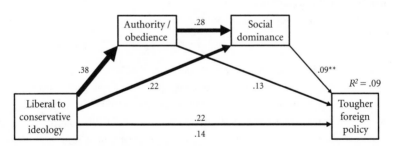

FIG. 3.11. Conservatives prefer tougher overall foreign policies more than liberals do, in part because they value authority more, in part because they desire to dominate other groups more, and in part because valuing authority more contributes to greater desires for group dominance.

Note: A sequential mediation model. ** $p < .01$, all other p's $< .001$. All three indirect paths were statistically significant. See SUP.org. Demographic covariates are not shown. *Data source:* OU Institute for US-China Issues, 2011.

THE FIRST DUTY

Civilization (*to China*)—*"That dragon must be killed before our troubles can be adjusted. If you don't do it I shall have to."*

FIG. 3.12. Conservatives fear revolution, value *authority*, and desire tougher foreign policies than liberals do, 1900.

Source: Udo J. Keppler, *Puck*, August 8, 1900. Image courtesy of the Library of Congress. LC-USZC2-1028.

with greater desires to dominate other social groups.

Udo Keppler illustrates the influence of the moral value of authority on American foreign policy in a *Puck* magazine cartoon from August 8, 1900 (Figure 3.12). It depicts a female figure referred to as "Civilization," but very much resembling Columbia, the female equivalent of Uncle Sam. She holds a spear and wears the helmet of an ancient warrior. Pointing at a dragon labeled "Boxer" hovering in the distance, she scolds a young emperor of China, "That dragon must be killed before our troubles can be adjusted. If you don't do it I shall have to." Clouds of smoke labeled "Anarchy," "Murder," and "Riot" hang over a city wall in the distance. Keppler is referring to the threat that the Boxer rebels, with imperial approval, were posing to the Americans, Europeans, and

Japanese besieged in Beijing's International Legation Quarter.

Keppler was prophetic: a military force of the Eight Nation Alliance quickly relieved the siege. The empress dowager and her court fled Beijing on August 15. Columbia will impose authority and her dominance if foreign governments will not.

LIBERAL AND CONSERVATIVE MORALITIES
AT HOME AND ABROAD

This chapter has argued that a major reason why American liberals and conservatives differ in their domestic and foreign policy preferences is that their moral values differ. Liberals tend to esteem the "individualizing" moral values of compassion and fairness more than conservatives do. Conservatives, by contrast, prize the "binding" moral values of authority, loyalty, and purity more than liberals do. Compassion and justice motivate liberals to approach the world (at home and abroad) to provide for it, while greater contamination disgust and desires for order motivate conservatives to avoid the world and protect a narrower in-group.

To make matters worse, liberals and conservatives have a hard time understanding each other's moral outlooks. This "moral empathy gap," psychologists Peter Ditto and Spassena Koleva argue, exacerbates partisan discord. Each side engages in hostile attribution, framing issues exclusively in its own moral terms and demonizing the other's motives.[58]

Disparate moral values undergird liberal-conservative differences in the various ideological domains. America's culture wars are driven to a substantial degree by liberal-conservative differences over the moral value of purity/sanctity. Differences in the social realm, such as on race and gender relations, are driven in part by the greater value that conservatives place on authority, and in part by the greater value that liberals place on fairness and compassion. Economically, our survey data supports the idea of "bleeding-heart liberals" more than that of "compassionate conservatives." Liberals value fairness and compassion more than conservatives do, contributing to greater desires for income redistribution at home and, as we shall see in the next chapter, greater support for humanitarian idealism in American foreign policy.

Moral values help account for liberal-conservative differences in overall feelings towards foreign countries and in foreign policy preferences. For instance, greater conservative coolness towards foreign countries in general is tied to the greater value they place on a narrow in-group loyalty. Conservatives, we shall see in the next chapter, are more patriotic and more nationalistic than liberals are. Greater liberal warmth towards foreign countries was partly accounted for by the greater value they place on compassion for the suffering of others, including that of foreigners and even enemies. Liberals are motivated to approach other nations and provide for them out of compassion, while conservatives are motivated out of loyalty to avoid other nations to protect the American in-group. Finally, because they value authority more, conservatives are more willing than liberals to endorse "tough love" policies to restore order and impose dominance—both at home and abroad.

4 The Foreign Policy Orientations of Liberals and Conservatives: Internationalism, Realism/Idealism, and Nationalism

Are there broad principles underlying the foreign policy preferences of the American people? If so, are they shaped by ideology?

This chapter explores how American liberals and conservatives differ on internationalism, realism/idealism, and nationalism. First, "internationalism" is often used synonymously with the three distinct concepts of (1) international activism/engagement, (2) multilateralism, and (3) diplomacy, and is thus juxtaposed against (1) isolationism, (2) unilateralism, and (3) the use of military force. We unpack these different "internationalisms," exploring the influence of both broad liberal-conservative ideology and our specific cultural, social, economic, and political dimensions of ideology on them. Second, American foreign policy idealisms, often juxtaposed against realism, come in humanitarian, religious, and political forms. Ideology, it turns out, has the largest influence on humanitarianism; liberals favor humanitarian interventions and foreign aid more than conservatives, who tend to oppose both. Third, nationalism moves beyond the love of country that is patriotism to a belief in American superiority over other countries. Conservatives, our data reveals, are both more patriotic and more nationalistic than liberals. The fourth and final section of this chapter explores the interrelationships among these many foreign policy orientations, identifying distinct Democratic and Republican foreign policy profiles.

THE MANY ENEMIES OF INTERNATIONALISM: ISOLATIONISM, UNILATERALISM, AND MILITARISM

"The point is a simple one: when our government meddles around the world, it can stir up hornet's nests and thereby jeopardize the safety of the American people. That's just common sense."[1]
—Congressman Ron Paul (Republican–Texas), 2008

> *"I know that now some say that times are so tough here at home that we can no longer afford to worry about what happens abroad. That maybe America needs to mind its own business. Well, whether we like it or not, there is virtually no aspect of our daily lives that is not directly impacted by what happens in the world around us. We can choose to ignore global problems, but global problems will not ignore us."*[2]
> —Senator Marco Rubio (Republican–Florida), 2011

Internationalism wears many hats. It can refer to international engagement/activism (opposed to isolationism), to multilateralism (opposed to unilateralism), or to diplomacy (opposed to militarism/force). It thus addresses a series of distinct questions. First, *should* the United States be actively involved in world affairs? Unlike Europe, America's relative isolation (thanks to the Atlantic and Pacific Oceans) has given it the luxury of asking a normative question about the desirability of active involvement in international affairs. Second, if America chooses to engage the world, *how* should it do so? Can it trust other countries enough to work multilaterally, whether through alliances, treaties, or international organizations? Or is it better to act alone? Third and finally, whether unilaterally or multilaterally, what is the best *means* to achieve U.S. foreign policy goals—diplomacy or the application of military force?

Our 2011 survey included six items tapping these three "internationalisms." International engagement/activism versus isolationism was captured by averaging together respondents' agreement with two items:

- *Our government should avoid international dealings.*
- *America should be actively involved in global affairs.* (reverse coded)

Multilateralism combined ratings of the importance of two items:

- *Strengthening international organizations.*
- *Supporting the United Nations.*

Finally, militarism/force combined ratings of the importance of two items:

- *Projecting our military power worldwide.*
- *Sustaining our military superiority.*

Item sequence was randomized, and all ratings were on seven-point scales. Although short, each scale was internally reliable.[3]

A series of multiple regressions controlling for the standard demographics revealed that in each case liberals were more internationalist than conservatives. The smallest effect was on isolationism/activism, with ideology accounting for 3 percent ($\beta = .18$) of the variance in attitudes towards international engagement. The influence of ideology on militarism and multilateralism was much larger. Ideology accounted for a substantial 13 percent ($\beta = .38$) of unique variance in support for militarism, confirming popular generalizations about liberal doves and conservative hawks. But ideology accounted for a remarkable 29 percent ($\beta = -.56$) of the variance in support for multilateralism. As we will see in Chapter 10, liberals support multilateral institutions like the United Nations, while conservatives do not trust them. These consistent and substantial ideological differences on internationalism demand explanation.

International engagement vs. isolationism. Writing during the George W. Bush administration, international relations theorist Michael Desch suggested that "Liberalism vacillates between isolationism when it cannot change the world and messianism when it can."[4] Such skepticism certainly appeared warranted during the Iraq War and the neoconservative ascendance.

The broader sweep of American diplomatic history, however, suggests that American ambivalence about the world leads the United States to pursue an activist foreign policy not when it is *able to*, but when it *must*. Prior to the twentieth century, Americans largely avoided international adventures, relying upon England to keep sea lanes open for American trade. In the twentieth century, with England's decline, Americans were ambivalent about the greater international role that many felt was forced upon them. As noted in the Introduction (see Figure 0.6), many Americans resisted entry into World War I, clinging to isolationism. Once the U.S. had joined the Great War, however, most Americans embraced international engagement. "No longer can any man live to himself alone, nor any nation," John D. Rockefeller declared in a wartime speech given in Denver. "The world has become a unit."[5]

After World War I, however, the U.S. Senate rejected President Woodrow Wilson's League of Nations, and America retreated into a comfortable isolationism. Republican senator Robert Taft argued that U.S. intervention in Continental troubles would be "more likely to destroy American democracy than to destroy German dictatorship."[6] Similarly, Republican senator Arthur Vandenberg supported the isolationist Neutrality Acts of the 1930s.

Many believe that American isolationism ended for good with Pearl Harbor. "There can be no peace for any part of the world," Vandenberg declared, "unless the foundations of peace are made secure throughout all parts of the world."[7] At the onset of the Cold War, Vandenberg, as chair of the Senate Foreign Relations Committee, worked across party lines with the Democratic Truman administration to construct a bipartisan American foreign policy. Indeed, it was Vandenberg who famously declared that "politics stops at the water's edge."

Isolationist sentiments nonetheless persisted after the war. As early as the Korean War, Senator Taft warned in his 1951 *A Foreign Policy for Americans* that the new policy of containing communism would mean entanglement in global affairs.[8] And as seen in the epigraph, Republican congressman Ron Paul has continued to preach anti-interventionism to this day.

By contrast, Republican senator Marco Rubio, also quoted above, argues that with the September 11 terrorist attacks of 2001, isolationism is no longer an option. Rubio thus agrees with Democrat Barack Obama, who argued in 2006 that "We cannot afford to be a country of isolationists right now. 9-11 showed us that, try as we might to ignore the rest of the world, our enemies will no longer ignore us."[9] Pearl Harbor and 9/11 were arguably external shocks that helped galvanize bipartisan—but far from unanimous or permanent—support for international engagement.

Despite such persistent elite contention, public opinion scholars have largely argued that there has been a postwar Main Street consensus in favor of international engagement. In *Misreading the Public*, Steven Kull and I. M. Destler lament that elites have reduced America's international engagement out of a mistaken belief in "public neoisolationism."[10] The American public itself, the authoritative *Public Opinion Quarterly* tells us, does not even realize just how committed to international engagement it really is.[11]

But the poor wording of poll questions may have inflated the impression of popular support for international engagement. For instance, polls have repeatedly forced respondents to choose between (1) the U.S. doing "its fair share" and (2) "withdrawing" from global affairs. Because all Americans are motivated to see the United States in a positive light—"We're not freeloaders!"—the question's wording likely introduced a systematic measurement bias, inflating the percentages of respondents choosing the normatively preferable "fair share" option. Yet scholars have repeatedly pointed to responses to this question to claim popular support for international engagement.[12]

In our spring 2011 survey, the mean score for all Americans on our two counterbalanced isolationism items was 3.42 on a 1 to 7 scale, where 4 is the scale midpoint, suggesting only slight overall support for international engagement. Liberals ($M = 2.87$) supported international engagement moderately more than conservatives did ($M = 3.68$), however.[13] What best accounts for this ideological difference?

A pair of multiple mediation models provides some answers. In one model, of the five moral foundations, only compassion/care was a statistically significant mediator of the relationship between ideology and isolationism.[14] Because they value compassion more, liberals appear to be more willing to approach a world seen as needing American help.[15]

In a second model, of the four dimensions of American ideology that we measured, social and political ideologies were statistically significant mediators of the relationship between ideology and isolationism, reducing the direct effect tenfold.[16] First, conservatives prefer greater isolationism than liberals do, in part because of their greater social dominance orientation. This is consistent with our finding at the outset of Chapter 2 that social dominance is associated with greater negativity towards free trade among nations. In both cases, the desire that "inferior groups stay in their place" is associated with a desire to avoid international contacts (recall Figure 2.3).

Second, conservatives are more isolationist than liberals, in part because of their greater average support for libertarianism. This is consistent with the nonioninterventionism promoted by libertarian elites like Ron and Rand Paul. It is certainly possible that the Pauls' German heritage has contributed to their isolationism. A 1941 wartime survey revealed that ethnicity shaped American attitudes towards the war: those of Allied parents (e.g., English descent) were much more likely to support intervention in the European war than those of Axis parents (e.g., German or Italian descent).[17] But it seems more likely that the Pauls' anti-interventionism today is a natural extension of their libertarian philosophy. As discussed in Chapter 2, libertarians believe that sovereign individuals should be free to do whatever they please—as long as they do not harm others. Non-interventionism abroad is a logical international extension of the nonaggression principle central to libertarian thought. Like Howard Roark in Ayn Rand's *The Fountainhead*, libertarians shun contact with society—domestically and internationally.

Multilateralism vs. unilateralism. When Americans do choose to engage the world, *how* should they do so? Should they follow the libertarian "Lone Ranger" ideal and go it alone? Or should they work together with other nations to better achieve American foreign policy goals?

Americans have long debated the relative merits of unilateralism and multilateralism. Perhaps the best-known debate was over the League of Nations. As we will discuss in Chapter 10, President Woodrow Wilson failed to win Republican backing for the league in the U.S. Senate, although he himself had been its champion during the Treaty of Versailles negotiations that followed World War I. Figure 4.1, from London's *Punch Magazine*, displays a British view of American ambivalence about multilateralism. Entitled "The Gap in the Bridge," it depicts a disdainful Uncle Sam resting against a keystone labeled "USA." He sits next to an unfinished "League of Nations Bridge" that looks ready to collapse without its keystone. A sign notes that the bridge "was designed by the President of the U.S.A.," suggesting that Americans are irresponsible for starting the multilateral project but failing to complete it.

Do Americans support multilateralism today? We saw in the Introduction (see Figure 0.3) that on average Americans feel cool to lukewarm towards the

THE GAP IN THE BRIDGE

FIG. 4.1. Unilateralism vs. multilateralism: A British view of American ambivalence towards the League of Nations, 1919.

Source: Punch Magazine, December 10, 1919. Image courtesy of the Internet Archive. Archive.org.

World Bank (36°), the United Nations (45°), and the European Union (46°). Average feelings towards these three international organizations (α = .80) account for 49 percent of the variance (β = .70) in support for multilateralism, which is lukewarm (M = 4.33) for the American population as a whole. Our gut feelings, the affect heuristic suggests, often drive our specific policy preferences.

Tepid overall American feelings towards the United Nations, which are replicated in Pew survey data, led pollster Andrew Kohut to conclude in 2006 that Americans suffer from "two-mindedness" when it comes to multilateralism. Americans, he lamented, maintain "quixotic and contradictory opinions" towards the United Nations.[18]

Americans are not schizophrenic about multilateralism. Instead, liberal and conservative Americans maintain consistently different views of international organizations. As we saw in the Introduction (see Figure 0.4), on average liberals (66°) felt an astounding 49° warmer towards the United Nations than conservatives (17°) did in 2011. By failing to acknowledge that ideology powerfully and consistently divides Americans in their views of multilateral institutions, Kohut misrepresents the American public as fickle and erratic.

As we will explore in greater detail in Chapter 10, liberal and conservative differences over multilateralism are natural extensions of their domestic ideologies. For instance, unilateralism flows from conservative individualism. "Modern-day conservatives laud the possibilities of individual action by persons and, internationally, by nations acting alone," political scientist Bruce Russett noted over twenty years ago. By contrast, "political liberals decry unfettered individualism as destroying natural bonds of community and mutual aid."[19] This contributes to a liberal embrace of multilateralism. As we will see in Chapter 10, the different dimensions of American ideology powerfully synergize when it comes to the United Nations and other international organizations, contributing to a massive overall difference between liberal and conservative attitudes towards multilateralism.

Diplomacy vs. military force. Whether unilaterally or multilaterally, if America is to act in the world, how should it do so? Can nations be persuaded through patient diplomacy to do America's bidding? Or is military force the best means to its foreign policy ends?

We have already seen that liberals are much more likely than conservatives to oppose spanking as a tool of child rearing. Liberals are also more likely to question both the efficacy and desirability of the use of force in international affairs. When President Barack Obama claimed in 2006 that Americans "instinctively understand that we cannot simply impose our will militarily on the entire globe," he was really speaking for liberal Americans, not all Americans.[20] In the liberal view, force is not just limited in its utility; it can also be questionable ethically. As we saw in the Bill Mauldin and Herblock cartoons in the previous chapter (see Figures 3.9 and 3.10), liberals do not generally glorify war. As Mauldin, who experienced the horrors of warfare firsthand in Europe, wrote in 1945:

> Some say the American soldier is the same clean-cut young man who left his home; others say morale is sky-high at the front because everybody's face is shining for the great Cause. They are wrong. The combat man isn't quite the same clean-cut lad because you don't fight a Kraut by Marquis of Queensberry rules. You shoot him in the back. . . . He does the same to you.[21]

Liberals tend to question both the efficacy and desirability of the use of force. They therefore tend to champion persuasion in the home and diplomacy abroad.

Conservatives, by contrast, are much more likely to embrace spanking as both an efficacious and an appropriate way to raise children. The same attitudes carry over to international affairs. The first sentence of the foreign policy section of the "2012 Republican Platform" begins boldly, "We are the party of peace through strength." It then advocates the maintenance of American "military superiority" to "deter aggression or defeat those who threaten our national security interests."[22]

The conservative view that force is both efficacious and normatively justified has a very long history. English Puritan Alexander Leighton declared in 1624 that "God is an excellent Man of War," and Puritans carried that view with them across the Atlantic. Puritans should "take, kill, burn, sink, destroy all sin and Corruption which are professed enemies to Christ Jesus," declared the Reverend Joshua Moodey in a 1674 sermon on the Indian Wars. They should not "pity or spare" the natives. "Following the Crusader's example, Puritan divines resurrected the idea of holy war against the unfaithful," writes historian Andrew Preston. "A nation could—indeed should—initiate war in pursuit of its mission."[23]

Over three centuries later, the first George W. Bush administration made military force the centerpiece of its foreign policy. "America has, and intends to keep, military strength beyond challenge," Bush stated in his commencement address at West Point in June 2002. U.S. military capabilities would deter rival states. "Our forces will be strong enough to dissuade potential adversaries from pursuing a military build-up in hopes of surpassing, or equaling, the power of the United States," states the September 2002 *National Security Strategy*, written at Condoleezza Rice's National Security Council. But force could also be used effectively against terrorists through the new doctrine of preemption. As Secretary of Defense Donald Rumsfeld put it, "The best and in some cases the only defense is a good offense."[24]

Of course, not all American Christians embrace the belligerent spirit of the Old Testament. The progressive Christianity of the New Testament has long been a mainstay of American pacifism. In the Introduction we saw that Democratic presidential candidate William Jennings Bryan was an anti-imperialist, opposing the U.S. colonization of the Philippines following the Spanish-American War of 1898. The Bible's command to "preach the gospel to every creature," Bryan famously declared, "has no Gatling-gun attachment."[25]

Thomas Nast captured the appeal of both diplomacy and military might in a series of engravings published in *Harper's Weekly* in the winter of 1874–75. The first, entitled "International Law—The Better Way," depicts a longboat named "The Arbitrator" flying a "Truce" flag landing in Geneva (Figure 4.2). Two female emissaries (the first as Columbia?) disembark, cordially received by various European dignitaries (including John Bull?) under a banner declaring, "Welcome to Peace Through Arbitration." *Harper's* includes a quotation from President Ulysses S. Grant: "The Nations are fast becoming so civilized as to feel that there is a better way to settle their difficulties than by fighting." War weary following the Civil War, Grant and his secretary of state, Hamilton Fish, relied on vigorous diplomacy to avoid wars with both Britain and Spain. They settled the Alabama Claims with Britain, which expressed its regrets and agreed to pay the U.S. government $15.5 million for damages done by warships built in Britain and sold to the Confederacy. With the 1871 signing of the Treaty of

INTERNATIONAL LAW—THE BETTER WAY
"The Nations are fast becoming so civilized as to feel that there is a better way to
settle their difficulties than by fighting."—U. S. Grant

FIG. 4.2. Diplomacy and international law, 1874.

Source: Thomas Nast, *Harper's Weekly*, November 14, 1874. Image courtesy of the Library of Congress. LOT 14012, no. 384.

Washington, the United States and Britain became close allies. Grant and Fish also negotiated a peaceful solution to the *Virginius* Affair, postponing a conflict with Spain over Cuba for a quarter century.

Military strength also has its appeal. A set of Nast engravings from February 1875 depict Columbia in a pair of contrasting poses (Figure 4.3). The print on the left, entitled "Peace Insecure—Afraid for Her Life," depicts a crouched Columbia with an anxious look in her eyes as she peers out from behind mock fortifications. A log pretends to be a cannon, and a scarecrow is propped up like a soldier. A U.S. flag hangs upside down, a sign of distress. American coastal defenses are clearly vulnerable. Nast may have been reacting to the military demobilization following the Civil War. Or he may have been fretting about how the many corruption scandals of the Grant administration might hollow out the U.S. Treasury and military.

By contrast, "Peace Secure—Safe and Protected," on the right of Figure 4.3, depicts Columbia standing resolutely beside a massive cannon, looking confidently out to sea. The U.S. flag flies briskly and upright over an armed sentry. Including an olive branch in her hand and doves flying near the fort's ramparts,

PEACE INSECURE—
AFRAID FOR HER LIFE

PEACE SECURE—
SAFE AND PROTECTED

FIG. 4.3. Military force: Peace through strength, 1875.

Source: Thomas Nast, *Harper's Weekly*, February 13, 1875. Images courtesy of the Library of Congress. LC-USZ62-129686 and LC-USZ62-129685.

Nast's drawing could be a visual representation of the declaration of "peace through strength" in the "2012 Republican Platform."

Given the large influence of ideology (β = .38) on support for "*Projecting military power*" and "*Sustaining military superiority*," it is not surprising that all four of the dimensions of American ideology contribute to this difference. The largest, however, were cultural traditionalism and social dominance, both of which are associated with aggression.[26] And of the five moral foundations, authority/discipline was by far the strongest mediator of the relationship. Conservatives, in other words, favor military power more than liberals do, in part because of the greater value they place on authority and their greater willingness to assert group dominance.

THE MANY ENEMIES OF REALISM:
HUMANITARIAN, POLITICAL, AND RELIGIOUS IDEALISMS

> "*Our foreign policy should promote traditional American ideals: democracy and human rights. . . . Human aspirations are universal—for dignity, for freedom, for the opportunity to improve the lives of our families*"[27]
>
> —Barack Obama, July 12, 2004

"I believe the desire for freedom is universal. History shows that, when given the chance, people of every race and religion take extraordinary risks for liberty."[28]
—George W. Bush, 2010

Unilateralism versus multilateralism and diplomacy versus military force address questions of *means*: How should the United States conduct its foreign policy? Realism versus idealism, by contrast, addresses the issue of *ends*: What foreign policy *goals* should the United States pursue? Should America seek to combat global hunger and disease? Should it promote democracy, human rights, and religious freedoms around the world? Or should its goals be limited to a national interest more narrowly defined in terms of U.S. economic and military security?

Our 2011 survey measured three distinct types of foreign policy idealisms—humanitarian, political, and religious—with three respective pairs of items. Participants were asked to rate the importance of the following on a seven-point scale:

- *Fighting diseases like AIDS and malaria in poor countries.*
- *Combating hunger in developing countries.*
- *Promoting and defending human rights in other countries.*
- *Helping to bring democracy to other nations.*
- *Defending religious freedom worldwide.*
- *Ending religious persecution around the world.*

Item sequence was randomized, and each pair was averaged together to create robust scales measuring humanitarian, political, and religious idealisms. The average score on each scale was substantially above the scale midpoint of 4, suggesting overall support for idealism in American foreign policy.[29]

There were significant differences between liberals and conservatives on two of the three idealisms. Ideology had a very large impact on humanitarian idealism and a small effect on political ideology, with liberals higher on both. It had no influence, however, on religious idealism.[30] We shall see that liberals and conservatives share a similar level of support for religious freedoms abroad—but for distinct reasons.

Humanitarian idealism. What best explains the very large influence of ideology on support for humanitarian idealism? Why would fighting disease and hunger around the world be a partisan issue? Anticipating this question, our survey included two items measuring endorsement of the "Protestant ethic" of self-help:

- *People are responsible for their own situation in life.*
- *People should not count on others to solve their problems.*

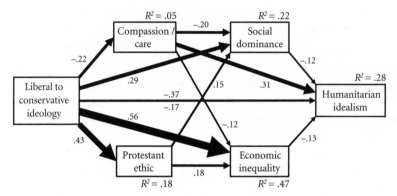

FIG. 4.4. Liberals are more supportive of humanitarian idealism in American foreign policy than conservatives are, in part because they place a greater value on compassion and oppose social dominance and economic inequality more; conservatives tend to oppose humanitarian idealism, in part because they favor the Protestant ethic of self-help more, and also support social dominance and income inequality.

Note: A path model. To reduce clutter, covariances and prediction error terms are not displayed. Model fit statistics are online at SUP.org. *Data Source:* OU Institute for US-China Issues, 2011.

Conservatives ($m = 5.79$) scored much higher than liberals ($m = 4.50$) on the resulting two-item "Protestant ethic" scale.[31] This is consistent with the U.S. data from the 2006 World Values Survey (WVS), implemented online by Knowledge Networks, in which Republicans ($m = 5.83$) scored much higher than Democrats ($m = 3.58$) on a ten-point scale from *"The government should take more responsibility to ensure that everyone is provided for"* to *"People should take more responsibility to provide for themselves."*[32]

A pair of multiple mediation models revealed that the ideological dimensions of social dominance and economic inequality, the Protestant ethic, and the moral value of compassion/care all mediated the impact of ideology on support for humanitarian idealism. Figure 4.4 combines these variables into a single path model that fit the data best. It reveals that opposing views of compassion and the Protestant ethic play a major role in dividing liberal and conservative attitudes towards humanitarian idealism. Liberal compassion for the suffering of others ($\beta = -.22$) both directly promotes support for humanitarian idealism ($\beta = .31$) and indirectly contributes to it via opposition to ideologies of social dominance ($\beta = -.20$) and economic inequality ($\beta = -.12$). By contrast, conservatives tend to be less concerned about the suffering of (foreign?) others ($\beta = -.22$) and much more concerned about upholding the Protestant ethic of self-help ($\beta = .43$). And belief in the Protestant ethic contributes to support for

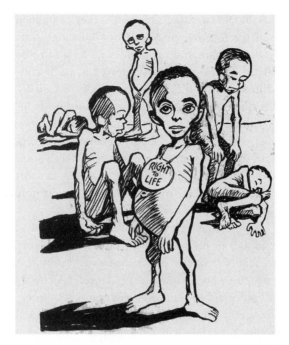

RIGHT TO LIFE

FIG. 4.5. Humanitarian idealism: Liberal compassion confronts the Protestant ethic and opposition to family planning, 1981.

Source: Copyright Bill Mauldin, 1981. Courtesy of the Bill Mauldin Estate LLC.

the maintenance of social ($\beta = .15$) and economic ($\beta = .18$) hierarchies, both at home and abroad.

Bill Mauldin captured the compassionate liberal view of humanitarian idealism in a haunting 1981 cartoon depicting starving children, likely from the famine then occurring in Uganda (Figure 4.5). He provocatively entitled it "Right to Life," a jab at the Reagan administration's cutoff of U.S. funding to all humanitarian NGOs that provide family planning—the "Global Gag Rule." "A cartoonist . . . [is a] lowly gadfly: circle and stab, circle and stab. Roughly put, our credo should be, If it's big, hit it," Mauldin had written twenty years earlier. "Having used the cartoon as a device to get the reader's attention on a subject, it doesn't really matter whether we needle him, amuse him, or infuriate him . . . if enough people get interested in an issue, the majority will come up with the right answer most of the time."[33]

By targeting compassion in his 1981 cartoon, however, Mauldin likely appealed more to fellow liberals than to the Christian conservatives who supported Reagan's "Global Gag Rule." Our 2011 survey respondents also rated the importance of the foreign policy goal of *"Promoting sexual education, family planning, and contraceptive use worldwide"* on a 1 to 7 scale. Not surprisingly, liberals (m = 5.56) strongly supported it, while conservatives (m = 2.97) opposed it, a massive difference statistically.[34] A mediation analysis revealed that this single item accounted for 90 percent of the relationship between ideology and humanitarian idealism.[35] In other words, vastly different views about sexual education, family planning, and contraceptive use accounted for most of the huge difference between liberals and conservatives on humanitarian idealism. The global sick and starving, in short, are hostage to the domestic American debate over whether sex for purposes other than procreation is sin.

Libertarians, by contrast, have long appealed to the Protestant ethic to oppose humanitarian aid. In his 1960 *The Conscience of a Conservative*, Barry Goldwater asserts that "Foreign aid has created a vast reservoir of anti-Americanism among peoples who . . . resent dependence."[36] As we shall see in the Chapter 6 discussion of aid to Haiti, Ron Paul objects to foreign aid on the grounds that income redistribution is immoral. For libertarians like Goldwater and Paul, the poor have the right to help themselves.

Political idealism. As revealed in the epigraphs, Presidents George W. Bush and Barack Obama share a common belief that promoting freedom and democracy are legitimate U.S. foreign policy interests. That belief likely contributed to their decisions to become militarily involved in Iraq and Libya, respectively.

Indeed, political idealism has long been used to justify American military interventions abroad. F. Victor Gillam's lithograph "A Plea for Cuba," published in an 1895 *Judge*, is an early example of political idealism (Figure 4.6). Columbia sleeps in an armchair. On an island just offshore a man labeled "Spain" in Spanish dress attacks a defenseless black woman labeled "Cuba" with the butt of a rifle. She is prone on the ground but holds up a banner reading, "Liberty or Death." Columbia holds a document in her hand that she was apparently reading before dozing off. "The Spanish rule in Cuba is a history of Tyranny and Brutality." The ghosts of French general Lafayette and German general von Steuben, who both served in the Continental Army during the American Revolutionary War, float behind Columbia. "What! Asleep with a cry for aid at your door! What would have been your fate if we had acted similarly in your hour of tribulation?" A *History of the Revolution* lies on the floor, opened to pages reading, "American revolutionists were recognized and aided by France and Germany. French sympathy, Lafayette's aid, and the aid of Germans were powerful factors in our struggle for Independence." Gillam even adds a bust

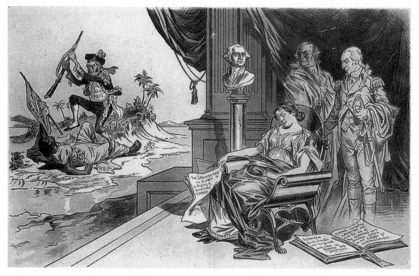

A PLEA FOR CUBA

Shades of Lafayette and Steuben (*to Columbia*)—"*What! Asleep with a cry for
aid at your door! What would have been your fate if we had acted similarly in
your hour of tribulation?*"

FIG. 4.6. Political idealism: The obligation to defend liberty abroad, 1895.

Source: F. Victor Gillam, *Judge*, October 19, 1895. Image courtesy of the Library of Congress. LC-
USZC4-4130

of President Washington to further appeal to Columbia's conscience: America
must help liberate Cuba!

A similar case would be made for U.S. intervention in World War I just
twenty years later. "The world must be made safe for democracy," President
Woodrow Wilson declared to a joint session of Congress in 1917. "Its peace must
be planted upon the tested foundations of political liberty."[37]

As noted above, liberals scored slightly higher than conservatives on support
for political idealism. Mediation analysis revealed that this difference was accounted for by the greater value that liberals place on compassion.[38] Liberals are
slightly more willing to promote human rights and democracy abroad because
they care more about the suffering of foreigners. American conservatives, by
contrast, appear more conflicted about political idealism. Cultural traditionalism has a small but statistically significant *positive* effect ($\beta = .11, p = .007$) on
support for political idealism, while political ideology (libertarianism) has a
small *negative* influence ($\beta = -.10, p = .002$); in effect, they cancel each other out.

Why would cultural conservatism be associated with political idealism? "I believe that God wants everyone to be free," President George W. Bush stated in a 2004 presidential debate with John Kerry. "And that's been part of my foreign policy. . . . Freedom . . . is a gift from the Almighty." Religious and political idealisms share about twice as much variation among conservatives (37%) as they do among liberals (19%). This suggests that the defense of religious liberty is a bigger reason for democracy promotion among conservatives than among liberals.[39]

Why would libertarianism be associated with less support for political idealism? One might think that defenders of individual liberty at home would support democracy promotion abroad. Instead, a mediation analysis revealed that their greater isolationism, discussed above, accounted for well over two-thirds of libertarian opposition to political idealism.[40]

Religious idealism. Religion has long played a major role in American foreign policy. The anti-imperialism of William Jennings Bryan, discussed in the Introduction, was motivated by his Christian beliefs. But President William McKinley defended the Philippine-American War on religious grounds as well. Believing Filipinos unfit for self-governance, McKinley argued that "there was nothing left for us to do but to . . . educate the Filipinos, and uplift and civilize and Christianize them, and by God's grace do the very best we could by them, as our fellow-men for whom Christ also died." McKinley was not alone in espousing a Christian imperialism at the turn of the century. "Providence has given the United States the duty of extending Christian civilization," argued Senator Knute Nelson of Minnesota, an abolitionist and Civil War veteran. "And we propose to execute it."[41]

Even during the height of the Cold War in the 1970s, when Realpolitik was ascendant, religious idealism survived and prospered. As we will see in Chapter 8, Senator Scoop Jackson was able to mobilize bipartisan opposition to Kissinger's détente with the Soviet Union on the basis of popular American unease about Soviet persecution of Jews. That attitude did not change in the 1980s. "Our people feel it keenly when religious freedom is denied to anyone anywhere," President Ronald Reagan declared in Moscow in 1988. All Russians, he argued, should "be able to practice their religion freely and openly."[42]

And religious idealism remains a foreign policy issue today. The section on "Protecting Human Rights" in the "2012 Republican Platform" actually focuses solely on religious liberty. "A Republican administration," it promises, "will return the advocacy of religious liberty to a central place in our diplomacy."[43]

Religious liberty thus appears to be a bigger issue for Republicans. Why then did our survey reveal no association between liberal-conservative ideology and support for religious idealism in our full sample? A series of regression analyses revealed that this statistical non-finding was hiding an interesting pattern. When controlling for warmth towards Christians, a negative association emerges, so that liberals appear to care more about religious freedom worldwide. But when controlling instead for humanitarian idealism, a positive association emerges, suggesting that conservatives care more about religious persecution.

How should this puzzling series of statistical findings be interpreted? Liberals and conservatives may have understood the same statements differently. When asked to rate the importance of *"Defending religious freedom worldwide"* and *"Ending religious persecution around the world"* as American foreign policy goals, the average conservative may think more about protecting fellow Christians from persecution. Thus, controlling for warmth towards fellow Christians pulls such conservative sentiments out of the relationship, allowing a liberal association to appear. When asked to rate the same two statements, the average liberal, lower on biblical literalism and religiosity, is likely less focused on the persecution of Christians in particular. Instead, they likely think about religious persecution more in terms of protecting persecuted peoples around the world. Thus, when controlling for the importance of more liberal humanitarian concerns like *"Combating hunger in developing countries"* and *"Fighting diseases like AIDS,"* a conservative association between ideology and religious idealism appears.

In short, both liberals and conservatives care about protecting religious freedom around the world—but for different reasons. "Religious liberty touched a nerve deep in the American worldview and was not bound by partisanship or ideology," writes historian Andrew Preston. "In the American tradition, religious liberty is perhaps the oldest and most sacrosanct of all human rights."[44] Our survey data suggests that Preston is right that liberal and conservative Americans share a desire to promote religious liberties abroad. But their motivations diverge: conservatives appear to be concerned primarily about the persecution of fellow Christians, while liberals view religious liberty through a broader humanitarian lens.

IDEOLOGIES OF AMERICAN NATIONAL IDENTITY: PATRIOTISM, NATIONALISM, AND NATIONAL NARCISSISM

"People of Berlin, people of the world, this is our moment. This is our time. [I come to you] as a citizen, a proud citizen of the United States and a fellow citizen of the world."[45]
　　　　　　　　　　　　　　　—Senator Barack Obama (Democrat–Illinois), 2008

"We must strengthen our unique American civilization. . . . Let me be clear: I am not a citizen of the world. . . . I am a citizen of the United States of America."[46]
　　　　　　　—Former Speaker of the House Newt Gingrich (Republican–Georgia), 2009

What does it mean to be an American? And how does being American shape one's attitudes towards the rest of the world?

Liberals like Barack Obama often identify with both America and humanity as a whole, acknowledging a degree of equality among nations. When asked in 2009 about his views on American exceptionalism, Obama replied, "I believe in American exceptionalism, just as I suspect that the Brits believe in British exceptionalism and the Greeks believe in Greek exceptionalism."

Conservatives, by contrast, tend to express how different they are as Americans from the rest of the world. "If everyone is exceptional, no one is," conservative pundit Charles Krauthammer countered Obama.[47] "American Exceptionalism," notably, is the title of the foreign policy section of the "2012 Republican Platform." And as the second epigraph reveals, Newt Gingrich prefers to identify solely with America, rejecting Obama's notion of being a citizen of the world.

These ideological differences are manifest in day-to-day life; they are not just hot air. "We don't like the World Cup. We don't like soccer," exclaimed Glenn Beck on his radio show in 2010. "Probably because the rest of the world likes it so much." If Beck's "we" was referring to his fellow conservatives, he was right. Our spring 2011 survey included a question asking respondents how much they agreed with the statement, "*I like international soccer and the World Cup.*" Even controlling for the standard demographics (including ethnicity: Hispanics are more liberal and like soccer more than non-Hispanics), liberals still scored substantially higher than conservatives on liking soccer.[48]

To explore liberal and conservative attitudes about being American, and the implications of those attitudes for foreign policy preferences, we measured American identities and national ideologies in three different ways. Following previous scholarship in political psychology, we distinguish between "patriotism" as love of country and "nationalism" as a belief in the superiority of one's own country over other countries.[49] This approach differs from lay usage of "patriotism" and "nationalism," generally used interchangeably to mean a strong identification with one's nation. Lay usage does distinguish, however, between patriotism as normatively good, and thus what "we" possess, and nationalism as normatively bad, and thus what "they" practice. We make no such normative distinction. Our survey measured patriotism with two items that cohered extremely well ($\alpha = .92$):

- *I love my country.*
- *I am proud to be American.*

Nationalism ($\alpha = .84$) was also measured with two items:

- *America is the best country in the world.*
- *The American system is superior to that of other countries.*

Patriotism and nationalism shared a remarkable 52 percent of their variance ($r = .72$) in our sample, suggesting that while conceptually distinct, among Americans they tend to go together.[50]

NEW YORK CITY'S AMERICAN MAYOR
Chorus of Naturalized Citizens—

He might have been a Rooshan,   *But in spite of all Temptations,*
A Frenchman, Turk or Prooshan,   *To belong to other Nations,*
Or perhaps an Irishman;   *He remains an American!*

FIG. 4.7. Patriotism and nationalism in a land of immigrants, 1888.

Source: F. Victor Gillam, *Judge*, March 31, 1888. Image courtesy of the University of Oklahoma Libraries, Nichols Collection. Color image online at SUP.org.

Why would patriotism and nationalism as an American tend to cohere? Social psychologists have demonstrated that the love of one's own social group does not necessitate competition with other groups.[51] One possibility may have to do with the demographics of American society. We are a nation of immigrants. First the colonies and then the United States were settled by wave upon wave of immigrants from different countries. American citizens frequently interacted with "foreign" immigrants of different races and languages, who confronted prejudice and the challenge of assimilation. This may have created a situation where a central way to express one's love of country was to assert its superiority over foreigners—both inside and outside the body politic.

F. Victor Gillam suggested as much in a brilliant editorial cartoon and farcical song published in an 1888 *Judge* magazine (Figure 4.7). New York City mayor Abraham Hewitt had issued a decree that "No flag will be hoisted on this City Hall but the American flag." Of English and French descent, Hewitt was well known for his nativist beliefs. Although he was a Democrat, he famously refused to review the city's St. Patrick's Day Parade honoring the Irish. Gillam draws Hewitt holding and wearing the red, white, and blue Stars and Stripes as a "chorus of naturalized citizens" serenades him. They include labeled English, German, Irish, and French men and an unlabeled Chinese man, easily recognizable from his national attire. The song they sing is Gillam's play on Gilbert and Sullivan's "For He Is an Englishman." Their 1878 comic opera *H.M.S. Pinafore* had become an international sensation in the 1880s. Gillam's lyrical alterations and engraving suggest that Hewitt's patriotism depends upon a nationalist ideology of superiority over other nations. "*He might have been a Rooshan, / A Frenchman, Turk or Prooshan, / Or perhaps an Irishman; / But in spite of all Temptations, / To belong to other Nations, / He remains an American!*" Part of Gillam's joke may also be that the previous year, during Queen Victoria's 1887 Golden Jubilee celebrations in New York, Mayor Hewitt had referred to her as "our Queen."[52] Hewitt's American nationalism is clearly that of the WASP variety. We will explore American attitudes towards "Mother England" further in Chapter 7.

Gillam depicts Mayor Hewitt with a peacock feather in his top hat, insinuating that excessive nationalism can degenerate into vanity. My colleague Huajian Cai and I call this phenomenon "national narcissism," an inflated view of one's own nation's importance and deservedness. It was measured with two items ($\alpha = .84$):

- *If America had a bigger say in the world, the world would be a much better place.*
- *I wish other countries would more quickly recognize American authority.*

Drawing on recent work in personality and social psychology on both individual level narcissism and "collective narcissism,"[53] we argue that national narcissism has two internal dimensions: national grandiosity and national entitlement, which differ in terms of their intra-national and inter-national orientations, respectively. To take the American case, national grandiosity shifts the subject from the individual level, "I am great," to the collective level, "We Americans are great"; and national entitlement, from "You owe me" to "The world owes us Americans."[54]

Samuel Ehrhart's cover illustration for a 1901 *Puck* magazine captures beautifully the grandiosity central to national narcissism (Figure 4.8). Entitled "Columbia's Easter Bonnet," it depicts Columbia gazing at herself in a mirror adoringly, a bayonet hanging from her waist. Like Mayor Hewitt in the Gillam illustration, she wears the red, white, and blue of the Stars and Stripes. Columbia is adjusting her hat, which is actually a small battleship labeled "World Power." Two of its four cannons are labeled "Army" and "Navy," and it belches smoke labeled "Expansion." The cartoon is likely a jab at President McKinley's imperialist foreign policy, from Cuba to Hawaii to the Philippines. "By the turn of the century . . . Americans had succumbed to the temptations of an assertively

COLUMBIA'S EASTER BONNET

FIG. 4.8. National narcissism: Imperial grandiosity and self-love, 1901.

Source: Samuel Ehrhart, *Puck* magazine cover, April 6, 1901. Image courtesy of the Library of Congress. LC-USZC4-6550. Color image online at SUP.org.

nationalist foreign policy," historian Michael Hunt writes. "Greatness abroad would glorify liberty at home . . . [and] liberty sanctified greatness."[55] The pursuit of national greatness, Ehrhart suggests, is little more than vanity.

But do patriotism, nationalism, and national narcissism really matter for the foreign policy preferences of the American people? Pew pollster Andrew Kohut claims that "Little hard data support the idea that . . . nationalism plays a significant role in Americans' actual opinions about . . . specific international issues."[56]

The survey data suggests otherwise. Patriotism, nationalism, and national narcissism *all* correlate positively and strongly with our measures of support for the use of military force (r = .49, .58, .55, respectively) and overall desires for tougher foreign policies (r = .21, .26, .27). Indeed, of the fifteen countries we measured foreign policy preferences towards, patriotism correlated significantly with all except South Korea, Japan, and Germany, nationalism with all except Japan and Germany, and national narcissism with all except England. In other words, these three different measures of Americanness correlated positively with desires for *tougher* policies towards specific foreign countries the vast majority of the time. In general, the correlations were the highest for countries seen as posing the greatest threats to the United States, such as Iran ($r = .34, .38, .28$, respectively) and North Korea ($r = .29, .29, .17$). As we will see in Chapter 8, the one exception was Israel: greater patriotism ($r = -.22$), nationalism ($r = -.30$), and national narcissism ($r = -.21$) as an American were associated with desires for *friendlier* policies towards Israel.

Do American liberals and conservatives differ in these national ideologies? Yes. Conservatives score moderately, massively, and much higher than liberals on patriotism, nationalism, and national narcissism, respectively.[57] This is consistent with the U.S. data from the 2006 World Values Survey, which revealed Republicans to be moderately more patriotic than Democrats.[58]

Because patriotism and nationalism correlate so highly with each other, controlling for either allows us to examine a more "pure" form of each. For instance, if we add nationalism to the demographic covariates in the first statistical analysis in the paragraph above on whether ideology shapes patriotism, the outcome actually *reverses*: liberals score slightly higher than conservatives on "pure patriotism."[59] What is "pure patriotism"? It is a love of or pride in America—after taking out the belief that America is better than or superior to other countries. In other words, while conservatives score higher than liberals on patriotism, liberals score higher than conservatives on a "pure patriotism," in which the sense of nationalist superiority has been removed.

What are the consequences of these ideological differences in patriotism and nationalism for the foreign policy preferences of the American people? Figure 4.9 displays a mediation model in which only one of the two indirect paths was statistically significant. Although conservatives are both more patriotic ($\beta = .31$) and more nationalistic ($\beta = .47$) than liberals, only their greater nationalism (the bottom path) accounts for the greater conservative than liberal desire for tougher foreign policies.[60] It is the externally oriented nationalist sense of superiority, and not the internally directed love of country, that appears to drive foreign policy preferences.

So what explains the very strong link between ideology and nationalism ($\beta = .47$) at the bottom left of Figure 4.9? Remarkably, all four dimensions of American ideology were statistically significant mediators, together accounting for over 90 percent of the relationship.[61] Different kinds of conservatives across the board are more nationalistic than liberals. Of the five moral values, however, only authority and purity were statistically significant mediators of the relationship between liberal-conservative ideology and nationalism.[62] Not surprisingly, they are the more traditional "binding" values. Presumably, conservatives endorse American superiority over other nations (nationalism) more than liberals do, in part because they value authority over foreigners more and in part

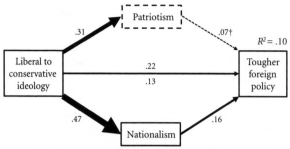

FIG. 4.9. Although conservatives are both more patriotic and nationalistic than liberals are, only their greater nationalism accounts for their greater desire for tougher foreign policies.

Note: A simultaneous mediation model. † p = .10. Only the indirect path through nationalism was statistically significant. Indirect effect statistics are online at SUP.org. Demographic covariates are not shown. Foreign policy scale is an average of fifteen countries (α = .83). *Data source:* OU Institute for US-China Issues, 2011.

because they prefer separation from them to maintain American purity and distinctiveness.

AMERICAN FOREIGN POLICY PROFILES

"Within America, there has long been a tension between those who describe themselves as realists or idealists—a tension that suggests a stark choice between the narrow pursuit of interests or an endless campaign to impose our values around the world. I reject these choices."[63]

—Democratic President Barack Obama, 2009

"I've never understood the division between so-called realists and so-called idealists. I don't know how you get up in the world every day, doing what I do, if you don't have some sense of idealism, because you have to believe that as hard as it is, you're going to prevent the dictator from oppressing his people, you're going to help to stop the war, you're going to figure out a way to get clean water to thirsty people and cure kids of disease. And at the same time, I don't know how you go through the day and expect to be successful without being very hardheaded and realistic. So for me, it's not an either/or."[64]

—Democratic Secretary of State Hillary Clinton, 2011

In *Special Providence*, diplomatic historian Walter Russell Mead lays out four distinct American schools or ways of thinking about foreign policy that express distinct "moral and political values as well as socioeconomic and political interests." *Hamiltonians* are commercial realists who advocate a strong alliance between the national government and big business to promote free trade and American commercial interests. *Wilsonians* are crusading moralists who, coming out of the American missionary tradition, oppose colonialism and support democracy. *Jeffersonians*, distrustful of large government and a standing army, and jealous of our fragile liberties at home, are democratic isolationists wary of international entanglements. *Jacksonian* populists value honor and military pride, and are willing to fight for both family and flag. These four schools, Mead argues, are not "blood types" but "ideal types": most Americans combine elements of each view in the ways that they think about foreign policy.[65]

Do different groups of Americans possess distinct foreign policy profiles? Cluster analysis, the statistical technique used in Chapter 2 to explore the ideological profiles of Democrats and Republicans, can be used to inductively address this question. We ran seven of our foreign policy orientations—isolationism, multilateralism, military force, humanitarian idealism, political idealism, religious idealism, and nationalism—in a series of two-step cluster analyses on our full U.S. sample and found that a three-cluster solution fit the data best.[66] As the bar chart in Figure 4.10 reveals, the largest group, representing about 40 percent of the American population, and labeled "idealistic doves," is relatively supportive of idealism in American foreign policy but is the lowest of all three groups of Americans on both nationalism and support for the use of military force. The second largest group, representing about a third of the U.S. population, is "idealistic hawks." They are the strongest supporters of all three types of idealism *and* are the most nationalistic, the most willing to use military force, and the least isolationist. Finally, the third group, representing about a quarter of the U.S. population, is "unilateralist hawks," the least idealist, most realist of all three groups. They are also by far the most unilateralist of all three groups, and the most isolationist.

Who are these people? The pie charts in Figure 4.10 display each group's composition by political party and religious identification. In terms of party identification, a majority (54%) of the idealistic doves are Democrats; only 11 percent are Republicans. By contrast, almost three times as many of the unilateralist hawks are Republicans (45%) as Democrats (16%). Idealist hawks, however, are a bipartisan mix: 36 percent are Democrats while 40 percent are Republicans. Substantial groups of both Democrats and Republicans have long supported the forceful promotion of democracy and religious freedom around the world.

In composition by religion, Evangelical Protestants make up the plurality of both groups of hawks. By contrast, those who self-identify as atheist, agnostic, or having "no religion" are most strongly represented among the idealistic doves. Mainline Protestants and Catholics stand between these two extremes, representing about the same portion of each foreign policy group.

Realist international relations theorists have recently argued that the American public is much more realist and much less idealist than are American political elites. "The overwhelming majority of Americans possess a Hobbesian world view," claims Tufts's Daniel Drezner. But this "realist mass public," he

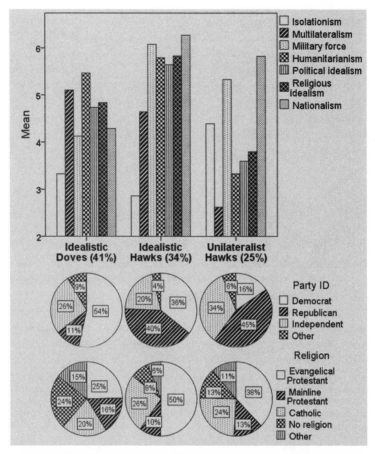

FIG. 4.10. American foreign policy profiles: While three-quarters of Americans support idealistic goals in U.S. foreign policy, divided mainly over nationalism and the use of military force, one quarter are "unilateralist hawks" fundamentally skeptical of multilateralism and idealism, and ambivalent about international engagement.

Note: There were massive differences between the three groups of Americans on all seven foreign policy orientations. The largest difference was on humanitarianism: $F(2, 1044) = 487.58, p < .001$, $\eta_p^2 = .48$, controlling for the seven standard demographics. *Data source:* OU Institute for US-China Issues, 2011.

laments, is "governed by a liberal internationalist elite."[67] Colin Dueck concurs, suggesting that "Foreign policy 'idealism' is to some extent a special preoccupation of party elites and party activists. . . . The general public is actually more realistic about foreign policy than is commonly believed."[68]

The data suggests otherwise. Three-quarters of Americans support idealism in American foreign policy, disagreeing only over how forcefully it should be pursued (Figure 4.10, two bar clusters to the left). Only one quarter of Ameri-

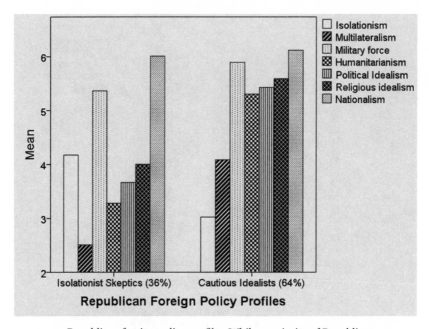

FIG. 4.11. Republican foreign policy profiles: While a majority of Republicans are *cautious idealists* willing to engage the world to improve it, a substantial minority are *isolationist skeptics* who disdain multilateralism and idealism, favoring isolationism.

Note: A two-step cluster analysis. There were no differences between the two groups of Republicans on nationalism: $F(1, 303) = .87$, $p = .35$. But there were moderate to massive differences on all other foreign policy orientations, especially political idealism and humanitarian idealism: $F(1, 303) = 225.38$, $p < .001$, $\eta_p^2 = .43$; and $F(1, 303) = 251.18$, $p < .001$, $\eta_p^2 = .45$, controlling for the seven standard demographics. *Data source:* OU Institute for US-China Issues, 2011.

cans, the unilateralist hawks, express ambivalence about idealism in American foreign policy in favor of realist caution.

Republican foreign policy profiles. To better understand *intra*party debates over U.S. foreign policy, we ran separate two-step cluster analyses for our Republican and Democratic subsamples. A two-cluster solution, displayed in Figure 4.11, fit the Republican subsample best. About a third of the Republicans were "isolationist skeptics," ambivalent about idealisms in American foreign policy, hostile to multilateral institutions like the United Nations, and unwilling to embrace an active role for the United States internationally. The other two-thirds of the Republicans were "cautious idealists," more willing to engage the world and support multilateral institutions, and accepting of idealist goals in U.S. foreign policy. Both groups were equally nationalistic.[69]

This quantitative finding of uniform Republican nationalism is consistent with Colin Dueck's qualitative historical analysis in *Hard Line: The Republican Party and U.S. Foreign Policy Since World War II*. "Whether the GOP pursues foreign policies characterized as isolationist or internationalist," Dueck concludes, "there is always a strong impulse of American nationalism that never waivers."[70] That is exactly what Figure 4.11 shows: while isolationist skeptics and cautious idealists differ on idealism versus realism and the various internationalisms, both groups of Republicans agree on American nationalism.

Democratic foreign policy profiles. A three-cluster solution fit the Democratic subsample best (Figure 4.12). Close to three-quarters of all Democrats were either "global citizens" or "forceful idealists," sharing a commitment to international activism, multilateralism, and humanitarian idealism. Forceful idealists, who might also be thought of as "humanitarian hawks," were somewhat

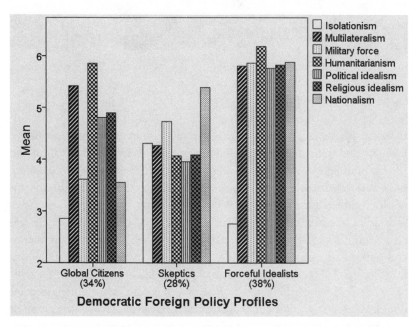

FIG. 4.12. Democratic foreign policy profiles: Democrats are about evenly divided between *global citizens*, who score low on nationalism and militarism but wish to work multilaterally on global challenges; *skeptics*, who are more nationalistic but skeptical about international entanglements; and *forceful idealists*, who believe that a strong America can work multilaterally to solve global problems.

Note: A two-step cluster analysis. There were large to massive differences between the three groups of Democrats on all seven foreign policy orientations. The largest was on humanitarianism: $F(2, 388) = 197.68, p < .001, \eta_p^2 = .51$, controlling for the seven standard demographics. *Data source:* OU Institute for US-China Issues, 2011.

FIG. 4.13. Forceful idealists in the Democratic Party: Obama's foreign policy team watches the raid that killed Osama bin Laden, May 2, 2011.
Source: Clifford Photo courtesy of whitehouse.gov.

more supportive of political and religious idealism than were global citizens, however, and were much more willing to embrace American nationalism and the use of military force. The remaining quarter of Democrats were "skeptics," more ambivalent about global engagement, multilateralism, and all three forms of idealism than other Democrats were.

The antiwar activism of George McGovern and Vietnam era liberals has created the impression that all Democrats are doves and all Republicans, hawks. Our 2011 data suggests some truth to the stereotype: *on average,* Republicans score substantially higher than Democrats on nationalism and support for military force.[71] However, this is another case where group means hide important differences within groups: our cluster analysis reveals that the largest group of Democrats was actually forceful idealists willing to embrace American nationalism and to deploy military force as a tool to achieve idealistic foreign policy goals.

In the 1990s, President William Clinton described America as the "indispensable nation," arguing that "When our national security interests are threatened, we will act with others when we can, but alone if we must. We will use diplomacy when we can, but force if we must."[72] His record, of course, was mixed: deploying the U.S. military to prevent further genocide in Bosnia, where his Republican predecessor George H.W. Bush had not, but failing to intervene in Rwanda.

Like Clinton, President Barack Obama and his secretary of state Hillary Clinton fit the "forceful idealist/humanitarian hawk" profile. As the epigraphs reveal, both Obama and Hillary Clinton reject the common juxtaposition of realism against idealism in American foreign policy. James Mann argues that Obama sought to blend the realism of Kissinger and Scowcroft with the idealism of Woodrow Wilson.[73] This is consistent with James Kloppenberg's argument that Obama is a philosophical pragmatist, open to different approaches to find what works. We have already seen that in March 2011 Obama ordered a U.S. military attack on the Libyan army that prevented a massacre in Benghazi. Less than two months later, Obama overrode the objections of Defense Secretary Robert Gates to authorize Operation Neptune Spear, in which U.S. Navy SEALs raided a compound in Abbottabad, Pakistan, killing Osama bin Laden (Figure 4.13).

Figure 4.12 suggests that Obama and the Clintons are not out of step with their party base. While about a third of Democrats are "global citizens," highly ambivalent about both American nationalism and the use of military force, another third are "forceful idealists," willing to use force in the pursuit of idealist goals.

5 Partisan Elites and Global Attitudes: Ideology in Social Context

In 1935 psychologist Kurt Lewin famously argued that most human behaviors are the product of both personal and environmental factors.[1] Demographics and ideology are what psychologists call "individual differences" variables, largely invariant characteristics or dispositions *within* the person. By contrast, the media and foreign contacts are "situational" variables *outside* of the person, which nonetheless shape attitudes and behaviors.

The dominant view in political science today is that since the American people do not know much about the world, their international attitudes must come from the external environment, specifically from partisan political elites and/or the media. This brief chapter first argues that while it is true that Americans are not very knowledgeable about the world, these situational explanations for international attitudes are not as powerful as a dispositionalist one, namely that ideology is a better predictor of the international attitudes of the American people than are elite cues or media exposure.

But the influence of ideology on international attitudes is best understood by putting "the mind in context."[2] Rather than simply replace a situational reductionism with a dispositional one, the second half of the chapter makes the case that a more complete understanding of the international attitudes of the American people requires exploring how ideological predispositions *interact* with situational factors. Describing "the power of social context" in a 2012 review of social science research, David Brooks writes in the *New York Times* that "We are influenced by a thousand breezes permeating the unconscious layers of our minds."[3] This chapter will explore how these many social breezes interact with our psychological predispositions to shape our international attitudes.

WHEN IGNORANCE IS BLISS: IDEOLOGY, MEDIA EXPOSURE, AND INTERNATIONAL ATTITUDES

In episode seven of the first season of the animated TV series *King of the Hill*, Hank Hill, a Texas propane salesman, gets new neighbors. Kahn and Minh Souphanousinphone and their daughter Connie are Laotians. Hank and his old friend Bill, a barber at the local military base, have a conversation with their new neighbor Kahn:

> *Hank*: So are you Chinese or Japanese?
> *Kahn*: I live in California last twenty year, but first come from Laos . . . We Laotian.
> *Bill*: The ocean? What ocean?
> *Kahn*: We are Laotian! From Laos, stupid! It's a landlocked country, in Southeast Asia. It's between Vietnam and Thailand, OK? Population 4.7 million!
> *Hank*: So are you Chinese or Japanese?[4]

The *King of the Hill* writers are clearly poking fun at American ignorance.

Our 2011 survey data supports the idea that Americans are not very knowledgeable about the world. The survey included five world-knowledge multiple choice questions, listed in Table 5.1. The average score on the quiz was 63 percent. This is consistent with the 60 percent average on the eight international items in Pew's News IQ survey of November 2011.[5]

Whether a D– is a good or bad score, of course, depends upon one's judg-

TABLE 5.1. World Knowledge Quiz:
Five multiple choice questions and percentage correct.

Question	Response choices	% ✓
1. *Where is the United Nations Headquarters located?*	New York/London/Paris/Brussels	71
2. *Which of the following countries is NOT communist?*	South Korea/Vietnam/Laos/Cuba	65
3. *Which of the following countries has the largest population?*	Indonesia/Australia/Thailand/Philippines	52
4. *Which of the following countries is NOT a member of the European Union?*	Israel/Czech Rep./Austria/Greece	65
5. *Which of the following countries is a permanent member of the UN Security Council?*	France/India/Japan/Germany	64
AVERAGE SCORE		63%

Note: Response choice sequence was randomized. Correct answer underlined and placed first here only. *Data source:* OU Institute for US-China Issues, 2011.

ment of the difficulty of the quiz. In our view, our questions (Table 5.1) and Pew's 2011 questions were not difficult. Furthermore, because both quizzes were multiple choice, with just four possible answers to choose from, pure chance alone would result in a score of 25 percent. It seems reasonable therefore to conclude that the American public is not very knowledgeable about the world. Of course, that is likely the case for people in most countries.

What are the implications of American ignorance about the world for their international attitudes? Christopher Gelpi repeatedly asserts that an uninformed American public "must inevitably rely on cues that they receive from elites."[6] Adam Berinsky refines this elite cues line of reasoning, highlighting the role of partisanship: "Citizens support wars championed by politicians they trust and rebuff conflicts associated with politicians they reject."[7] Matthew Baum and Tim Groeling counter the "conveyor belt" view of the media as faithfully transmitting elite cues, arguing that the media have an independent role in shaping popular attitudes: "Citizens learn virtually everything they know about foreign policy from the mass media."[8]

This chapter, by contrast, argues that ideology is a better predictor of international attitudes and foreign policy preferences than is media exposure, partisanship, or even partisan media exposure. Our survey measured *media exposure* ($\alpha = .65$) with two items:

- *Would you say you follow what's going on in government and public affairs?*
- *On an average day over this past week, how much time did you spend paying attention to international news?*

To measure the nature or partisanship of media watched, we also asked:

- *If you had to watch cable news, would you prefer to watch more MSNBC (e.g. Rachel Maddow) or FOX (Glenn Beck, Bill O'Reilly)?*

To create a *partisan media exposure* variable combining both quality and quantity, we first centered answers to the MSNBC-Fox question (from −2 to +2), and then multiplied it by the quantity of time paying attention to international news (0–6) item, resulting in a twenty-five-point variable from −12 to +12. *Partisanship* was measured on a single seven-point scale from "strong Democrat" to "strong Republican."

We decided to explore the predictive power of these variables against our overall feelings towards fifteen foreign countries scale and a more specific foreign policy variable. By April 2011 American attention had largely shifted from Iraq to the counterinsurgency campaign in Afghanistan. Thirty thousand additional American troops had been sent there the previous year. We therefore included two seven-point disagree-agree items ($\alpha = .81$) on separate pages, tapping the degree of support for increasing the U.S. military presence in Afghanistan:

- *The U.S. should expand its military presence in Afghanistan.*
- *We should reduce our military involvement in Afghanistan.* (reverse coded)

In a pair of regressions, media exposure did *not* predict either overall feelings towards foreign countries or Afghanistan policy preferences.[9] Our partisan media exposure variable did better, however, with greater exposure to Fox (as opposed to MSNBC) predicting both coolness towards foreign countries (β = −.17) and support for an expanded U.S. military presence in Afghanistan (β = .26). However, when ideology (β = −.26) was added to the first regression, partisan media exposure became nonsignificant (p = .62). In the second regression, on Afghanistan, the inclusion of ideology (β = .30) overwhelmed partisan media exposure, reducing its impact from β = .26 to just β = .09. Even self-identified Democrat-Republican partisanship could not compete with ideology in accounting for either overall warmth towards foreign countries or Afghanistan policy preferences.[10]

In short, the survey data suggests that it is ideology and not media exposure, partisan media exposure, or even partisanship itself that, in the absence of much knowledge about the world, most powerfully shapes the international attitudes and foreign policy preferences of the American people. Why? The "affect heuristic" discussed in Chapter 1 suggests that when confronted with difficult specific questions that we lack the knowledge needed to answer directly, we subconsciously substitute easier questions about how we feel about the topic—and our preexisting ideologies powerfully shape our gut feelings about foreign affairs.

THE MIND IN CONTEXT

How do individual differences and situational variables combine to produce the international attitudes of the American people? For instance, our data reveals that Americans raised in more-urban areas tend to feel greater overall warmth towards foreign countries than those raised in rural areas. It turns out that both personal and situational factors help account for this effect. As displayed in Figure 5.1, ideology and foreign contacts both mediate the relationship between rural-urban upbringing and warmth towards foreign countries. Foreign friends, travel, and contact were measured with three items (α = .71):

- *Have you ever traveled outside of the U.S. or Canada?*
- *How frequently do you have contact with foreigners?*
- *Do you have many friends who are from foreign countries?*

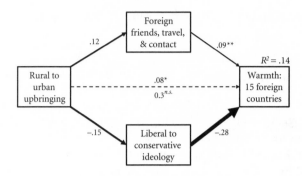

FIG. 5.1. Americans raised in more-urban environments feel slightly warmer towards foreign countries than those raised in more-rural areas, in part because they have more foreign friends and contacts, and in part because they are more liberal.

Note: A simultaneous mediation model. * $p < .05$, ** $p < .01$, all other p's $< .001$. Both indirect paths were statistically significant. See SUP.org. Seven demographic covariates are not shown. *Data source:* OU Institute for US-China Issues, 2011.

Not surprisingly, the top path of Figure 5.1 reveals that Americans who grew up in more-urban environments experienced more foreign contacts and travel ($\beta = .12$), contributing to greater warmth towards foreign countries ($\beta = .09$). "Travel is fatal to prejudice, bigotry and narrow-mindedness, and many of our people need it sorely on these accounts," Mark Twain wrote in his 1869 travelogue *Innocents Abroad*. "Broad, wholesome, charitable views of men and things cannot be acquired by vegetating in one little corner of the earth all one's lifetime."[11]

Ideology also mediated the relationship between rural-urban upbringing and warmth towards foreign countries (bottom path in Figure 5.1). Those Americans who grew up in more-urban environments tended to be more liberal than those who grew up in more-rural environments ($\beta = -.15$), also contributing to greater warmth towards foreign countries ($\beta = -.28$). Together, these dispositional and situational factors reduced the direct relationship between rural-urban upbringing and warmth towards foreign countries fivefold.[12]

Can we explore the *interaction* of individual differences and situational variables? Sometimes different types of people respond to the same experiences differently. For example, personality psychologists would predict that an extrovert attending a party would get excited, while an introvert attending the same party would get anxious. Similarly, our data reveals that cultural conservatives, high on traditionalism, respond to greater foreign travel and contacts differently from cultural liberals, low on traditionalism (Figure 5.2).

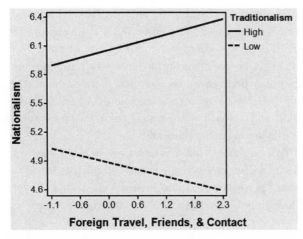

FIG. 5.2. As foreign travel, friends, and contacts increase, nationalism *increases* among cultural conservatives, but *decreases* among cultural liberals.

Note: A moderation analysis. Interaction ΔR^2 = .01, $F(1, 996)$ = 6.61, p = .01. The positive and negative slopes for cultural conservatives (B = .14, p = .07) and liberals (B = −.12, p = .09) were both statistically significant, but only marginally so. *Data source:* OU Institute for US-China Issues, 2011.

Specifically, cultural conservatives become *more* nationalistic as a consequence of foreign contacts, while cultural liberals become *less* so. Cultural ideology thus moderates the influence of foreign travel and contacts on nationalism as an American.

This finding is consistent with work on the social psychology of intergroup relations. Following Gordon Allport's "contact hypothesis," during the civil rights movement psychologists initially advocated busing and other integration policies to increase contact and reduce racism.[13] What they discovered, however, was that the quantity of contact was indeterminate in its impact on prejudice. It was the quality of intergroup contacts that was vital: when blacks and whites were forced together in high schools without sufficient attention to the quality of their interactions, increased contacts could *increase* racial prejudice. But when the contacts were of a better quality, and all parties felt respected and treated as equals, increased intergroup contact would often *reduce* prejudice and conflict.

In our 2011 survey, there were no differences between either liberals and conservatives or Democrats and Republicans in the quantity of their foreign travel, contacts, and friends.[14] In a 2008 Internet survey, the Program on International Policy Attitudes specifically asked, "*In the last five years have you travelled to another country, or not?*" There were no partisan differences among the Americans in their sample either.[15]

So ideology and/or partisanship are not associated with *how much* Americans travel or have contact with foreigners. But they do appear to *moderate* the impact of travel or foreign contact on international attitudes.[16] In addition to its polarizing effect on nationalism, foreign contact also appears to polarize some foreign policy preferences. For instance, greater foreign contacts are associated with desires for *tougher* policies towards American foes (Iran, North Korea, Pakistan, and China; $\alpha = .80$) among cultural conservatives, but slightly *friendlier* policies among cultural liberals.[17]

Different types of liberals and conservatives, in short, may respond to the same situations in distinct ways. Further research is needed to better understand how such "person by situation" interactions shape the international attitudes and foreign policy preferences of the American people.

Part 2

CASES

6 Latin America: Liberal and Conservative Moralities of Immigration and Foreign Aid

"'Think of the cats staying up all night,' whispered Dean [after crossing into Mexico from Laredo, Texas]. *'And think of this big continent ahead of us with those enormous Sierra Madre mountains we saw in the movies, and the jungles all the way down, and the whole desert plateau as big as ours and reaching clear down to Guatemala and God knows where, whoo! What'll we do? What'll we do? Let's go!'"*[1]
—Jack Kerouac, 1953

"Let's be clear right off the top: People who want this country to secure its borders are not racist. Nor are they bigots, hatemongers, xenophobes, or un-American. There is a difference between the law-abiding Ellis Island immigrants and those who came here in the dark of night and slip into the shadows; but it's not the color of their skin."[2]
—Glenn Beck, 2007

When Americans ponder the world south of the border, what do they feel and think? Are they full of curiosity and wonder like Dean in Jack Kerouac's *On the Road*? Or are they defensive about their racial views, like Glenn Beck, who appears to protest too much?

Three of the fifteen foreign countries in our 0°–100° cool-to-warm "feeling thermometer" were from Latin America. Overall, Americans felt cool to tepid towards Mexico (40°), Haiti (44°), and Brazil (52°), located in North America, the Caribbean, and South America, respectively (see Figure 0.3).

These mean scores, however, hide consistent and substantial ideological differences among Americans in their feelings towards these three Latin American countries. As revealed in Figure 0.4, liberals felt 22° warmer than conservatives did towards both Haiti (55° vs. 33°) and Brazil (62° vs. 40°) and a full 28° warmer towards Mexico (53° vs. 25°), differences that ranged from medium-large to very large statistically.[3] In short, liberals felt lukewarm to warm towards these Latin American countries, while conservatives felt cool to downright frigid towards them.

These stark ideological differences extend beyond broad feelings of warmth and coolness to specific emotions. Susan Fiske, a Princeton social psychologist, argues that assessments of the intentions (based upon feelings of warmth or friendliness) and capabilities (competence, strength) of other social groups

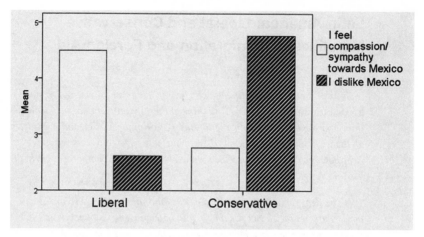

FIG. 6.1. Liberals tend to feel some compassion for Mexico and do not dislike it; conservatives tend to dislike Mexico and not feel sympathy towards it.

Note: $F(1, 419) = 111.38$, $p < .001$, $\eta_p^2 = .21$ and $F(1, 419) = 136.33$, $p < .001$, $\eta_p^2 = .25$ for compassion and dislike, respectively. Both ANCOVA control for seven standard demographics. *Data source:* OU Institute for US-China Issues, 2011.

together predict specific intergroup emotions and action tendencies. Her stereotype content model (SCM) predicts that we will pity social groups that we perceive as friendly but incompetent, such as the elderly or the disabled. But we will dislike and even feel disgust towards groups that we may feel are hostile and incompetent, such as drug addicts.[4] Hypothesizing that all Americans would view Mexico as a relatively weak, incompetent country but would differ systematically by ideology in their warmth towards Mexico, we extended the SCM to American attitudes towards Mexico by including two additional seven-point disagree-agree items in our survey:

- *I feel compassion/sympathy towards Mexico.*
- *I dislike Mexico.*

As expected, liberals scored vastly higher than conservatives did on feeling compassion for Mexico, while conservatives scored vastly higher than liberals on disliking Mexico (Figure 6.1).

The large ideological impact on feelings towards these Latin American countries, furthermore, had foreign policy consequences. On our 1–7 "much friendlier" to "much tougher" rating scale, conservatives desired substantially tougher foreign policies towards all three of these countries than liberals did.[5] As will be discussed in detail below, our survey also measured two specific policy issues: Mexican border policy and aid to Haiti. Among white Americans, the impact of ideology on these policy items was enormous. Specifically, we will see that white conservatives were vastly more likely than white liberals to prefer a tougher Mexican border policy and restricting aid to Haiti.[6]

What best explains this persistent pattern of substantial ideological differences in American feelings and foreign policy preferences towards these Latin American countries? This chapter argues that differing moral values and differences in cultural, socio-racial, economic, and political ideologies each contribute to differences between liberals and conservatives over Latin America. First, when it comes to general feelings towards these Latin American countries, among whites it is differing attitudes towards proper race relations that matter most. Of our four ideological dimensions, *only* social dominance orientation is associated with feelings towards these countries, and differing liberal and conservative moralities of compassion and authority undergird this ideological difference. Second, white conservative preferences for tougher border policies are partially explained by their greater social dominance but also by their greater cultural traditionalism. Cultural conservatives appear to fear the impact of Mexican immigration on Christian values and a WASP American national identity more than cultural liberals do. Third, among whites, three of our four ideological dimensions mediate the relationship between ideology and preferences for aid for Haiti: social, economic, and political ideologies each contribute to a conservative desire to limit aid. The chapter concludes with a brief exploration of how Hispanic American and African American views of Latin America differ from those of their white compatriots.

RACE AND AMERICAN FEELINGS ABOUT LATIN AMERICA

> *"The Darkey [is] but a few generations removed from the wildest savagery."*[7]
> —Republican President Theodore Roosevelt, 1900

> *"The future, ladies and gentlemen, is going to be very different for this hemisphere from the past. These states lying to the south of us, which have always been our neighbors, will now be drawn closer to us by . . . sympathy and understanding. . . . We must prove ourselves their friends and champions upon terms of equality and honor."*[8]
> —Democratic President Woodrow Wilson, 1913

What drives white conservative coolness towards Latin America? Of the four dimensions of American ideology we measured in our 2011 survey, *only* social dominance orientation—the desire that *"Inferior groups should stay in their place"*—mediated the relationship between ideology and feelings towards Mexico and Haiti.[9] For Brazil, none of the four dimensions of American ideology mediated the relationship, but social dominance was by far the strongest, approaching marginal significance.[10] Perhaps the much greater percentage of whites in Brazil (48%) than in Mexico (18%) or Haiti (less than 5%) dilutes the influence of race on white American feelings towards Brazil. Brazil has the third largest white population in the world, after the United States and Russia.

Chapter 3 argued that conservatives are much more likely than liberals to value order and authority, contributing to a preference for social dominance—the maintenance of social hierarchies and domination of subordinate social groups. Liberals, for their part, are more likely than conservatives to value fairness and compassion, leading them to oppose racial hierarchies and support the equality of racial groups (see Figure 3.4).

These differing liberal and conservative views of race relations have long influenced American views of Latin America. "Color-conscious Americans" in the nineteenth century, historian Michael Hunt argues, were horrified by "the wholesale miscegenation that had further blacked [Latinos] both literally and figuratively. With appalling freedom, white Spaniards had mixed with enslaved blacks and native Indians to produce degenerate mongrel offspring. This sexual license among the races set an example particularly disturbing to Americans dedicated to defending the color line at home."[11] As the epigraph reveals, President Theodore Roosevelt believed that colored peoples were racially inferior and thus incapable of self-government.

Other Americans, of course, opposed the "color line" both at home and abroad. Race was central to the turn-of-the-century debates over American empire discussed in the Introduction. Fairness and compassion were values that animated anti-imperialists like politician William Jennings Bryan and philanthropist Andrew Carnegie. "What response will the heart of the Philippine Islander make, as he reads Lincoln's Emancipation Proclamation?" asked Carnegie in 1898. "Are we to practice independence and preach subordination, to teach rebellion in our books, yet to stamp it out with our swords, to sow the seed of revolt and expect the harvest of loyalty?"[12]

Competing turn-of-the-century visions of proper U.S.–Latin American race relations were displayed on the covers of two 1901 *Puck* magazines (Figure 6.2). On the left, Udo Keppler depicts a black boy labeled "Cuba" making a sandcastle on a beach. Labeled "Cuban Independence," it resembles a capitol building. Uncle Sam, perhaps representing President William McKinley or Vice President Theodore Roosevelt, looks down on the child, wagging a finger: "That's right, my boy! Go ahead! But, remember, I'll always keep a Father's eye on you!" Entitled "Encouraging the Child," the drawing is a strikingly paternalistic representation of an American father's properly superior position vis-à-vis his new Caribbean son.

Samuel D. Ehrhart's "Pan-American Puck," from just a month and a half later, depicts a strikingly different vision of North-South relations (Figure 6.2, right). A white Columbia welcomes a colored woman labeled "South America" to the Pan-American Exposition in Buffalo, New York. Although Columbia is

ENCOURAGING THE CHILD

Uncle Sam—*"That's right, my boy! Go ahead! But, remember, I'll always keep a Father's eye on you!"*

PAN-AMERICAN PUCK

FIG. 6.2. Paternal and sisterly American visions of North-South race relations, 1901.

Sources: Udo Keppler, *Puck*, February 27, 1901, and Samuel D. Ehrhart, *Puck*, May 8, 1901. Both images courtesy of the Library of Congress. LC-DIG-ppmsca-25502 and LC-DIG-ppmsca-25525.

foregrounded and larger than the dark woman, they smile at each other while holding each other's hands. The gesture is one of sisterly equality and friendship.

As the second epigraph reveals, President Woodrow Wilson would promote a similar vision of equality and friendship in U.S.–Latin American relations a dozen years later. Wilson's racism is well known. However, his egalitarian vision of North-South relations would anticipate the "Good Neighbor Policy," which President Franklin D. Roosevelt would champion two decades later. "The essential qualities of a true Americanism must be the same as those which constitute a good neighbor, namely, mutual understanding, and, through such understanding, a sympathetic appreciation of the other's point of view," Roosevelt declared to the Pan-American Union in Washington, DC, on "Pan-American Day," April 12, 1933. "Your Americanism and mine must be a structure built of confidence, cemented by a sympathy which recognizes only equality and fraternity."[13]

But racism against Latin Americans persisted. Opposition to Wilson's League of Nations was often framed in terms of race. Speaking on the Senate floor on May 26, 1919, conservative Democrat James Reed of Missouri objected that Haiti, with its barbarous voodoo, would be treated as an equal to the United States: "These baby murderers, these creatures of the forest who sacrifice children to their idols, are to have a place in the council of nations, and their vote is to be the equal of the vote of the United States."[14] As we shall see in Chapter 10, Republican senator Henry Cabot Lodge also appealed to racial prejudices in opposing the league.

American ambivalence about proper North-South race relations would persist during the Cold War. President John F. Kennedy launched the Alliance for Progress in 1961 to promote liberty and equality in Latin America. But racism endured even within the Kennedy and Johnson administrations. "I know my Latinos," declared Thomas C. Mann, a Texan who served as U.S. ambassador to Mexico and assistant secretary of state for inter-American affairs in the 1960s. "They understand only two things—a buck in the pocket and a kick in the ass."[15] Meanwhile, opponents of the civil rights movement at home opposed African independence movements as threatening to racial hierarchies in the American South. Segregationists like George Wallace praised the anticommunism of the white South African government, while taking heart in the endurance of apartheid.[16]

Our 2011 survey revealed that conflicting ideologies of race relations continue to divide Americans in their views of colored Latin America today. We saw in Chapter 3 that conservatives value authority and are more likely to support hierarchies of race, while liberals, more concerned about fairness and compassion, are more likely to support racial equality. The survey data presented here shows that these divergent ideologies and moralities of race relations shape specific attitudes and foreign policy preferences towards Latin America.

MEXICAN BORDER POLICY: LIBERAL AND CONSERVATIVE MORALITIES OF IMMIGRATION

"The bosom of America is open to receive not only the Opulent and respectable Stranger, but the oppressed and persecuted of all Nations and Religions; whom we shall welcome to a participation of all our rights and privileges."[17]

—President George Washington, 1783

"America must be kept American."[18]

—Republican President Calvin Coolidge, 1924

Americans have been debating immigration since colonial times. Early settlers from England were soon joined by immigrants from other northern European countries. By the mid-1850s, the nativist "Know Nothing Party," whose membership was limited to WASP males, targeted Catholic immigrants from Germany and Ireland. Catholics were seen as beholden to the Pope in Rome, and thus both treasonous and a threat to the republican values associated with Protestantism.

Southern and Eastern Europeans dominated immigration in the early twentieth century. Republican president Herbert Hoover, of German descent, was contemptuous of the more recent Italian immigrants. "Italians are predominantly murderers and bootleggers," he wrote in anger to his fellow Republican Fiorella LaGuardia. "You should go back to where you belong."[19]

Immigration to the United States over the last half century has been dominated by Asians and especially Mexicans and Latin Americans. Radio talk show host Rush Limbaugh, also of German descent, has targeted much of his nativism against Mexicans. "You're a foreigner," Limbaugh declared of Mexicans on his April 6, 2006, show. "You shut your mouth or you get out, and if you come here illegally, you go straight to jail and we're going to hunt you down 'til we find you."[20]

In a comprehensive review of the history of immigration to America, historian Lawrence Fuchs argues that three distinct ideas have dominated American debates over immigration, each of which he associates with an early American colony.[21] The "Virginia idea," based on the plantation economy and its need for manual labor, promoted immigration without assimilation, first of indentured servants from the Old World and later of slaves from Africa. Even after the Civil War and slavery, businessmen continued to look to immigration to keep the cost of labor down. F. Victor Gillam captures the "Virginia idea" in an 1888 *Judge* magazine (Figure 6.3). "Supply and Demand—Shall Immigration Be Restricted?" depicts two groups of workers on a balance. A large and diverse group of immigrants labeled "pauper labor" outweigh a sullen group of American workmen striking against low wages. "As long as I am plentifully supplied with Immigrant Labor," declares a wealthy businessman happily, "I shall be deaf to the demands of the native workingman." In 2012 former Republican congressman and anti-immigration crusader Tom Tancredo of Colorado lamented that little has changed: "The Republican Party looks at massive immigration, legal and illegal, as a source of cheap labor, satisfying a very important constituency."[22]

The "Pennsylvania idea" also welcomed immigration—but on the basis of equality and acceptance. As President George Washington suggested in the epigraph, settlers would be welcome to live, speak, and worship as they pleased in an open and tolerant America. The Pennsylvanian Germans, for instance, would not be forced to speak English.

The "Massachusetts idea," by contrast, was more restrictive, limiting immigration to those willing to adhere to Puritanism. This approach would later expand into the view that only those willing to learn English, assimilate, and adopt WASP values should be allowed to immigrate to the United States. This

SUPPLY AND DEMAND—SHALL IMMIGRATION BE RESTRICTED?
Employer—"As long as I am plentifully supplied with Immigrant Labor, I shall
be deaf to the demands of the native workingman."

FIG. 6.3. The "Virginia idea": Immigration and labor, 1888.

Source: F. Victor Gillam, Judge, February 11, 1888. Image courtesy of the University of Oklahoma
Libraries, Nichols Collection.

nativist strain runs from the Know Nothing movement through Presidents
Coolidge and Hoover to Rush Limbaugh today.

To explore popular American attitudes towards immigration from Mexico
today, we included two items in our 2011 survey:

- *The U.S. needs to improve its border security to prevent illegal immigration
  from Mexico.*
- *We do NOT need to tighten security along the Mexican border.* (reverse
  coded)

Among whites, conservatives preferred a vastly tougher Mexican border policy
than liberals did.[23]

What best explains this massive ideological effect? We ran a pair of mediation analyses on our white subsample and found that of the four dimensions

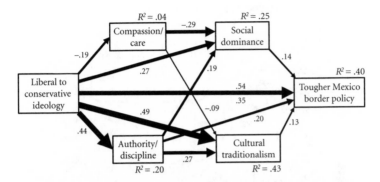

$R^2 = .04$ Compassion/care

$-.29$

$R^2 = .25$ Social dominance

$-.19$

$.14$

$.27$

$.19$

$R^2 = .40$ Tougher Mexico border policy

Liberal to conservative ideology

$.54$

$.35$

$-.09$

$.49$

$.20$

$.13$

$.44$

Authority/discipline

$R^2 = .20$

$.27$

Cultural traditionalism

$R^2 = .43$

FIG. 6.4. Among white Americans, differing liberal and conservative moralities of compassion and authority help account for their disagreement over Mexican border policy.

Note: A path model. To reduce clutter, covariances and prediction error terms are not displayed. Model fit was very good. Statistics online at SUP.org. *Data source:* OU Institute for US-China Issues, 2011.

of ideology that we measured, only social and cultural ideology mediated the relationship. And of the five moral values, only compassion and authority did so. Figure 6.4 combines these four mediators within one path model. It reveals that differences in social dominance orientation and cultural traditionalism, undergirded by differing moralities of compassion and authority, together accounted for three-quarters of the direct effect of liberal-conservative ideology on Mexican border policy preferences.[24]

The indirect path at the top of Figure 6.4 reveals that liberals are more likely than conservatives to buy into the open and tolerant Pennsylvania idea of immigration. More compassionate towards the suffering of strangers than are conservatives ($\beta = -.19$), liberals are more likely to prefer the equality of different social and racial groups ($\beta = -.29$), contributing to their opposition to tougher border security ($\beta = .14$).

Cartoonist Andy Singer captures this liberal view of immigration in a 2005 "No Exit" (Figure 6.5). Entitled "The First Illegal Immigrants," it depicts Pilgrims arriving in the New World. A group of Native Americans are there to greet them, sternly demanding, "No green cards? No visas? I'm sorry . . . but we need to see some identification." The Indians carry tomahawks, bows, and arrows, and the family of Pilgrims are wide-eyed in fright. Singer is decrying white hypocrisy and lack of compassion for immigrants today.

The post–hardcore band the Desaparecidos express a similar liberal dismay at the ill treatment of Hispanics in America today in their 2012 song "MariK-

FIG. 6.5. On immigration, liberals value compassion and decry hypocrisy, 2005.
Source: Andy Singer, July 22, 2005. Image courtesy of www.andysinger.com.

KKopa," an angry retort to Sheriff Joe Arpaio of Maricopa County, Arizona. "I've seen with my own eyes how our unjust immigration system tears these families apart, separating mothers and fathers from their children and leaving all involved in a state of helplessness and despair," Nebraskan singer-songwriter Conor Oberst told the *Huffington Post*. "I'll never understand how destroying families through deportation benefits our society. How we treat the undocumented says a great deal about us as a people and whether or not we'll continue to fulfill the fundamental American promise of equality and opportunity for all."[25]

The top path in Figure 6.4 reveals that liberals feel greater compassion for the *suffering* of Hispanic immigrants, contributing to opposition to social dominance and desires for a more relaxed border policy. But both Singer and Oberst also highlight the *injustice* of the current immigration situation. So why didn't fairness/justice emerge as a third moral value mediating the relationship between ideology and border policy preferences? A closer look at our 2011 survey data suggests that fairness was not statistically significant because both liberals and conservatives view the issue as one of fairness—but from opposing perspectives that canceled each other out. White liberals see the issue as unfair from the perspective of vulnerable immigrants, while white conservatives view it as unfair from the perspective of white Americans.

Among white conservatives ($n = 158$), valuing fairness predicts *support* for tougher border policies ($\beta = .15$, $p = .048$). Lending anecdotal support to this statistical finding, conservative anti-immigration advocates chose to name their organization "FAIR," the Federation for American Immigration Reform. Similarly, the "2012 GOP Platform" opposes amnesty and advocates tougher immigration policies on the grounds of fairness, both to legal immigrants and to American workers.[26]

If the moral value of loyalty is allowed to mediate the relationship between fairness and tougher border policy preferences for all whites, however, the direct relationship goes from statistically insignificant ($p = .44$) to both significant and *negative* ($\beta = -.12$, $p = .001$).[27] In other words, if you pull loyalty (which conservatives value more than liberals) out of the relationship between fairness and immigration policy, what's left is a liberal conception of fairness *from the perspective of the immigrant* that *opposes* tougher border policies. Singer, Oberst, and other liberals oppose tougher immigration policies out of compassion *and* a sense of injustice/fairness from the perspective of the immigrant, a perspective that conservatives are likely to view as disloyal.

The survey data also suggests that conservatives are more likely to buy into the more restrictive Massachusetts idea of immigration, as the indirect path at the bottom of Figure 6.4 reveals. More concerned about maintaining authority than are liberals ($\beta = .44$), conservatives are more likely to support racial hierarchies ($\beta = .19$) and cultural traditionalism ($\beta = .27$), both of which contribute to desires for tougher border policies ($\beta = .14$, $.13$, respectively).

Social psychologists John Duckitt and Chris Sibley have shown that while both social dominance and cultural traditionalism predict prejudice, they are driven by distinct psychological dynamics. Conservatives high in social dominance view the social world as a competitive jungle, so seek to maintain group dominance. Those high in traditionalism, by contrast, tend to view the world as a dangerous place requiring the vigorous defense of traditional values.[28] Both ideologies, our data reveals, contribute to greater conservative support for tougher Mexican border policies.

Grant E. Hamilton's 1891 "Where the Blame Lies" captures this conservative morality of immigration (Figure 6.6). It depicts a horde of grubby immigrants arriving in New York City. They are variously labeled "German socialist," "Russian anarchist," "Polish vagabond," "Italian brigand," "English convict," and "Irish pauper." A well-dressed man points at the mob and declares to a worried Uncle Sam, "If Immigration was properly Restricted you would no longer be troubled with Anarchy, Socialism, the Mafia and such kindred evils!"

WHERE THE BLAME LIES
"If Immigration was properly Restricted you would no longer be troubled with Anarchy, Socialism, the Mafia and such kindred evils!"

FIG. 6.6. A conservative morality of immigration: The challenge to authority and social order, 1891.

Source: Grant E. Hamilton, *Judge*, April 4, 1891. Image courtesy of the Library of Congress. LC-USZC4-5739.

This view of immigrants as a threat to public order lives on in American discourse on Mexican immigration today. For instance, Proposition 187, the ballot initiative that Californians overwhelmingly passed in 1994, began with the declaration that "The People of California . . . have suffered and are suffering personal injury and damage caused by the criminal conduct of illegal aliens in this state."[29]

In this white conservative view, however, the threat of immigration is not just to physical security but to cultural security as well. Immigrants threaten WASP values. "The citizenship of a nation," Republican congressman Walter Chandler of New York declared in 1921, "like the morals of character or the blood of the body, should be kept free from poison, corruption, and contamination."[30] Hispanic immigration "threatens to divide the United States into two peoples, two cultures, and two languages," Harvard political scientist Samuel Huntington has more recently warned, because Hispanics reject "Anglo-Protestant values."[31] The "English as the official language" movement seems motivated by a similar desire to protect WASP culture from foreign contamination.

For instance, while campaigning for the Republican presidential nomination in March 2012, Rick Santorum declared that Puerto Rico must adopt English as its official language to become a U.S. state. In the white conservative view, a tougher border policy is needed not just to maintain authority and protect Americans from Mexican gangs and violence, but to protect America's WASP national identity.

AID FOR HAITI: RACE AND REDISTRIBUTION

"Throughout Latin America . . . millions of men and women suffer the daily degradations of poverty and hunger. . . . Therefore I have called on all people of the hemisphere to join in a new Alliance for Progress . . . to satisfy the basic needs of the American people for homes, work and land, health and schools."[32]

—Democratic President John F. Kennedy, 1961

"Morally, I cannot justify the violent seizure of property from Americans in order to redistribute that property to a foreign government."[33]

—Congressman Ron Paul (Republican–Texas), 2008

Americans have long debated the merits of foreign aid to Latin America. During the Cold War, both Democrats and Republicans supported aid to avert the spread of communism. Franklin D. Roosevelt's Good Neighbor Policy of nonintervention was replaced by a more active U.S. role in the region. John F. Kennedy's Alliance for Progress, cited above, was an outgrowth of Republican initiatives under the Dwight D. Eisenhower administration. "There is absolutely no doubt in my mind that revolution is inevitable in Latin America. The people are angry. They are shackled to the past with bonds of ignorance, injustice, and poverty," Milton Eisenhower, the president's brother and roving ambassador for Latin America, wrote in his 1963 *The Wine Is Bitter.* "The United States has a crucial role in this drama. Our aid can be decisive in helping Latin Americans build better institutions, increase income, and purge injustice from their society. We must be swift and generous."[34]

With the end of the Cold War and the reduced need to combat communism in Latin America, partisan divisions over foreign aid have reemerged. The "2012 Democratic Party Platform" states that "Together with the American people and the international community, we will continue to respond to humanitarian crises around the globe."[35] The "2012 GOP Platform," by contrast, argues for "limiting foreign aid spending" in favor of private charity work. Its section on foreign aid is nonetheless entitled "America's Generosity," opening with the claim that "Americans are the most generous people in the world."[36]

To examine popular American attitudes towards foreign aid to Latin America today, we included two questions in our April 2011 survey about a real-world crisis. In January 2010, a magnitude 7.0 earthquake struck the most populated area of Haiti, just west of the capital, Port-au-Prince. Hundreds of thousands of Haitians were killed and over a million made homeless. The ongoing tragedy was a major media story in the United States, so we decided to measure attitudes towards helping Haiti with two items ($\alpha = .87$):

- *Our government should provide more aid and assistance to Haiti.* (reverse coded)
- *We should NOT provide more aid to Haiti.*

Among whites, liberals were immensely more supportive of increased aid to Haiti than conservatives were.[37] This finding is consistent with data from the Chicago Council's 2010 survey, which asked half of its respondents whether they favored or opposed:

- *Food and medical assistance to people in needy countries.*
- *Aid that helps needy countries develop their economies.*
- *Aid to help farmers in needy countries become more productive.*

Liberals were 12 percent, 26 percent, and 25 percent more likely than conservatives to favor these three types of foreign aid, respectively.[38]

What best explains the very large ideological cleavage among American whites over aid to Haiti? Three of our four dimensions of ideology were statistically significant mediators of the relationship between ideology and positions

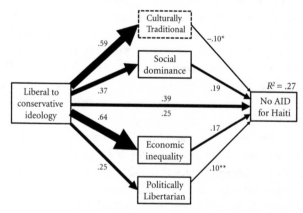

FIG. 6.7. Among whites, social, economic, and political ideologies all contribute to greater conservative opposition to aid for Haiti; cultural ideology does not.

Note: A simultaneous mediation model. * $p < .05$, ** $p < .01$, all other p's < .001. Only the indirect path through cultural traditionalism was not statistically significant. See SUP.org for indirect effect statistics. Five demographic covariates (age, gender, education, income, and region) are not shown. Aid for Haiti is a two-item scale ($\alpha = .87$). *Data source:* OU Institute for US-China Issues, 2011.

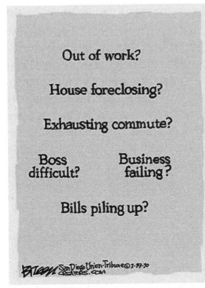

FIG. 6.8. Liberals support foreign aid out of compassion, 2010.

Source: Steve Breen, *San Diego Union-Tribune*, January 19, 2010. Image courtesy of Steve Breen and the *San Diego Union-Tribune*.

on aid to Haiti (Figure 6.7). Together, they accounted for over 80 percent of the relationship.[39]

First, we have already seen that social dominance orientation helped account for ideological differences in feelings towards Mexico and Haiti, and Mexican border policy preferences. It is thus not surprising that group dominance also accounts for preferences regarding aid for Haiti. As we saw in Chapter 3, the greater value that conservatives place on authority helps explain their preference for racial hierarchies, while the greater value that liberals place on compassion and fairness helps account for their opposition to hierarchy and preference for the equality of social and racial groups.

Steve Breen captures this liberal compassion in a thoughtful cartoon published in the *San Diego Union-Tribune* just a week after the earthquake hit Haiti (Figure 6.8). A young black woman holding a baby sits on a cement block amidst the ruins of the earthquake. She is wearing a ragged dress and is barefoot. The accompanying text reads, "Out of work? House foreclosing? Exhausting commute? Boss difficult? Business failing? Bills piling up? . . . She'd trade places with you in an instant." It's a powerful statement of compassion for the suffering of others—regardless of race. "A theme of my work is to remind Americans how easy we have it compared to the rest of humanity," Breen later wrote.[40]

Second, in Chapter 4 we saw that their greater opposition to income redistribution helps account for greater conservative opposition to humanitarian idealism. Figure 6.7 replicates this finding in the specific case of aid to Haiti. In an October 2011 Republican presidential primary debate, Ron Paul declared that "To me, foreign aid is taking money from poor people in this country and giving it to rich people in poor countries."[41] From Paul's perspective, economic redistribution is immoral, as the epigraph also suggests. It is immoral in part because it violates the Protestant ethic of self-help. As noted in Chapter 4 (see Figure 4.4), agreement with "*People are responsible for their own situation in life*" and "*People should not count on others to solve their problems*" mediated the relationship between ideology and support for economic inequality. From the perspective of economic conservatives, Haitians should be allowed to stand alone and help themselves.

Third, Figure 6.7 reveals too that conservatives' greater average libertarianism also helps account for their greater opposition to helping Haiti. "No government can impose prosperity or benign thinking on masses of people," Bill O'Reilly wrote in his 2006 *Culture Warrior*. "It is simply impossible."[42] Foreign aid, from the libertarian perspective, is both normatively wrong and practically impossible. The communitarian perspective, by contrast, is less skeptical about the efficacy and desirability of helping others, contributing to greater liberal support for increased aid to Haiti.

Fourth, the top path of Figure 6.7 reveals that while cultural traditionalism was significantly correlated with both conservatism and support for *increased* aid for Haiti, the combined indirect effect was not statistically significant. It is intriguing, however, that the negative sign of traditionalism's effect on Haiti aid preferences ($\beta = -.10$, $p < .05$) was the *opposite* of the other three dimensions of ideology, suggesting a suppression effect.[43] Indeed, when traditionalism is run as the sole mediator of the relationship between liberal-conservative ideology and aid to Haiti preferences, the strength of the direct relationship *increases* slightly.[44] So it appears that if it were not for the fact that conservatives on average maintain more traditionalist attitudes than liberals do, conservative opposition to aid for Haiti would be *even stronger*.

A benign interpretation of this possible suppression effect points to Christian charity. While Habitat for Humanity may be associated with Jimmy Carter and mainline or liberal Protestant denominations, conservative Protestants also support aiding the downtrodden, both at home and abroad. Similarly, Catholics who might be high on traditionalism, disagreeing strongly with statements like "*There is nothing wrong with premarital sexual intercourse*," might also be strong supporters of the disaster relief and refugee resettlement work of religious groups like Catholic Charities.

The conservative anti-immigration group FAIR suggests a more malign interpretation, however. "The era of mass international migration to the United States as a solution to international problems must come to an end," FAIR declares on its website. "Problems of poverty and overpopulation must be vigorously confronted *where people live*, rather than ... by ... the importation of masses of people."[45] For some cultural conservatives, reducing immigration to the United States could be the real driver of desires to provide aid to Haitians *in Haiti*. Supporting this interpretation, the moral value of purity mediates the relationship between ideology and aid to Haiti, also suppressing the full impact of conservatism on opposition to helping Haiti.[46] Fleeing poverty and political instability, Haitian immigrants had been entering the United States long before the 2010 earthquake. For some white cultural conservatives, desires to maintain WASP purity by limiting black Haitian immigration to the United States could contribute to support for aid to Haitians in Haiti.

Finally, it is noteworthy that the large influence of ideology on views of how much aid we *should* provide to countries like Haiti is also associated with beliefs

"From now on it'll be skimmed."

FIG. 6.9. Liberals think that the United States should provide more foreign aid than conservatives do, 1963.

Source: Copyright Bill Mauldin, 1963. Courtesy of the Bill Mauldin Estate LLC.

about how much aid we actually *do* provide. A fall 2010 Program on International Policy Attitudes Internet survey revealed Democrats, on average, scoring 5 percent higher than Republicans in their mean responses to both "*What percentage of the federal budget goes to foreign aid?*" (30% vs. 25%) and "*What do you think would be an appropriate percentage?*" (15% vs. 10%), small but statistically significant partisan differences.[47] This suggests that ideology shapes not just our attitudes and policy preferences but also our very beliefs about the nature of the world we live in.

The greater liberal than conservative preference for more foreign aid is captured in a 1963 Bill Mauldin cartoon (Figure 6.9). Entitled "From Now on It'll Be Skimmed," it depicts an endless line of people holding empty buckets while a man milks a cow labeled "U.S. Foreign Aid." Supply does not meet demand. By contrast, as the "2012 GOP Platform" cited above suggests, conservatives are more likely to believe that "generous" Americans provide too much aid and that it should be reduced. In the 2006 World Values Survey, Democrats (74%) were almost 50 percent more willing than Republicans (26%) "*to pay higher taxes in order to increase your country's foreign aid to poor countries.*"[48]

HISPANIC AMERICAN AND AFRICAN AMERICAN VIEWS OF LATIN AMERICA

American blacks and Hispanics, not surprisingly, maintain distinct feelings and policy preferences towards different parts of Latin America. For instance, while both blacks ($\beta = .16$) and Hispanics ($\beta = .16$) feel warmer than nonblacks and non-Hispanics towards Mexico, only Hispanics ($\beta = -.10$) oppose a tougher Mexican border policy. Indeed, blacks are slightly supportive of tougher Mexican border policies ($\beta = .06, p = .04$). Competition for jobs or concerns about the downward pressure that immigration places on wages may counteract black warmth towards Mexico. Among our black subsample ($n = 110$), only age ($\beta = .53$) and being from the South ($\beta = .18, p = .03$) predicted support for tougher border policies. Perhaps older blacks and those from the South have felt employment competition from Mexicans the most keenly. Or they may simply be more prejudiced against Hispanics.

By contrast, only blacks ($\beta = .21$) and not Hispanics ($p = .89$) felt more warmly towards Haiti. And while blacks were very opposed to limiting aid to Haiti ($\beta = -.29$), Hispanics were only marginally opposed to it ($\beta = -.05, p = .08$).

Similarly, only blacks ($\beta = .10$) and not Hispanics ($p = .65$) felt warmer towards Brazil. Perhaps because of the language barrier (Spanish vs. Portuguese), Hispanic Americans may not identify with Brazilian mestizos, while language may not be an issue for American blacks who can identify positively with Brazilian blacks. It is also possible that those Hispanic Americans originally from South America fear Brazilian regional hegemony.[49]

Another possible interpretation of the lack of Hispanic American warmth towards Brazil has to do with gender and cultural traditionalism. Hispanic women (50°) felt 7° cooler towards Brazil than Hispanic men (57°) did.[50] A mediation analysis revealed, however, that differences in traditionalism accounted for this small-to-medium-sized gender difference.[51] Hispanic women held more traditional attitudes towards nudity, sex, drugs, and alcohol than Hispanic men ($\beta = -.24$) did, contributing to much cooler feelings towards Brazil ($\beta = -.56$). This might be labeled a "Carnival" effect: Brazil is known for skimpy bikinis and hedonism. Hispanic American women might disdain Brazilian women as libertines, or view them as competitors for Hispanic men.

Immigration generation had a remarkably strong influence on how Hispanics felt about Mexico. Our survey asked all respondents, "Which of these statements best describes you?"

1. "*Immigrant citizen (naturalized) or non-citizen*": I am an immigrant to the USA.
2. "*First generation*": I was born in the USA but at least one of my parents is an immigrant.
3. "*Second generation*": My parents and I were born in the USA but at least one of my grandparents was an immigrant.
4. "*Third generation*": My parents, grandparents and I were all born in the USA.

Seventy-two percent of the whites and 81 percent of the blacks in our sample chose "*Third generation*," resulting in skewed distributions of limited use for correlational analysis. But our Hispanic subsample ($n = 101$) was remarkably well distributed across all four categories, at 29 percent, 32 percent, 16 percent, and 23 percent, respectively. A regression analysis revealed that the more generations an Hispanic American's family had lived in the United States, the more coolly they felt towards Mexico ($\beta = -.32$).

Intriguingly, this generational effect on Hispanic American feelings towards Mexico would be even stronger if it were not for a suppression effect involving cultural ideology. When traditionalism is included as a mediator, the direct relationship between immigrant generation and feelings towards Mexico actually *increases* in absolute size, accounting for about a third more variance.[52] This may be due to a secularizing influence of living in a family with longer roots in the United States. More generations in the United States is associated with reduced ($\beta = -.13$) traditionalism. And given that traditionalism is a powerful predictor of coolness ($\beta = -.49$) towards Mexico, the combined indirect effect is positive, the *opposite* of the direct effect, which was negative. In other words, if it were not for the fact that more time in the United States contributes to Hispanic Americans becoming more culturally liberal, they would feel even cooler towards Mexico over time.

THE POLITICS OF IMMIGRATION REFORM

"We've gotta get rid of the immigration issue altogether."[53]

—Fox News political commentator Sean Hannity, 2012

Following President Obama's reelection in November 2012, Republican postmortems focused on the Hispanic vote. Appealing to conservatives during the Republican primaries, Mitt Romney had argued for making life so difficult for undocumented immigrants that they would pursue "self-deportation." The Hispanic vote went 71 percent to Obama and just 27 percent to Romney. "If Republicans do not do better in the Hispanic community," Republican senator Ted Cruz of Texas warned, "in a few short years Republicans will no longer be the majority in our state." Sean Hannity of Fox News, who had been a venomous critic of "amnesty" policy proposals for years, made a public about-face on immigration immediately after the election, claiming that his views had "evolved."

Our 2011 survey data suggests that a Republican Party makeover on immigration will be easier said than done. Conservatives on average felt a frigid 25° towards Mexico and scored a full 6.56 on a seven-point scale tapping preferences for a tougher Mexican border policy. And the problem is even worse when we home in on the Republican primary voters that Republican congressmen and senators fear most. Teavangelical Republicans (24°), highly motivated to vote in Republican primaries, felt 12° cooler towards Mexico than moderate Republicans (36°) did. Teavangelicals also desired a substantially tougher border policy than did moderate Republicans.[54]

Efforts by Republican elites to soften their party's position on immigration are likely to be met with hostility by a wide variety of conservative primary voters. This chapter has argued that conservative antipathy towards Latin America is driven by all four of the dimensions of American ideology that we measured. Libertarians and economic conservatives oppose foreign aid to places like Haiti out of a belief in the Protestant ethic of self-help and opposition to income redistribution. And cultural conservatives fear the impact of Mexican immigration on Christian values and a WASP American national identity. But it is social dominance that has the most pervasive influence on white conservative antipathy towards Latin America. Desires for law and order and the maintenance of racial hierarchies continue to shape white conservative views of the world south of the border.

7 Europe: Socialist France, Mother England, Brother Germany, and the E.U. Antichrist

"Americans are from Mars and Europeans are from Venus," foreign policy analyst Robert Kagan claimed in 2002. The George W. Bush administration's "war on terror" had opened up an alarming transatlantic divide, as Europeans, sympathetic with America following the September 11 terrorist attacks, had begun questioning Bush's turn to unilateralism and the use of force. "It is time to stop pretending that Europeans and Americans share a common view of the world," Kagan declared. Because the balance of military power had shifted from Europe to the United States, first during the Cold War and even more so afterwards, Americans and Europeans, he argued, had developed opposing views of force. Americans were "realists" like Kagan himself, inhabiting a Hobbesian world where might makes right; Europeans, by contrast, were driven by a "psychology of weakness." They were "idealists" promoting diplomacy and Kant's "Perpetual Peace."[1]

Kagan's argument did not go unchallenged. Daniel Drezner noted Kagan's failure to address Europe's still formidable economic power, "a key error of omission."[2] Robert Jervis questioned whether Europeans are really so averse to the use of force.[3] Both sides of the debate, however, tended to anthropomorphize both "America" and "Europe," generalizing about each as if it were a unitary actor.

This chapter, by contrast, argues that to understand trans-Atlantic relations, neither "America" nor "Europe" should be treated as an undifferentiated whole. First, not all Americans view Europe in the same way: liberals tend to feel warmer towards the Old World than conservatives do. Second, in American eyes, Europe is not of a piece: liberals and conservatives of different stripes view various European countries in distinct ways that reflect their many ideologies.

In our 2011 survey, the average American felt tepid (51°) to lukewarm (57°) to warm (69°) towards France, Germany, and England, respectively (see Figure 0.3). The Chicago Council had reported 56°, 63°, and 73° mean feelings towards those same countries a year earlier.[4] This is consistently about 5° higher than our figures, likely because its measure asked for assessments of both "countries and peoples," while ours asked solely about "countries." In our survey, Americans also felt warmer towards "Europeans" (63°) as people than towards the "European Union" (47°).

These mean scores hide ideological differences. While liberals felt only 5° warmer towards England than conservatives did, they felt 12° warmer towards Germany and a remarkable 27° warmer towards France (see Figure 0.4).[5] Liberals also felt 13° warmer towards Europeans as a people, and a whopping 37° warmer towards the European Union than conservatives did—medium-large and massive differences statistically.[6]

This chapter seeks to explain this pattern of ideological differences. It first argues that the very large gap between liberal Francophiles and conservative Francophobes reflects a synergy between the economic and cultural dimensions of American ideology. Economic conservatives revile a "socialist" France seen as redistributing income, while economic liberals appreciate the benefits of its social welfare state. Culturally, those liberals low on "traditionalism" are more likely than cultural conservatives to enjoy the fine arts, fashion, food, and wine—and to feel warmly towards France. The coolness that cultural conservatives feel towards France may also be driven by its perceived secularism and sexual permissiveness. Conservatives, furthermore, prefer a much tougher foreign policy towards France than liberals do, in part due to their greater average nationalism and greater desire for group dominance. Ideology appears to shape how Americans respond to Gaullist assertions of French *grandeur*; conservatives are outraged while liberals appear merely bemused.

Attitudes towards England present us with a puzzle. Liberals feel slightly warmer than conservatives towards England, but conservatives prefer a slightly friendlier foreign policy. Both liberal and conservative Anglophiles thus appear to drive the "Special Relationship" today, but for different reasons. Nationalism and perceived cultural and political commonalities appear more important for conservative than liberal Anglophiles.

The cultural and economic dimensions of American ideology work against each other when it comes to feelings towards Germany, effectively canceling each other out. Cultural conservatism is associated with greater *coolness* towards Germany, perhaps because those high on traditionalism are particularly sensitive to threats to their worldviews and may view German culture as too sexually permissive. Economic conservatism, by contrast, is associated with greater *warmth* towards Germany, perhaps because of its association in the American mind with Angela Merkel and fiscal conservatism (in opposition to French "socialism"). Supporting these interpretations, "Teavangelical" Republicans felt warmer towards Germany than did purely "cultural" Republicans.

Finally, conservatives felt massively cooler towards the European Union than liberals did, in part because they felt much cooler towards international organizations in general, in part because they felt cooler towards Europeans as a people, and in part, remarkably, because of their greater belief in the Devil. Our 2011 survey data suggests that dispensationalist books and movies by Christian Zionists like Hal Lindsey and John Hagee appear to have successfully popularized an "End of Times" narrative in which the Antichrist will emerge out of the European Union.

France, England, Germany, and the European Union will each be addressed in turn. Overall, American views of the Old World are marked by a projection of domestic ideologies onto a European looking glass. Liberal and conservative Americans see in Europe their fears and fantasies about the USA.

SOCIALIST, SECULAR, AND GAULLIST FRANCE: LIBERAL HEAVEN, CONSERVATIVE HELL

> *"France has neither winter nor summer nor morals—apart from these drawbacks it is a fine country."*[7]
>
> —Mark Twain

> *"American tourists in Paris are reported to be being yelled at, spit upon, and attacked by the French. Thank God things are getting back to normal."*[8]
>
> —Jay Leno, 2003

> *"Just like John Kerry, [Mitt Romney] speaks French!"*[9]
>
> —Newt Gingrich attack ad, 2012

Anticipating that our survey would reveal large differences in liberal and conservative warmth towards France (which it did—a 27° gap), we decided to explore specific emotions as well. As noted in Chapter 6, psychologist Susan Fiske argues that assessments of the intentions (based upon feelings of warmth) and capabilities (strength) of other social groups together predict both specific intergroup emotions and action tendencies. Her stereotype content model predicts specific attitudes towards not just weak groups like Mexico but also stronger groups like France. Specifically, it suggests that we will admire or take pride in social groups that we perceive as both friendly and competent, such as Christians or the middle class. But we will envy or resent powerful groups whose intentions we suspect, such as rich businesspeople.[10] Hypothesizing that all Americans would view France as a relatively powerful country but would differ systematically by ideology in their warmth of feelings, we included two additional items in our survey:

- *I feel admiration/respect towards France.*
- *I feel irritated/annoyed by France.*

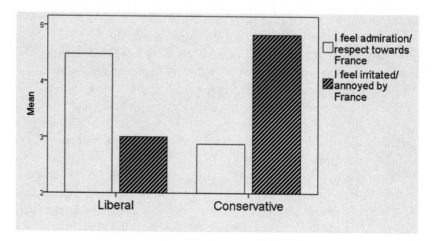

FIG. 7.1. Liberals respect and are not annoyed by France; conservatives are annoyed by France and do not respect it.

Note: $F(1, 419) = 114.28$, $p < .001$, $\eta_p^2 = .21$ and $F(1, 419) = 118.61$, $p < .001$, $\eta_p^2 = .22$ for admire and annoyed by, respectively. Both ANCOVA control for seven standard demographics. *Data source:* OU Institute for US-China Issues, 2011.

As expected, liberals scored much higher than conservatives did on feeling "*admiration/respect*" while conservatives scored much higher than liberals on feeling "*irritated/annoyed*," differences that were very large statistically (Figure 7.1). Liberals, in other words, respect and are not irritated by France, while conservatives are annoyed by France and do not respect it.

What best explains these consistently large differences between liberal Francophiles and conservative Francophobes? The simplest explanation—lingering conservative anger at French opposition to the Republican Bush administration's 2003 invasion of Iraq—is not supported by existing longitudinal survey data. The Chicago Council reports that mean American feelings towards France (as a country and a people) were 55° in 1994, 1998, and 2002, dropping to 47° in 2004 but then recovering to 56° by 2010.[11] So the events of 2003 had a small, but only temporary influence on American feelings towards France.

This section will instead locate more-enduring sources of liberal-conservative differences over France in socialism, secularism, and Gaullism. First, differences in economic ideology have the biggest influence; economic liberals admire the French social welfare state, while economic conservatives revile it as "socialist." Second, cultural ideology also divides Americans on France; cultural liberals delight in French high culture, and cultural conservatives are threatened by French secularism and possibly hedonism. Third and finally, conservatives, who are higher on nationalism, are infuriated by Gaullist provocations, while liberals, lower on nationalism, tend to laugh them off, contributing to very different policy preferences towards France.

Socialist France. The French Revolution followed quickly upon the heels of the American, and our Founding Fathers watched the upheavals in France attentively. As we saw in Chapter 2, the second and third U.S. presidents did not always agree about what they saw. Federalist John Adams feared the radicalism of the French revolutionaries, especially their efforts to redistribute property. But Republican Thomas Jefferson was less troubled by economic redistribution and more optimistic about the prospects for liberty in France.

Of the wave of revolutions that swept Europe in 1848, Americans followed the events in Paris the most intently. The administration of Democratic president James Polk immediately recognized the new regime in France, and the Senate unanimously approved a resolution applauding the French people's "success in their recent efforts to consolidate liberty." But the Whig opposition was anxious about the new government's promised economic reforms. Whig senator Daniel Webster of Massachusetts decried the new French constitution's guarantee "to all Frenchmen, not only liberty and security, but also, employment and property."[12]

With the Paris Commune of 1871, many Americans came to associate France with socialism. The new transatlantic cable supplied the daily news from France to a growing American commercial press, which highlighted violence and the threat of redistribution. "Property throughout France will be seized and distributed to the rabble should the Reds extend and maintain their power," warned the *Cleveland Leader*. The Paris Commune, the *New York Times* similarly declared, "is a socialistic outbreak, a stroke at property itself."[13]

The American left objected to this media coverage. "The commune in Paris gave the American Press a fresh opportunity to renew their venomous attacks, calumniations & execrations of the Parisian Workingmen, our [International Workingmen's] Association . . . and its members," lamented German American labor leader Friedrich Sorge.[14]

Remarkably, the divisive economic issues of property and redistribution continue to shape American feelings towards France today. Of the four dimensions of ideology that we measured in our 2011 survey, only beliefs about economic inequality mediated the very large correlation between ideology and feelings towards France, accounting for over two-thirds of the relationship.[15] Specifically, conservative support for economic inequality contributed to coolness towards France, while liberal opposition to inequality (i.e., support for redistribution) contributed to warmth towards France.

The conservative American economic position on France is frequently on display on the editorial pages of the *Wall Street Journal*, which has never been shy about its defense of property. "We believe in the individual, in his wisdom and his decency. We oppose all infringements on individual rights," editor William H. Grimes proclaimed in 1951. "We are radical ... [and] make no pretense of walking down the middle of the road."[16] It is thus not surprising that the *Journal*'s editorial page frequently projects its economic fantasies and fears onto France. When the center-right Nicolas Sarkozy won the French presidency in 2007, *Journal* editors rejoiced about the vote as a "French Revolution." Sarkozy had lambasted France's social welfare state as "unjust" and "financially untenable" for "discourag[ing] work and job creation." Echoing the *Journal*'s own views, Sarkozy had instead proposed a "new social contract founded on work, merit and equal opportunity."[17] In short, business-conservative heaven.

But when Sarkozy lost to the Socialist Francois Hollande in 2012, the *Journal*'s editorial page went into denial, declaring in an editorial entitled "Socialist France" that "the French vote for Mr. Hollande is less a lurch to the socialist left than it is a desire not to reward [Sarkozy's] failure."[18] In "France's Class Warrior," they had already branded Hollande "a socialist of the very old school: a high-taxing, rich-bashing, inflation-tolerating class warrior." In short, Obama and business-conservative hell.

Chuck Asay captured the conservative American economic view of France and European "socialism" in a 2010 editorial cartoon (Figure 7.2). The top panel, "France Today," depicts the general strikes that were then occurring in major French cities against a government proposal to raise the retirement age. A mob of French union workers battles the police and holds signs reading, "Don't Mess with My Pension" and "Worker's Unite!" The bottom panel, "California Tomorrow," is virtually identical, showing a mob of California liberals battling police and holding up similar signs reading, "Don't Mess with My Pension" and "Worker's Unite!" Asay cannot resist, however, adding to the latter, "You've got nothing to lose but the economy!" From Asay's conservative perspective in Colorado Springs, American coastal liberals are little different from French socialists: a violent mob seeking to violate property rights through redistribution.

Economic liberals don't buy it: the "fiscal scolds" actually bash France because it has balanced its budget through raising taxes rather than gutting its social welfare state. "France has committed the unforgivable sin of being fiscally responsible without inflicting pain on the poor and unlucky," writes Paul Krugman in a November 2013 op-ed for the *New York Times*. "And it must be punished."[19]

FIG. 7.2. "Socialist" France: Conservatives associate France with strong unions, strikes, and the social welfare state, which they decry at home as well, 2010.

Source: Chuck Asay, October 10, 2010. By permission of Chuck Asay and Creators Syndicate, Inc.

Indeed, economic liberals view the redistribution of income as both compassionate and fair (recall Figure 3.6), so they praise French and European social welfare states. "Despite the fact that Americans work . . . more than workers in virtually every western European nation by a considerable margin, these same states somehow sponsor far more generous programs of training and job mobility, and pay generous unemployment benefits," extols Eric Alterman in *Why We're Liberals.* "Europeans also enjoy high-quality public health and education provisions, and all manner of public services, from parks to efficient and inexpensive public transportation systems, that are not available anywhere in the United States."[20] In short, liberal economic heaven.

Secular France. Cultural ideology also divides Americans over France. Popular culture certainly suggests as much. For instance, in his 2011 *Midnight in Paris,* Woody Allen depicts American conservatives as philistines who dislike French culture. "I will always take a California wine" over a French one, declares the conservative businessman John, the bride-to-be's father. The conservative *Washington Times* countered in a review that *Midnight in Paris* "taps into a timeless American [read liberal] attraction to the City of Light as a cultural beacon, a place even ordinary artists can visit and emerge reborn." A *Times* reader commented to the review that Woody Allen's "morals are reprehensible. It's no wonder this movie flatters France and batters the U.S. because France tolerates perverted reprobates like Monsieur Allen. Quel dommage!"[21]

We decided to explore the idea that attitudes towards high culture might shape American views of France by including two high-culture items in a rating scale of "personal likes and dislikes" in our 2011 survey:

- *I enjoy gourmet foods and fine wines.*
- *I enjoy the fine arts (like painting) and/or high fashion.*

The resulting "high culture" scale correlated positively ($r = .23$) with warmth towards France, stronger than its relationship with feelings towards any of the other fifteen countries we measured.

We also measured "openness to new experience," which, as noted in Chapter 1, is the personality trait most consistently related to ideology:

- *I see myself as open to new experiences, complex.*
- *I see myself as conventional, uncreative.* (reverse coded)

The resulting "openness" personality scale also correlated positively ($r = .12$) with feelings towards France.

For a psychological variable as deep and enduring as the personality trait of openness to correlate with feelings towards any foreign country demands explanation. A serial mediation model revealed that cultural traditionalism and enjoyment of high culture accounted for virtually all of the direct relationship between an open personality and feelings towards France (Figure 7.3).[22] Americans with personalities characterized by greater "openness to new experience" felt

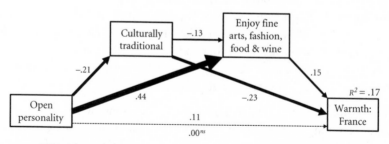

FIG. 7.3. Midnight in Paris: Cultural traditionalism and attitudes towards high culture help account for the positive association between an open personality and warmth towards France.

Note: A serial mediation model. All three indirect paths were statistically significant. See SUP.org for details. Seven demographic covariates are not shown. Warmth towards France is a three-item scale ($\alpha = .85$). *Data source:* OU Institute for US-China Issues, 2011.

"She's not naked, Jake, she's French."

FIG. 7.4. On France, liberals enjoy the fine arts, and are not as concerned about nudity and traditional values, 2005.

Source: Michael Crawford, *New Yorker,* October 17, 2005. Image courtesy of the Cartoon Bank.

warmer towards France than those with more conventional personalities did, in part because they were also more culturally liberal, in part because they tended to enjoy the fine arts, fashion, food, and wine more, and in part because being more culturally liberal contributed to their greater enjoyment of high culture.

Cultural conservatives tend to feel otherwise. Asked in 2005 about having to sit through a modern dance and poetry performance at a NATO summit in Prague, Bush administration secretary of defense Don Rumsfeld replied, "I'm from Chicago."[23] To Rumsfeld, it was self-evident that culturally conservative, heartland Americans would dislike high culture.

How should we interpret the even stronger direct path ($\beta = -.23$) from cultural traditionalism to feelings towards France? A 2005 *New Yorker* cartoon is suggestive (Figure 7.4). Standing in front of a large painting of a reclining nude, a father says to his son, "She's not naked, Jake, she's French." Liberals enjoying a painting is an example of how a greater appreciation of the fine arts helps account for their greater warmth towards France (the mediated relationship at the top right of Figure 7.3). But the fact that it is a *nude* painting points to the idea that attitudes towards traditional values are directly involved as well. As noted in Chapter 2, cultural traditionalism was measured with items that touched upon attitudes towards drugs, alcohol, nudity, and premarital sex. Could it be, as the comment to the *Washington Times* cited above suggests, that cultural conservatives view the French as sacrilegious and degenerate? Our survey included a measure of feelings towards "Christians" that we used to explore this question. Those feelings, it turns out, were a *positive* predictor of feelings towards England ($\beta = .14$) but a *negative* predictor of feelings towards France ($\beta = -.13$). It could be French Catholicism (as opposed to English Protestantism) that explains this negative association between American feelings towards "Christians" and feelings towards France, but it could also be a view of France as a secular Babylon. "One place where France has gone astray," Republican president Dwight D. Eisenhower told a group of fellow Republicans in 1952, is that "50 per cent of their people [are] agnostics or atheists." French "moral fiber," he concluded, "has disintegrated."[24] More recently, Ann Coulter has asserted that "The French Revolution is the godless antithesis to the founding of America."[25] That France has harbored child rapist Roman Polanski for decades, receiving public support from liberal Hollywood and enmity from the U.S. heartland, certainly does not help. Perceived French secularism and hedonism are likely the best interpretation of the direct relationship between cultural traditionalism and coolness towards France.

Gaullist France. While economic and cultural ideologies do the best job accounting for American *feelings* towards France, it is social dominance orientation that mediates the relationship between ideology and *foreign policy preferences* towards France. Conservatives desired tougher policies towards France than liberals did due in part to their greater need for group dominance. The desire that *"Inferior groups should stay in their place"* captures a degree of aggression, so it makes sense that it might relate to an action tendency or policy preference rather than feelings. But where does this aggressive impulse to put France back in its place come from?

The data suggests that it comes in part from a nationalist response to French Gaullism. Figure 7.5 reveals that nationalism (as an American) and social dominance orientation act as sequential mediators of the relationship between ideology and foreign policy preferences towards France, accounting for two-thirds of the relationship.[26] Conservatives desired a tougher foreign policy towards France than liberals did, in part because of their greater nationalism, in part because of their greater desire for group dominance, and in part because greater nationalism contributes to greater social dominance.

One way that some Frenchmen have coped with France's relative decline over the past century has been to cherish the glory of French civilization and to thumb their nose at the global hegemon, the United States. "All my life I have thought of France ... as dedicated to an exalted and exceptional destiny," Charles de Gaulle wrote in his *Memoires de Guerre*. "France cannot be

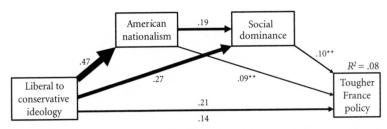

FIG. 7.5. Conservatives desire a tougher foreign policy towards France than liberals do, in part because of their greater average nationalism and social dominance orientation.

Note: A serial mediation model. ** $p \leq .01$, all other p's $< .001$. All three indirect paths were statistically significant. See SUP.org for details. Demographic covariates are not shown. *Data source:* OU Institute for US-China Issues, 2011.

France without *la grandeur*."[27] Infuriated that he was excluded from the 1945 Yalta Conference, in which Roosevelt, Churchill, and Stalin, representing the "Big Three," decided the fate of postwar Europe, de Gaulle fiercely defended France's postwar independence, often defying his American and British Cold War allies. When France first tested an atomic bomb in 1960, de Gaulle declared that he would aim his bombs "in every direction." In 1966 he withdrew France from NATO, expelling U.S. forces from the French soil they had liberated from Nazi rule just two decades earlier. In a letter to President Lyndon B. Johnson, de Gaulle proclaimed that "France intends to recover, in her territory, the full exercise of her sovereignty, now impaired by the permanent presence of Allied [read U.S.] military elements."[28]

Gaullism did not die with de Gaulle. In 2003, Prime Minister Jacques Chirac and his foreign minister, Dominique de Villepin, were the most outspoken opponents of the Bush administration's decision to invade Iraq, thwarting Bush's desire for U.N. authorization. Bush was forced to put together his own "Coalition of the Willing" composed primarily of U.S. and British troops. "France remains loyal to its friends and to the values it shares with them," Prime Minister Nicholas Sarkozy declared at the United Nations on September 25, 2007. "But loyalty is not the same as submission."[29] The Gaullist insistence on equality and even French superiority clearly persists.

Our survey data suggests that Americans differ systematically in how they respond to Gaullist provocations. Conservatives, higher in nationalism and desires to put perceived inferior groups back in their place, appear more likely to respond with anger. In 2003, Republicans in the U.S. House of Representatives changed the name of French fries to "freedom fries" in the House cafeteria, a symbolic but satisfying snub. "We lost 3,000 Americans on September 11 and I

"I tell you Khrushchev is a chicken!"

FIG. 7.6. American responses to French Gaullism: Liberals laugh while conservatives bristle in anger? 1962.

Source: Copyright Bill Mauldin, 1962. Courtesy of the Bill Mauldin Estate LLC.

think many Americans, [and] I'm one of them, are very disappointed about the attitude of the French," complained Republican congressman Walter B. Jones Jr. of North Carolina.[30]

Other conservatives went significantly further. Fox's Bill O'Reilly led a nationwide campaign to boycott French products. Historians John Miller and Mark Molesky were so angered by French opposition to the Iraq War that they decided to rewrite the entire history of Franco-American relations. "The French attitude toward the United States consistently has been one of cultural suspicion and political dislike, bordering at times on raw hatred," they wrote in their 2004 *Our Oldest Enemy: A History of America's Disastrous Relationship with France.* "France is not America's oldest ally, but its oldest enemy."[31] In a review for *Foreign Affairs,* Harvard historian Stanley Hoffmann judged the book "shoddy and biased," concluding that "Ultimately, this book is a contribution to our understanding only of U.S. neoconservatism, not of Franco-American relations."[32]

American liberals, lower on nationalism, appear less inclined to anger and more disposed to laugh off Gaullist irritants. Bill Mauldin captured this liberal attitude in a 1962 cartoon (Figure 7.6). "I Tell You Khrushchev Is a Chicken!"

depicts Charles de Gaulle as a tiny mouse. Standing atop an imposing eagle of "U.S. power," he waves his tiny fist, full of bluster. It is a comic dismissal of a silly French nationalist. "De Gaulle," Mauldin wrote tongue in cheek the next year, "was very hard to please."[33]

Johnny Carson also loved to poke fun at Gaullism, and several late-night comedians took up that cause again in 2003 over the Iraq controversy. "You know why the French don't want to bomb Saddam Hussein?" asked Conan O'Brien. "Because he hates America, he loves mistresses, and wears a beret. He *is* French, people."

Liberal comedians are often as bemused by conservative American Francophobes as they are by French Gaullists, however. "In protest of France's opposition to a U.S. war on Iraq, the U.S. Congress' cafeteria has changed French fries and French toast to 'freedom fries' and 'freedom toast,'" deadpanned *Saturday Night Live*'s Tina Fey on a 2003 "Weekend Update." "Afterwards, the congressmen were so pleased with themselves, they all started freedom kissing each other. In a related story, in France, American cheese is now referred to as 'idiot cheese.'"[34]

MOTHER ENGLAND:
LIBERAL AND CONSERVATIVE ANGLOPHILES

"The People of the United States are kindred of the People of Great Britain. With all our distinct national interests, objects, and aspirations, we are conscious that our moral strength is largely derived from that relationship."[35]

—Republican President Abraham Lincoln, 1861

"There is always in this country a certain amount of criticism of and superficial ill feeling towards the British, in time of danger something deeper comes to the surface, and the British and we stand firmly together, with confidence in our common heritage and ideas."[36]

—Eleanor Roosevelt, 1949

Anglophilia and Anglophobia have long coexisted in the New World, both within individuals and between different groups of Americans. The 1776 Declaration of Independence first decried the tyranny of King George: "The history of the present King of Great Britain is a history of repeated injuries and usurpations, all having in direct object the establishment of an absolute Tyranny over these States."[37] Countless loyalist Tories fled or were tarred and feathered during the revolution.

But the founders ended up establishing a political system that resembled Britain's in many ways. The American presidency, argues historian Frank Prochaska, is a "disguised monarchy" given "quasi-regal status and the trappings of royalty." In 1789 Thomas Jefferson wrote that "We were educated in royalism. No wonder, if some of us retain that idolatry still." Over a century later, on

February 9, 1896, the *Knoxville Journal* claimed that "Great Britain is a republic with a hereditary president, while the United States is a monarchy with an elective king."[38]

In addition to shared politics, American Anglophiles also treasure shared lineage, language, and Protestant culture. Presenting his credentials to King George III as the first U.S. ambassador to Britain in June 1785, John Adams declared that "I shall esteem myself the happiest of men, if I can be instrumental in . . . restoring . . . the old good humor between people who, though separated by an ocean and under different governments, have the same language, a similar religion, and kindred blood." In his 1856 "English Traits," Ralph Waldo Emerson similarly wrote, "Every book we read, every biography, play, or romance, in whatever form, is still English history and manners."[39]

Anglophobia generally took two forms. Populist Anglophobes of the late nineteenth and early twentieth centuries objected to the association between the WASPs who ran America—the business and political elites—and things British. American elites wore English suits and affected English manners, leading to a populist backlash, especially among the largely agrarian People's Party at the turn of the century. Irish Anglophobes had more direct grievances against England itself. Irish immigrants who settled in the United States following the famine at home maintained a bitter animosity towards England. "I wanta make the King of England keep his snoot out of America," declared Chicago mayor Big Bill Thompson in 1927.[40] Irish American politicians and newspapers fused Anglophobia with Irish American identity, even for postimmigrant generations.

Frank Hutchins captured "Two Kinds of Fool Americans" in a playful 1895 editorial cartoon for *Puck* magazine (Figure 7.7). A child Puck holds up two large sheets of paper. The one on the left, entitled "The Jingoes," depicts a mob of American Anglophobes yelling, throwing their hats, and shaking their umbrellas in outrage. Republican Whitelaw Reid, who had already served as U.S. ambassador to France and would go on to serve as ambassador to Great Britain, holds a flag reading, "We Will Stand No Nonsense from Tyrannical England!!! Our Blood Is Always Boiling!!" An eagle tagged "U.S." but looking more like a vulture perches upon John Bull, who lies stiff as if in rigor mortis. The sheet of paper on the right is titled "The Anglo-Maniacs." Dressed in English suits and dresses, American Anglophiles bow down before an "English Butler," an "English Lord," and an "English Actor," all with a stiff upper lip and noses held high. Even more lofty are "English Clothes," "English Manners," and a portrait of "'is Royal 'ighness," in a dismissive play on an English accent.

Following World War II, both Anglophile and Anglophobe passions appear to have waned. In the early postwar, "American references to England as 'moth-

TWO KINDS OF FOOL AMERICANS

FIG. 7.7. American Anglophobes and Anglophiles, 1895.

Source: Frank M. Hutchins, *Puck*, April 24, 1895. Image courtesy of the Library of Congress. LC-DIG-ppmsca-29003.

er country' were less often heard and calls to Anglo-Saxon racial unity had less charm," argues Prochaska. By the 1980s, "Rally calls to the unity of the English-speaking people . . . were by now unfashionable. Diversity was in. WASPs were out."[41] With the Belfast "Good Friday Agreement" of 1998, the "Troubles" were largely resolved and Irish American Anglophobia faded. And the populist association between the American elite and England appears to have dissipated as well.

What can our 2011 survey tell us about American feelings and policy preferences towards England today? As noted in the Introduction, Americans as a whole felt substantially warmer towards England (69°) than they did towards any other foreign country we measured (see Figure 0.3). And the ideological gap on England was the smallest of all foreign countries measured, with liberals (74°) feeling just 5° warmer towards England than conservatives (69°) did, a small but statistically significant difference.[42]

While none of our four ideological dimensions mediated the small relationship between ideology and feelings towards England, nationalism did, *suppressing* it: including nationalism as a mediator actually *increased* the influence of ideology, more than doubling it.[43] Specifically, controlling for nationalism in-

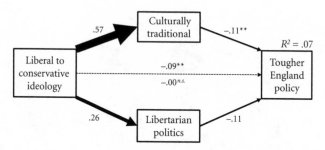

F I G . 7.8. Conservatives desire an even friendlier policy toward England than liberals do, in part because of their greater traditionalism and libertarianism.

Note: A simultaneous mediation model. ** $p < .01$, all other p's $< .001$, $^{n.s.}$ = not significant. Both indirect paths were statistically significant. Details are online at SUP.org. Demographic covariates are not shown. *Data source:* OU Institute for US-China Issues, 2011.

creased the gap between liberal (77°) and conservative (66°) feelings towards England to 11°.[44] In other words, if it were not for the fact that conservatives are more nationalistic than liberals, they would feel even cooler towards England vis-à-vis liberals.

How should this suppression effect be interpreted? Nationalism, as discussed in Chapter 4, is defined and operationalized in political psychology as a belief in the *superiority* of one's own country over other countries. Nationalism as an American, it turns out, correlates positively only with feelings towards Israel ($r = .30$) and England ($r = .11$), and negatively or not at all with feelings towards all other countries. This suggests that England is included in the American "we" that is activated by items like "*The American system is superior to that of other countries.*" Central to the "Special Relationship" is the idea that the United States and "Mother England" share a political system committed to protecting individual liberties. Supporting this interpretation, of the four dimensions of ideology, none of which mediated the relationship between ideology and feelings towards England, libertarian politics came the very closest, approaching marginal significance ($\beta = .05, p = .11$).

Libertarianism, it turns out, also plays a role in American foreign policy preferences towards England. While both liberals and conservatives desired a friendlier England policy, conservatives desired a slightly friendlier policy than liberals did.[45] A mediation analysis revealed that of the four dimensions of ideology that we measured, only culture and politics were statistically significant.[46] As displayed in Figure 7.8, their greater average traditionalism and libertarianism helped account for why conservatives desired an even friendlier policy toward England than liberals did, reducing the direct effect of ideology to statistical nonsignificance.

It thus appears that conservatives today embrace a shared WASP culture and perceived libertarian politics with England more than liberals do. "Our founding fathers were God fearing descendants of Puritans and other colonial Christians," Ann Coulter writes in her 2011 *Demonic*. "The dominant American culture was Anglo-Saxon and Christian. Even while fighting 'the British,' as we now call them, Americans considered themselves British with the rights of Englishmen."[47] Coulter thus echoes Benjamin Franklin, who argued over two centuries earlier that the War of Independence was fought for English political values: "It was a resistance in . . . favor of the liberties of England."[48]

The synergy of culture and politics in conservative Anglophile views of England is nicely captured in a pair of speeches given on Queen Victoria's Golden Jubilee in 1887. "Everywhere mother [England] and daughter [America] have carried the atmosphere of free speech, free thought, and freedom to worship God, according to conscience," declared Seth Low, former Republican mayor of New York City. "The two nations have had their differences; but behind them all beat, as I believe, two kindred hearts." A pastor in Texas agreed: "We are part of Great Britain—that earth-encircling family of English speaking nations, the planting and nurture of which is the most remarkable of God's modern miracles," declared the Reverend C. I. Scofield of Dallas's First Congregational Church. "One hundred years ago He broke the bond of authority which bound us to the mother land, but He left unbroken and unbreakable five gentle and unfretting links of union—the link of race, the link of law, the link of language, the link of literature and the link of liberty."[49]

There is also some evidence that partisanship played a small role in accounting for the slightly greater conservative desire for a friendlier policy towards England. While party identification is usually not as strong a predictor of international attitudes as ideology, in the case of policy towards England it is.[50] Just as American feelings towards France cooled after 9/11, warmth towards Britain increased.[51] A cult of Prime Minister Tony Blair emerged, especially among conservatives appreciative of his support for President Bush. Conservative historians Miller and Molesky, incensed at France, wrote approvingly of Blair: "Despite the British public's misgivings about the wisdom of invading Iraq, Prime Minister Tony Blair acted with a solid appreciation of America's positive role in the world and a firm understanding of common values and mutual interests."[52]

Republicans in Congress also promoted the cult of Blair. Curt Weldon of Pennsylvania declared Blair "the Winston Churchill of the 21st Century."[53] Senator Elizabeth Dole of North Carolina introduced a bill to award a congressional gold medal to Blair in March 2003. During House debate over the bill in June, Pete King of New York proclaimed:

Throughout our history, there has probably been no country that the United States has had a closer relationship with than Great Britain. Certainly we share certain immutable, transcendent values. Throughout our history we have stood together in a number of noble causes, probably dramatically manifested during World War II when Prime Minister Churchill and President Roosevelt stood together to defeat the forces of fascism and Nazism. But there is probably no British Prime Minister who has been there when America needs him more than Tony Blair.[54]

The bill passed both houses and was signed into law by President Bush on July 17, 2003.

Why liberals felt slightly warmer towards England than conservatives did while conservatives desired a slightly friendlier policy towards England remains a puzzle. For the foreign countries that we measured, on average feelings accounted for a very substantial 21 percent of policy preferences. But feelings towards England accounted for just 8 percent of policy preferences towards England, the lowest for all fifteen countries. It could be that gratitude towards Blair along with Republican partisanship kicks in when conservatives ponder foreign policy towards England, but not when judging overall feelings towards England.

It does seem clear from Figure 7.8, however, that a greater cultural and political affinity for England accounts for the even greater conservative than liberal desire for friendlier policies towards England. "I absolutely agree with you as to the importance . . . of a growing friendship between the English-speaking peoples," Republican president Teddy Roosevelt wrote in reply to a letter from King Edward VII in 1905. "The larger interests of the two nations are the same; and the fundamental, underlying traits of their characters are also the same."[55]

BROTHER GERMANY: "*HEIL HITLER!*"

"*The President should learn a lesson from the 'German Miracle.*'"[56]
—Congressman Joe Wilson (Republican–South Carolina), 2011

"*You must buy health insurance or pay the new Gestapo—the IRS.*"[57]
—Governor Paul LePage (Republican–Maine), 2012

Germans were the first and largest immigrant group in America. They were initially met with ambivalence. In tolerant colonies, German immigrants were welcomed to come and live as they pleased. Pennsylvania Germans, for instance, were not forced to speak English. Less tolerant colonies like Massachusetts, however, tended to limit immigration to those willing to speak English and assimilate into WASP values. Benjamin Franklin initially belonged to the less tolerant camp. Of English descent, he was wary of "swarthy" German immigrants. "Why should Pennsylvania," Franklin asked in 1751, "founded by the

English, become a Colony of *Aliens*, who will shortly be so numerous as to Germanize us instead of our Anglifying them, and will never adopt our Language or Customs, any more than they can acquire our Complexion?"[58]

By the midnineteenth century, however, the arrival of newer waves of even more "swarthy" immigrants, from Southern Europe and Asia, appears to have contributed to WASP acceptance of German Americans—and a positive view of Germany itself. In 1866 *The Nation* described Germans as "the most learned, patient, industrious, civilized people on the face of the globe, which has achieved the highest distinction in arts, science, in arms, [and] literature."[59] In 1883 *Puck* celebrated "The 200th birthday of the healthiest of Uncle Sam's adopted children." Germans had apparently first arrived in the New World in 1683.[60] By 1900, German Americans constituted 10 percent of the American population. Because turn-of-the-century Americans "had neighbors of German birth and ancestry . . . and liked them . . . as good citizens and friendly neighbors," wrote historian and journalist Mark Sullivan three decades later, "the natural disposition of America was to think well of Germany."[61]

That changed with two world wars in the twentieth century. At the turn of the century, rising German bellicosity under Kaiser Wilhelm II raised questions about the loyalty of German Americans. Udo Keppler, himself of Austrian descent, captured the problem in a pair of 1900 editorial cartoons for *Puck*, which his father Joseph had founded three decades earlier as a German-language weekly in St. Louis. In "Our Beloved German-American" at the left of Figure 7.9, a rotund man smokes a pipe while reading about "American politics" in a newspaper. He wears oversized spectacles labeled "Made in Germany." The caption declares that "He would have a happier time if he looked through American-made spectacles." This German American is misguided but harmless.

In "The Real German-American," on the right of Figure 7.9, a stout and resolute man casts his vote for president with his right hand while using his left hand to hold back Wilhelm II and Carl Schurz. "Kaiser Bill" is lampooned in the spiked helmet or *Pickelhaube* then worn by the German military. Schurz was the first German-born American elected to the United States Senate. He was famous both for his anti-imperialism and his advocacy of a dual German American identity. "He who calls himself a German now must never forget his honorable obligation to his name; he must honor Germany in himself," Schurz had declared at the Chicago World's Fair in 1893. "The German-American can accomplish great things for the development of the great composite nation of the new world [the United States], if in his works and deeds he combines and welds the best that is in the German character with the best that is in the American."[62]

Keppler's German American voter thinks otherwise. He stands in front of

OUR BELOVED GERMAN-AMERICAN
*"He would have a happier time if he looked
through American-made spectacles."*

THE REAL GERMAN-AMERICAN
*"He does his own thinking, and will
do his own voting."*

FIG. 7.9. German Americans: Traitors or Patriots? 1900.

Sources: Udo Keppler, *Puck*, May 9, 1900, and October 31, 1900. Images courtesy of the Library of Congress. LC-DIG-ppmsca-25419 and LC-DIG-ppmsca-25469.

a banner displaying images of President William McKinley and Vice President Theodore Roosevelt, suggesting that the patriotic German American vote for the Republican ticket in 1900 rather than the anti-imperialist Democrat William Jennings Bryan. Keppler's caption reads, "He does his own thinking, and will do his own voting."

The efforts of Keppler and others appear to have been largely successful in dispelling WASP doubts about German American loyalty. Because "Germans were thought to be basically 'like us,'" historian Michaela Moore argues, "the American public was not predisposed to hate or fear Germany." As a result, in the twentieth century, wartime U.S. governments were forced to *construct* enemy images of Germany—twice. George Creel's Committee on Public Information first portrayed the "Huns" as bent on global domination during World War I. Then, during World War II, the Office of War Information labored to explain to the American people "Why We Fight" against the Nazis. Moore argues that central to this latter project was distinguishing between the German people, who were good, and Adolf Hitler and the Nazi regime, which were evil.[63]

As we will see in the next chapter, historian John Dower has argued that ra-

FIG. 7.10. German American Bund parade in New York City, October 30, 1939.
Source: Photo courtesy of the Library of Congress. LC-USZ62-117148.

cial thinking is a big reason why the War in the Pacific was so much more brutal than the European theater of World War II. American wartime propaganda demonized the "Japs" as an Asian racial group, while demonizing only Hitler and the Nazis in Europe, retaining some humanity for the German people. "U.S. citizens of Japanese extraction were treated with greater suspicion and severity than German or Italian aliens," Dower writes, "despite the fact that the German-American Bund had agitated on behalf of Hitler in the United States prior to the outbreak of war, and despite the fact that there never was, at Pearl Harbor or later, any evidence of organized subversion among the Japanese community."[64] Figure 7.10 is a photograph of an October 30, 1939, German American Bund parade on East Eighty-sixth Street in New York City. A Swastika flag is clearly visible. Moore argues that there was a degree of "whitewashing" of the reality of the Third Reich and the Holocaust in the United States during the war that had its origins in race: "the 'whiteness' of the Germans helped to exculpate them."[65]

So how do Americans feel about Germany today? The mediation model displayed in Figure 7.11 reveals that the cultural and economic dimensions of ideology push in *opposite* directions, canceling each other out. They cannot therefore account for the 12° of greater warmth towards Germany among liber-

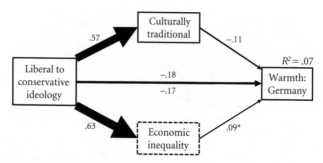

FIG. 7.11. Conflicted American feelings towards Germany: Cultural and economic ideologies offset each other.

Note: A simultaneous mediation model. * $p < .05$, all other p's $< .001$. Only the indirect path through traditionalism was statistically significant. See SUP.org. Seven demographic covariates are not shown. *Data source:* OU Institute for US-China Issues, 2011.

als relative to conservatives. Cultural conservatism ($\beta = -.11$) is associated with *coolness* towards Germany, while economic conservatism ($\beta = .09$, $p < .05$) is associated with *warmth* towards Germany.

Economic ideology's *suppression* effect (the coefficients .63 and .09 at the bottom of Figure 7.11 combine to create a positive number, while the direct effect, −.18, is a negative number) may be the easier of the two indirect effects to interpret.[66] Although Germany is a social welfare state, Americans today likely see it as more economically conservative than its continental European neighbors, especially Greece, Spain, and France. Many Americans view German chancellor Angela Merkel as a champion of fiscal conservatism, turning Germany's role in the European fiscal crisis into a proxy war between American liberals and conservatives over domestic economic policy. "Growth or austerity?" posed the *Wall Street Journal* in its 2012 editorial "Europe's Phony Growth Debate." "Mrs. Merkel's government did the world an additional favor in 2009, amid the financial crisis, by rejecting calls from the International Monetary Fund, then British Prime Minister Gordon Brown, President Obama, Treasury Secretary Tim Geithner and the same dominant Keynesian consensus to join the global spending party."[67] Republican congressman Steve King of Iowa similarly held up Merkel's austerity as a model: "It ought to hit home to our president of the United States. It ought to hit all of us here in this country."[68]

Economic liberal Paul Krugman of the *New York Times* countered that "tales of German austerity are greatly exaggerated." Foisting austerity on Greece, Spain, and other European countries, Krugman argued, would only worsen their plight. The United States, for its part, needed more economic stimulus, not less.[69]

By contrast, the top path of Figure 7.11 reveals that cultural traditionalism helps account for greater conservative *coolness* towards Germany.[70] How should this be interpreted? As noted in Chapters 2 and 6, social psychologists have demonstrated that conservatives, high in traditionalism, tend to view the world as a dangerous place full of threats to their worldviews.[71] Perhaps cultural conservatives are more likely than cultural liberals to view Germany through the threatening prism of Hitler and the Nazis. Fundamentalist Christians appear to equate their enemies with Hitler more often than do other Americans. As we will read in the next chapter, Christians United for Israel's John Hagee declared in 2007 that "Iran is Germany and Ahmadinejad is the new Hitler."[72]

More broadly, Beverly Crawford and James Martel have argued that popular Hollywood images of Germany have returned to the "evil Nazi" view of Germans that prevailed during World War II. With the onset of the Cold War and West Germany becoming a U.S. ally against the Soviet Union, Nazi atrocities were downplayed in favor of depictions of the "Good German," or at least the harmless German. For instance, the 1951 film *Desert Fox* portrayed Erwin Rommel as a good general, who in the end tries to assassinate Hitler. Similarly, Sergeant Schultz of the 1960s TV comedy *Hogan's Heroes* was depicted as a bumbling and foolish—but harmless—traditional Bavarian. Later, at the height of the Cold War, the idea of "totalitarianism" conflated Nazism and communism in movies like *The Spy Who Came in from the Cold* (1965) and *Dr. Strangelove* (1964).

With détente and then the end of the Cold War, however, Hollywood revived the evil German Nazi as villain in movies like *Marathon Man* (1976) and *Raiders of the Lost Ark* (1981). Other Hollywood villains were not necessarily Nazis but were Aryans with thick German accents, such as in Bruce Willis's *Die Hard* (1988) and the James Bond film *Tomorrow Never Dies* (1997), in which 007 takes on a megalomaniac German media mogul and his Aryan henchmen. "Because of America's complex identifications with Germans and Germany," Crawford and Martel conclude, "the postwar film industry has been obsessed with German, not Japanese images as representations of evil."[73] Perhaps these renewed negative images of Germany emanating from Hollywood have had a greater influence on cultural conservatives than on cultural liberals due to the formers' greater sensitivity to threat.

It is also possible that cultural liberals and conservatives differ over Germany for some of the same reasons that they appear to differ over France, such as perceived high rates of abortion and cohabitation outside of marriage, and the legalization of gay marriage. "Religious conservatives have a hard time with secular German society," historian of German American relations Thomas Adam writes.[74] "Berlin"—like "Paris" and "Los Angeles"—may act as an urban symbol of the sexual politics central to the American culture wars.

Regardless of how we interpret these two indirect effects, economic ideology clearly *suppresses* the full influence of cultural ideology on feelings towards Germany. In other words, if it were not for the fact that economic conservatives celebrate Chancellor Merkel's austerity policies, the average conservative would feel even cooler towards Germany. Supporting this finding, the "Teavangelical" Republicans (58°) we identified in Chapter 2 felt 8° warmer towards Germany than did our more purely "cultural" or religious right Republicans (50°), a substantial difference statistically.[75] Angela Merkel's advocacy of austerity presumably appeals more to the greater economic conservatism and libertarianism of the Teavangelical Republicans (see Figure 2.10), while cultural Republicans may care less about economic policy and harbor greater fears about fascist and secular German threats to WASP American values.

THE E.U. ANTICHRIST

"We believe that the Common Market and the trend toward the unification of Europe may well be the beginning of the 10-nation confederacy predicted by Daniel and the Book of Revelation."[76]

—Hal Lindsey, *The Late, Great Planet Earth*, 1970

"In Revelation 13, we have a description of the Antichrist, who will be the head of the European Union."[77]

—John Hagee, *Jerusalem Countdown*, 2006

"The United States congratulates the European Union on being awarded the Nobel Peace Prize," reads an October 2012 Obama White House press release. "It reflects the spirit and dedication of the Europeans to coexist peacefully in a society that draws strength from the diversity of its people, its languages and its cultures."[78] The editorial page of the *New York Times* agreed: "the E.U. is a remarkable achievement."[79]

Conservatives disagreed. "Why on Earth give a prize to the unaccountable bureaucrat jamboree in Brussels known as the European Union?" asked Christian Whiton for Fox News. "The awarding of the Nobel Peace Prize to the European Union itself is the latest grotesque act of self-indulgence by Old Europe's political class."[80] Whiton was not alone. On October 12, 2012, the *Wall Street Journal* asked its online readers a loaded question: "Did the European Union deserve to win the Nobel Peace Prize?" Two weeks later, 87 percent of 1,537 *Journal* reader-respondents had answered "no."[81]

These opposing reactions to the E.U.'s Nobel Prize are indicative of broader ideological differences in how Americans view the European Union. As noted above, liberals (64°) felt a remarkable 37° warmer towards the European Union than conservatives (27°) did. As the multiple mediation model displayed in Figure 7.12 reveals, part of this difference is the result of the big gap between liberal and conservative feelings towards international organizations like the

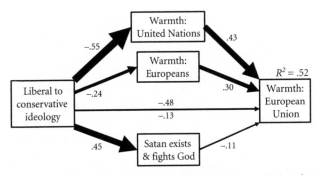

FIG. 7.12. Conservatives feel much cooler towards the European Union than liberals do, in part because they feel much cooler towards international organization like the United Nations, in part because they feel cooler towards Europeans as a people, and in part because of their greater average belief in the Antichrist.

Note: A simultaneous mediation model. All three indirect paths were statistically significant. Statistics are online at SUP.org. Seven standard demographic covariates are not shown. Data source: OU Institute for US-China Issues, 2011.

United Nations, which we will explore in greater detail in Chapter 10. Greater conservative coolness towards Europeans as a people also helps account for their greater coolness towards the European Union. Finally, and perhaps most remarkably, the greater conservative belief in the Devil—"*The basic cause of evil in this world is Satan, who is still constantly & ferociously fighting against God*"—also accounts for greater conservative coolness towards the European Union. Together, these three mediators reduce the gap between liberal and conservative feelings towards the European Union from a massive 37° to just 12°.[82]

That belief in the Devil uniquely predicted feelings towards the European Union—even when covarying for the powerful effects of feelings towards the United Nations and the European people—is truly remarkable, demanding explanation. As the first epigraph reveals, Christian Zionist Hal Lindsey popularized the notion of the European Union as the source of the Antichrist in his 1970 dispensationalist blockbuster *The Late, Great Planet Earth*. Since then, he has continued to claim that the Bible predicts that Europeans are forming a revived Roman Empire out of which the Antichrist will emerge. "There is a potential dictator waiting in the wings somewhere in Europe who will make Adolf Hitler and Josef Stalin look like choir boys," Lindsey wrote in his 1994 *Planet Earth—2000 A.D.*[83]

Lindsey is not alone. John Hagee, televangelist and founder of Christians United for Israel, is another Texas-based Christian Zionist who has popularized the idea of the European Union as the source of a future "Antichrist." In Hagee's 2001 movie *Vanished*, the Antichrist is portrayed as the "President of the European Union." A revived Roman Empire, the European Union is depicted as a "Fourth Reich" seeking global domination. Other dispensationalists also popularize this view of the European Union online. "The Rise of the European Super-State" is one of the "Strategic trends" that you can follow on the large website of "Koinonia House," the ministry of Chuck and Nancy Missler. Based on their reading of the Bible, they claim that the European Union will be the source of "the Antichrist," who will rise prior to Christ's Second Coming.[84]

A EUROPEAN LOOKING GLASS

This chapter first sought to demonstrate broad liberal-conservative differences in American feelings towards Europe. It then showed how different kinds of American liberals and conservatives view various European countries in distinct ways. Greater cultural conservatism was associated with desires for a friendlier policy towards Mother England but with coolness towards secular France, Germany, and the European Union. Economic conservatism was associated with warmth towards fiscally austere Germany but coolness towards "socialist" France. Greater conservative nationalism was associated with warmth towards liberal England but coolness towards Gaullist France.

When Robert Kagan claimed in 2002 that "Americans are from Mars and Europeans are from Venus," he was distancing himself from France by conflating "America" with conservatives like himself who revile French "socialism" and Gaullism. American liberals, we have seen, are more likely to be Francophiles. If Americans are Martians, therefore, Mars has multiple races.

8 The Middle East: Christian Zionism, the Israel Lobby, and the Holy Land

In a series of articles and a book on the Israel lobby, realist international relations theorists John Mearsheimer of the University of Chicago and Stephen Walt of Harvard argued in 2006–7 that America's virtually unqualified support for Israel was damaging the U.S. national interest. "Now that the Cold War is over, Israel has become a strategic liability for the United States," they argue. "Washington's close relationship with Jerusalem makes it harder, not easier, to defeat the terrorists who are now targeting the United States."[1] America's disastrous Middle East policy, they further contend, is best explained by the pernicious influence of the "Israel lobby" in Washington, especially the right-wing American Israel Public Affairs Committee (AIPAC).

The outraged response came fast and furious. Several former U.S. diplomats took it personally. Dennis Ross, who worked under Presidents George H.W. Bush and Bill Clinton, insisted that "never in the time that I led the American negotiations on the Middle East peace process did we take a step because 'the lobby' wanted us to."[2] Princeton's Aaron Friedberg, who served under Vice President Dick Cheney during the George W. Bush administration, was indignant: "Sadly, their argument here is not only unscientific, it is inflammatory, irresponsible, and wrong."[3]

Two Israelis hit back where it hurt most, arguing that U.S. Middle East policy was actually driven by a realist calculus. Shlomo Ben-Ami, former Israeli foreign minister, maintained that America's Israel policy was grounded in "shared interests and considerations of realpolitik."[4] Historian Michael Oren, who would later become the Israeli ambassador to the United States, argued that "Arab oil (and not Israel) was America's persistent focus in the Middle East." Furthermore, U.S. "presidents have supported Israel for strategic and moral reasons, not political ones."[5]

Other critics turned their attention from K Street to Main Street. "In the United States, a pro-Israel foreign policy does not represent the triumph of a small lobby over the public will," diplomatic historian Walter Russell Mead argued in *Foreign Affairs*. "It represents the power of public opinion." Indeed, "the ultimate sources of the United States' Middle East policy lie outside the Beltway and outside the Jewish community." Specifically, U.S. Middle East policy cannot be understood apart from the long-standing but evolving Protestant American affinity for Israel.[6]

Mead is right that Mearsheimer and Walt err in reducing U.S. Middle East policy to an Israel lobby, especially one too focused on AIPAC and wealthy Jews.[7] American foreign policies in the region should be understood within the context of broader American public opinion. But Mead goes a bit too far when he claims that support for Israel in the United States "commands broad public support."[8] Political scientist Michael Koplow certainly errs when he goes even further, asserting that support for Israel in the United States is "broad and deep" and even "crosscutting."[9]

This chapter uses public opinion survey data to demonstrate that Americans are actually *divided* in their feelings and policy preferences towards Israel, Iran, the Palestinian people, and Muslims in general. While American conservatives today tend to feel quite warmly towards Israel, American liberals are more ambivalent and do not desire a friendlier Israel policy. The survey data suggests that Mead is more accurate when he acknowledges that "U.S. opinion on the Middle East is not monolithic."[10]

LIBERALS, CONSERVATIVES, AND THE MIDDLE EAST

In our spring 2011 survey, the average American felt lukewarm ($59°$) towards Israel, cool towards "the Palestinian people" ($41°$) and "Muslims" ($38°$), and downright frigid towards Iran ($19°$). This is largely consistent with the 2010 Chicago Council survey, which found average feelings of $57°$, $32°$, and $27°$ towards Israel, the "Palestinian Authority," and Iran, respectively.[11] On Middle East policy, our 2011 survey also revealed that the median, or most typical, American was neutral about U.S. policy towards Israel, desiring it to be neither friendlier nor tougher. But the typical American did desire a "tougher" policy on Iran.

Ideology, however, systematically divides Americans in their feelings towards Middle Eastern countries and peoples (Figure 8.1). Conservatives ($74°$) felt $22°$ warmer towards Israel than liberals ($52°$) did. However, liberals felt $13°$, $28°$, and $32°$ warmer than conservatives towards Iran, the Palestinians, and Muslims, respectively. Data from both the 2009 Program on International Policy Attitudes and 2010 Chicago Council surveys replicate this robust pattern of ideological polarization; conservatives felt warmer than liberals towards Israel but cooler

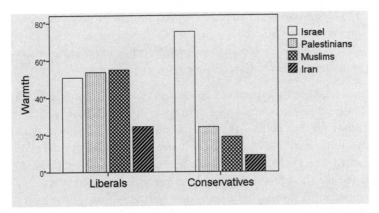

FIG. 8.1. Ideology polarizes American feelings towards Middle Eastern countries and peoples: Conservatives feel much warmer than liberals do towards Israel, but much cooler towards Palestinians, Muslims, and Iran.

Note: Israel: $F(1, 419) = 64.62$, $p < .001$, $\eta_p^2 = .13$; Palestinians: $F(1, 419) = 146.27$, $p < .001$, $\eta_p^2 = .26$; Muslims: $F(1, 419) = 194.37$, $p < .001$, $\eta_p^2 = .32$; Iran: $F(1, 419) = 47.83$, $p < .001$, $\eta_p^2 = .10$. All four ANCOVA include seven standard demographic covariates. *Data source:* OU Institute for US-China Issues, 2011.

towards Palestinians.[12] Similarly, liberals reported feeling substantially more favorable towards the Palestinian people than conservatives did in a September 2011 CNN telephone poll.[13]

Broad ideological differences in warmth were matched by differences in specific emotions. As noted in Chapter 7's discussion of France, psychologist Susan Fiske's stereotype content model predicts that we will admire or take pride in social groups that we perceive as both friendly and competent, such as Christians or the middle class. But we will envy or resent powerful groups whose intentions we suspect, such as rich businesspeople.[14] Hypothesizing that all Americans would view Israel as a relatively powerful and competent country but would differ systematically by ideology in their warmth towards Israel, we included two additional items in our survey:

- *I feel admiration/respect towards Israel.*
- *I feel irritated/annoyed by Israel.*

As expected, conservatives greatly admired Israel and did not feel irritated by it; liberals, by contrast, were ambivalent, feeling neither admiration nor annoyance towards Israel. The ideological differences on both items were very large.[15]

In addition to the Israel and Iran items in our fifteen-country "much friendlier" to "much tougher" foreign policy rating scale, our 2011 survey included two specific Israel policy items:

- *The U.S. government should implement a more severe and uncompromising policy towards Israel.*
- *Our government should adopt a more supportive and obliging foreign policy towards Israel.* (reverse coded)

Averaged together, the three Israel policy items formed a robust scale.[16] American conservatives, it revealed, desired a vastly friendlier Israel policy—and a much tougher Iran policy—than liberals did.[17] This is consistent with other surveys. In the 2011 CNN telephone poll mentioned above, 53 percent of liberals favored *"the establishment of an independent Palestinian state on the West Bank and the Gaza Strip,"* while only 26 percent of conservatives did.[18] In a November 2011 CBS telephone poll, conservatives scored substantially higher than liberals on a four-point assessment of Israel, from "enemy" to "unfriendly" to "friendly but not an ally" to "ally."[19]

What best explains this consistent pattern of ideological differences in how Americans view the Middle East? This chapter will argue that while all four dimensions of American ideology contribute to liberal-conservative differences in feelings and policy preferences towards Israel, the Palestinians, Muslims, and Iran, it is differences in cultural and social ideology, along with nationalism, that matter the most. Differences in biblical literalism between cultural conservatives and cultural liberals contribute to their very different feelings and policy preferences towards both Israel and the Muslim world. And differences in social dominance orientation divide liberals and conservatives in their views of the Arab-Israeli conflict. A conservative morality of authority contributes to a view of Israel as the David and the surrounding Muslim world as the Goliath. Liberal moralities of compassion and justice, by contrast, contribute to a view of the Palestinians as the David resisting an oppressive Israeli Goliath. Finally, conservatives' greater nationalism contributes to greater conservative than liberal warmth towards Israel and desires for tougher Iran policies.

The chapter begins with a brief overview of the history of American engagement with Jews, Muslims, and the Middle East. It then turns to an analysis of our 2011 survey data, exploring how liberal-conservative differences on Israel policy are driven by differences in their feelings towards both Israel and the Palestinians, as well as differences in biblical literalism, libertarianism, and social dominance orientation. The final section explores how nationalism divides American liberals and conservatives in both their feelings towards Israel and their Iran policy preferences.

GENTILES, JEWS, AND MUSLIMS:
AMERICA'S EPIC ENCOUNTER WITH THE MIDDLE EAST

"We Americans are the peculiar, chosen people—the Israel of our time; we bear the ark of the liberties of the world."[20]

—Herman Melville, 1850

"The Egyptian, the Babylonian, and the Persian rose, filled the planet with sound and splendor, then faded to dream-stuff and passed away; the Greek and the Roman followed, and made a vast noise, and they are gone; other peoples have sprung up and held their torch high for a time, but it burned out, and they sit in twilight now, or have vanished. The Jew saw them all, beat them all, and is now what he always was, exhibiting no decadence, no infirmities of age, no weakening of his parts, no slowing of his energies, no dulling of his alert and aggressive mind. All things are mortal but the Jew; all other forces pass, but he remains. What is the secret of his immortality?"[21]

—Mark Twain, 1899

The first Jews to arrive in North America landed on Manhattan Island in September 1654. New Netherlands governor Peter Stuyvesant promptly declared the twenty-three immigrants "hateful enemies and blasphemers of the name of Christ." He then petitioned the Dutch West India Company for permission to deport them.[22]

The first president of the United States was more welcoming. "May the children of the stock of Abraham who dwell in this land continue to merit and enjoy the good will of the other inhabitants," George Washington declared to a Jewish leader in Newport, Rhode Island, in 1790. Washington also took the opportunity to champion both the freedom of religion and the separation of church and state: "The United States is not a Christian nation, any more than it is a Jewish or Mohammedan nation."[23]

Many Americans nonetheless came to view their revolution and national mission through the lens of the Christian Bible. King George of England was the Pharaoh of Egypt, and the American colonists were the "New Israel" triumphing—with divine assistance—over tyranny. For instance, in 1776 Benjamin Franklin proposed that the Great Seal of the new United States of America evoke Exodus and the story of the Israelites. With the motto "Rebellion to tyrants is obedience to God," it would depict Moses parting the Red Sea, saving the fleeing Israelites while drowning the Pharaoh and his pursing troops. As in the Old Testament, in the "New Israel" of the United States, liberty would defeat tyranny.

Gentile American ambivalence about the Jews in their midst intensified in the midnineteenth century with the arrival of new Jewish immigrants from Eastern Europe and Russia. Both anti-Semitism and biblical literalism shaped early views of Palestine. The 1878 publication of *Jesus Is Coming* launched Wil-

STOP YOUR CRUEL OPPRESSION OF THE JEWS
"Now that you have peace without, why not remove his burden and have peace within your borders?"

FIG. 8.2. Religious liberty and American compassion for the Jews, 1905.
Source: Emil Flohri, *Judge*, 1905. Image courtesy of the Library of Congress. LC-DIG-ppmsca-05438.

liam E. Blackstone's career as a prophet of the Second Coming and a Christian Zionist. But in his famous 1891 memorial to President Benjamin Harrison urging U.S. support for a Jewish homeland in Palestine, he began with a little-disguised appeal to the anti-Semitism of his fellow Gentile elites: "What shall be done for the Russian Jews?" asked Blackstone. Rather than assimilating them into America, "Why not give Palestine back to them?" Only then did he appeal to humanitarianism and the authority of the Bible, arguing that Palestine was the Jews' "inalienable possession, from which they were expelled by force." He closed his argument with an appeal to Christian guilt: "Let us now restore them to the land of which they were so cruelly despoiled by our Roman ancestors."[24]

In the twentieth century, Americans often viewed the plight of the Jews in Europe through the prism of religious liberty. At the turn of the century, the harassment of American Jews traveling in czarist Russia became a major diplomatic issue. In April 1904, the U.S. Congress approved a resolution calling upon the czar to respect U.S. citizens regardless of faith. Emil Flohri addressed the issue in the editorial cartoon "Stop Your Cruel Oppression of the Jews" for a 1905 *Judge* magazine (Figure 8.2). An old man with a long white beard wears a yarmulke. Labeled "Russian Jew," he strains under a large bundle labeled "Oppression" that he carries on his back. Weights added to his burden are labeled "Cruelty," "Autocracy," "Robbery," "Assassination," "Deception," and "Murder." A mother and daughter follow him, fleeing a burning village in the distance. U.S. president Theodore Roosevelt resolutely declares to the emperor of Russia, Nicholas II: "Now that you have peace without, why not remove his burden and have peace within your borders?"

American concerns for the Jews persisted during the Cold War. As noted in Chapter 4, Henry Kissinger's proposed rapprochement with the Soviet Union in 1973 was derailed when Senator Henry "Scoop" Jackson mobilized opposition to détente based upon the Soviet Union's continued persecution of Russian Jews.

Postwar changes in American Protestantism had a profound influence on evolving and diverging American views of Israel. In the first quarter century following World War II, the then dominant mainline and liberal Protestant denominations shifted from anti-Semitism to embracing Jews and support for Israel. For instance, Democratic president Harry Truman supported the creation of Israel out of humanitarianism. A devout Christian, Truman declared in 1945 that he could not "stand idly by while the victims of Hitler's madness were not allowed to build new lives. The Jews needed someplace where they could go."[25]

By the 1980s, however, the rise of Evangelical and fundamentalist Protestantism and the slow decline of mainline and liberal denominations fundamentally altered American views of Israel. The newly dominant conservative Protestantism was much more preoccupied with personal salvation and prophesy.[26] Taking heart in Israel's occupation of Jerusalem in the 1967 Six-Day War, Christian Zionists eagerly awaited the End of Days, refusing compromise on the newly occupied territories in the West Bank and Gaza.

American attitudes towards Muslims and the Arab world have an equally long lineage. Historian Andrew Preston argues that "The Puritans of colonial New England had thought of Muslims as a satanic force and the Ottoman empire as a hellish source of earthly evil."[27] Michael Oren suggests that attacks by the Barbary pirates of North Africa on American merchants in the Mediterranean helped motivate the newly independent Americans to convene a Constitutional Convention. The Articles of Confederation were no longer sufficient: a stronger federal government and a U.S. Navy were needed to defend American honor from Barbary affronts. Referring to "Algerian Corsairs and the Pirates of Tunis and Tripoli," New York's John Jay wrote that "The more we are ill-treated abroad the more we shall unite and consolidate at home." Though wary of federal power, James Madison argued during the Constitutional Convention itself that the United States required a navy, as "weakness will invite insults." Oren concludes that "A threat from the Middle East had played a concrete role in creating a truly *United* States, a consolidated nation capable of defending not only its borders at home but its vital economic interests overseas."[28]

American fears of Islam persisted long after the threat of the Barbary pirates had receded. Conservative Protestants tended to have an antagonistic relationship with Islam, seen as led by a rival and false prophet. For instance, at the turn of the century, Presbyterian missionary to India E. M. Wherry depicted Christianity as in an existential battle against the "Moslem peril," a battle that could only be won "with the Sword of the Spirit."[29] American liberals, by contrast, tended to view Islam as a threat to Enlightenment values and modernity. "Islam is intellectually stagnant, an ironic punishment for a religion which . . . for centuries carried the lamp of learning," *Time* magazine lamented in 1951. Islam had "deliberately turned its back upon reason as the enemy of faith."[30]

In his masterly 2007 ride through America's tumultuous history in the Middle East, *Power, Faith, and Fantasy*, Michael Oren argues that in the American imagination, Christian fears of Islam have long coexisted with a romance with both the Arab, seen as a fellow David fighting against the Goliath of colonial oppression, and the Arab world, seen as a land of forbidden pleasures. On the former, he cites Bentley, an American journalist in the 1962 film *Lawrence of Arabia*: "We Americans were once a colonial people and we naturally feel sympathetic to any people, anywhere, who are struggling for their freedom." On the latter, he cites the popular 1970s song "Midnight at the Oasis," sung by the sensuous Maria Muldaur. "You won't need no harem, honey, when I'm by your side," she purred. "And you won't need no camel, no, no, when I take you for a ride."[31]

For many Americans, "Orientalist" fantasies about the Arab world were shattered with the Iranian Revolution and subsequent hostage crisis. Fifty-two American diplomats from the U.S. Embassy in Tehran were held captive for 444 days, from November 1979 to January 1981. "The actions of Iran have shocked the civilized world," President Jimmy Carter stated during a press conference on November 28, 1979. "For a government to applaud mob violence and terrorism . . . violates not only the most fundamental precepts of international law but the common ethical and religious heritage of humanity."[32] The Iran hostage crisis was one of the most widely covered stories in U.S. television history, rivaling Vietnam and Watergate. The nightly coverage highlighted the suffering of the U.S. diplomats and the fanaticism of Iran and Islam. Melani McAlister argues that this TV news coverage, along with subsequent movies like the 1986 Chuck Norris and Lee Marvin revenge fantasy *Delta Force*, cemented a link between terrorism, Iran, and Islam in the American imagination.[33]

THE SOURCES OF U.S. ISRAEL POLICY PREFERENCES

"To stand against Israel is to stand against God."[34]
—The Reverend Jerry Falwell, 1980

"I turn back to your ancient prophets in the Old Testament and the signs foretelling Armageddon, and I find myself wondering if—if we're the generation that's going to see that come about."[35]
—Republican President Ronald Reagan, 1983

Why do conservatives desire a vastly friendlier Israel policy than liberals do? Would feelings towards the Palestinian people and Muslims in general matter for the Israel policy preferences of the American people, or would they be overwhelmed by feelings towards Israel? A mediation analysis revealed that both feelings towards the Palestinians/Muslims *and* feelings towards Israel helped account for liberal-conservative differences on Israel policy. We then ran a pair of multiple mediation models in which our four dimensions of American ideology were used to account for the impact of broad liberal-conservative ideology on feelings towards these two groups. They revealed that cultural, economic, and political ideologies mediated the influence of ideology on feelings towards Israel, while cultural, social, and economic ideologies mediated the impact of ideology on feelings towards Muslims and the Palestinians, though the economic effect was quite small.

Why would cultural traditionalism help account for conservative *coolness* towards Muslims and the Palestinians and *warmth* towards Israel? As noted in Chapter 2, traditionalism was measured with three statements assessing attitudes towards nudity, sex, drugs, and alcohol. Our 2011 survey also measured biblical literalism:

- *The Bible is literally true, from Genesis to Revelation, from Adam and Eve to Armageddon.*
- *I have no doubt at all that God exists.*
- *Whenever science and scripture conflict, science is right.* (reverse coded)
- *The basic cause of evil in this world is Satan, who is still constantly & ferociously fighting against God.*

Participant assessments of these four statements cohered very well ($\alpha = .88$), and the resulting biblical literalism scale shared about half of its variance ($r = .71$; $R^2 = .50$) with traditionalism. But biblical literalism was a stronger mediator of the influence of ideology on feelings towards Israel than was traditionalism. It appears, therefore, that traditionalism mediated the relationship between ideology and feelings towards Israel not so much because of respondents' attitudes towards sex and drugs but because those higher or lower on traditionalism also tended to be higher or lower on biblical literalism.

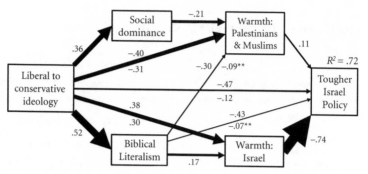

FIG. 8.3. The socio-racial and biblical sources of conservative coolness towards Palestinians and Muslims, warmth towards Israel, and desires for a friendlier Israel policy.

Note: A mixed multiple mediation model. ** $p < .01$, all other p's $\le .001$. Standardized β coefficients above an arrow indicate the unmediated relationship; those below an arrow reflect the inclusion of the mediator(s). With the exception of the two indirect paths via SDO only and via SDO and warmth towards Israel, all indirect paths were statistically significant. Indirect effect statistics are online at SUP.org. Policy and warmth towards Israel are both three-item scales (both $\alpha = .88$). Biblical literalism is a four-item scale ($\alpha = .88$), not including the Palestine item. Demographic covariates, none of which were statistically significant, are not shown. *Data source:* OU Institute for US-China Issues, 2011.

Figure 8.3 combines four of these mediators—feelings towards Israel and the Palestinians/Muslims, social dominance orientation, and biblical literalism—into a single mediation model. Remarkably, where liberal-conservative ideology alone accounted for 20 percent of the variance in Israel policy preferences in an unmediated model, the addition of these four mediators reduced its effect to just 1 percent.[36] So our four mediators account for 95 percent of ideology's massive influence on Israel policy preferences.

We begin with warmth towards Israel at the bottom right of Figure 8.3, which was by far the most powerful predictor ($\beta = -.74$) of Israel policy preferences. Given the affect heuristic discussed in Chapter 1, it is not surprising that feelings towards Israel strongly shape the policy preferences towards Israel of the American people.

Biblical literalism, bottom left, was associated with warmth towards Israel ($\beta = .17$). But it also had a direct influence on preferences for a friendlier Israel policy ($\beta = -.43$), even after controlling for warmth towards Israel ($\beta = -.07, p = .002$).

How should these two effects of biblical literalism be interpreted? The direct effect of biblical literalism on opposition to a tougher Israel policy seems best attributed to the Christian Zionist prophetic belief that Israel must hold on to the occupied territories to prepare for Christ's Second Coming. Israel's occupation of Jerusalem, the West Bank, and Gaza during the Six-Day War in

1967, Jerry Falwell avowed in 1988, is "the single greatest sign indicating the imminent return of Jesus Christ."[37] In his 2006 sensation *Jerusalem Countdown*, John Hagee similarly declares that "God's word is very clear! There will be grave consequences for the nation or nations that attempt to divide up the land of Israel."[38] Former Arkansas governor Mike Huckabee has been one of the most public and outspoken defenders of the Israeli settlements, arguing both that outsiders should not tell Israelis where they should live in their own country, and that Palestinians should settle in Arab countries outside of Israel.

Our 2011 survey included the item "*God gave Palestine (today's Israel) to the Jewish people.*" Not surprisingly, the degree of agreement with this statement accounted for 95 percent of the relationship between greater biblical literalism and opposition to a tougher Israel policy.[39] "Much of America's blessing as a nation can be traced to its benevolent treatment of the Jews and Israel," writes Pastor Mark Hitchcock of Faith Bible Church in Edmond, Oklahoma. But "if America continues on its current path and fails to bless the Jewish people, the final vestige of God's blessing on our nation could be withdrawn, and the end could come quickly—very quickly."[40] In *Allies for Armageddon*, Victoria Clark suggests that a fear of the "wrath of God" plays a major role in Christian Zionist support for Israel: "if America abandons Israel, then God will cancel America's Most Divinely Favored Nation status."[41]

But not all conservative Christians believe that the End of Days is imminent. They likely feel warmly towards Israel ($\beta = .17$; Figure 8.3, bottom center) out of gratitude, remorse, or desires for personal salvation. Gratitude and love stem from a deep sense of religious affinity. "Christians and Jews are united," John Hagee proclaimed at AIPAC in 2007. "We are indivisible, we are bound together by the Torah—the roots of Christianity are Jewish. We are spiritual brothers."[42] Mike Huckabee was even more effusive during a trip to Israel in 2010. "I worship a Jew!" Huckabee proclaimed. "I have a lot of Jewish friends, and they're kind of, like, 'You evangelicals love Israel more than we do.' I'm, like, 'Do you not get it? If there weren't a Jewish faith, there wouldn't be a Christian faith!'"[43]

Guilt also contributes to conservative Christian warmth towards Israel. Christianity scholar Stephen Spector reports that his "evangelical informants repeatedly expressed their deep remorse for the Church's abuse of Jews in the name of Christ." In this view, Martin Luther was an anti-Semite, and the Church was complicit in the Holocaust. In his 1973 *The Promised Land: The Future of Israel Revealed in Prophesy*, radio Bible teacher Derek Prince repented that "the Nazis merely reaped a harvest that the Church had sown."[44] John Hagee's 2006 *Jerusalem Countdown* similarly contains several contrite chapters chronicling Christian anti-Semitism. "For centuries, the Jews have been beaten, murdered, robbed, and raped while fanatics have screamed, 'You are the Christ killers!'"[45]

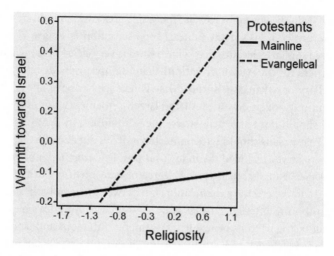

FIG. 8.4. Among American Protestants, religiosity dramatically increases warmth towards Israel, but only for those of Evangelical denominations.

Note: A moderation analysis. Interaction $\Delta R^2 = .01$, $F(1, 468) = 5.97$, $p = .015$. The positive slope for Evangelical Protestants was statistically significant: $B = .32$, $p < .001$; the slope for mainline Protestants was not: $B = .02$, $p = .82$. Religiosity = frequency of (1) church attendance, (2) prayer, and (3) importance of religion. *Data source:* OU Institute for US-China Issues, 2011.

Biblical literalism may also contribute to Christian conservative warmth towards Israel out of a more self-interested desire for God's blessings. In Genesis 12:3, the Lord says to Abram, "I will bless those who bless you, and I will curse him who curses you." The desire for personal salvation likely contributes to Christian warmth towards Israel. "God promised long ago that those who bless Abraham and his descendants will be blessed, and those who curse them will be cursed," writes Oklahoma pastor Mark Hitchcock.[46] The 2012 "Texas GOP Platform" opposes "pressuring Israel to make concessions it believes would jeopardize its security, including the trading of land for the recognition of its right to exist." Why? The Platform is explicit: "Our policy is based on God's biblical promise to bless those who bless Israel and curse those who curse Israel."[47]

As noted in Chapter 2, *religiosity*—the frequency and importance of religious practice—is conceptually distinct from the set of beliefs that is *biblical literalism*. But they are highly intercorrelated ($r = .71$), and they correlate similarly with feelings towards Israel ($r = .33, .32$). However, when set against each other, biblical literalism accounts for almost twice the variance in feelings towards Israel than religiosity does.[48] What best accounts for this pattern? A moderation analysis revealed that among Protestants the influence of religiosity on warmth towards Israel depends upon denomination (Figure 8.4). Greater religiosity was only associated with increased warmth towards Israel among Protestants of

Evangelical denominations. Greater frequency of church attendance or prayer had no effect on feelings towards Israel among Protestants of mainline or liberal denominations; hence, the stronger influence of biblical literalism. In other words, the kind of church an American Protestant attends has powerful implications for his or her feelings towards Israel.

Although greater average biblical literalism accounted for some of why conservatives felt warmer towards Israel than liberals did, it did not account for all of it. How should we interpret the substantial remaining direct relationship ($\beta = .30$) between conservatism and warmth towards Israel? Although not included in Figure 8.3, to reduce clutter, greater libertarianism (political ideology) also mediated the relationship between conservatism and warmth towards Israel. Many conservatives follow Benjamin Franklin in viewing America as the New Israel, not so much in religious terms as in the political terms of freedom triumphing over tyranny. House majority leader Tom DeLay emphasized this libertarian theme in a remarkable speech to the Israeli Knesset on July 30, 2003:

> I stand before you today, in solidarity, as an Israeli of the heart. The solidarity between the United States and Israel is deeper than the various interests we share. It goes to the very nature of man, to the endowment of our God-given rights to life, liberty and the pursuit of happiness. It is the universal solidarity of freedom. It transcends geography, culture and generations. It is the solidarity of all people—in all times—who dream of and sacrifice for liberty. It is the solidarity of Moses and Lincoln. Of Tiananmen Square and the Prague Spring. Of Andrei Sakharov and Anne Frank.[49]

To DeLay, a Manichean view of freedom against tyranny appears to provide an overarching libertarian framework to understand the entire world and its history. With Israel firmly lodged on the side of liberty, there can be no doubt about where his loyalties lie. Mike Huckabee has similarly argued that "Even if there was nothing about eschatology involved, the reason this [Israel], as an American, matters to me is because freedom and liberty matter to me." For conservatives like Huckabee, support for Israel is driven by multiple dimensions of his ideological profile.

Many American liberals, by contrast, question whether Israel really is a David fighting heroically against an Arab Goliath. With the 1967 Six-Day War and the Israeli occupation of the West Bank and Gaza, liberals now often suggest that the Israeli David has become a Goliath oppressing the Palestinian people in the occupied territories. Bill Mauldin captured this liberal view of Israel in a 1978 cartoon entitled "Endangered Species" (Figure 8.5). It depicts two birds in hats labeled "Israel's doves." The olive branches they hold in their beaks are wilting. With Israeli successes in the 1967 and 1973 wars, Israeli pacifists were

ENDANGERED SPECIES

FIG. 8.5. David no more: A liberal view of Israel as Goliath, 1978.
Source: Copyright Bill Mauldin, 1978. Courtesy of the Bill Mauldin Estate LLC.

approaching extinction. "To me the great charm of the Israelis when I was there before, during, and after the Six Day War was that they disliked militarism but knew how to handle it," Mauldin later wrote. "I wondered if eventually all those wars might turn them into Spartans. To a degree it seems to have happened."[50] Greater liberal than conservative coolness towards Israel may in part be due to a view that Israelis have changed from doves into hawks.

BIBLICAL LITERALISM AND FEELINGS TOWARDS ISRAEL AND THE PALESTINIANS

"The first thing, then, which the Lord will do, will be to purify His land (the land which belongs to the Jews) of the Tyrians, the Philistines the Sidonians—of all the wicked, in short, from the Nile to the Euphrates."[51]
—John Darby, 1840

Figure 8.3 revealed that biblical literalism predicts not just warmth towards Israel ($\beta = .17$) but also coolness towards the Palestinians ($\beta = -.30$). Figure 8.6 depicts the relationship between biblical literalism and feelings towards Israel and the Palestinians by American religious group. The two lines represent how coolly or warmly each religious group feels towards Israel and the Palestinians.

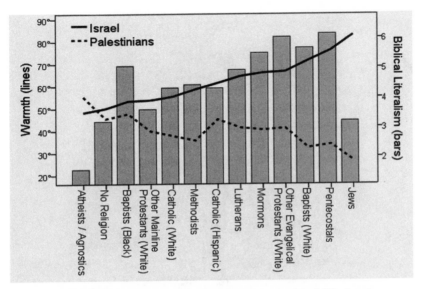

FIG. 8.6. Biblical literalism (bars) and feelings towards Israel (solid line) and
the Palestinians (dashed line) by American religious group: Jews and Evangelical
Protestants feel the warmest towards Israel and the coolest towards the Palestinians;
atheists and nonreligious Americans are the most ambivalent towards both groups.

Note: Israel: $F(12, 789) = 7.45, p < .001, \eta_p^2 = .088$; Palestinians: $F(12, 789) = 5.09, p < .001, \eta_p^2$
$= .062$; biblical literalism (four-item scale, $\alpha = .88$): $F(12, 890) = 43.48, p < .001, \eta_p^2 = .37$. All
ANCOVA control for seven standard demographics. Survey ($N = 1,050$) oversamples Jews and
Mormons. *Data source:* OU Institute for US-China Issues, 2011.

The bars represent each group's mean level of biblical literalism. The sequence
of religious groups is in ascending left-to-right order of warmth towards Israel;
atheists and those Americans claiming no religion are first, and Evangelical
Christians and American Jews, last.

The value added in Figure 8.6 over Figure 8.3 is that the former simultane-
ously displays the general pattern of the polarizing influence of biblical literalism on feelings towards Israel and the Palestinians of Americans of different
religious groups, on one hand, and the outliers to the pattern, on the other. For
example, American Jews (at the far right) are a clear exception to the rule. Not
surprisingly, they feel the warmest of all religious groups towards Israel and the
coolest of all towards the Palestinians—even though they score as low on our
biblical literalism scale (which included an item on Revelation from the New
Testament) as those Americans who report no religion at all.

At the opposite extreme, atheists, agnostics, and those Americans reporting
no religion are not just the coolest towards Israel of all religious groups but also
the warmest towards the Palestinians. They appear to be "religion blind," refus-

"Do I detect a Middle Eastern accent?"

FIG. 8.7. Secular liberals disregard cultural/religious differences, 2001.
Source: Robert Weber, *New Yorker,* July 23, 2001. Image courtesy of the Cartoon Bank.

ing to allow religious or cultural differences to shape their views of Israel or the Palestinians. Robert Weber mocks this secular American position in a 2001 cartoon for the *New Yorker* (Figure 8.7). A Caucasian American man wearing a suit is at an outdoor cocktail party. He faces a woman covered in a head-to-toe burka, with only her eyes peeking out, and asks, "Do I detect a Middle Eastern Accent?" Weber is poking fun at liberals for their willful blindness to cultural and religious differences. The cartoon is particularly poignant, as it was published just a month and a half before the September 11 terrorist attacks on New York City and Washington, D.C.

By contrast, Figure 8.6 also reveals that Pentecostals, white Baptists, and other white Evangelical Protestants are the highest on biblical literalism *and* display the largest gaps (with the exception of American Jews) between their warmth towards Israel and their coolness towards Palestinians. As the epigraph from John Darby, the father of modern dispensationalism, suggests, prophesy-writers have long identified Muhammad and Islam with the Gog and Magog of the Bible, contributing to conservative Protestant prejudice against Arabs and Palestinians.

More recently, Florida pastor Terry Jones has given voice to Evangelical Protestant hostility towards Islam. By burning a Koran and provoking Muslim violence, and promoting slogans like "Everything I need to know about Islam, I learned on 9–11," Jones has sought to link Islam with violence and terrorism. Other conservative Christians have similarly expressed deep skepticism about the "Arab Spring," which first erupted in Tunisia in late 2010. In his 2012 *Middle East Burning*, Evangelical pastor Mark Hitchcock writes that "It's likely that the Arab awakening will be hijacked and exploited by murderous Islamists and jihadists who are more oppressive and dangerous than the despots they replace."[52]

Race is an outlier that Figure 8.6 highlights. White and black Baptists do not differ in their average religiosity, and white Baptists score just slightly higher than black Baptists on biblical literalism.[53] But there are large differences in their feelings towards the Middle East. White Baptists (71°) feel 17° warmer than black Baptists (54°) towards Israel, while black Baptists (47°) feel 15° warmer than white Baptists (32°) towards the Palestinian people, both medium-large differences statistically.[54]

Race appears to drive this difference in black and white Baptist feelings towards the Palestinians. We created a composite variable of mean feelings towards the eleven non-white countries in our 2011 survey. Added to the standard demographics as another control variable, feelings towards these colored countries reduced the 15° difference between white and black Baptists on feelings towards the Palestinian people to zero.[55] In other words, if we could remove their different feelings about colored countries, black and white Baptists would feel similarly cool (38°) towards the Palestinians. As anthropologist Melani McAlister argues in *Epic Encounters*, racial politics at home has powerfully shaped how black and white Americans understand the Middle East.[56]

The same is true of the small but statistically significant 6° difference between white Catholic (38°) and Hispanic Catholic (44°) feelings towards the Palestinian people, also displayed in Figure 8.6.[57] When feelings towards colored countries is added to the analysis as a control variable, the difference between white (39°) and Hispanic (40°) Catholics is reduced to a statistically nonsignificant 1°.[58] Race matters for American views of the Middle East.

ISRAEL AND THE PALESTINIANS: DAVID AND GOLIATH?

"It will be a tragedy—for the Israelis, the Palestinians, and the world—if peace is rejected and a system of oppression, apartheid, and sustained violence is permitted to prevail."[59]

—Former Democratic President Jimmy Carter, 2006

"As you travel through the West Bank, you get a sense of the differences between life for Palestinians and Israelis in this region. Palestinians have to suffer through the checkpoint system, the barriers, the fenced-in wall that exists just to get to their job, often times to travel from north and south even within the West Bank. It's created enormous hardship for them."[60]

—Senator Barack Obama (Democrat–Illinois), 2006

The top left corner of Figure 8.3 reveals that another reason that American conservatives feel cooler than liberals do towards the Palestinians and Muslims is because of their greater average social dominance orientation (SDO), the desire that *"Inferior groups should stay in their place."* This finding replicates the work of social psychologists who have also found, with American samples, that greater SDO predicts greater prejudice against Muslims.[61]

Chapter 3 argued that differing moral psychologies partially account for liberal-conservative differences in SDO (see Figure 3.4). Conservatives value authority more than liberals do, contributing to their greater desire for group dominance. Liberals, by contrast, value justice and compassion more than conservatives do, contributing to their greater opposition to social dominance and greater support for the equality of racial and social groups.

Conservatives feel cooler than liberals do towards the Palestinians and Muslims, in part because they are more sensitive to threats to authority and social order. Harvard sociologist Theda Skocpol and her colleague Vanessa Williamson attended local Tea Party meetings in Massachusetts, Virginia, and Arizona in 2010 and 2011, and concluded that the dominant sentiment was fear. "A sense of 'us versus them' along racial and ethnic fault lines clearly marks the worldview of many people active in the Tea Party," Skocpol and Williamson write. "Fear and hatred of Islam and Muslims were commonly expressed."[62]

Some politicians have sought to harness this widespread conservative fear of Islam. "We have been under attack by the irreconcilable wing of Islam since the Iranians illegally seized our embassy in 1979," Newt Gingrich wrote in his 2010 *To Save America*. "For thirty-one years our enemies have been plotting and maneuvering to kill us. Time is not on our side. We have to defeat them decisively before they acquire weapons that could destroy our very civilization."[63] From this conservative perspective, the Israelis are in the front line of a battle to keep the Palestinians and other Muslims from upsetting the global pecking order. If the Israelis need to rule the occupied territories with an iron fist to maintain law and order, so be it.

Gingrich actually builds on a conservative tradition of viewing Israel as a model for the forceful response to perceived Muslim threat that dates to the late 1960s—not just 1979. The 1967 Six-Day War thrilled American conservatives, not just because of biblical prophecy but also because of Israel's remarkable military victory. In the late 1960s, conservatives celebrated Israeli military successes as a way to counter the antiwar movement at home. Melani McAlister argues that after Vietnam, "Israel and its military played a key symbolic role for those who advocated the remilitarization of U.S. policy."[64] For instance, conservative hawks could bask in the reflected glory of the dramatic Israeli rescue of over one hundred Israeli hostages in Entebbe, Uganda, in July 1976. Walter Russell Mead similarly argues that following the 1967 war, "Jacksonian" conservatives—nationalists favoring a strong military—formed a negative view of Arabs as terrorists and a positive view of Israeli uses of overwhelming force.[65]

By contrast, the greater value that liberals place on compassion and fairness contributes to their opposition to what they view as Israeli domination over the Palestinians in the occupied territories. Compassion is displayed in the second epigraph as Barack Obama speaks of the suffering and hardship of the Palestinian people living in the West Bank. And justice is frequently invoked by liberals seeking a more balanced policy towards the Palestinian question. "If we Americans are to be successful peace brokers, we have to be as sensitive toward Arab concerns and aspirations as we are to the Israelis," George McGovern wrote in 2011. "I believe it is in the best interest of America for us to be equally fair to the Israelis and the Arabs."[66]

For some liberals, the prolonged Israeli occupation of the West Bank and Gaza and ongoing settlement activity make the Israelis as bad as Palestinian terrorists. Herblock captured this liberal view in a 1994 cartoon for the *Washington Post* (Figure 8.8). It depicts two similarly gruff and battle-hardened men carrying smoking machine guns. The only difference between them is that one is labeled "Israeli fanatics" while the other is labeled "Palestinian terrorists." Entitled "Blood Brothers," it is a clear statement of moral condemnation.

But it is former president Jimmy Carter who best expressed liberal unease with Israeli treatment of the Palestinians in his highly controversial 2006 book *Palestine: Peace Not Apartheid*. As noted in the epigraph, Carter views the situation in the West Bank and Gaza as "a system of oppression, apartheid, and sustained violence." He later explained that "I intended the word *apartheid* to describe a situation where two peoples dwelling on the same land are forcibly segregated from each other, and one group dominates the other."[67] Like Carter, many liberals oppose such group dominance, contributing to their greater relative warmth towards the Palestinians (see top of Figure 8.3).

Jimmy Carter is certainly not alone. Mainline Protestant denominations have begun protesting Israeli treatment of the Palestinians. In 2004, during the second Palestinian intifada, the General Assembly of the Presbyterian Church voted 413–62 to divest from multinational corporations doing business in Israel. Methodists and Episcopalians soon followed suit. More recently, on October 5, 2012, fifteen mainline Protestant leaders sent a letter to Congress claiming that U.S. aid to Israel was in violation of U.S. foreign aid laws concerning hu-

BLOOD BROTHERS

FIG. 8.8. Israelis and Palestinians: A liberal view of moral equivalence, 1994.
Source: A 1994 Herblock Cartoon, © The Herb Block Foundation.

man rights violations. "As Christian leaders in the United States, it is our moral responsibility to question the continuation of unconditional U.S. financial assistance to the government of Israel."[68]

LIBERALS, CONSERVATIVES, AND IRAN'S NUCLEAR WEAPONS PROGRAM

"The red line is now, because the Iranians now are deepening their fortifications, deepening their underground laboratories, deepening their commitment to nuclear weapons while we talk."[69]

—Republican presidential candidate Newt Gingrich, 2012

"Let's just stop throwing the word 'war' around so casually."[70]

—Senate majority leader Harry Reid (Democrat–Nevada), 2012

Iran was a major issue in the lead-up to the 2008 presidential election. Speaking in January 2007 at the Herzliya Conference in Israel, Republican presidential primary candidate Mitt Romney declared that "It is time for the world to speak three truths: (1) Iran must be stopped; (2) Iran can be stopped; (3) Iran will be stopped!"[71] Iran was also center stage at the annual AIPAC conference back in Washington, D.C., just two months later. "Iran poses a threat to the State of Israel that promises nothing less than a nuclear holocaust," asserted John Hagee of Christians United for Israel (CUFI). "Iran is Germany and Ahmadinejad is the new Hitler."[72]

Iran returned as an even bigger issue in the 2012 presidential election, when many politicians reenacted their earlier roles in the political theater. The Republican primary contenders competed to be seen as the most hawkish on Iran. Rick Santorum accused President Obama of engaging in "appeasement." Mitt Romney told the March 2012 AIPAC meeting that "the only thing respected by thugs and tyrants is our resolve, backed by our power and our readiness to use it." Newt Gingrich, whose campaign was largely funded by the pro-Israel billionaire Sheldon Adelson, argued that the time for talk was over: Iran's nuclear program should be attacked now (see epigraph).

Democrats fought back, accusing Republicans of saber rattling and politicizing national security. "Distorting the president's position and needlessly dividing Americans on a critical national security question may score political points with some, but it doesn't serve the national interest," declared Democratic senator Jack Reed of Rhode Island on March 5, 2012.[73] And as the second epigraph reveals, Senator Harry Reid sought to paint the Republican presidential contenders as reckless warmongers who would drag the American people into another war in the Middle East.

The American debate over Iran policy reaches well beyond Washington. Alarmed by "increasingly inflammatory rhetoric that could spark military action and war against Iran," in July 2012 a coalition of Oklahomans raised money to pay for three antiwar billboards in Oklahoma City, in the heart of the Bible Belt (Figure 8.9). "Americans Against the Next War" included Oklahomans from both the left and the right. "We are especially concerned that a constant state of war now seems normal to a whole generation of Americans," said Nathaniel Batchelder, director of Peace House in Oklahoma City. "The same people who were cheerleading for the Iraq War are now fear-mongering about the threat from Iran," said Katherine Scheirman, a retired U.S. Air Force colonel. "I agree with Ron Paul who said that the threat to U.S. national security is not Iran, but endless wars."[74]

What can our 2011 survey data tell us about the Iran policy preferences of the American people? Why did conservatives desire a much tougher Iran policy than liberals did? Given that Iran's nuclear program is a potential threat to both Israel and the United States, we were interested to see whether American na-

FIG. 8.9. Middle East policy debated in the heartland: Oklahoma City billboard, October 25, 2012.

Source: Photo courtesy of the author.

tionalism and feelings towards Israel would be sources of Iran policy preferences. Figure 8.10 depicts the results of a statistical analysis in which nationalism and feelings towards Israel sequentially mediate the relationship between ideology and desires for a tougher Iran policy, accounting for 80 percent of the direct relationship.[75] Conservatives desired a tougher Iran policy than liberals did, in part because they were more nationalistic, in part because they felt warmer towards Israel, and in part because their greater nationalism contributed to greater warmth towards Israel.

In political psychology, patriotism is understood and operationalized as the internally oriented love of country, while nationalism is the externally oriented belief in the superiority of one's country over other countries. In Chapter 4 we saw that only nationalism and not patriotism accounts for the greater conservative than liberal preference for tougher overall foreign policies (see Figure 4.9). It is not surprising, therefore, that Figure 8.10 reveals that nationalism as an American kicks in ($\beta = .32$) when confronted by the threat that Iran poses to American superiority. Indeed, of the fifteen countries that we measured foreign policy preferences towards, nationalism as an American correlated the strongest with Iran ($r = .38$), likely seen as the greatest threat to the United States.[76]

Given the centrality of Israel to the Iran policy debate among American elites, it is not surprising that warmth towards Israel also mediated the relationship between ideology and Iran policy preferences. When Senator Joe Lieberman told AIPAC in 2012 that "The United States will prevent Iran from

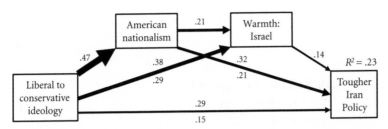

FIG. 8.10. Greater nationalism and warmth towards Israel help account for greater conservative than liberal desires for a tougher Iran policy.

Note: A serial mediation model. All three indirect paths were statistically significant. Indirect effect statistics are online at SUP.org. Warmth towards Israel is a three-item scale ($\alpha = .88$). Seven demographic covariates are not shown. *Data source:* OU Institute for US-China Issues, 2011.

acquiring a nuclear-weapons capability, by peaceful means if we can, but with military force if we absolutely must," he was representing the views of many of his fellow Jewish Americans. "As an American Jew who has children and grandchildren living in Israel, I have seen firsthand the threat that the people of Israel face from their Middle East neighbors," Harvey Caras wrote in a March 12, 2012, letter to *USA Today*. "Obama has done nothing to earn the trust of Israelis or American Jews." Of course, the feelings towards Israel of Gentile elites from Mike Huckabee to Jimmy Carter also find their analogues in Protestant American discourse on Israel.

Of the three indirect paths in Figure 8.10, perhaps the most interesting is the longest one running from ideology to nationalism ($\beta = .47$) to feelings towards Israel ($\beta = .21$) to Iran policy ($\beta = .14$). As noted in Chapter 7, nationalism as an American only correlated *positively* with warmth towards two of our fifteen foreign countries, England ($r = .11$) and Israel ($r = .30$). Given that nationalism correlated *negatively* with warmth towards eleven other countries, this finding demands explanation.[77] A multiple mediation model reveals that the cultural, economic, and libertarian dimensions of American ideology all mediate the substantial positive relationship between American nationalism and warmth towards Israel.[78] Not surprisingly, the effect of cultural ideology was the largest, and is likely best interpreted by the cultural affinity that many American Christians feel towards Israel and Judaism, leading them to incorporate Israel into their Christian nationalism. Indeed, Israeli flags often hang side by side with U.S. flags at many Christian Zionist events. The mediating role of libertarianism, for its part, is likely best interpreted by the widespread view of America as a New Israel. As Tom DeLay's passionate 2003 speech to the Israeli Knesset quoted above suggests, many Americans internalize Israel into their view of America as a David fighting for freedom against the Goliath of tyranny. For both cultural and political conservatives, in short, nationalism as an American contributes to warmth towards Israel and desires for tougher Iran policies.[79]

CONCLUSION: THE ISRAEL LOBBY AND THE ELECTORAL CONNECTION

"The so-called Israel lobby succeeds in Washington for exactly the same reason that Mothers Against Drunk Driving has succeeded in their lobbying: because it has public opinion on their side."[80]
—Congressman Steve Rothman (Democrat–New Jersey), 2008

"I believe it is vitally important that we cast our ballots for candidates who base their decisions on biblical principles and support the nation of Israel."[81]
—The Reverend Billy Graham, 2012

This chapter has argued that American liberals and conservatives differ substantially in their feelings and foreign policy preferences towards the Middle East. Conservatives feel warmer towards Israel but cooler towards Iran, the Palestinians, and Muslims, more broadly, than liberals do.

It has further argued that these differences have their origins in many of the same ideological fissures that cleave domestic American politics. The same culture wars that divide Americans on abortion, gay marriage, and prayer in public schools also divide them over Israel, Iran, and the Palestinians. For instance, our 2011 survey reveals that biblical literalism is a powerful predictor of both opposition to abortion ($\beta = .62$) and warmth towards Israel ($\beta = .36$). Similarly, the racial politics that has divided Americans from the civil rights movement of the 1960s to the affirmative action battles of today also divides liberals and conservatives in their feelings towards Palestinians and Muslims. Conservatives tend to view them as threats to both Christianity and established authorities, while liberals have a greater tendency to view their plight in the West Bank and Gaza as analogous to segregation or even apartheid, triggering moralities of compassion and social justice. Finally, the same nationalism that divides Americans on flag burning and defense spending also divides them over Iran policy.

What are the policy implications of the polarizing influence of ideology on American attitudes towards the Middle East? Because America is a democracy and its elected leaders are accountable to their constituents, the "electoral connection" ensures that American public opinion is a vital driver of U.S. foreign policy.[82] I thus agree with Walter Russell Mead, first in that John Mearsheimer and Stephen Walt are too reductionist in their narrow focus on American Jews and AIPAC as drivers of U.S. Middle East policy, and second that greater attention should be paid to the role of broader American opinion, especially that of the Christian majority.

But Michael Koplow goes too far, not just when he argues that American opinion on Israel is uniformly positive but also when he promotes the influence of public opinion to the exclusion of other sources of U.S. policy towards the Middle East, asserting, for instance, that "pro-Israel lobbying does not drive policy decisions."[83] A more nuanced understanding of U.S. Middle East policy must be multicausal, including public opinion, vital lobbying groups like AIPAC, CUFI, and J Street, as well as the roles of individual politicians (e.g., Tom DeLay, Newt Gingrich), media personalities (Mike Huckabee), religious leaders (Jerry Falwell, John Hagee), and even campaign donors (Sheldon Adelson). Thomas Friedman was on to something when he wrote in a March 2012 *New York Times* column that "The Israel lobby—both its Jewish and evangelical Christian wings—has never been more influential." But that is not just "because of its ability to direct campaign contributions to supportive candidates."[84] It is also, this chapter argues, because of the "electoral connection": politicians cater to the citizens who vote for them.

The influence of American opinion on Israel policy, however, is not uniform. Due to gerrymandering and the ongoing ideological sorting of the American electorate, very few congressional races today are competitive. The only challenge most incumbents face comes from potential primary challengers *within their own party*. As a result, the "electoral connection" does *not* mean that politicians heed the opinions of their average constituent. Instead, politicians seek the support of their primary voters, usually the ideological extremes of their parties.

A similar dynamic also plays out in presidential elections. During the 2008 and 2012 Republican primaries, most candidates sought to portray themselves as strongly pro-Israel to appeal to highly conservative primary voters, who, this chapter has argued, are extremely pro-Israel. It is not surprising, therefore, that Mitt Romney was extremely pro-Israel and hawkish on Iran during the 2012 Republican primaries. Romney later tacked back to the center during the third and final presidential debate on foreign policy, however. At that point, Romney was competing with President Obama for undecided voters in the center. By stating that he supported sanctions against Iran, Romney hoped to neutralize Obama's argument that Romney and the Republicans were warmongers who would lead the country into a war with Iran.

More difficult to explain is why Democratic elites have been pulled so far to the right on Middle East policy. The Chicago Council's 2008 survey data reveals that liberals then (50°) felt 17° cooler towards Israel than conservatives did (67°), differences consistent with our 2011 and their 2010 survey data.[85] So if Democratic primary voters were ambivalent in their feelings towards Israel, why didn't we hear more from the 2008 Democratic primary candidates about a more balanced approach to resolving the Arab-Israeli issue?

It could be that the more ambivalent nature of liberal opinion on Israel makes it harder for lobbying groups like J Street and politicians like Jimmy Carter and George McGovern to mobilize liberal support for a two-state solution. But other factors could play a role as well. Jews, while a tiny portion of the U.S. population overall, represent a larger proportion of the much smaller pool of Democratic primary voters, especially in swing states like Florida. American Jews also represent a surprisingly large percentage of Democratic campaign volunteers and donors.[86]

Mearsheimer and Walt's real gripe is not with the existence of an Israel lobby but with the dominance of its right wing, with CUFI and AIPAC lining up behind Likud and right-wing Israelis.[87] They would prefer J Street and other, more liberal elements of the Israel lobby to predominate, enabling a two-state solution that they believe would ease tensions in the Middle East and thus serve the U.S. national interest. By demonstrating that American opinion on the Middle East is divided along ideological lines, I hope that this chapter has shown that the dominance of the right wing of the Israel lobby today does not represent the subversion of the democratic process by an elite few, but is instead the natural product of an American electoral system that caters to the extreme ends of Main Street.

9 East Asia: Red China, Free Asia, and the Yellow Peril

"The plight of the people of Tibet is a challenge to the conscience of the world. The United States must be prepared to confront the Chinese government when they violate the human rights of their people."[1]

—Speaker of the House Nancy Pelosi (Democrat–California), 2008

"It is time to hold the Chinese government accountable for failing to match its peaceful rhetoric with its robust military spending and belligerent behavior, manipulating currency, violating the human rights of its own people, sending our citizens toxic drywall, and standing in the way of peaceful solutions on a range of issues from growing tension in Iran to violence in Syria."[2]

—Congressman Randy Forbes (Republican–Virginia), 2012

Both the Democratic and Republican Parties are internally divided over China. On the left, some Democrats argue for a pro-China policy of engagement to better integrate China into the global economic, political, and security orders. Other Democrats, concerned about human rights issues, advocate for tougher China policies. For instance, California congresswoman Nancy Pelosi, quoted above, has been a frequent critic of Chinese human rights abuses. Yet other Democrats on Capitol Hill, many from heavily blue collar districts, join Big Labor in condemning unfair Chinese trade practices and advocating tougher U.S. trade policies towards China.

On the right, Republicans in Washington are equally divided on China policy. Business conservatives have historically promoted a friendlier China policy conducive to increased trade, investment, and profits. For instance, the U.S.-China Business Council and AmCham China, which lobby on behalf of U.S. companies doing business with China, have worked closely with many Republicans on the Hill to support pro-China and block anti-China legislation. Military hawks and Christian conservatives, however, usually argue for tougher China policies. Congressman Randy Forbes of Virginia, quoted in the epigraph, serves on the House Armed Services Committee and cochairs the House's China Caucus, and frequently promotes tougher positions on China. New Jersey congressman Christopher Smith, who has held dozens of hearings on Capitol Hill to deplore China's lack of religious freedoms, has also advocated a tougher U.S. China policy, but for very different reasons. "China's continued repression of religion is among the most despotic in the world," Smith, a Christian conservative who founded the

House Pro-Life Caucus, argues. "Today, numerous underground Roman Catholic priests and bishops and Protestant pastors languish in the infamous concen-
tration camps of China for simply proclaiming the Gospel of Jesus Christ."[3]

If Democratic and Republican Party elites are internally divided over China,
are Main Street liberals and conservatives also internally divided? If so, do the
China policy preferences of the left and right simply wash out?

In their 2010 *Living with the Dragon: How the American Public Views the Rise
of China*, political scientists Benjamin Page and Tao Xie repeatedly claim that
individual differences like ideology have "little impact" on the China attitudes
of the American public. Americans, they assert, share the same basic views of
China.[4]

The survey data suggests otherwise. This chapter argues that ideology has
a substantial influence on the China and broader Asia attitudes of the American people. In our spring 2011 survey, the average American felt cool (35°)
towards China (see Figure 0.3), but the average conservative (22°) felt a full
18° cooler towards China than the average liberal (40°) did (see Figure 0.4), a
large difference statistically.[5] By contrast, Americans felt substantially warmer
towards the East Asian democracies of Taiwan (49°), South Korea (50°), and
Japan (60°), with conservatives feeling just 6°, 6°, and 8° cooler than liberals did towards each.[6] These results are largely consistent with those from the
Chicago Council's 2010 global views survey, Pew's 2010 global attitudes survey,
and a 2011 CNN poll.[7]

What's more, the large ideological cleavage on feelings towards China has
policy consequences. In addition to the "China" item in our 1–7 "much friendlier" to "much tougher" rating scale of foreign policy preferences towards fifteen countries, we included two additional 1–7 "strongly disagree" to "strongly
agree" items in our survey:

- *The best way to deal with China is to build up our military to counter
  Chinese power.*
- *The U.S. government should pursue a tougher China policy.*

The resulting three-item scale revealed that on average, conservatives desired a
great deal tougher China policy than liberals did.[8]

This chapter seeks to understand the sources of these substantial ideological
differences among Americans on China and Asia policy. It begins with a brief
review of the history of America's encounter with the "Orient" and "Orientals,"
both at home and abroad. It then disaggregates "China" into the "Chinese people" and the "Chinese government," exploring two distinct pathways to China
policy preferences. Conservatives desire a tougher China policy than liberals
do, in small part because, on average, they maintain slightly more prejudicial

attitudes towards Asians in general and the Chinese in particular. However, in larger part conservatives desire a tougher China policy than liberals do because on average they maintain much more negative attitudes towards communist countries in general and the Chinese government in particular. The chapter then turns to a closer examination of how all four dimensions of American ideology that we measured in our 2011 survey contribute to ideological polarization over China. For instance, cultural conservatives and libertarians may disagree over what they most dislike about China, but they can agree that they dislike China more than liberals do.

While internal ideological predispositions are powerful predictors of China attitudes, the external social world matters too (see Chapter 5). The chapter then explores how variations in social experiences, like travel, direct contacts with Chinese, and media exposure shape the China attitudes of the American people. Not all people respond to the same situations in the same ways: ideological predispositions can interact with situational variables to produce different China attitudes.

The chapter then turns to a brief comparative exploration of how ideology shapes American feelings towards the East Asian democracies of Japan, South Korea, and Taiwan. As was the case with China, slightly greater prejudice against "Orientals" contributes to greater average conservative than liberal coolness towards these East Asian countries. But their greater average libertarianism leads conservatives to feel warmer than liberals do towards these fellow democracies in "Free Asia." Social and political ideologies, in other words, counteract each other, reducing overall liberal-conservative differences in American feelings towards the East Asian democracies.

The chapter concludes by returning from Main Street public opinion back to Capitol Hill, speculating on the policy implications of American ideological divisions over China. Following the Global Financial Crisis, China has become more assertive in both economic and security matters, and U.S. Big Business is no longer as united in support of China. Greater average conservative coolness towards China, therefore, may begin to be more clearly expressed in the Capitol Hill politics of U.S. China policy.

"CHINKS" AND "JAPS": ORIENTALS AT HOME AND ABROAD

"Christian Civilization will bring to China a truer conception of the nature of man, a better understanding of his relations and his duties, of his dignity and his destiny."[9]
—D. Z. Sheffield, Presbyterian missionary to China, 1900

"Once a Jap, always a Jap! You can't any more regenerate a Jap then you can reverse the laws of nature."[10]
—Congressman John Rankin (Democrat–Mississippi), 1942

Eighteenth-century Americans first encountered Asia indirectly via European writings about China. To extol the virtues of Liberty, Enlightenment thinkers like Montesquieu constructed the foil of "Oriental despotism." China was both an ancient civilization with cultural achievements worthy of admiration—and a land of tyranny to be despised.

In the nineteenth century, direct American missionary contacts with China and the Chinese people increased. "In the early nineteenth century the image of a China distant, refined, and exotic began to give ground to that of a China repulsive, reactionary, and heathen as . . . missionaries broadcast their impressions back home," writes historian Michael Hunt. For instance, to demonstrate the defects of the "Chinese racial character" and justify his Christian civilizing mission, Connecticut missionary Arthur Smith wrote home about "Orientals" as "two-faced" and duplicitous.[11]

By the late nineteenth century, immigration had led to unprecedented direct American contacts with Chinese workers on American soil. Part of a Republican strategy to gain access to the China market and hold down domestic wages following the slaughter of the Civil War, the 1868 Burlingame Treaty allowed unrestricted Chinese immigration. This gave rise to a nativist backlash, which Democrats sought to capitalize on. They could play to the prejudices of their party base—white racism in the South and among Catholics in northern cities—and appeal to new swing voters in the West, where party loyalties remained weak. In 1879 the Democratic-controlled House and Senate passed the "Fifteen Passenger Bill," barring vessels from transporting more than fifteen Chinese at a time. Republicans then sought to neutralize the immigration issue with equally anti-Chinese rhetoric.[12]

Some progressives objected to the growing anti-Chinese sentiment. Massachusetts senator Charles Sumner, an antislavery advocate both during and after the Civil War, championed the rights not just of blacks but of Chinese immigrants as well. In 1868 and 1869 Sumner introduced bills to remove the word "white" from naturalization laws. Neither bill came to a vote. "Senators undertake to disturb us . . . by reminding us of the possibility of large numbers swarming from China," Sumner lamented in 1870. "But . . . the Chinese . . . are peaceful and industrious; how can their citizenship be the occasion of solicitude?"[13]

James Wales captured the late-nineteenth-century politics of anti-Chinese prejudice for an 1880 *Puck* (Figure 9.1). His cartoon depicts the two presidential candidates at the time, James Garfield and Winfield Hancock, nailing a Chinese man between two large "Anti-Chinese" boards labeled "Republican Plank" and "Democratic Plank." The caption reads, "Where Both Platforms Agree—No Vote—No Use to Either Party." The cartoon was not really about the Chinese

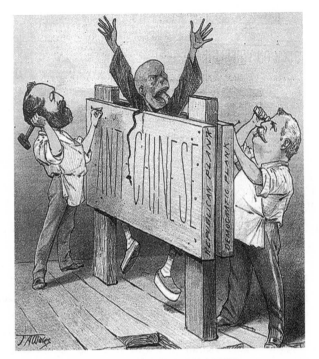

WHERE BOTH PLATFORMS AGREE.—
NO VOTE—NO USE TO EITHER PARTY

FIG. 9.1. Bipartisan anti-Chinese prejudices, 1880.

Source: James Albert Wales, *Puck*, 1880. Image courtesy of the Library of Congress. LC-DIG-ds-00868.

immigrants themselves, but about how both parties were seeking to capitalize upon widespread anti-Chinese prejudices.

Garfield won the election but was assassinated just two hundred days after taking office. His running mate, Chester Arthur, became president in 1881 and signed the Chinese Exclusion Act the following year. But neither anti-Chinese sentiment nor its political use diminished. In 1888, Democratic president Grover Cleveland declared Chinese immigrants "dangerous to our peace and welfare." Not to be outdone, his Republican challenger, Benjamin Harrison, claimed that the assimilation of such an "alien" race was "neither possible nor desirable."[14]

By the turn of the twentieth century, historian Christopher Jespersen argues, American attitudes towards China were driven by "two powerful but contradictory impulses." On the one hand, "God and Mammon" conspired to draw American missionaries and merchants to China to save the Chinese from hell and to capture profits from the "China market." "Hardly a town in our land was

without its society to collect funds and clothing for Chinese missions," statesman Dean Acheson later recalled about the early 1900s, "to educate the minds
and heal the bodies as well as save the souls of the heathen Chinese." On the
other hand, Jespersen writes, a "virulent racism" and "fear of a Yellow Peril"
persisted.[15] The 1882 Chinese Exclusion Act was only repealed in 1943.

The Japanese were the second group of "Orientals" to find a place in the
American imagination. In 1854, Commodore Matthew Perry of Newport,
Rhode Island, forced Japan open at cannon point. Japan's successful Westernization during the Meiji Restoration then evoked much paternalistic American
pride. But increased Japanese immigration in the early twentieth century led
to an anti-Japanese backlash on the same West coast soils where anti-Chinese
nativism had flourished just decades earlier. "As had happened with other foreign peoples, the closer the contact and the larger the numbers," Michael Hunt
maintains, "the more elaborate and negative the American appraisal."[16]

While both Chinese and Japanese continued to be the objects of American
prejudice, the twentieth century witnessed an ongoing exchange of Chinese-
Japanese, good guy–bad guy roles in the American imagination. During the
Boxer Rebellion at the turn of the century, the Chinese acted the barbarians
while the Japanese joined the good-guy Westerners in the Eight-Nation Alliance to relieve the siege of Beijing. But with the rise of Japanese fascism and
Japan's invasion of China in the 1930s and 1940s, the "Japs" were dehumanized
while Generalissimo and Madame Chiang Kai-shek of Nationalist China were
lionized as Christian redeemers. "It seems that by juxtaposing these two oriental peoples Americans had found a means of keeping their hopes and anxieties
in equilibrium," Hunt surmises. "While oriental villains served as the lightning
rod of American racial fears, more worthy Orientals could be summoned up to
keep alive liberal dreams of a prosperous, stable, and democratic East Asia."[17]

The wartime American press and propaganda machine dehumanized the
"Japs" as monkeys, rats, insects, and snakes. "A viper is nonetheless a viper
wherever the egg is hatched," claimed the *Los Angeles Times* in 1942. "So a Jap-
anese-American, born of Japanese parents, grows up to be a Japanese not an
American."[18] Such blood-is-destiny racism was used to justify the internment
of over 100,000 Japanese Americans during the war, as the epigraph from Mississippi congressman John Rankin suggests. Figure 9.2 is a detail from a photograph that Ansel Adams took in 1943 at the Manzanar "War Relocation Center"
at the foot of the Sierra Nevada in eastern California. It was one of ten camps
where Japanese Americans were incarcerated during the war.

In his moving *War Without Mercy*, historian John Dower argues that the war
in the Pacific was more brutal than the war in Europe because both Americans
and Japanese dehumanized and even demonized each other. Surrender thus

FIG. 9.2. Japanese Americans interned at the Manzanar "War Relocation Center,"
California, 1943.

Source: Ansel Adams photo, courtesy of the Library of Congress. Prints & Photographs Division,
LC-DIG-ppprs-00229.

became unthinkable, and the extermination of the vermin enemy a moral obligation. "Louseous Japanicas . . . inhabits coral atolls in the South Pacific, particularly pill boxes, palm trees, caves, swamps, and jungles," read the March 1945 *Leatherneck* magazine of the U.S. Marines. "Flamethrowers, mortars, grenades and bayonets have proven to be an effective remedy. But before a complete cure may be effected, the origin of the plague, the breeding grounds around the Tokyo area, must be completely annihilated."[19] On a single night of firebombing, March 9–10, 1945, 100,000 "Louseous Japanicas" were exterminated in Tokyo.

The 1949 establishment of the People's Republic of China (PRC) added communism to the mix of factors shaping American views of Asia. The Cold War, Republican president Dwight D. Eisenhower declared in 1953, was a "war of light against darkness, freedom against slavery, Godliness against Atheism."[20] "Red China" on the mainland was juxtaposed against "Free China" on Taiwan, even though first Chiang Kai-shek and then his son Chiang Ching-kuo maintained strict authoritarian rule in the Republic of China.

Racial images of the "Yellow horde" persisted in the form of a "Red Menace." "The dragon had awakened, and, rather than turning out to be a friendly one predisposed towards the United States, it instead seemed to confirm the anxieties of those who had looked across the Pacific in fear," Jespersen writes.[21] The danger was quickly hammered home with the Korean War. "It required an experience as jolting as that in Korea to introduce . . . new images of the Chinese as warriors, for the contrary images of the Chinese as unaggressive,

non-mechanical, and un-martial, are among [our] oldest and most deeply im-
bedded," wrote journalist and China hand Harold Isaacs in 1957. "'The Yellow
tide' in Korea swept up all sorts of ancestral memories . . . that had lain long in
the recesses of time and the mind. The Mongol hordes had reappeared."[22]

In his thoughtful *China and the American Dream*, sociologist Richard Madsen argues that the Tiananmen Square Massacre of June 4, 1989, had a profound
impact on American views of China, and that changed American attitudes had
less to do with China than with American national identity itself. For Americans, the moral drama of Tiananmen involved an exercise in navel gazing, of
"dreaming their social selves in face of the realities of the other."[23] Specifically,
Americans had reveled in China's reform and opening of the 1980s, projecting
their Liberal myths onto China and Deng Xiaoping, who was even declared
Time magazine's "Man of the Year" in 1985. China's perceived embrace of the
market was seen as affirming American capitalism and democracy. Tiananmen
shattered that illusion, as the American image of Deng shifted abruptly from
a capitalist "just like us" to that of a "communist tyrant," the very antithesis of
American Liberty.

RED CHINA AND THE YELLOW PERIL

*"The Communists are moving fast towards their goal of world revolution. Perhaps God
brought you to the kingdom for such an hour as this—to stop them. In doing so, you
could be the man that helped save Christian civilization."*[24]
— The Reverend Billy Graham to Democratic President Lyndon B. Johnson, 1965

Why do conservatives today desire so much tougher a China policy than liberals do? Does the "Yellow Peril" continue to shape American views of China?
Or have the civil rights movement and racial integration since the 1960s elimi-
nated race as an influence on American views of Asia? After thirty-five years of
"reform and opening," China today is communist in name only. Do liberal and
conservative feelings about "red communism" nevertheless continue to shape
their China policy preferences?

To best answer these questions, we decided to measure how the American
people feel about the Chinese people and the Chinese government separately.[25]
In addition to our 0°–100° feeling thermometer item on "China," therefore,
we added "the Chinese people" and "the Chinese government." And to reduce
measurement error and increase the internal reliability of these two measures,
we also added a pair of more cognitive items that were evaluated on the standard seven-point "strongly disagree" to "strongly agree" rating scale:

- *The Chinese GOVERNMENT is trustworthy.* (reverse coded)
- *The Chinese GOVERNMENT is devious.*

- *The Chinese PEOPLE are trustworthy.* (reverse coded)
- *The Chinese PEOPLE are devious.*

Item sequence was randomized. After reverse-coding the feeling thermometer and trustworthy items, we standardized and averaged them together to form three-item "prejudice against the Chinese people" and "negative attitudes towards the Chinese government" scales, both of good internal reliability.[26]

Americans felt a whopping 34° cooler towards the Chinese government (21°) than towards the Chinese people (55°), an extremely large difference statistically.[27] Just as conservatives felt 18° cooler than liberals towards "China," they felt 11° cooler towards "the Chinese people" and 15° cooler towards "the Chinese government," medium and large differences statistically.[28] Our survey also included thermometers measuring feelings towards "Asians" and "Communist countries." On average, conservatives scored 5° and 19° cooler than liberals on these two items, small and large differences statistically.[29]

Would cooler conservative than liberal feelings towards the Chinese people and their government, and Asians and communist countries more broadly, help account for conservatives' preference for a tougher China policy? Figure 9.3 reveals that they did: the inclusion of these four mediators accounts for a full three-quarters of the direct relationship between ideology and China policy preferences.[30]

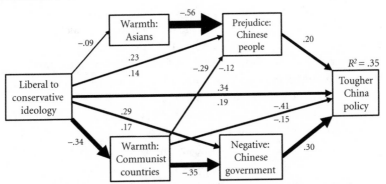

FIG. 9.3. Conservatives desire a tougher China policy than liberals do, in small part because of their greater average prejudice against Asians in general and the Chinese people in particular, and in larger part because of their greater average coolness towards communist countries in general and the Chinese government in particular.

Note: A mixed multiple mediation model. With the exception of the two indirect paths via Asians only and via Asians and negative attitudes towards the Chinese government, all indirect paths were statistically significant. Indirect effect statistics are online at SUP.org. All three China measures are three-item scales. Seven demographic covariates, none of which were statistically significant, are not shown. *Data source:* OU Institute for US-China Issues, 2011.

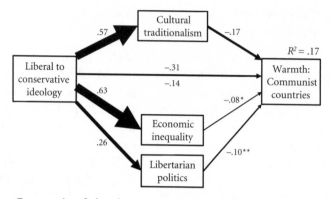

FIG. 9.4. Conservatives feel cooler towards communist countries than liberals do, in part because of their greater average cultural traditionalism, opposition to income redistribution, and libertarian politics.

Note: A simultaneous mediation model. * $p < .05$, ** $p < .01$, all other p's $< .001$. All three indirect paths displayed were statistically significant. Statistics are online at SUP.org. Social dominance, which was not a statistically significant mediator, and seven standard demographic covariates are not shown. Older people felt cooler ($\beta = -.09$) and those with greater education felt warmer ($\beta = .11$) towards communist countries. *Data source:* OU Institute for US-China Issues, 2011.

Figure 9.3 also reveals that there are two largely distinct pathways to China policy preferences. Liberals and conservatives can differ on China policy because of small differences in their average warmth towards Asians in general and the Chinese people in particular (the top path in the model). As the consistently thicker lines along the bottom path in the model reveal, however, on average liberals and conservatives differ on China policy in larger part because of their greater differences in warmth towards communist countries in general and the Chinese government in particular.[31]

Prejudice against "Orientals," we have seen, has been a persistent theme in American history, and as James Wales reminded readers in 1880 (see Figure 9.1), it has often been a source of bipartisan agreement. However, our 2011 data is consistent with work in social psychology demonstrating that on average conservatives are slightly more prejudiced against Asians ($\beta = -.09$, top left of Figure 9.3) than liberals are.[32] As discussed in Chapter 3, differing racial attitudes are in part due to the greater moral value that liberals place on fairness and compassion than conservatives do (see Figure 3.4). For instance, missionaries from liberal and mainline Protestant denominations frequently opposed discrimination against Asians on the basis of compassion. "The status of inferiority thus far imposed upon these people by the West must come to an end," the ecumenical Foreign Missions Conference of North America declared in November 1949, one month *after* the establishment of the People's Republic.

"Asiatics, no less than ourselves, are children of the Heavenly Father and, as such, are entitled to be dealt with on the basis of racial equality."[33]

But it is greater conservative (13°) than liberal (32°) coolness towards communist countries ($\beta = -.34$, bottom left of Figure 9.3) that plays the larger role in accounting for overall liberal-conservative differences over China policy. The ideological sources of American feelings about communism therefore merit closer examination. A multiple mediation analysis revealed that three of the four dimensions of American ideology that we measured contributed to the substantial 19° gap between liberal and conservative feelings towards communist countries. As shown in Figure 9.4, only social dominance orientation did not mediate the relationship, which makes sense as communism is not a racial issue. Together, the three mediators accounted for over 90 percent of the direct relationship between liberal-conservative ideology and warmth towards communist countries.[34]

Cultural traditionalism, the top path in Figure 9.4, was the most powerful mediator of the relationship between ideology and feelings towards communist countries. Christian conservatives have long viewed communism as an atheistic threat to God and Christian values. "Communism is not only an economic interpretation of life," the Reverend Billy Graham declared in 1949. "Communism is a religion that is inspired, directed and motivated by the Devil himself who has declared war against Almighty God."[35] In his famous 1983 "Evil Empire" speech given to the National Association of Evangelicals, cited in Chapter 2, President Ronald Reagan similarly equated the fight against communism with the fight against "evil." "Fighting communism was a religious duty, and the American government was engaged in the work of the Lord when it opposed the Soviet Union," historian Daniel Williams writes in *God's Own Party: The Making of the Christian Right*. "The 'American way of life' was therefore the Christian way of life, and a threat to one was a threat to the other."[36]

Communism is primarily, however, an economic theory; Marx was an economic historian. It is not surprising, therefore, that differences between economic liberals and conservatives over income redistribution would also help account for overall ideological differences over communism (Figure 9.4, middle path). "Fundamentally there are only two ways of coordinating the economic activity of millions," Milton Friedman wrote in *Capitalism and Freedom*. "One is central direction involving the use of coercion—the technique of the army and of the modern totalitarian state. The other is voluntary co-operation of individuals—the technique of the marketplace."[37] The same disagreements that liberals and conservatives have about taxes, social welfare spending, and income redistribution at home, our survey data suggests, also shape their feelings towards "communist countries" abroad.

The political division between libertarians and communitarians also shapes feelings towards communist countries, as the bottom path in Figure 9.4 reveals. In his 1975 *The Broken Covenant*, sociologist Robert Bellah argued that although many Americans dislike communism for economic and religious reasons, it is communism's perceived threat to cherished American liberties that stings the most. "Though 'revolutionary' and 'atheistic' would continue to be negative terms used to characterize socialism, it was the attribute of collectivism or statism, in contrast to allegedly American individualism, that would be the central negative image."[38] Remarkably, our 2011 survey data exactly confirms Bellah's argument that there are three (economic, religio-cultural, and libertarian) distinct ideological ways that Americans think about communism. Historian Andrew Preston has more recently but similarly argued that a libertarian ethic rooted in Protestantism "made Americans suspicious about other nations that relied too heavily upon concentrations of power, be they religious (the Catholic Church) or political and economic (the Communist Party)."[39] Libertarians don't like democratic governments, let alone communist party-states.

LIBERAL PANDA-HUGGERS AND
CONSERVATIVE DRAGON-SLAYERS

"A Bible-believing Christian Conservative, by definition, is anti-Communist, and therefore anti-Red China."[40]
—Evangelist Billy James Hargis, 1972

Broad feelings about "Asians" and "communist countries" thus help account for more-specific feelings towards the Chinese people and their government, respectively, contributing to ideological differences in China policy preferences. As discussed in Chapter 1, when confronted with difficult specific questions like, "How much do you agree or disagree with the statement, 'The U.S. government should pursue a tougher China policy?'" we frequently resort to "affect heuristics," substituting easier and broader questions about our gut feelings like, "How do I feel about Asians?" or "How do I feel about communist countries?" Such heuristic devices, social psychologist Daniel Kahneman has argued, help us "generate intuitive opinions on complex matters."[41] This helps explain how Americans, in the absence of much knowledge about China, can nonetheless form consistent opinions about it.

Why do different kinds of American liberals and conservatives differ so systematically in their intuitive opinions about China? The path model in Figure 9.5 reveals that all four of the dimensions of American ideology that we measured in our 2011 survey shaped China policy preferences. Furthermore, all four operate in the same direction. In other words, conservatives of different stripes may disagree over why they desire a tougher China policy than liberals do, but

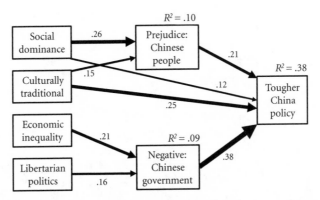

FIG. 9.5. Negative attitudes towards the Chinese people and government act as separate pathways for four dimensions of American ideology to shape China policy preferences.

Note: A path model. All three China measures are three-item scales. Covariances and prediction error terms are not displayed. Model fit was excellent and all indirect paths were statistically significant. Statistics are online at SUP.org. *Data source:* OU Institute for US-China Issues, 2011.

they can agree on a tougher policy. Similarly, different kinds of liberals may differ over why they want a friendlier China policy than conservatives, but they can agree on a friendlier policy. The intensity of the ideological disagreement on China policy is due in part to the four dimensions of American ideology working together rather than against one another.

The top path in Figure 9.5 reveals that the same racial politics that divides Americans today on domestic issues like affirmative action also shapes their feelings towards the Chinese people (β = .26) and policy preferences towards China (β = .12). A closer look at the substantial influence of social dominance orientation—the belief that *"Inferior groups should stay in their place"*—on prejudice against the Chinese people is revealing. Of the five moral values, compassion and loyalty mediated the relationship between group dominance and anti-Chinese prejudice, and authority was a marginally significant mediator as well.[42] Liberals, generally lower on social dominance, value compassion more than conservatives do, leading them to oppose anti-Chinese prejudice. For their part, conservatives, generally higher on social dominance, value loyalty to the in-group and authority more than liberals do, fostering greater prejudice against the Chinese people.

Thomas Nast captured the competing moral values shaping American feelings towards Chinese immigrants in a pair of editorial cartoons for *Harper's Weekly* (Figure 9.6). The 1870 cartoon at the left depicts a group of Caucasians atop "The 'Chinese Wall' Around the United States of America." They throw

THROWING DOWN THE   E PLURIBUS UNUM
LADDER BY WHICH THEY ROSE   (EXCEPT THE CHINESE)

FIG. 9.6. Chinese immigration: Conservatives value in-group *loyalty* and out-group *obedience*, while liberals value *compassion*, 1870 and 1882.

Sources: Thomas Nast, *Harper's Weekly*, July 23, 1870, and April 1, 1882. Both images courtesy of the University of Oklahoma Libraries.

down a ladder labeled "emigration" as Chinese workers sporting long Manchu queues look up helplessly from below. The Caucasians above celebrate having kept the Chinese in their subordinate place. Nast objects out of compassion for the Chinese immigrants. A flag on the wall refers to the 1870 "Know-Nothings," "Pres. Patrick, Vice Pres. Hans," a clear reference to the Irish and German immigrants who had been persecuted by WASP nativists just a decade earlier. Nast makes his moral stance explicit with his caption, "Throwing Down the Ladder by Which They Rose." He wants his reader to feel compassion for the Chinese victims of the hypocrisy of earlier Irish and German immigrants.

Nast made the same point a dozen years later (Figure 9.6, right). A castle flying an American flag and labeled "The Temple of Liberty" is surrounded by a deep moat. A guard scrutinizes a Chinese immigrant's passport, blocking his entry. Nast's caption again makes his objection explicit: "E Pluribus Unum (Except the Chinese)." White racism is not just doing violence to American democratic values, but harming vulnerable Chinese as well.

A similar clash of moral values was on display in a 2011 controversy over Rush Limbaugh's derogatory parody of Chinese president Hu Jintao speaking Chinese. On his January 19, 2011, radio show, Limbaugh spoke of watching an

Obama-Hu press conference: "Hu Jintao, he was speaking, and they weren't translating. . . . Hu Jintao was just going . . . 'chin chang chin chan chong chang chi bababba chi chike zhing zha zhe zhike rroooor ji kedi ba baba.'" Limbaugh's racist gibberish immediately produced a liberal outcry. "Calling the Chinese names and imitating the Chinese language was a childish and offensive tactic," said Democratic congresswoman Judy Chu of California, the first Chinese American woman elected to the U.S. House of Representatives. "It is one thing to disagree with a nation and criticize its policies, but it is another thing to demonize an entire people. Over the last 150 years, Chinese in America have faced severe racial discrimination. It wasn't that long ago that the Chinese in America were . . . called racial slurs, were spat upon in the streets, derided in the halls of Congress and even brutally murdered."[43] Our survey data suggests that Limbaugh and Chu were not disconnected from Main Street: differing beliefs about proper racial and social hierarchies, and the differing moral values that undergird them, continue to divide American liberals and conservatives today in their feelings towards the Chinese people.

Figure 9.5 reveals that cultural liberals and conservatives also differ in their views of both the Chinese people and U.S. China policy. For cultural traditionalists, Chinese immigrants, like the Mexican immigrants discussed in Chapter 6, may be viewed as a threat to traditional WASP values, contributing to anti-Chinese prejudice ($\beta = .15$) and subsequent desires for tougher China policies ($\beta = .21$). The stronger direct path ($\beta = .25$) from cultural traditionalism to preferences for tougher China policies may reflect a fear-driven response to a rising China seen as different and dangerous. Social psychologists have demonstrated that when confronted by perceived threats to shared cultural beliefs, values, or norms, cultural conservatives are more likely than cultural liberals to respond with aggression.[44]

Many cultural conservatives advocate tougher China policies. As noted above, Republican congressman Christopher Smith deplores the persecution of Christians in China. Smith serves as cochair of the House Pro-Life Caucus and as a member of its Taiwan Caucus, which generally promotes tougher China policies. Smith is not unusual in linking these seemingly disparate issues. Our 2011 survey included the abortion question *"Are you more pro-life or pro-choice?"* Answers to this intensely personal question were a substantial predictor ($\beta = .22$) of the China policy preferences of the American people, even after controlling for the standard demographics.

Economic ideology, by contrast, has no influence on feelings towards the Chinese *people*. Its effect on China policy preferences is instead mediated through feelings towards the Chinese *government* ($\beta = .21$, Figure 9.5, near-bottom left). Not surprisingly, liberal-conservative disagreements over whether

"*The government should decrease income differences*" also shape their attitudes towards the "communist" Chinese government. While business conservatives often support pro-China policies out of a material self-interest in profiting from trade and access to the China market, economic conservatism as an ideology is marked by an antipathy towards governments—especially socialist governments—that tax, spend, or redistribute income, all lamented as violations of free market principles.

In Chapter 7 we saw that the *Wall Street Journal* editorial page frequently comments on the economic policies of European countries like France, Britain, and Germany as proxy battles in domestic economic wars. Its editorials on China often serve the same function. In its June 1, 2011, editorial "Red Ghost over China," the *Journal* frets that free market capitalism may be on the defensive in China. "Leftist thinkers are genuinely trying to turn the Party back toward Marxist ideology." Worse yet, "Wu Bangguo, the Party's No. 2 man, recently gave a speech in which he attacked private property." Domestic American debates over economic stimulus were similarly exported to China the next year. "While it must be tempting to goose GDP once more, Mr. Wen and his colleagues should think twice about another round of stimulus," the editorial board argued in its May 23, 2012, "China Is Stimulused Out." "Now is not the time to try to reinflate the economy with more wasteful spending and investment." Economic liberals, by contrast, were more inclined to praise Chinese efforts at economic stimulus during the onset of the Global Financial Crisis in 2008 and 2009—and to advocate more stimulus at home.

Like economic ideology, communitarian-libertarian political ideology is not associated with prejudice against the Chinese *people*; its influence on China policy preferences is instead mediated through feelings towards the Chinese *government* (β = .16, Figure 9.5, far-bottom left). Greater libertarian agreement that "*Individuals should be free to follow their own dreams in their own ways, without interference from government*" leads to suspicion and hostility towards the American government, which is democratic. It is not surprising, therefore, that libertarians would also tend to feel cooler than communitarians towards the Chinese government, which is authoritarian.

William Allen Rogers captured libertarian fears of "Oriental despotism" in a 1900 *Harper's Weekly* (Figure 9.7). The Boxer Rebels had been killing Christian missionaries and their Chinese converts in North China since 1898, and foreigners sought refuge in the legation quarters in Beijing in June 1900. The Empress Dowager Cixi of the Qing Dynasty then decided to throw her support behind the Boxers by declaring war on the foreign powers in China. An Eight-Nation Alliance of American, European, and mostly Japanese troops soon broke the siege of Beijing. Rogers's July 28 drawing depicts President William McKinley

IS THIS IMPERIALISM?
*"No blow has been struck except for liberty and humanity,
and none will be."*—William McKinley

FIG. 9.7. Libertarian fears of Oriental despotism, 1900.

Source: William Allen Rogers, *Harper's Weekly*, July 28, 1900. Image courtesy of the University of Oklahoma Libraries.

and Uncle Sam doing battle against crazed Boxers. Severed Western heads are held high on pitchforks, and one Chinese rebel is about to sink a dagger into a prostrate and helpless white woman. Next to her, a white baby lies (dead?) under an American flag. McKinley resolutely holds an American flag that is inscribed with the words "Life, Liberty, and Pursuit of Happiness Under Treaty Rights." The illustration is entitled "Is This Imperialism?" Rogers quotes President McKinley to answer his own question with a resounding no: "No Blow Has Been Struck Except for Liberty and Humanity, And None Will Be." Americans are not imperialist aggressors in China; they are defenders of liberty against a tyrannical Chinese government that has unleashed its fanatical people.

Libertarian fears of the Chinese government persist today, contributing to conservative desires for tougher China policies (Figure 9.5, bottom path).

"Remember, there are reasons why Communist China remains under an arms embargo," Republican congressman Dana Rohrabacher of California said at an April 2, 2009, congressional hearing on export controls. "The Tiananmen Square massacre, where the tyrannical and brutal Chinese government murdered thousands of peaceful reformers, changed the course of history."[45] Note both the reference to "Communist China" and the clear distinction drawn between the "tyrannical and brutal Chinese government" and the Chinese people, described as "peaceful reformers." Libertarians, Figure 9.5 reveals, do not harbor prejudices against the Chinese people. Their fears, instead, are directed against governments, especially strong authoritarian governments like that of "Communist China."

GLOBALIZATION AND U.S.-CHINA RELATIONS: CONTACT, KNOWLEDGE, AND AMERICAN ATTITUDES TOWARDS CHINA

"I am convinced that as the Chinese study abroad, trade with free nations, build enterprises, and become increasingly exposed to people and cultures around the world, they will demand freedom and genuine democratic reforms."[46]

—Republican presidential candidate Mitt Romney, 2010

Ideological predispositions are powerful predictors of the China policy preferences of the American people. But they are not the only source of American attitudes towards China. Globalization is increasingly compressing both time and space, bringing the world closer and closer together.[47] Airplane travel and new communications technologies such as e-mail and Skype now allow Americans and Chinese to interact more directly and frequently than ever before. Television, movies, and the Internet are dramatically increasing indirect contacts as well.

Do these growing interactions shape how Americans and Chinese feel and think about each other? Americans like Mitt Romney, quoted above, believe that increased contacts will be a good thing, leading Chinese to embrace American-style democracy. "The exposure of the Chinese people to our way of life can be the greatest force for change in their country," the "2012 Republican Platform" similarly declares. "We should make it easier for the people of China to experience our vibrant democracy and to see for themselves how freedom works."[48]

The Chinese government seems to have embraced a similar logic: if only Americans knew more about China, they'd like China more. Since 2004, the PRC Ministry of Education has launched hundreds of Confucius Institutes around the world, aggressively promoting Chinese language education as well as renewed international academic and cultural exchanges. The underlying assumption appears to be that increased contact with and knowledge about China will improve foreign attitudes toward China.

TABLE 9.1. China Knowledge Quiz:
Five multiple choice questions and percentage correct.

Question	Response choices	% ✓
Which of the following is a current leader of China?	Hu Jintao/Mao Zedong/Jiang Zemin/Deng Xiaoping	41
The dominant ethnicity/race in China is the	Han/Manchu/Hui/Zhuang	33
Which of the following countries does NOT border China?	Singapore/Mongolia/India/N. Korea	38
The Three Gorges Dam, a massive construction project begun in 1994, is located on which of these Chinese rivers?	Yangzi River/Yellow River/Pearl River/ West River	61
What is the name of the political party that governs the People's Republic of China today?	The Communist Party of China The Chinese Republican Party The Democratic Progressive Party of China The Nationalist Party of China	41
AVERAGE SCORE		43%

Note: Response choice sequence was randomized. Correct answer underlined and placed first here only. *Data source:* OU Institute for US-China Issues, 2011.

We decided to test this assumption by measuring both knowledge about China and contacts with Chinese in our 2011 survey. The average American scored a 43 percent on our five-item China knowledge quiz. The five questions are listed in Table 9.1 for readers to judge for themselves the difficulty of the quiz. It covered basic politics and geography, and in our judgment was not too difficult. With just four response choices each, pure chance alone would have resulted in a score of 25 percent, so we interpret the 43 percent to mean that Americans on average are not very knowledgeable about China. This interpretation is arguably supported by a 2013 Pew Internet survey, which found that only 57 percent of Americans could correctly identify the flag of the People's Republic of China when shown images of the four very different flags of the PRC, Turkey, Japan, and South Africa.[49] Overall, the American public does not appear to be very knowledgeable about either China or the world (see Table 5.1).

Indeed, there are areas where the American public is clearly *misinformed* about China. Our 2011 survey measured the perceived economic power of foreign countries on a seven-point "extremely weak" to "extremely strong" scale. Of the fifteen countries we measured, China and the United States were seen as the two most economically powerful countries, with China seen, on average, as slightly *more* economically powerful than the United States.[50] GDP and GDP per capita are two of the better objective measures of national economic power. According to the International Monetary Fund, in 2011 the nominal U.S. GDP ($15 trillion+) was over twice that of China ($7 trillion+), and the U.S. GDP

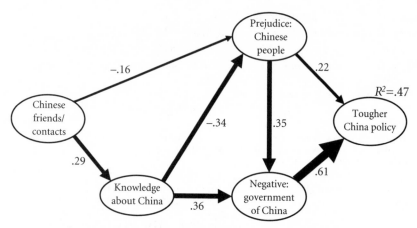

FIG. 9.8. When knowledge is a double-edged sword: Contact with Chinese increases knowledge about China, which *decreases* prejudice but *increases* negativity towards the Chinese government.

Note: A structural equation model. Ovals are latent variables. To reduce clutter, observed variables, and measurement and prediction error terms, are not displayed. Model fit was excellent and all indirect paths were statistically significant. Statistics are online at SUP.org. *Data source:* OU Institute for US-China Issues, 2011.

per capita ($48,000+) was six times higher than China's ($8,000+).[51] In the spring of 2011, however, U.S. unemployment was high and media coverage of China highlighted Chinese purchases of American debt, China's favorable balance of trade with the United States, and China's high growth rate, all of which likely contributed to the widespread American *misperception* that China was economically more powerful than the United States.

Our 2011 survey also included two items measuring the quantity and quality of direct contacts with Chinese:

- *How frequently do you have contact with Chinese?*
- *Do you have many friends who are from China?*

Responses were averaged together to form a two-item "Chinese friends/contacts" scale of good internal reliability.[52]

Do contacts then with Chinese and knowledge about China shape the China attitudes and policy preferences of the American people? The statistical model displayed in Figure 9.8 reveals that they do, but that increased knowledge about China is indeterminate when it comes to U.S. China policy. Greater knowledge about China is associated with substantially *decreased* ($\beta = -.34$) prejudice against the Chinese people, but substantially *increased* ($\beta = .36$) negative attitudes towards the Chinese government. The former contributes to desires for *friendlier* (β = .22) China policies, while the latter contributes to desires for much *tougher* (β = .61) policies towards China.

The reduced prejudice finding is consistent with half a century of scholarship in social psychology on the intergroup "contact hypothesis." In 1954 Gordon Allport proposed that increased contact between racial groups living in close proximity would increase their knowledge about each other, decreasing prejudice.[53] Allport's influential hypothesis contributed to social policy, as busing and integration were implemented during the U.S. civil rights movement in an attempt to reduce prejudice between American racial groups. Decades of research and policy experiments have revealed that increased intergroup contact, under the right conditions, can reduce prejudice. Increased contact under the wrong conditions, however, can exacerbate conflict and prejudice, as Michael Hunt suggested in the context of Chinese and Japanese immigration to the United States. Psychologists Thomas Pettigrew and Linda Tropp have noted in a recent meta-analysis that along with perspective taking and anxiety reduction, knowledge is a mediator of the relationship between intergroup contact and prejudice reduction.[54]

Figure 9.8 reveals, however, that while increased knowledge about China decreases prejudice against the Chinese people, it increases negativity towards the Chinese government. From a theoretic perspective, this finding has two implications. First, contact theory can travel from prejudice reduction between groups *within* nations (such as blacks and whites in the United States) to prejudice reduction between groups *across* nations (such as the United States and China). Contact theory, in other words, has international wings. Second, the increased knowledge that follows from increased intergroup contacts only improves attitudes towards certain types of out-groups. Our analysis above suggests that it may be the association with "communism" that contributes to greater American knowledge about China leading to greater negativity towards the Chinese government. But psychologists may wish to explore whether there are more generalizable features of the kinds of out-groups to which contact theory applies.

From a policy perspective, Figure 9.8 reveals that the Chinese government's massive investment in Confucius Institutes and educating Americans about China is a mixed bag. On the one hand, increasing positive contacts with Chinese can increase knowledge and reduce prejudice, contributing to desires for *friendlier* China policies. On the other hand, greater knowledge about China contributes to greater negativity towards the Chinese government, fostering desires for *tougher* China policies. Greater knowledge about China can thus be a double-edged sword.[55]

Different kinds of people can also respond to the same social experiences in very different ways. In Chapter 5 we saw that as foreign travel, friends, and contacts increase, nationalism *decreases* among cultural liberals but *increases* among cultural conservatives (see Figure 5.4). Cultural ideology, in other words, polarizes the effect of foreign contacts on American nationalism. Similarly, ideology also moderates the influence of contact on China attitudes. A statistical analysis revealed that as foreign and Chinese friends, contacts, and travel increase, desires for tougher China policies decrease—but only among cultural liberals and not among cultural conservatives.[56] This could be based in personality: it may be that greater average liberal than conservative "openness to new experience" leads cultural liberals to embrace contacts with Chinese more, increasing their warmth towards China.

Finally, media exposure appears to act as a kind of indirect contact, having similar effects on China attitudes as did direct contacts with Chinese. As discussed in Chapter 5, our 2011 survey included two items measuring time *"paying attention to international news"* and the degree of *"interest in news and public affairs."* Averaged together, they formed a "media exposure" scale which predicted *decreased* prejudice against the Chinese people ($\beta = -.11$, $p = .003$) but *increased* negativity towards the Chinese government ($\beta = .26$) in a pair of regressions controlling for the seven standard demographics. This is consistent with the "double-edged sword" of direct contacts with Chinese people on China policy preferences discussed above. So media exposure acts as a type of indirect intergroup contact polarizing American attitudes towards the Chinese people and their government.

FREE ASIA AND THE YELLOW PERIL

> "When Japanese pilots were flying suicide missions into American battleships, it seemed impossible that six decades later Japan would be a democracy, a lynchpin of security in Asia, and one of America's closest friends."[57]
>
> —Republican President George W. Bush, 2008

> "America and Taiwan are united in our shared belief in fair elections, personal liberty, and free enterprise."[58]
>
> —"2012 Republican Party Platform"

What influence does ideology have on American feelings towards the East Asian democracies of Japan, Taiwan, and South Korea? Statistical analysis revealed that of the four dimensions of American ideology that we measured in our survey, only social dominance orientation and communitarian-libertarian politics mediated the relationship between ideology and warmth towards these three East Asian countries (Figure 9.9). But the two indirect effects canceled each other out.

Greater average conservative than liberal social dominance ($\beta = .36$) con-

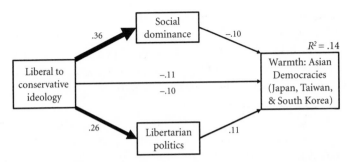

FIG. 9.9. Conflicted American feelings towards Asian democracies: Socio-racial and political ideologies counteract each other.

Note: A simultaneous mediation model. All p's $\leq$ .001. Both indirect effects were statistically significant, but the total indirect effect was not. Statistics are online at SUP.org. Seven demographic covariates are not shown. *Data source:* OU Institute for US-China Issues, 2011.

tributed to conservatives' greater *coolness* ($\beta = -.10$) towards these three Asian lands (Figure 9.9, top path). Chinese are thus not the only Asian objects of prejudice in America today. "It's because of you little motherfuckers that we're out of work!" Ronald Ebens yelled at Vincent Chin outside a nightclub in Detroit in 1982. Ebens, an autoworker, thought that Chin, a Chinese American, was Japanese, and hence the source of Detroit's economic woes. Ebens and his stepson, Michael Nitz, tracked Chin down later that night and bludgeoned him to death with a baseball bat. Ebens and Nitz were not sentenced to prison time, provoking Asian American outrage and greater Asian American involvement in the civil rights movement.[59] Thirty years later, Assistant Attorney General Thomas E. Perez of the U.S. Department of Justice's Civil Rights Division marked Chin's death by writing, "In a diverse, democratic nation like ours, we all must be able to live and work in our communities without fear of being attacked because of how we look, what we believe, where we are from, or who we love."[60] Differences among Americans today about proper race relations at home, our survey reveals, also shape their feelings not just towards China but towards other Asian countries as well.

Greater average conservative libertarianism ($\beta = .26$), however, contributed to greater conservative *warmth* towards these Asian democracies ($\beta = .11$), *suppressing* the overall effect of ideology (Figure 9.9, bottom path). In other words, if it were not for the fact that conservatives tend to be more libertarian than liberals, on average conservatives would feel more coolly towards these Asian democracies. For libertarians, the success of Japan, Taiwan, and South Korea represents the triumph of freedom in East Asia. When promoting the democratization of the Middle East, President George W. Bush frequently extolled

Japan and Germany as "great democracies" capable of "sustaining democratic values."[61] "Today the great powers are also increasingly united by common values, instead of divided by conflicting ideologies. The United States, Japan and our Pacific friends, and now all of Europe, share a deep commitment to human freedom," Bush declared in his 2002 commencement address at West Point. "And the tide of liberty is rising."[62]

Taiwan—"Free China"—has also long been held up by American libertarians as a beacon of liberty in the Chinese world. "Taiwan is one of the strongest democratic partners of the United States in the Asia-Pacific region and serves as a model of freedom and democracy," Republican senator Jim Inhofe of Oklahoma wrote in 2008.[63] Although the state of Oklahoma has few commercial or other ties with Taiwan, Inhofe has served on the Senate Taiwan Caucus since its founding in 2003, and is currently its cochair. Supporting Taiwan appears to be a way for some American politicians to express their antipathy towards Chinese communism. "I want to express my strong support for Taiwan," Republican congressman Michael McCaul of Texas declared in 2009. "We like our independence in Texas and I think that's what we have in common. America stands for freedom and democracy and the fight against oppression and dictatorships. And so we stand with you."[64]

Japan, Taiwan, and South Korea thus appear to receive a libertarian boost for being democratic or capitalist that counteracts the negative influence of lingering racism. Turning to South Asia, India receives a similar democratic/capitalist boost: greater libertarian warmth ($\beta = .07$) towards India partially counteracts the negative influence of racism/social dominance ($\beta = -.14$) on feelings towards India. The suppression effect of greater conservative libertarianism helps explain why the overall ideological gap between liberals and conservatives on these Asian democracies is much smaller than that between them on communist countries like China and North Korea. Our survey data thus supports Michael Hunt's contention, noted above, that American hopes for a "democratic East Asia" and "racial fears" about "oriental villains" exist in equilibrium—or at least coexist.

MAIN STREET, WALL STREET, AND U.S. CHINA POLICY

"America's relations with other countries—particularly a Communist country
like China—must rest on a solid foundation of public opinion. When the Chinese
government resorts to the wanton violation of human rights, it will inevitably pay a
price with the American public and its elected representatives."[65]

—Congressman Stephen Solarz (Democrat–New York), 1989

This chapter has argued that while conservatives feel somewhat cooler than liberals towards "Free Asia," they feel much cooler towards "Red China." It further argued that the sources of these ideological differences in attitudes towards Asian countries can be found in many of the same issues that divide them on domestic politics.

One source of greater overall conservative coolness towards Asian countries is conservatives' greater average prejudice. "I think one man is just as good as another so long as he's honest and decent and not a nigger or a Chinaman," future president Harry Truman wrote in 1911. "Negroes ought to be in Africa, yellow men in Asia and white men in Europe and America."[66] While such overt prejudice has declined over the last century, our survey reveals that it does persist, and that greater average conservative than liberal prejudice has a small but statistically significant influence on American attitudes towards Asian countries.

But communism was an even larger source of ideological differences over China. For cultural, social, economic, and political reasons, conservatives felt cooler than liberals towards both communist countries in general and the Chinese government in particular. By contrast, their greater libertarianism warmed conservatives towards the Asian democracies of Japan, Taiwan, and South Korea, attenuating the overall ideological gap.

If ideology powerfully divides Americans on China, why is that division not more clearly reflected on Capitol Hill? First, ideology is not the sole determinant of American attitudes towards China. This chapter has shown that variations in contact with Chinese and knowledge about China mold the China attitudes of the American people as well. Further research is needed to better understand how such external situational variables interact with internal ideological predispositions to shape the China attitudes of the American people.

Second, public opinion is not the sole determinant of the policy preferences of our elected representatives. As noted in the discussion of the Israel lobby in Chapter 8, campaign contributors and special interest groups can exert an independent influence on members of both the legislative and executive branches. It may be that the pro-China advocacy of business groups like the U.S.-China Business Council and AmCham China has been able to neutralize the anti-China leanings of congressional Republicans and their conservative constituents. Similarly, the anti-China advocacy of Big Labor has likely counteracted the greater liberal warmth towards China within the Democratic Party.

Will this delicate balance endure? While candidates from both political parties have long sought to use China against their political opponents in their political campaigns, Republican politicians today appear to have begun utilizing anti-China tactics more frequently. Republican campaign ads often invoke the "Red Menace" and "Yellow Hordes" views of China, appealing to their conservative constituents' fears of both communism and Asians.

Meanwhile, pro-China business groups, so united in the 1990s as apologists for China during the fight against President Clinton over China's most-favored-nation status, may now be dividing over China. During the Global Financial Crisis in 2008–9, the Chinese government made the case to its people that the Chinese economic model was superior to the West's, contributing to greater Chinese assertiveness and tougher policies towards the Western business world. "In my more than two decades in China, I have seldom seen the foreign business community more angry and disillusioned than it is today," China business expert James McGregor wrote for *Time* magazine in 2010. "Anti-foreign attitudes and policies in China have been growing and hardening since the global economic crisis."[67]

This recent development raises an important question. If business Republicans become divided on China policy and stop counterbalancing the anti-China leanings of Main Street conservatives and their elected representatives, what is to keep the Republican Party from moving towards a substantially tougher China policy? We may be poised for a significant change in the politics of China policy on Capitol Hill.

10 International Organizations and Treaties: Blue Helmets, Black Helicopters, and Satanic Serpents

"We have restored America's leadership at the U.N. by cooperating with our partners there when we can and respectfully disagreeing with them when we must, reversing the previous administration's disdain for the U.N."[1]

—2012 "Democratic Party Platform"

"As long as some of the world's worst tyrants hold seats on its Human Rights Council, and as long as Israel is treated as a pariah state, the U.N. cannot expect the full support of the American people."[2]

—2012 "Republican Party Platform"

On December 4, 2012, thirty-eight Republican senators voted against a United Nations treaty on the rights of the disabled, leaving it five votes short of the two-thirds majority required for ratification. The international treaty is modeled on the Americans with Disabilities Act, which Republican president George H.W. Bush signed into law on July 26, 1990, with broad bipartisan congressional support. Former senator and 1996 presidential candidate Bob Dole, a disabled veteran, appeared on the Senate floor to appeal to his fellow Republicans to support the treaty—to no avail.

Although the treaty lacks enforcement powers, merely suggesting that the disabled not be discriminated against, Republican senators claimed it would infringe upon American sovereignty. "I do not support the cumbersome regulations and potentially overzealous international organizations with anti-American biases that infringe upon American society," Senator Jim Inhofe of Oklahoma declared on the Senate floor. Senator Mike Lee of Utah went further, claiming that the nonbinding treaty would nonetheless lead to "the constant looming threat of state interference" in home schooling—and a rise in abortions.[3]

Democrats were dumbstruck. "I ask [my] colleagues to do for the world what they've done for America," Senator John Kerry of Massachusetts implored his colleagues. "Raise your voice and vote for millions who are voiceless in their own lands. Stand up for those who cannot stand up for themselves."[4] After the vote, majority leader Harry Reid of Nevada wrote, "It is a sad day when we cannot pass a treaty that simply brings the world up to the American standard for protecting people with disabilities because the Republican Party is in thrall to extremists and ideologues."[5]

Do the sharply opposed views of these Democratic and Republican senators reflect the views of their constituents? Is Main Street as divided over international organizations and treaties as Capitol Hill is?

Scholars of American public opinion have generally argued that unlike American elites, the American public is *not* divided: it is united in support of multilateral institutions. In his 2006 *The Foreign Policy Disconnect: What Americans Want from Our Leaders but Don't Get*, Benjamin Page argues that "Again and again over the years, large majorities of Americans—often in contrast to government officials—have expressed a high level of regard for the U.N."[6] In 2012, Joshua Busby and Jonathan Monten argued that Republican elites like Jesse Helms and John Bolton have attacked multilateralism despite "mass public support for the U.N."[7]

Pollsters largely agree. On the basis of its 2012 survey, the Chicago Council on Global Affairs declared that "U.S. participation in multilateral treaties receives majority support" among Democrats and Republicans. The media's focus on popular polarization, it claims, is "exaggerated."[8]

This chapter argues that these political scientists and pollsters have misinterpreted the public opinion data: whether on Capitol Hill or on Main Street, American liberals and conservatives today are strikingly *divided* in their views of international organizations and treaties. In our 2011 survey, liberals (66°) felt a remarkable 48° warmer towards the United Nations than conservatives (18°) did, a truly massive difference statistically.[9] Liberals (42°) also felt 21° warmer towards the World Bank than conservatives (21°) did, a very large difference.[10] This ideological gap is not new but may be growing. For instance, liberals (68°) felt 23° warmer towards the United Nations than conservatives (45°) did in the Chicago Council's 2004 survey, a large difference statistically.[11]

These feelings, moreover, had policy consequences. As noted in Chapter 4, our survey included two items assessing the importance of "strengthening international organizations" and "supporting the United Nations" that cohered well. Liberals scored massively higher than conservatives on the resulting "support for multilateralism" scale.[12] These findings are consistent with data from the Chicago Council. In its 2010 survey, liberals scored much higher than conservatives did on a three-point ("not" to "somewhat" to "very" important) assessment of "strengthening the United Nations" as a U.S. foreign policy goal.[13] It also asked half of its respondents whether seven "international institutions" (WTO, ICC, WHO, IMF, WB, U.N., and IAEA) "need to be strengthened or not." Liberals scored vastly higher than conservatives on overall support for strengthening these international institutions.[14] Similarly, in a 2013 Gallup landline and cell phone poll, 87 percent of liberals agreed that the United Nations played a "necessary role" in the world today, while only 56 percent of conservatives did—a substantial 31 percent difference. And whereas a large majority (67%) of conservatives felt the United Nations was doing a "poor job," a small majority of liberals (56%) felt it was doing a "good job."[15]

There is also substantial polarization in popular American attitudes towards international treaties. In our 2011 survey, conservatives scored immensely higher than liberals on an "opposition to international treaties" scale consisting of two items[16]:

- *International treaties cannot be trusted to safeguard U.S. national security.*
- *International treaties are one of the best ways to maintain America's national security.* (reverse coded)

The massive ideological difference on these items provides powerful support for Brian Rathbun's recent argument that ideology can serve as a proxy for generalized trust, and that "multilateralism is the expression of trust."[17] Data from a 2007 Program on International Policy Attitudes survey similarly reveals Republicans to have been 15 percent, 28 percent, and 24 percent more likely than Democrats to oppose treaties (1) prohibiting attacks against satellites, (2) implementing a nuclear test ban, and (3) bilaterally (with Russia) reducing nuclear stockpiles.[18]

This chapter further argues that these deep disagreements over international organizations and treaties have their origins in many of the same values and beliefs that divide liberal and conservative Americans over domestic issues like God and gun control. Cultural conservatives view international organizations like the United Nations as part of a secular humanist agenda to replace reliance upon God with reliance upon man. Cultural liberals, by contrast, tend to view international organizations as a means to spread a progressive vision of mankind's common humanity. Domestic disagreements over racial politics also shape attitudes towards the United Nations. For their part, economic conservatives and libertarians view international organizations as a threat to property and individual liberty. Economic liberals and communitarians, by contrast, view international organizations as a means to promote social justice and the equality of men.

Different kinds of liberals and conservatives may therefore disagree amongst themselves about *why* they like or dislike the United Nations, but they can largely agree in their basic normative position. This synergy of views contributes to the formation of a deep ideological divide: liberals like the United Nations; conservatives truly dislike it.

This chapter begins with a brief review of the history of America's dealings with international organizations and treaties. It then explores cultural politics in some depth, arguing that debates over American involvement in international organizations have been part of the broader battle between religious fundamentalists and modernists for much of the past century. Next it briefly examines the surprising persistence of race as a factor in American views of international organizations. It then turns to economic ideology and the idea of the United Nations as a "global social welfare state." This is followed by an exploration of the political dimensions of ideological debate over the United Nations, focusing on libertarian objections to the United Nations' "Agenda 21" and the perceived threat of "blue helmets" and "black helicopters." A final section briefly examines how ideology interacts with gender, education, and partisan media exposure to shape attitudes towards the United Nations. The concluding section addresses the implications of divided American opinion on multilateral treaties and institutions for U.S. foreign policy.

FROM THE LEAGUE OF NATIONS TO THE UNITED NATIONS

"A general association of nations must be formed under specific covenants for the purpose of affording mutual guarantees of political independence and territorial integrity to great and small states alike."[19]

—Democratic President Woodrow Wilson, 1918

"We have abstained from joining the League of Nations mainly for the purpose of avoiding political entanglements and committing ourselves to the assumption of the obligations of others . . . in which we have no direct interest."[20]

—Republican President Calvin Coolidge, 1923

As noted in the first paragraph of the Introduction, in his 1796 "Farewell Address" President George Washington cautioned against foreign entanglements. By that point, however, the young United States had already signed bilateral treaties with France, the Dutch Republic, Sweden, Britain, Prussia, Morocco, Algeria, Spain, and Tripoli.

American diplomacy in the nineteenth century would continue to be marked by a series of mostly bilateral treaties. For instance, in Chapter 9 we saw that the 1868 Burlingame Treaty promoted U.S. trade with China and opened U.S. borders to Chinese immigration. In Chapter 4 we also saw how, following the Civil War, a war-weary President Ulysses S. Grant and his secretary of state Hamilton Fish relied upon vigorous diplomacy to avoid another war with Britain, settling the Alabama Claims and signing the 1871 Treaty of Washington.

As U.S. power grew in the twentieth century, so did its involvement in bilateral treaty making. In 1906 President Theodore Roosevelt won the Nobel Peace Prize for brokering an end to the Russo-Japanese War. Clifford Berryman celebrated Roosevelt's efforts in a pair of editorial cartoons for the *Washington Post* in the summer of 1905 (Figure 10.1). The cartoon on the left depicts Roosevelt as

NAMING THE BABY

FIG. 10.1. President Theodore Roosevelt wins the 1906 Nobel Peace Prize for brokering the 1905 Russo-Japanese Portsmouth Treaty, 1905.

Sources: Clifford Berryman, *Washington Post,* June 17 and September 2, 1905. Both images courtesy of the National Archives. ARC 6010593 and 6010615.

a smiling Uncle Sam holding out two small chairs for Japan and Russia, depicted as diminutive children. Russia is bearded and beaten up. A peace dove with an olive branch in its beak sits overhead as Uncle Sam smiles, "The pleasure is all mine, gentlemen." "Naming the Baby," at right, depicts a wholesome woman labeled "Portsmouth" carrying a healthy baby labeled "Treaty." Roosevelt and Uncle Sam look on as two other men debate what to name their offspring. Both cartoons radiate paternalistic pride in America's accomplishment.

American involvement in multilateral treaties and institutions also increased in the twentieth century. Following World War I, Democratic president Woodrow Wilson played a major role at the Paris Peace Conference, which drafted the Treaty of Versailles and the Covenant of the League of Nations. As his 1918 "Fourteen Points" speech, quoted in the epigraph, suggests, Wilson was a strong advocate of a powerful league that would ensure a postwar peace. He was awarded the 1919 Nobel Peace Prize for his efforts.

Wilson failed, however, to win Senate ratification of the covenant, and the United States never joined his League of Nations. Senate majority leader and Foreign Relations Committee chairman Henry Cabot Lodge of Massachusetts led the Republican opposition and appealed to isolationism and American sovereignty. "Are you ready to put your soldiers at the disposition of other na-

ALL DRESSED UP AND NOWHERE TO GO

FIG. 10.2. President Woodrow Wilson fails to win Senate ratification of the Covenant of the League of Nations, which he helped craft at the Paris Peace Conference, 1920.

Source: Clifford Berryman, *Washington Evening Star,* April 5, 1920. Image courtesy of the National Archives. ARC 6011598.

tions?" Lodge asked the president.[21] On November 19, 1919, the final day of Senate debate over the league, Republican William E. Borah of Idaho gave one of the Senate's most famous speeches, making an eloquent case against ratification. Like Lodge, Borah highlighted the threat to American sovereignty, arguing that "This treaty . . . imperils . . . the right of our people to govern themselves free from all restraint, legal or moral, of foreign powers."[22]

On Easter Sunday, 1920, Washington, D.C., was hit by rains that forced a cancellation of the annual Easter festivities on the White House lawn. Clifford Berryman thought the disappointment of the children matched the disappointment of liberal internationalists who had hoped that the United States would join Wilson's League of Nations. In "All Dressed Up and Nowhere to Go," Berryman depicts President Wilson as a youthful Uncle Sam ready to play with the "Peace Plans" he had carefully prepared in his Easter egg basket (Figure 10.2). Buffeted by the "Anti-Treaty Storm," however, Uncle Sam stands forlorn, unable to play. Berryman's trademark teddy bear stands in solidarity with Wilson in the rain, making plain Berryman's sympathy for the president.

The situation was dramatically different thirty-five years later at the conclusion of World War II. President Franklin D. Roosevelt had first described the allied powers as the "United Nations" in 1941, and negotiations over the shape of a postwar international organization by that name began in 1944 at the Dumbarton Oaks estate in Georgetown, continuing at the Yalta Conference in early 1945. On June 26, 1945, fifty nations signed the Charter of the United Nations in San Francisco. Just one month later, on July 28, the U.S. Senate ratified the charter by an overwhelming vote of 89 to 2. "The action of the Senate," Democratic president Harry S. Truman rejoiced, "substantially advances the cause of world peace."[23]

But the United Nations, like the League of Nations that preceded it, proved to be a contentious political issue. For instance, Republican senator Jesse Helms of North Carolina used his position as chair of the Senate Foreign Relations Committee from 1995 to 2001 to block the payment of U.S. dues to the United Nations. His jealousy of U.S. sovereignty echoed that of Senator Lodge and the other Republican "Irreconcilables," who had opposed the League of Nations eighty years earlier. "The United Nations is being transformed from an institution of sovereign nations into a quasi-sovereign entity in itself," Helms lamented in a 1996 *Foreign Affairs*. "The United Nations has moved from facilitating diplomacy among nation-states to supplanting them altogether."[24]

John Bolton, a President George W. Bush recess appointment as the U.S. ambassador to the United Nations from August 2005 until December 2006, was also an outspoken critic. In 1994 he joked that "The Secretariat Building [of the U.N.] in New York has 38 stories. If you lost ten stories today, it wouldn't make a bit of difference." Senate Democrats successfully filibustered Bolton's confirmation as U.N. ambassador.

"THIS SATANIC SERPENT":
GOD'S RULE AND THE RULE OF MAN

"Christianity should be used to set things right here. It should be used to purify the world. We should rectify it by social actions."[25]

—Governor Woodrow Wilson (Democrat–New Jersey), 1911

"The League of Nations is doomed to signal failure for the simple reason that there has been a most conspicuous ignoring of the fact of God on the part of any, and all, of the men at the peace table."[26]

—*Presbyterian of the South* magazine, September 3, 1919

Why are Main Street liberals and conservatives today so divided over international treaties and institutions? Figure 10.3 reveals that all four of the dimensions of American ideology that we measured in our 2011 national survey were unique predictors of warmth towards the United Nations. Together with the standard demographic covariates, these four ideological predispositions accounted for a remarkable 35 percent of the variance in American feelings

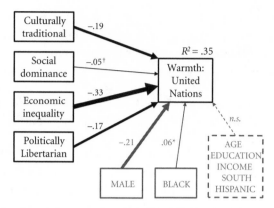

FIG. 10.3. Cultural, social, economic, and political ideologies each uniquely predict warmth towards the United Nations.

Note: A regression analysis. † $p = .058$, * $p < .05$, all other p's $< .001$. *Data source:* OU Institute for US-China Issues, 2011.

towards the United Nations. By contrast, the situational variables that we measured were weak predictors of feelings towards the United Nations. For instance, when exposure to and interest in international news, and direct foreign contacts, friends, and travel were added to the regression, they contributed just 1 percent of additional variance.

This section explores the top path in Figure 10.3: why cultural liberals and conservatives differ in their feelings towards the United Nations. The next sections will turn to the other three paths in the figure, exploring why social, economic, and political liberals and conservatives differ over the United Nations.

The serial mediation model in Figure 10.4 reveals that cultural conservatives felt cooler towards the United Nations than cultural liberals did, in large part because of their greater biblical literalism, which is partially accounted for by the greater value they placed on a morality of purity.

How should this statistical finding be interpreted?

Historian Markku Ruotsila has advanced the provocative argument that over the past century, Christian anti-internationalism has been part of a wider fundamentalist reaction against the Social Gospel, modernist theology, and even secular humanism more broadly. The League of Nations controversy was the pivotal starting point. Religious conservatives and modernists had mostly confined themselves to debating theological issues prior to World War I. Following the league debates, however, they began publicly contesting domestic political issues. For instance, in Chapter 2 we discussed William Jennings Bryan and the 1925 Scopes Trial, which upheld a Tennessee law prohibiting the teaching of evolution and was central to the broader fundamentalist/modernist con-

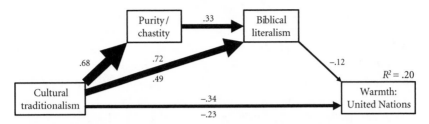

FIG. 10.4. Cultural conservatives feel cooler towards the United Nations than cultural liberals do, in part due to their greater biblical literalism, which is in part accounted for by the greater value they place on purity.

Note: A serial mediation model. Indirect path via purity only was not statistically significant; the other two indirect effects were. Statistics are online at SUP.org. Seven demographic covariates are not shown. *Data source:* OU Institute for US-China Issues, 2011.

troversy of the 1920s and 1930s. "The evangelical critique of the League of Nations survived throughout the interwar years and [was] carried over, largely in toto, into the cold war experiment with the United Nations," Ruotsila contends, "and resurfaced in early-twenty-first century debates."[27]

This section argues that our mediation analysis lends empirical support to Ruotsila's contention. Religious differences on international organizations persist in our 2011 survey data: in Figure 10.4, the inclusion of biblical literalism and the moral value of purity as mediators accounts for over three-quarters of the direct relationship between traditionalism and feelings towards the United Nations.[28]

Progressive Christians were strong supporters of the League of Nations. At the turn of the century, "Kingdom Theology" promoted the *post*millennial pursuit of a perfect world. "No visible return of Christ to earth is to be expected, but rather the long and steady advance of the spiritual kingdom," wrote William Newton Clarke, member of the New York chapter of the Brotherhood of the Kingdom.[29] The Social Gospel promoted a liberal, universalistic view of the brotherhood of all peoples, regardless of race or religion. In his seminal 1917 *A Theology for the Social Gospel*, Walter Rauschenbusch declared that "Before the war the social gospel dealt with social classes; today it is being translated into . . . a Christianizing of international relations."[30]

The religious underpinnings of liberal internationalism have been embodied in the persons of numerous American statesmen over the past century. As the epigraph suggests, President Woodrow Wilson viewed progressive Christianity as a redemptive force that could be used to "purify the world." Wilson was a devout Presbyterian thoroughly steeped in the Social Gospel tradition. Indeed, historian Andrew Preston argues that Wilsonianism was a "global application of progressive Christianity."[31]

While modernist Protestants lost the League of Nations ratification fight, they were successful advocates of the United Nations system created after World War II. John Foster Dulles, who would go on to become secretary of state under President Dwight D. Eisenhower in the 1950s, ran the Federal Council of Churches' influential Commission on a Just and Durable Peace, and he helped draft the preamble to the United Nations Charter in the 1940s. Like Wilson before him, Dulles was a liberal Presbyterian who endorsed the Social Gospel view of the brotherhood of man. Americans, he argued, should "use our power, not to perpetuate itself, but to create, support, and eventually give way to international institutions drawing their vitality from the whole family of nations."[32]

The internationalism of President Barack Obama is also best understood in light of his religious beliefs. As argued in the Introduction and in Chapter 4, Obama is no liberal dove. Instead, he has embraced the fighting Christianity of the Social Gospel. Like Dulles before him, Obama has not abandoned Christian love but has transformed it into a Christian realism suitable to action within an imperfect world.

Over the past century, the conservative Christian response to the progressive Christian embrace of liberal internationalism has been marked by three interweaving themes. The first views international organizations through the lens of premillennial dispensationalism, depicting them as the work of the Antichrist. For the most part, this appears to have been a minority fundamentalist view. A second and more widely embraced conservative perspective portrays international organizations as a secular humanist challenge to God's rule. A third view condemns international organizations out of opposition to the mixing of Christian and non-Christian peoples. Appealing to popular prejudices, this view of international organizations may extend beyond conservative Christians to a broader Christian public.

Satan and the Second Coming. Our five-item biblical literalism scale included one item specifically tapping belief in the Devil: "*The basic cause of evil in this world is Satan, who is still constantly & ferociously fighting against God.*" One reason that our biblical literalism scale helped account for greater cultural conservative coolness towards the United Nations may be that some fundamentalists view the United Nations as the work of the Antichrist.

With the rapid social change that accompanied industrialization at the turn of the century, the United States was ripe for fundamentalism. Biblical prophecy, Ruotsila argues, brought "order, predictability, and clear causality to modern chaos."[33] As noted in the Chapter 7 discussion of the European Union, premillennial dispensationalists preached that in the last seven years before the Second Coming, an anti-Christian world empire would attempt the purification and perfection of the world through secular human effort. Republican senator Warren Harding of Ohio, who would go on to succeed Wilson as president, was a Baptist who objected to the League of Nations' presumption to achieve goals that could only be reached on "the millennial day that marks the beginning of heaven on earth."[34] During the League of Nations ratification fight, the World Christian Fundamentals Association was among the most passionate of the naysayers.

The premillennial dispensationalist view of international organizations did not die with the League of Nations. "Scripture does prophesy" the establishment of world government, Iowa fundamentalist preacher M. G. Hatcher declared in 1943, "mak[ing] possible for the World Dictator, the Anti-Christ, to take over control."[35] Dispensationalist animus was directed at the United Nations during and after the Cold War. Fundamentalist televangelist Pat Robertson, who competed for the 1988 Republican presidential nomination, was well known for his prophesy beliefs. In his 1991 bestseller *The New World Order*, Robertson asserted that international organizations like the United Nations were actually seeking the creation of "a new order for the human race under the domination of Lucifer and his followers."[36]

Robertson is not alone. In their wildly successful *Left Behind* series of fictional prophecy novels, evangelist Tim LaHaye and Jerry Jenkins tell the story of Armageddon, in the style of Tom Clancy. Their books depict the U.N. secretary general as the Antichrist. He is seen as marshaling the evil forces of world government against the followers of Jesus Christ. Seven of the sixteen novels in the *Left Behind* series reached number one on national best-seller lists, and over 65 million total copies have been sold. There have also been three film adaptations as well as several video games.

In Chapter 8 we explored how premillennial dispensationalism contributes to conservative Christian warmth towards Israel. Warmth towards Israel appears to contribute to conservative Christian hostility towards the United Nations as well. In 1986 Pat Robertson described the United Nations as "a sounding board for anti-American, anti-Western, and anti-Israel propaganda."[37] In his 2006 *Jerusalem Countdown*, pastor John Hagee of Christians United for Israel wrote that "The U.N. has labeled *Zionism* as *racism*, which means it has a longstanding documented hatred for Israel."[38] In 2012, pastor Mark Hitchcock of Faith Bible Church in Edmond, Oklahoma, similarly described the United Nations as an "Israel-despising body."[39]

This linkage of feelings towards Israel and feelings towards the United Nations is not confined to Evangelical pastors. In a 2008 address to the Knesset in Jerusalem, President George W. Bush declared that "We consider it a source of shame that the United Nations routinely passes more human rights resolutions against the freest democracy in the Middle East than any other nation in the world." As noted in the epigraph to this chapter, the "2012 Republican Platform" explicitly links American support for the United Nations to its treatment of Israel.

The Israel-U.N. link extends beyond religious and political elites to broader American public opinion. In our 2011 survey, warmth towards Israel was a substantial predictor ($\beta = -.26$) of opposition to "strengthening international organizations" and "supporting the United Nations." Perhaps even more indicative of the continuing influence of End of Days prophesy belief on American attitudes towards the United Nations today, a mediation analysis revealed that only the item "*God gave Palestine (today's Israel) to the Jewish people*" and *not* a four-item measure of biblical literalism (tapping belief in God, Satan, the Bible, and the Bible's superiority to science) mediated the relationship between cultural traditionalism and warmth towards the United Nations.[40] The Israel-U.N. link clearly runs deep.

Satan and secular humanism. Central to conservative Christian anti-internationalism is the more widespread belief that international organizations represent a secular challenge to God's rule on earth. Following World War I, many conservative Protestants were outraged that neither the Treaty of Versailles nor the Covenant of the League of Nations contained the words "God" or "Deity." Baptist J. C. Massee depicted the league as "a deliberate effort to dethrone God in the earth." Like the Tower of Babel, it sought to "make the judgment of the crowd a moral law." Cortland Myers, also a Baptist, went considerably further, at least rhetorically, denouncing the league covenant as "the most atheistic, infidel document that was ever printed in this world." Although most Methodists then were proud advocates of progressive Christianity and the league, conservative Eugene Thwing used the league issue to resist the modernist turn in his denomination. In his 1919 *The League of Nations as a Moral Issue*, Thwing decried the league as an anti-Christian "device of man's contrivance, which was built without recognition of God's governing hand in the affairs of men."[41] For conservative Protestants like Massee, Myers, and Thwing, fighting the league was an international front in the domestic battle against progressive Christianity and the Social Gospel.

Chapter 1 suggested that liberals and conservatives differ in their intuitive feelings about human nature. Liberals tend to view mankind as basically good, and the world as therefore perfectible through human effort, while conservatives generally view man as born in sin, and therefore reliant upon God for salvation. This cleavage has implications for liberal and conservative attitudes towards both national and international governance. "Conservatives tend to take a pessimistic stance regarding the possibilities for transforming the international system," writes Colin Dueck in *Hard Line*. "Their view of human nature leads them to skepticism regarding schemes for permanent peace through international organizations, treaties, or political reform."[42]

Christian conservatives often based their opposition to the League of Nations on mankind's selfish and sinful nature. "Universal domain and perfect peace are beyond the reach of man," *Presbyterian* magazine declared in January 1919. "They will never be accomplished save by the power and personal presence of him who has the right to reign." In his *The League of Nations in the Light of the Bible*, dispensationalist Arno Gaebelein similarly mocked the "great delusion that man, by his power . . . will succeed in making the world better."[43] Only Christ can save the world.

These hostile views of the League of Nations were echoed in conservative religious criticisms of the United Nations during the Cold War. In 1950, evangelist Louis Bauman condemned the United Nations as "Man's supreme attempt to bring 'on earth peace, good will among men' without the partnership of Him whom Almighty God has ordained as 'The Prince of Peace.'" Early Cold War dispensationalist Wilbur Smith referred to the United Nations as "this satanic serpent" for a false humanitarianism that actually seeks to "mock God and deify man." In his 1970 best seller *The Late Great Planet Earth*, evangelist Hal Lindsey condemned the United Nations because "Jesus has been excluded from the premises." To Christian nationalist Rousas John Rushdoony, writing in 1978, the United Nations had developed a new "religion of humanity" involving a "faith in humanity as such, not in a transcendental moral or spiritual order."[44] The United Nations, Rushdoony argued, was fundamentally a religious issue.

Does this conservative Christian view of international organizations like the United Nations persist today? Our biblical literalism scale included the item "*I have no doubt at all that God exists.*" One likely reason our biblical literalism scale accounted for over three-quarters of the relationship between cultural ideology and feelings towards the United Nations (see Figure 10.4) is that for some Americans at least, belief in God's rule and belief in secular governing bodies can be zero-sum.

A group of social psychologists led by Aaron Kay at Duke University have recently conducted research that lends support to this interpretation. Earlier psychologists had demonstrated that feelings of personal control over one's destiny are associated with mental health, while the loss of personal control is associated with feelings of helplessness and depression.[45] Kay and colleagues first demonstrated that when feelings of personal control diminish, people are more likely to turn to external sources of control in a process they call "compensatory control."[46] They later argued that just as internal and external sources of control are substitutable, two different sources of *external* control—God and government—are also interchangeable. In a remarkable series of experiments,

Kay and his colleagues were able to manipulate beliefs in government stability, leading subjects to temporarily increase or decrease their belief in God's controlling hand. The process, furthermore, is bidirectional: another experiment manipulated beliefs in a divine hand in the operation of the universe, altering levels of support for government. Beliefs in the controlling hand of God and government, in other words, exist in "hydraulic" relationship: as one increases, the other tends to decrease.[47]

Our survey data suggests that Kay's work on God and national governments as external sources of control may extend to the "World Government" that is the United Nations. The mediating role of biblical literalism in Figure 10.4 could reflect cultural traditionalists' greater reliance on God as an external source of control in the world, compared to "human" institutions like "world government." By contrast, cultural liberals may rely more on national and international governments (such as the United Nations) as sources of external control.

Pagans and Christians. "Be ye not unequally yoked together with unbelievers, for what fellowship hath righteousness with unrighteousness?" reads 2 Corinthians 6:14. "And what communion hath light with darkness?" A third theme of Christian anti-internationalism condemns international organizations out of opposition to the mixing of Christians and pagans. Condemning the "Yoke fellowship" is one way that Christian anti-internationalists have appealed to desires for Christian purity among the fundamentalist faithful, as well as popular prejudices within the broader Christian public.

Advocates of the League of Nations appealed to the brotherhood of man central to the Social Gospel. "My dream," President Woodrow Wilson declared on July 4, 1914, "is that America will come into the full light of day when her flag is the flag not only of America, but also of humanity."[48] The inclusive nature of the league would realize that dream.

Christian conservatives viewed Wilson's universalism as apostasy. "How can God bless these nations, who continue in idolatries, who defy His laws?" asked Arno Gaebelein. "Can He bless professing Christian nations, banded together in pact with heathen nations?" Cooperating with non-Christians was a threat to Christian purity. "If this nation is to be Christian," Baptist minister Russell H. Conwell of Philadelphia roared in a sermon, "we will build a Christian navy, and we will have a Christian army . . . that shall ever set its face against the infidels and against the heathen, and never, never, permit them to weaken us."[49]

The conservative Protestant aversion to a "mixed world" could extend beyond contacts with non-Christians to contacts with other, less "pure" Christians as well. A significant subtheme in arguments against the league was that it would be dominated by Catholic countries and become an instrument of the Pope. For instance, Weert Janssen, a Lutheran pastor from Missouri, warned that the league would become a "society of nations under control of the Pope, that is the aim and hope of the Catholic Church today." Anti-Catholic sentiment undergirded many criticisms of the league. The Pope and Rome were depicted as the Antichrist, and the League of Nations as its demonic institution.[50]

The aversion to "Yoke fellowship" continued as a source of Cold War Christian antipathy towards the United Nations. "The majority vote in the U.N. is now being cast by heathen peoples from Asia and Africa," lamented Pentecostal R. A. Kerby in 1963. Together with mainline Protestants and secular liberals, Kerby claimed, these heathens worshiped the United Nations as a false idol.[51]

Our 2011 survey data suggests that desires to defend Christian purity continue to shape cultural conservative coolness towards the United Nations today. The moral value of purity accounted for three-quarters of the direct relationship between cultural ideology and biblical literalism (Figure 10.4, top left), which then shaped feelings towards the United Nations.[52] "While the notion of compromise is central to the U.N.'s mission, it is for the most part incompatible with Christian conservatism," historian Andrew Preston argues. "Indeed, the very bases of evangelicalism and fundamentalism are ideological, theological, and cultural *purity* grounded in a refusal to compromise with the irreligious and immoral forces of liberalism."[53]

"A COLORED LEAGUE OF NATIONS": RACE AND INTERNATIONAL ORGANIZATIONS

"The majority of the nations composing the League do not belong to the white race of men. On the contrary, they are a conglomerate of black, yellow, brown, and red races, frequently so intermingled and commingled as to constitute an unclassifiable mongrel breed."[54]
— Senator James Reed (Democrat–Missouri), 1919

"The American people have rejoiced to see the people of the old colonial empires attain their independence. This movement is in our tradition. It fulfills on a grand scale that prophetic phrase in our Declaration of Independence that all men—not just Americans—are created equal and have unalienable rights. . . . Our posture in the United Nations is based on the belief, so amply justified year after year, that the interests which we hold in common with the great majority of nations—regardless of size, power, population, race or region—are so much stronger than the interests which divide us."[55]
— U.S. Ambassador to the United Nations Adlai Stevenson, 1962

Social dominance orientation, the belief that *"Inferior groups should stay in their place,"* was also a small but statistically significant predictor of feelings towards the United Nations (see Figure 10.3). "Undoubtedly, the least researched,

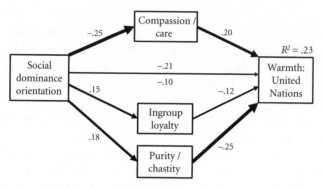

FIG. 10.5. Americans higher on social dominance feel cooler towards the United Nations than those lower on it, in part because they value compassion less, and loyalty and purity more.

Note: A simultaneous mediation model. All three indirect paths shown here were statistically significant. Fairness and authority were not and are not displayed. Indirect effect statistics are online at SUP.org. Seven demographic covariates are not shown. *Data source:* OU Institute for US-China Issues, 2011.

understood, or discussed factor in the evolution of American attitudes towards international institutions is race," argues Edward Luck, former president of the United Nations Association of the USA.[56] Though small, the influence of race on feelings towards the United Nations merits closer consideration.

Why would social dominance orientation shape feelings towards the United Nations? As displayed in Figure 10.5, of the five moral values that we measured in our 2011 survey, three were statistically significant mediators of the relationship. Americans higher on social dominance orientation felt cooler towards the United Nations than those lower on it, in part because they valued *compassion* less, and in part because they valued *purity* and in-group *loyalty* more. Together, moral values accounted for over 80 percent of the direct relationship.[57]

These conflicting moral values have been enduring themes in American debates over international organizations. As noted in the discussion of Haiti in Chapter 6, race was central to the Senate debate over the League of Nations. Speaking on the Senate floor, conservative Democrat James Reed of Missouri argued against joining "a colored League of Nations." As the epigraph reveals, Reed appealed to racial *purity*, warning against the dangers of contact with a "mongrel breed."

Republican Henry Cabot Lodge, who led the Senate opposition to joining the league, also appealed to racism. Invoking in-group *loyalty*, he warned that signing the covenant would lead to a flood of immigration: "Are we ready to leave it to other nations to determine whether we shall admit to the United

States a flood of Japanese, Chinese, and Hindi labor?" Lodge further claimed that immigration was an issue not just of labor but also of the need to "maintain the *purity* of our race."[58]

As noted in Chapter 6, race became a foreign policy issue during the civil rights movement of the 1960s and 1970s. Segregationists "argued that decolonization gave control of the U.N. to Third World nations with an ingrained hatred of whites," historian Thomas Noer writes. African countries, segregationists claimed, were "obsessed with revenge against Caucasians."[59] In 1963, Republican congressman James B. Utt of Orange County, California, claimed that "a large contingent of barefooted Africans" was training in Georgia as part of a United Nations military exercise to take over the United States. In 1971, conservative Democrat John Rarick of Louisiana objected to the U.N.'s "aggressive program . . . to mobilize the people of the world to combat racism."[60]

In 1962 Republican senator John Tower of Texas warned against the Kennedy administration's support for anticolonial independence movements in Africa, for "no importance is given to the primitive state of millions of tribesmen, or their age-old feuds which will erupt as the Afro-Europeans are driven out." As the epigraph reveals, Adlai Stevenson, Kennedy's ambassador to the United Nations, defended the administration's position by appealing to a common humanity—regardless of race. Stevenson was advocating compassion for the Africans and downplaying the value of a narrow in-group loyalty. In 1965 Secretary of State Dean Rusk similarly claimed that "This is the last nation on the face of the earth to shun diversity, or to reject the open forum, or to fear the growth of democratic processes."[61]

Figure 10.3 also reveals that blacks in our 2011 survey felt slightly warmer (β = .06, $p < .05$) towards the United Nations than nonblacks did. Looking instead at whites and controlling for age, gender, education, income, and being from the South, whites (43°) felt 6° cooler towards the United Nations than nonwhites (49°) did, a small but statistically significant difference.[62] When it comes to the United Nations, in short, both race and racism matter.

A "GLOBAL SOCIAL WELFARE STATE":
THE UNITED NATIONS AND NORTH-SOUTH REDISTRIBUTION

"Like a shipwrecked, exhausted Gulliver on the beach of Lilliput, America is to be tied down with threads, strand by stand, until it cannot move when it wakens . . . our sovereignty is being surrendered . . . America has ensnared itself in a web that restricts its freedom of action, diminishes its liberty, and siphons off its wealth."[63]
—Republican Pat Buchanan, 1998

Fundamentalist Protestants and racial segregationists are not the only conservatives who take issue with international organizations. Figure 10.3 reveals that economic and political ideology were also unique predictors of feelings towards the United Nations. Economic ideology divides Americans over the United Nations: economic conservatives oppose international organizations for their perceived efforts to redistribute income. These organizations seek American wealth, Pat Buchanan claimed in 1998: "the transfer of money, prestige, power and sovereignty from America to a new class of parasite-mandarins."[64]

Conservatives have long feared that international organizations seek to milk American riches. In a 1927 book on the League of Nations, A. Cressy Morrison, the president of the New York Academy of Sciences, lamented that among foreigners "There is a united sentiment that anything which can be done to distribute our prosperity throughout the world, and advance other nations by tapping our sources of income is a perfectly normal and proper thing to do."[65]

This fear intensified with rapid decolonization in Africa and Asia following World War II. "Under the control of the numerous Third World nations, the U.N. has been actively promoting a comprehensive and totalitarian system of global management," the Cato Institute's Doug Bandow warned in 1985. "If the Group of 77 gets its way, such resource transfers will be carried out as a matter of right by U.N. institutions controlled by a Third World majority."[66]

While the Cato Institute's rhetoric was alarmist and overblown, there is little denying that with decolonization and the doubling of U.N. membership by 1960, the U.N. General Assembly came to be dominated by developing nations sharing a common postcolonial ideology. As Daniel Patrick Moynihan, U.S. ambassador to the United Nations under President Gerald R. Ford, argued in a discerning 1975 article for the neoconservative *Commentary* magazine, these new U.N. member states inherited the progressive welfare state philosophy of the British left. Ideas about class conflict within nations were internationalized, with the global "North" seen as exploiting the global "South." In this view, helping the developing world, in the words of the Indian food minister, was "*not* ... charity but deferred compensation*" for past exploitation. Moynihan called for a frontal U.S. assault on the "tyranny of the U.N.'s 'new majority,'" with its "redistributionist bias."[67]

Congressman Ron Paul agrees with Moynihan's diagnosis of the redistributionist disease, but not his prescription: rather than confront the U.N. majority, the United States should instead quit the United Nations. "There is no way that you can have the concept of private property rights" under the United Nations, Paul argued in a 1998 John Birch Society video. "They believe in welfare redistribution, socialist redistribution—everybody owns everything—and they would take from the wealthy and give to the poor to get an equal balance."[68] Paul first introduced his "American Sovereignty Restoration Act" in 1997 to withdraw the United States from the United Nations and to remove the U.N.

headquarters building from New York City. He resubmitted the bill in every subsequent Congress until his retirement in 2013.

BLUE HELMETS AND BLACK HELICOPTERS:
WORLD GOVERNMENT AND INDIVIDUAL LIBERTY

"Just a generation ago, this place was called America. Now, after the worldwide implementation of a U.N.-led program called Agenda 21, it's simply known as 'the Republic.' There is no president. No Congress. No Supreme Court. No freedom. There are only the Authorities."[69]

—Glenn Beck and Harriet Parke, 2012

Like the wildly successful *Hunger Games* trilogy, *Agenda 21* is a dystopian novel starring a teenage heroine and set in the police state that America will soon become. Unlike *Hunger Games*, however, *Agenda 21* includes a number of far-right conspiracy theories about radical environmentalism, such as the privileging of animal rights over human rights. In the first chapter, a man is sentenced to death for running over a snake. And in his afterword (the novel itself is written by Harriet Parke), Glenn Beck declares the U.N.'s real Agenda 21 as "evil," "anti-free market," and "anti-American."[70]

What is Agenda 21? It is a nonbinding U.N. resolution from the 1992 Rio "Earth" Summit that advocates smart, sustainable growth for the twenty-first century. Many libertarians, however, interpret "sustainable" to mean "socialist," and the U.N.'s Agenda 21 as part of a broader conspiracy to create a communist world government. In a 2012 video, the John Birch Society argues that Agenda 21 will involve, among other things, the "seizure of private property" and "relocating people from rural areas to cities." It urges Americans to "Choose Freedom" by opposing Agenda 21 locally.[71] Many Tea Party activists have done so, disrupting county and city urban planning meetings across the country.

Beck's fiction has been matched by mass market nonfiction. In 2012, HarperCollins published Fox News analyst Dick Morris's *Here Come the Black Helicopters! U.N. Global Governance and the Loss of Freedom*. The front flap declares in full-capitals, "Warning: Our National Sovereignty and Our Freedom Are in Grave Danger." The copy then explains that "Stealthily advancing, the globalists and socialists at the United Nations, and in the United States itself, are trying to dilute our national sovereignty, undermine our democratic values, and mandate massive transfers of our wealth and technology to third world countries." The back flap concludes, "They call it 'global governance.' We call it the end of freedom. . . . The day when the virtual black helicopters land."[72]

This was not the first time that far-right conspiracy theories about the United Nations entered mainstream popular culture. In February 1987, ABC aired a prime-time television miniseries called *Amerika* set ten years after a Soviet conquest. The "United Nations Special Service Unit" acts as "peacekeepers" policing a demoralized America. Composed primarily of Eastern Europeans, this U.N. "Special Service" (SS) is reminiscent of the Nazi Schutzstaffel (SS).

Amerika aired at a time when the Reagan administration was getting tough on the United Nations. In 1982, U.S. ambassador to the United Nations Jeane Kirkpatrick derided the U.N.'s regulatory philosophy as "global socialism." In 1984 President Reagan withdrew the United States from participation in UNESCO, claiming that it was hostile to the "basic institutions of a free society, especially a free market and a free press."[73] And following the airing of *Amerika* in February 1987, Alan Keyes, the ranking State Department official in charge of U.N. affairs, told a House subcommittee that the miniseries was only "*probably going too far*" in "portray[ing] the United Nations as the rubric under which the liberties of this country are finally subverted and destroyed." Nonetheless, "those tendencies exist."[74]

But libertarian fears of the United Nations are having a greater impact on state and national politics today. The 2012 Texas GOP Platform declares that "We support the withdrawal of the United States from the United Nations and the removal of U.N. headquarters from U.S. soil. We oppose implementation of the U.N. Agenda 21 Program." In June 2012 Alabama governor Robert Bentley signed State Bill 477 prohibiting the state from implementing any policy recommendations "originating in, or traceable to 'Agenda 21,' adopted by the United Nations."[75] The Alabama House and Senate had both approved the bill *unanimously*. In April 2013, the Republican majority House and Senate in Missouri passed a similar measure.

Libertarian fears of Agenda 21 are increasingly influencing national politics as well. The *national* "2012 Republican Platform" states, "We strongly reject the U.N. Agenda 21 as erosive of American sovereignty, and we oppose any form of U.N. Global Tax."[76]

Why are libertarians today so much more hostile towards the United Nations than are communitarians? Two themes dominate libertarian rhetoric about the United Nations: the futility and danger of contact with communist countries, and the threat that the United Nations poses to U.S. sovereignty, self-defense, and "freedom of action." Our survey included a measure of warmth towards "Communist countries," but it did not include any direct measures of attitudes towards sovereignty or self-defense. It did, however, include measures of the Protestant ethic of self-help, and of attitudes towards gun control that can serve as proxies for sovereignty and self-defense. Figure 10.6 reveals that each of these variables acted as unique mediators of the relationship between political ideology and feelings towards the United Nations. Together, they accounted for three-quarters of the direct relationship.[77]

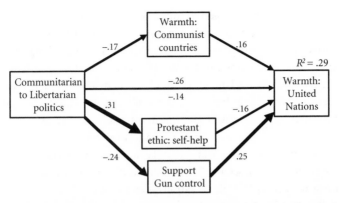

FIG. 10.6. The Nanny State: Libertarians feel cooler toward the United Nations than communitarians do, in part because of their greater anticommunism and greater concerns about sovereignty and self-defense.

Note: A simultaneous mediation model. All three indirect paths were statistically significant. Indirect effect statistics are online at SUP.org. Seven standard demographic covariates are not shown. Data source: OU Institute for US-China Issues, 2011.

Anticommunism. Anticommunism has long been central to libertarianism in the United States; it has also been central to libertarian critiques of international organizations. During the debate over the League of Nations in 1919, David Jayne Hill of the Independence League decried both the proposed League of Nations and International Labor Organization as part of a "Socialized State" that would threaten individual liberty. A former assistant secretary of state, Hill warned that these new international organizations would seek "absolutism under omnipotent government control."[78]

Libertarian fears of communism and international organizations intensified with the onset of the Cold War. "Hardcore anticommunists," Edward Luck argues, "came to see the U.N. as a modern day Trojan horse, offering a means for spies and subversives to infiltrate American soil."[79] The United Nations was implicated in the "McCarthyism" of the first half of the 1950s. In 1952, the U.S. Senate held hearings on "Activities of U.S. Citizens Employed by the U.N.," seeking to expose American communists at the United Nations. Alger Hiss, later charged with giving state secrets to the Soviet Union, had represented the State Department at the 1945 San Francisco conference founding the United Nations.

For some on the libertarian right, the U.N.'s communist member states made it contaminating. "The United Nations," Senator Barry Goldwater wrote in his 1960 *The Conscience of a Conservative*, "is in part a Communist organization."[80] After the United Nations admitted Red China in 1971, expelling Taiwan, Goldwater declared that "The time has come, for us to cut off all financial help, withdraw as a member, and ask the United Nations to find a headquarters location outside the United States that is more in keeping with the philosophy of the majority of voting members, someplace like Moscow or Peking."[81] Goldwater's views were not confined to the political elite. "Militant anticommunism contributed to fears of the United Nations," argues historian Lisa McGirr about grassroots conservatives in the 1960s. "After all, since the Right opposed diplomatic overtures with the Soviet Union, summit talks, and treaties, it logically followed that it would oppose an organization in which . . . socialist nations had membership."[82] Many elite and popular libertarians, in other words, were *in principle* opposed to a secular "Yoke fellowship" between the democratic and communist worlds. "The United Nations does not represent people," Kirkpatrick rightly noted in 1996 Senate testimony, "and it cannot be said to represent people until all the governments present there are representative democracies."[83]

There was also a *practical* libertarian objection: communists were using the United Nations as a bullhorn. "By recognizing the right of Communist regimes to participate in the U.N. as equals," Goldwater argued, "we grant Communist propaganda a presumption of reasonableness it otherwise would not have."[84] Republican Robert Taft of Ohio agreed, arguing in 1975 that the United Nations was "a propaganda forum for the Communist powers."[85]

Libertarian fears of the U.N.'s propaganda value to communist tyrants have not dissipated with the end of the Cold War. On December 22, 2011, the U.N. General Assembly observed a moment of silence to mark the passing of North Korean leader Kim Jong-il. U.N. offices later lowered their flags to half-mast to mark Kim's funeral. Many American conservatives were outraged. "In dipping its flag to half mast, the U.N. is effectively delivering a message of encouragement to a North Korean regime which sustains itself by way of repression, murder and nuclear proliferation," former *Wall Street Journal* editorial writer Claudia Rosett wrote on her blog. "A U.N. flag that is lowered to half-mast for Kim Jong Il is a flag [that] does not deserve to fly at all."[86] By memorializing Kim, the United Nations had revealed itself to be a morally bankrupt organization, a body which could be used as a megaphone for communist tyrants, undermining the cause of liberty.

Sovereignty and self-defense. Figure 10.6 also reveals that belief in the Protestant ethic of self-help and positions on gun control also mediate the relationship between political ideology and feelings towards the United Nations. As noted in Chapters 4 (see Figure 4.4) and 6, our survey measured endorsement of the Protestant ethic with two items: "*People are responsible for their own situation in life*" and "*People should not count on others to solve their problems.*" Respondents also located their position on a "gun control" placement ruler anchored by "strongly oppose" and "strongly support." Our mediation analysis suggests that these items act as proxies for sovereignty/liberty and the right to self-defense.

Debates over the United Nations have long echoed domestic debates over the proper balance between individual liberty and the greater good. "American ambivalence towards government at home is paralleled," Edward Luck rightly notes, "in American attitudes towards global governance and intergovernmental institutions."[87] Libertarians, jealous of their individual liberties at home, are equally jealous of U.S. national sovereignty abroad. Communitarians, by contrast, see government as playing a greater role in providing collective goods like security, and so view both individual liberty and national sovereignty as less absolute.

The core libertarian fear is one of loss of *control*, whether of the individual to the U.S. government, or of the United States to a world government. In 1962, Congressman Utt introduced one of many bills to revoke U.S. membership in the United Nations, claiming, "This nation cannot survive as a Republic as long as we are *shackled* to an organization by a treaty which supersedes the Constitution."[88] In 1971, conservative Democrat John R. Rarick of Louisiana proposed legislation to "remove the United States from the U.N. and the U.N. from the United States, thus freeing our people from the *ever tightening yoke* of international controls and the erosion of national sovereignty and constitutional government."[89] Note that "shackled" and "yoke" are both metaphors of control.

Americans, from the libertarian perspective, should not cede their sovereignty but embrace the Protestant ethic of self-help. "International organizations—whether the United Nations, the World Trade Organization, or any others—will not protect American interests. Only America can do that," Republican senator Bob Dole declared in 1995. "U.S. sovereignty must be defended, not delegated."[90] Dole could not have been too surprised when Senate Republicans voted down the U.N. disability treaty he later championed in 2012.

The National Rifle Association (NRA) has been one of the American right's most vociferous critics of the United Nations. The NRA's Wayne LaPierre dedicated his 2006 *The Global War on Your Guns: Inside the U.N. Plan to Destroy the Bill of Rights* to fellow NRA members who "have thus far safeguarded American freedom from the global offensive of the United Nations." The book's description invokes the menace of "an armed U.N. platoon of blue helmets [that] can knock on your door to take your guns." During a 2007 book tour, LaPierre told the *Liberty Sentinel* of Florida that "Our freedom and the Bill of Rights are what make our country the greatest in the world, and the last thing Americans want is to let the U.N. succeed in taking that away."[91] More recently, on July 26, 2012, Republican senator Jerry Moran of Kansas sent a letter cosigned by fifty other senators to President Obama and Secretary of State Clinton warning of the danger that the U.N. Arms Trade Treaty poses to the Second Amendment: "Our country's sovereignty and the constitutional protection of these individual freedoms must not be infringed."[92]

Supporters of international organizations have tended to view U.S. sovereignty in less zero-sum terms. "When we ratify the San Francisco charter and become a member of the international organization, we lose no American rights, we surrender no American sovereignty, and invite no interference or meddling with American domestic affairs," Democrat Joseph Hill of Alabama claimed during the U.S. Senate ratification of the U.N. Charter in 1945. "We continue [to be] the master of our own household."[93]

Underlying the more communitarian view of international organizations is a greater recognition of interdependence—that in a nuclear world U.S. security is bound up with the security of other nations. "Only the creation of a world government can prevent the impending self-destruction of mankind," Albert Einstein warned in 1952.[94] "The science of weapons and war has made us all, far more than eighteen years ago in San Francisco, one world and one human race with one common destiny," President John F. Kennedy similarly declared in 1963. "In such a world, absolute sovereignty no longer assures us of absolute security."

From a communitarian perspective, some restrictions on liberty actually serve the cause of liberty, whether at the domestic or international level. "We are every day, in one sense, accepting limitations upon our complete freedom of action," Secretary of State Dean Rusk noted thoughtfully in testimony before the Senate Foreign Relations Committee in 1965. "Law is a process by which we increase our range of freedom . . . by being able to predict what others are going to do."[95] Rusk was talking about the United Nations and U.S. national sovereignty, but he could have been making a communitarian case for gun control.

A DOG THAT BARKED, AND ONE THAT DIDN'T

We have already seen that in our 2011 survey blacks felt warmer towards the United Nations than whites did. Two other demographic variables in Figure 10.3 also merit closer examination.

Gender ($\beta = -.21$) was a dog that barked loudly. Controlling for age, education, income, and being black, Hispanic, or from the South, women (53°) still felt 15° warmer towards the United Nations than men (38°) did.[96] In Chapter 1, we saw that men are more conservative than women (see Figure 1.3). Adding ideology as an additional covariate, however, only reduced the gender gap to 12°, still a medium-sized difference.[97] Further research is needed to better understand the reasons for the gender gap in feelings towards the United Nations.

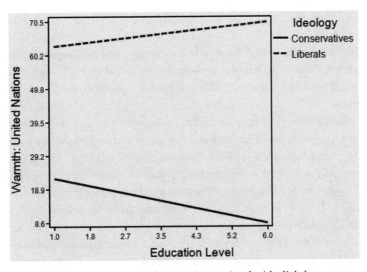

FIG. 10.7. Among liberals, greater education is associated with slightly greater *warmth* towards the United Nations; among conservatives, greater education is associated with greater *coolness* towards the United Nations.

Note: A moderation analysis. Interaction $\Delta R^2 = .01$, $F(1, 413) = 8.47$, $p = .004$, controlling for six demographics (education excluded). Both slopes were statistically significant: $B = 1.76$, $p = .099$, and $B = -2.51$, $p = .02$, although the positive slope for liberals was only marginally so. *Data source:* OU Institute for US-China Issues, 2011.

Education was a dog that did *not* bark. In Figure 10.3, education level was not a statistically significant predictor of feelings towards the United Nations for the full U.S. population. Averages can be deceiving, however. A moderation analysis revealed that for the self-identified liberal and conservative subpopulations, there *were* significant correlations between education and feelings towards the United Nations. They were in the *opposite* directions, however, canceling each other out at the aggregate level (Figure 10.7). Among liberals, greater education was associated with slightly greater warmth towards the United Nations. Among conservatives, by contrast, greater education correlated with greater *coolness* towards the United Nations. Ideology, in other words, polarized education's influence on feelings towards the United Nations.

This finding is consistent with research on the relationship between education, partisanship, and attitudes towards global warming. Education is associated with belief in global warming among liberals and Democrats, but not among conservatives and Republicans.[98] Journalist Chris Mooney has labeled this phenomenon a "smart idiot" effect among Republicans. He suggests that greater exposure to right-wing news and opinion may lead more-educated conservatives to better know what other conservatives think on the issue, and thus be more motivated to seek out confirmatory evidence while dismissing contrary facts.[99]

While Mooney's "smart idiot" jibe is a bit silly, and group polarization effects and the confirmation bias are not limited to the right, his idea is worth exploring in the context of education and partisan feelings towards the United Nations.

As noted in Chapter 5, our 2011 survey included a measure of partisan media exposure: "*If you had to watch cable news, would you prefer to watch more MSNBC (e.g. Rachel Maddow) or FOX (Glenn Beck, Bill O'Reilly)?*" This item allows us to put Mooney's idea to a partial test. A pair of mediation analyses revealed that a greater preference for partisan media sources partially accounts for why ideology polarizes the influence of greater education on feelings towards the United Nations. Among conservatives, a greater preference for Fox partially mediated the impact of greater education on coolness toward the United Nations.[100] Among liberals, however, a greater preference for MSNBC did *not* mediate the relationship.[101] Perhaps Fox's conservative antipathy to the United Nations is more infectious than MSNBC's more positive liberal view. Alternatively, as noted in Chapter 1, psychologist John Jost has argued that conservatives have a greater relational need for belonging than liberals do. Perhaps this makes Fox viewers more susceptible to group polarization effects than MSNBC viewers are.

The influence of partisan media exposure on conservative feelings towards the United Nations is an example of the kind of "person-by-situation" interactions addressed in Chapter 5. While ideological predispositions are powerful predictors of international attitudes, future work can gain further leverage by exploring how the broader social context (like the media) interacts with individual differences variables (like gender, education, and ideology) to shape American attitudes towards not just the United Nations but foreign affairs more broadly.

GOD, GUNS, AND THE UNITED NATIONS

"*Why in the name of minimal common sense does our government allow itself to be denounced, vilified and lied about day after day in the halls of the United Nations by a mob of terrorists, savages, revolutionaries, bankrupts, demagogues, voluptuaries, and half-educated opportunists masquerading as representatives of newborn sovereign nations?*"[102]

—James Burnham for the *National Review*, 1965

This chapter has argued that ideology powerfully divides Americans over international organizations and treaties. The survey evidence is overwhelming: liberals like the United Nations; conservatives dislike it.

Writing about the 1960s, historian Lisa McGirr argues that "For conservatives across the spectrum, from religious conservatives to libertarians, the United Nations was potentially dangerous to U.S. interests and sovereignty."[103] Our 2011 survey data suggests that the same is true today, half a century later. All four of the dimensions of American ideology that we measured in our 2011 national survey point in the same direction: liberals are warmer towards the United Nations, and conservatives are cooler. Cultural liberals and conservatives differ over the United Nations, in large part because of their differences in biblical literalism (see Figure 10.4). Premillennial dispensationalists believe that the United Nations will join Satan's forces during Christ's Second Coming. Conservative Christians are also more likely than liberal Christians or nonreligious Americans to view the United Nations as a secular threat to God's rule on earth. Some conservatives may also fear that interacting with pagans in the United Nations may dilute Christian purity. Although the effect was small, racial thinking also divides Americans in their views of the United Nations today, as social conservatives are loath to participate in a "colored U.N." The impact of differences in economic ideology is stronger, for conservatives are more suspicious than liberals that the United Nations seeks to redistribute income on a global scale. Finally, libertarians' greater anticommunism and jealousy of national sovereignty and individual liberty contributes to greater libertarian than communitarian paranoia about "blue helmets" and "black helicopters."

These highly polarized popular attitudes have foreign policy consequences. The thirty-eight U.S. senators who blocked ratification of the U.N. disabilities treaty discussed at the beginning of this chapter were not "disconnected" from Main Street voters.[104] Instead, they were hyperattuned to the preferences of their voters: most come from "deep red" hyperpartisan states and so fear being "primaried" more than losing a general election. It is therefore the anti–Agenda 21 fervor of the Tea Party activists who vote in Republican primaries that they dread most.

The rising influence of ideologically extreme primary voters is increasingly alienating mainstream party members. Moderate Republicans like David Brooks understandably felt snubbed by the Republican senators who voted against the disabilities treaty. "It's an embarrassment for the country. This was a treaty that could have given Afghan vets who have lost limbs the greater ability to go abroad and live with dignity," Brooks declared on the December 7, 2012, *PBS NewsHour*. "And to do it for black helicopter reasons, to vote against this, it is an embarrassment." Liberal Mark Shields concurred: "This was a profile in cowardice. Republicans who are terrified of a primary, of a challenge on their right. Blue-helmeted U.N. soldiers coming into homeschooling parents and ripping their child away, having disembarked from the black helicopters."

That Republican Brooks and Democrat Shields were lining up together against the thirty-eight Republican senators who voted against the U.N. treaty on the disabled suggests just how narrow a slice of the U.S. electorate the Republican senators were catering to. Brooks is right that the vote was an embarrassment, but from an electoral perspective the Republican senators were acting rationally, currying favor with the "blue helmets" and "black helicopters" crowd on the far Tea Party right of the Republican Party.

Political polarization has contributed to treaty gridlock in the U.S. Senate, and presidents increasingly rely on executive agreements rather than treaties to conduct U.S. foreign policy. Despite Democratic control of the Senate, the two-thirds requirement for treaty passage has led Barack Obama to submit just four treaties to the Senate per year, down from twenty-four per year under the Bush administration.[105] Ideological polarization is thus weakening the Senate's "advice and consent" function, undermining the system of checks and balances so central to our democracy.

Conclusion: Ideology—Why Politics Does *Not* End at the Water's Edge

"Foreign policy should be the policy of the whole nation and not the policy of one party or the other. Partisanship should stop at water's edge."[1]
—Democratic President Harry S. Truman, 1948

This book does not advance a theory of American foreign policy, the sources of which are complex and multiple. For instance, special interests and bureaucratic politics at home, and the balance of power abroad, powerfully shape the making of American foreign policy. These topics are beyond the scope of this monograph.

Instead, this book has focused more narrowly on the ideological foundations of partisanship over American foreign policy. While Democrats and Republicans in Washington, D.C. sometimes argue over foreign policy out of petty partisan desires that their party win and the other side lose, their disagreements are more often rooted in deeper ideological differences. Elite partisanship over foreign policy is usually a reflection of the disparate international attitudes of the Main Street liberals and conservatives who elect them.

This book thus disagrees with the Chicago Council on Global Affairs, which has been surveying the global views of the American people for decades, and declared in 2012 that "Democrats and Republicans are very similar in their views on foreign policy." Media claims of "political polarization," therefore, are "exaggerated."[2] Pew's Andrew Kohut agrees, arguing that Americans are "realistic centrists," and that for the most part "partisan differences are slight." Neither religion nor nationalism, Kohut further claims, shapes American views on foreign affairs.[3]

Most political scientists agree with these pollsters. For instance, public opinion scholar Benjamin Page, who has worked extensively with the Chicago Council, claims that partisanship and ideology have "limited effects" on foreign policy preferences, making them "quite different from opinions about domestic policy."[4] Writing for *Foreign Affairs* in 2012, three international relations scholars even declared in their title that "American Foreign Policy Is Already Post-Partisan: Why Politics Does Stop at the Water's Edge."[5]

These arguments are flawed. The idea that there is little partisanship in American foreign policy does not survive a reality check. Americans know from personal experience that their liberal and conservative relatives, colleagues, and neighbors differ over foreign affairs, and even the casual observer can tell that foreign policy is a contentious issue on Capitol Hill. The elites who make foreign policy and experience its intense partisanship firsthand would likely be dumbfounded by the "post-partisan" argument. Little wonder political science has little policy influence: policy makers are rightly skeptical of claims that do not pass the common sense test.

The "post-partisan" argument does not pass the social science test either. The *Foreign Affairs* piece was based upon a nonrepresentative convenience sample of just forty-three foreign policy professionals. The external validity of such a survey is questionable. The more common problem with existing surveys of international attitudes is not generalizability, however, but internal validity or measurement. Problems of question design (such as variables that lack sufficient variation) and wording (such as loaded diction, or answer categories that overlap) contribute to substantial measurement error, attenuating the observed relationships among measures of ideology and international attitudes. Poor measurement has likely contributed to the dominant—but incorrect—view that partisan differences over foreign affairs are slight.

This book presents new survey evidence of divided American public opinion over international affairs, helping explain why politics in the United States does *not* end at the water's edge. Combining the strengths of psychological survey methodology (namely, measurement) and political science/sociology survey methodology (namely, sampling), we implemented our own nationally representative U.S. survey in the spring of 2011. While a careful inductive analysis of the existing survey data—Chicago Council, Pew, Program on International Policy Attitudes, CNN, and other surveys—is sufficient to debunk the "post-partisan" argument, our survey was the first to combine extensive questions about ideology and international attitudes within a single sample. This allowed us to explore their interrelationship in greater depth.

Utilizing this new survey data, this book has argued that American liberals and conservatives maintain consistent—if consistently different—international attitudes and foreign policy preferences. With the exception of Israel, which conservatives felt much warmer towards, liberals felt warmer towards *all* of the countries and international organizations that we measured. This included large ideological disparities on countries like Russia, China, Haiti, and Brazil, very large gaps on France and Mexico, and truly massive differences on international organizations like the European Union and especially the United Nations (see Figure 0.4).

The ideological gap in feelings towards foreign countries and international organizations, furthermore, is consequential for the foreign policy preferences of the American people. Feelings towards foreign countries, through the "affect heuristic," powerfully shape foreign policy preferences (see Figure 1.9). This contributes to large-to-massive differences in liberal and conservative foreign policy preferences towards countries like China (Figure 9.3) and Israel (Figure 8.3), and specific foreign policies like whether to expand our military presence in Afghanistan.

Ideology also divided Americans on broad foreign policy orientations, with liberals very much more supportive of humanitarian idealism (Figure 4.4) and multilateralism, and conservatives much more supportive of uses of military force. Conservatives also scored higher than liberals on patriotism and especially nationalism (Figure 4.9), although liberals scored slightly higher on a "pure" patriotism that controlled for the sense of superiority over other countries which is central to nationalism.

Main Street differences over foreign affairs are matched on Capitol Hill. Charles Kupchan and Peter Trubowitz have argued, primarily on the basis of the analysis of congressional voting patterns, that "'Red' and 'Blue' America disagree about the nature of U.S. engagement with the world."[6] This book provides public opinion evidence that elite partisanship over foreign affairs is not disconnected from a "centrist" American public, as Kohut puts it; instead, elite partisanship reflects the views of a divided American public.

Ideology's influence on foreign policy seems similar to its influence on domestic policy. Benjamin Page appears mistaken when he claims that the determinants of domestic and foreign policy opinions are "quite different."[7] Instead, Adam Berinsky is likely right that "public opinion about war is shaped by the same attitudes and orientations that shape domestic politics."[8] Indeed, this book extends Berinsky's point well beyond war to foreign affairs more broadly: the same ideological cleavages that animate domestic policy debates also animate foreign policy debates.

Although ideology (widely shared and systematic beliefs about how the world works) and partisanship (the degree of party identification and loyalty) are highly intercorrelated, postwar scholarship in American politics has consistently privileged the latter. Following the "Michigan model," for the past fifty years students of American voting and political behavior have largely dismissed ideology in favor of the study of partisanship.[9] In 1964 Phillip Converse claimed that the attitudes of the vast majority of the American people were not constrained by ideology; scholarship in American public opinion since then has largely upheld Converse's view.[10]

This book, by contrast, focuses on the ideological underpinnings of partisanship. Ideology is more psychologically and even physiologically fundamental, value laden, and complex than partisanship. Psychologically, liberals and conservatives differ systematically in their fundamental epistemic needs for certainty, existential needs for security, and relational needs for solidarity.[11] As the product of both nature and nurture—for parental and peer socialization impact gene expression—ideological differences are even associated with physiological distinctions. Greater conservative than liberal sensitivity to threat, for example, is reflected in a stronger startle reflex and a larger right amygdala.[12]

Ideologies are also value laden. Liberal and conservative Americans often infuriate each other because of their differing moral values. Righteous anger contributes to extreme rhetoric on issues like abortion, where the demonization of the other side as "baby killers" or as waging a "War on Women" creates enemies with whom compromise becomes impossible. In research using convenience samples, moral psychologists have shown that liberals value the "individualizing" moralities of *fairness* and *compassion* more than conservatives do, while conservatives value the "binding" moralities of *loyalty, authority,* and especially *purity* more than liberals do. Our nationally representative U.S. sample replicated this finding (see Figure 3.1) and demonstrated that the different moral constellations of liberals and conservatives can help account for their divergent foreign policy preferences. For instance, liberals' greater compassion for the suffering of strangers contributes to greater liberal than conservative warmth towards foreign countries in general, while conservatives' greater in-group loyalty contributes to greater conservative coolness towards those same foreign countries (Figure 3.8). And the greater value that conservatives place on authority and obedience helps account for their greater support for tough, "hard-line" foreign policies (Figure 3.11).

Ideologies are also complex. While the common unidimensional liberal-to-conservative measure of ideology is a powerful predictor of a wide variety of political attitudes, we gain even greater leverage on the role of ideology in shaping our attitudes by disaggregating it into its component dimensions. A number of political scientists have advocated a two-dimensional approach to ideology, focused on economics and the culture wars.[13] This book goes a step further, exploring four dimensions—cultural, social, economic, and political—of American ideology (see Figure 2.4). This approach gives us greater leverage to better understand the diverse ways that our ideologies shape our international attitudes.

First, *cultural ideology.* Morris Fiorina is wrong and Alan Abramowitz is right: the "culture wars" are no myth.[14] Religiosity does divide Americans on issues like abortion. Indeed, differing religious beliefs divide Americans, not just on abortion, gay marriage, and school prayer but on foreign affairs as well.

Cultural conservatives value purity much more than cultural liberals, who value fairness and justice more (see Figure 3.2). Cultural conservatives thus feel cooler towards Mexico and fear Mexican immigration more than cultural liberals do, and are more anxious about threats to authority and America's WASP identity (Figure 6.4); cultural liberals, for their part, decry the injustice and heartlessness of current U.S. immigration policies. Cultural conservatives also appear to feel cooler than cultural liberals do towards more secular and sexually permissive countries like France (Figure 7.3) and Germany (Figure 7.11). And fundamentalist religious beliefs contribute to conservative hostility towards the European Union (Figure 7.12) and the United Nations (Figure 10.4), both seen by some biblical literalists as serving the Antichrist during the End of Days. A more widespread Christian conservative belief is that the United Nations represents a secular affront to God's rule on earth. Secular Americans and liberal Christians, by contrast, have greater faith in the ability of the United Nations and other worldly governments to improve mankind's destiny through human effort. Cultural conservatives also feel substantially warmer towards Israel than cultural liberals do, largely because of their greater biblical literalism (Figure 8.6). And cultural conservatives are wary of "godless" communism (Figure 9.4), contributing to greater conservative than liberal antipathy towards "Red China" (Figure 9.5) and North Korea (Figure 1.7).

Second, *social ideology*. Both race and racism continue to shape the international attitudes of the American people. Greater average social dominance orientation—the belief that "*Inferior groups should stay in their place*"—was a major driver of greater conservative coolness towards the "colored" developing world. Social dominance was the only dimension of American ideology to account for greater conservative coolness towards Mexico and Haiti. Greater liberal compassion contributed to their greater opposition to social dominance (Figure 3.4), support for intergroup equality, and desire for more aid to Haiti (Figure 6.7) and a less restrictive Mexican border policy (Figure 6.4). Greater social dominance also contributed to greater conservative than liberal racial prejudice against Chinese (Figure 9.5) and other Asians (Figure 9.10). More surprisingly, greater social dominance had a small but statistically significant impact on conservative antipathy towards the United Nations (Figure 10.5).

Third, *economic ideology* has a pervasive influence on the international attitudes of the American people. The greater value that liberals place upon fairness and compassion contributes to their greater support for income redistribution at home (Figure 3.6) and humanitarian idealism abroad (Figure 4.4). Economic conservatives, by contrast, are more likely to oppose aid to places like Haiti (Figure 6.7), disdain countries like France that are seen as socialist, and despise communist governments like China's (Figure 9.5). Economic ideology even divides Americans on the United Nations (Figure 10.3). Economic conservatives view it as seeking to engage in income redistribution on a global scale, transferring resources from the advanced industrial countries of the North to the developing countries of the South.

Fourth and finally, *political ideology* was operationalized with a communitarian-to-libertarian scale. Though it was not related to prejudice against different kinds of *people*, it had a substantial influence on attitudes towards various kinds of *governments*. Libertarians don't like the American government, let alone authoritarian governments like China's (Figure 9.5). They also felt cooler towards communist countries in general (Figure 9.4) and the United Nations and other forms of "world government" (Figure 10.6). However, greater libertarianism was associated with greater warmth towards the "free" Asian democracies of Japan, South Korea, Taiwan, and India (Figure 9.10).

Each American, of course, varies across each of these four dimensions of ideology. In Chapter 2 we saw that Democrats tend to cluster into two broad ideological profiles, "moderates" and "liberals," with the latter more culturally, socio-racially, and economically liberal (see Figure 2.10). Republicans tend to cluster into three ideological profiles. "Cultural" Republicans score the highest on traditionalism but the lowest on libertarianism. "Teavangelicals" score the highest on libertarianism and support for income inequality. And "moderate" Republicans score the lowest on cultural traditionalism, and near scale midpoints on social and economic ideology. These different types of Democrats and Republicans can differ substantially in their international attitudes. For instance, we saw that Teavangelical Republicans desired a substantially tougher Mexican border policy and felt substantially cooler towards the United Nations than moderate Republicans did. Liberal Democrats, for their part, felt substantially warmer towards the United Nations than moderate Democrats did.

Democrats and Republicans, we saw in Chapter 4, also clustered into distinct foreign policy profiles. Democrats were fairly evenly divided between three groups (see Figure 4.12). The largest was "forceful idealists" like Obama and the Clintons, nationalists willing to deploy force if needed to pursue humanitarian foreign policy goals. The next largest group of Democrats was "global citizens" ready to pursue humanitarian missions through multilateral institutions like the United Nations, but less willing to deploy military force and much less nationalistic. The smallest group of Democrats was the "skeptics," more ambivalent about international engagement and the pursuit of idealism in U.S. foreign policy. While one third of Republicans might be called "isolationist skeptics," unwilling to support the United Nations or pursue idealistic foreign policy goals, the other two-thirds were characterized as "cautious idealists," ambivalent about multilateralism but willing to pursue humanitarian, political, and religious idealisms as U.S. foreign policy goals (Figure 4.11).

These cleavages *within* the Democratic and Republican parties mean that we have to be careful about overly broad generalizations. For instance, while the average conservative is more libertarian than the average liberal, cultural/ religious right Republicans appear to be even more communitarian than most Democrats—very different from Teavangelical Republicans, who are much more libertarian. Similarly, while conservatives generally support the use of force more than liberals do, "forceful idealists" within the Democratic Party are willing to deploy force when necessary to achieve humanitarian aims, such as preventing a massacre in Benghazi, Libya, in 2011.

We also have to be careful about overly strong causal claims. As noted in Chapter 3, the mediation models in this book are best understood as revealing syndromes of variables that go together—not definitive causal chains. Further experimental research is still needed to pin down the exact causal mechanisms suggested by our cross-sectional survey data.

BEYOND THE MEDIAN VOTER:
PUBLIC OPINION AND FOREIGN POLICY IN A DIVIDED AMERICA

Public opinion is but one of several drivers of U.S. foreign policy. However, because the United States is a democracy, it is an important one. The "electoral connection" ensures that politicians who want to be reelected will pay careful attention to the international attitudes of their core constituents.[15]

For the most part, however, the views of the average voter no longer matter. The "median voter" is less and less relevant today because the majority of House and Senate districts have become hyperpartisan. The South's partisan realignment, begun during the civil rights movement, is now largely complete. And Americans are increasingly choosing to live in communities of the like-minded: liberals on the coasts or in big cities, conservatives in the heartland or the suburbs. With this ideological self-sorting and gerrymandering, the majority of congressional districts have become so deeply blue or red that the general election outcome is a foregone conclusion.

The action in American electoral politics today is largely in the primaries. And primary voters, political scientist Gary Jacobson has shown, are more ideologically extreme than general election voters, especially in the Republican Party.[16] To avoid being "primaried," therefore, politicians today increasingly pander to the ideological extremes of their parties. This exacerbates conflict and gridlock, not just on domestic economic and cultural issues like the budget and abortion but on foreign policy as well.

This has serious implications for the U.S. national interest. As David Boren wrote in the Foreword, "When foreign policy becomes partisan, the national interest suffers." There is a reason why Senator Arthur Vandenberg, President Harry Truman, and Secretary of State Hillary Clinton all pleaded with their colleagues to leave partisanship "at water's edge": discord over foreign policy hurts the United States.

For instance, Teavangelical antipathy towards the United Nations can help explain why, as discussed in the Introduction and Chapter 10, Senate Republicans have consistently and overwhelmingly blocked ratification of U.N. treaties on issues like the law of the sea (UNCLOS) and the rights of the disabled. Such actions appear both irrational and cruel. UNCLOS serves U.S. economic and security interests and has been promoted by both the U.S. Chamber of Commerce and the Pentagon, groups that Republicans usually support. And the treaty on the rights of the disabled promotes decent treatment of the disabled worldwide—at no material cost to the United States.

These Republican senators, however, were acting consistently with Teavangelical antipathy towards the United Nations. That the American public as a whole—the "median voter"—was neutral towards the United Nations was irrelevant, as was Democratic warmth. To be reelected, these Republican senators do not need to represent the median voter in their district, let alone their Democrats. Instead, they need to mollify the Tea Party activists who they believe show up at Republican primaries.

Our survey data supports these senators' belief that Republican primary voters are largely Teavangelicals. Harvard's Theda Skocpol argues that the grassroots Tea Party activists of the Republican Party today are older, white, and very conservative Americans driven by fear of a rapidly changing society.[17] Many are rather communitarian conservative Protestants who would fall into our "cultural" cluster of Republicans discussed in Chapter 2. Others are former Goldwater supporters and John Birch Society members, much higher on libertarianism. While both groups are much more conservative than "moderate" Republicans, it is the more libertarian Teavangelicals who express the greatest interest in *"what's going on in government and public affairs."*[18] The 10 percent of Americans who fell into our "Teavangelical" Republican category appear to be the most likely Republican primary voters.

It is noteworthy, therefore, that Teavangelical Republicans do not just differ massively from Democrats and independents in their international attitudes; they also differ substantially from *other Republicans*. For instance, Teavangelical Republicans (17°) feel 24° cooler towards the United Nations than moderate Republicans (41°) do; they are also much less supportive of international organizations and substantially less trusting of international treaties.[19] When Republican senators vote against U.N. treaties, they are *representing* the preferences of Teavangelical primary voters. They are hyperattuned to, not disconnected from, their core constituents. As we saw in Chapter 10, when it comes to the United Nations, Teavangelical primary voters fear "blue helmets" and "black helicopters." Republican senators thus have good electoral reasons to oppose international treaties.

The rising political influence of the ideological extremes undermines the national interest. When UNCLOS cannot pass the U.S. Senate, U.S. business and national security interests are harmed. And when international treaties are unlikely to pass the Senate, the U.S. president is forced to utilize executive agreements instead.[20] This sends a clear signal to the world that the United States is internally divided, and that those cleavages can be exploited. It also undermines the system of advice and consent so central to our democracy.

Scholars and policy makers would be wise to acknowledge that real differences on foreign affairs exist between liberals and conservatives, on Capitol Hill *and* on Main Street. Because of the perverse incentives of the electoral connection today, divided American public opinion on foreign affairs has real foreign policy consequences. Students and practitioners of American foreign policy would be wise too not to dismiss the influence of ideology on the international attitudes of the American people.

Acknowledgments

This book could not have been written without the help of many people and institutions.

I am grateful to Harold and Ruth Newman for their generosity in endowing the Chair I was hired to fill, and funding the Institute for US-China Issues, which I was hired to create. The Institute funded the 2011 national survey that is the basis of this book. Working with and getting to know Harold and Ruth has been a true pleasure.

University of Oklahoma President David Boren solicited the Newmans' donation and has long championed international studies at OU. He is also passionate about the dangers of excessive partisanship in American politics. I thank him for his service to OU and the nation—and for contributing the Foreword to this book.

This book began with a grant from the Smith Richardson Foundation. I thank Allan Song for his patience as the project—and my skill set—evolved. I hope the book was worth the wait.

The Tower Center at Southern Methodist University in Dallas hosted a book manuscript workshop in April 2013. I thank Jim Hollifield, Hiroki Takeuchi, Matthew Wilson, Luigi Manzetti, and Sandy Thatcher for their thoughtful comments. Matthew's careful reading of the first draft was particularly valuable. I am fortunate to have Hiroki as a colleague and friend.

I take full responsibility for the arguments advanced in this book. I cannot take full credit, however, for all of the research that went into it. When I use the first-person plural—"we" or "our"—in the text, it is usually in reference to research collaborators: colleagues at OU and around the world, and postdocs and graduate assistants in my "Political Psychology of U.S.-China Relations" research lab.

This book would not have been possible without my OU colleague Mike Crowson, who first taught me statistics and then became a close research collaborator and coauthor. His enthusiasm for statistics and the study of ideology has been infectious. But his friendship has been more valuable.

I thank graduate research assistants Zach Stokes-Avery, Karina Legradi, and David

Stroup in particular for their willingness to undertake the oddest of tasks. Postdocs in my lab played an even greater role. I am indebted to Darshon Anderson, Matthew Sanders, and especially Collin Barnes, who contributed immensely to both survey design and the initial data analysis.

Geoffrey Burn at Stanford University Press was everything that an author could hope for in an acquisition editor: thoughtful and responsive. His close read of the text and enthusiasm for the project is what sold me on SUP. James Holt and John Feneron expertly managed a complex text. And Jeff Wyneken did a close copy edit of the entire manuscript. All have been a pleasure to work with. I look forward to working with Mary Kate Maco on publicity. Brian Rathbun and Paul Kowert, I now know, were SUP's external reviewers. Both provided thoughtful and encouraging comments, for which I am truly grateful.

There are also many people I do not know personally who nonetheless influenced this book. All mediation and moderation analyses were conducted using Andrew Hayes's invaluable PROCESS plug-in for SPSS. Thank you, Andrew! Historian Michael Hunt and sociologist Richard Madsen gave me confidence that studying China provided a unique perspective on America. Bob Putnam and David Campbell's *American Grace* reassured me that "applied political science" does not have to be an oxymoron. And the breathtaking scope of Andrew Preston's *Sword of the Spirit, Shield of Faith*, and Steven Pinker's *The Better Angels of Our Nature* inspired me to be ambitious.

The reader will see that my understanding of ideology is greatly indebted to the research of John Jost and Jonathan Haidt and their armies of graduate students and collaborators. But I also learned a great deal about how the moral values of compassion and fairness undergird "small *l*" liberalism from Jon Stewart and his team at the *Daily Show*. And the *New York Times* columns of Paul Krugman and David Brooks presented contrasting liberal and conservative moral visions on an almost daily basis.

Pop culture was also a source of inspiration. Hank Hill and Dale Gribble of *King of the Hill* taught me much about cultural traditionalism and libertarianism. And Ned Flanders and Lisa Simpson of *The Simpsons* provided insights into Christian conservatism and liberal compassion. My daughter Julia provided companionship as I studied these texts.

My wife Mônica, daughter Julia, and our collie Zeus allowed me to work in our home office, while always encouraging me to come out and play. This book is dedicated to my father, David Gries, for his unwavering encouragement and support.

Statistical Glossary

ANCOVA (Analysis of covariance). A statistical technique used to test the relationship between one or more categorical independent variables (such as gender) and one continuous dependent (or criterion) variable, controlling for the effects of covariates (such as demographics) of lesser interest.

Beta (β) coefficient. An index of the predictive relationship between standardized predictor (independent) and criterion (dependent) variables in regression analysis. When multiple predictors are present, this index reflects the predictive relationship between a single predictor and the criterion variable after controlling for the remaining predictor variables. Standardized *β* (partial coefficients) of .1, .3, and .5 can be considered small, medium, and large, respectively (see Kline 2005).

Cluster analysis. A statistical technique that classifies individuals into groups on the basis of their scores on a set of measured variables. Cluster members exhibit high levels of similarity on measured variables within their cluster, and high levels of dissimilarity to those in other clusters (see Hair and Black 2000).

Correlation (r). An index of the association or relationship between two standardized variables. Correlation coefficients can range from –1.00 (a perfect negative relationship) to +1.00 (a perfect positive relationship). In the social sciences, Pearson's *r* values of .1, .3, and .5 (in absolute value) are considered to be small, medium, and large, respectively (see Cohen 1988).

Cronbach's alpha (α). An index of the internal consistency or reliability of the items that together form a scale. Values range from 0 to 1, with those closer to 1 reflecting less random "noise" (i.e., unreliability) in the measure. Alphas of .60 or higher are generally desirable. However, longer scales artificially inflate the alpha, so lower scores on shorter scales can also be acceptable.

Factor analysis. A statistical technique used to uncover the latent dimensions or unobserved variables (called factors) that explain variation in a larger number of measured (i.e., observed) variables.

Mediation analyses are utilized to test whether one or more variables "transmit" some or all of the variation from a predictor to a criterion variable. They thus explore the mechanism(s) or pathway(s) through which two variables relate to one another (see Hayes 2013). Establishing causal mediation is extremely difficult. First, it is nearly impossible to anticipate and measure all possible mediators of a relationship, so one cannot be completely certain that the mediators tested are the true drivers of an indirect relationship. Second, with correlational data, one can never be sure of the exact causal sequence (see Green, Ha, and Bullock 2010).

Moderation analyses are utilized to test whether the relationship between two (or more) variables is conditioned upon (i.e., dependent upon) the level of a third variable. For instance, one might ask whether the relationship between education level and feelings towards the United Nations differs for liberals and conservatives (third variable = ideology; see Figure 10.7). Moderation analyses thus address the boundary conditions or circumstances under which a relationship between two variables holds (see Hayes 2013).

Partial eta squared (η_p^2). An effect size statistic used in reporting of analysis of variance (ANOVA) results. A η_p^2 of .1 can be interpreted as small, .06 as medium, and .14 as large.

Probability value (p value). The likelihood that an observed relationship between variables within a sample is due to sampling fluctuation (i.e., chance) as opposed to capturing a true relationship within the full population sampled. If a p value is not reported in this book, the reader should assume it to have been less than .001. In other words, the likelihood that the observed relationship is actually due to pure chance is less than 1 in 1,000.

Regression. A statistical technique used to estimate the relationship between one criterion (dependent or outcome) variable and one or more independent or "predictor" variables.

Suppressor. A third variable whose inclusion allows the true nature of the relationship between two variables to become more fully apparent. In mediation analyses, a "suppression effect" occurs when the inclusion of a mediator increases rather than decreases, or changes the direction of, the direct relationship between two variables (see Rucker, Preacher, Tormala, and Petty 2011).

Type I error. A *false positive* in the context of statistical significance testing. This error involves an assertion on the researcher's part that a significant (i.e., non-zero) relationship exists between two (or more) variables within the population when the converse is actually true (i.e., the actual relationship is zero).

Type II error. A *false negative* in the context of statistical significance testing. This error involves an assertion on the researcher's part that a nonsignificant (i.e., zero) relationship exists between two (or more) variables within the population when the converse is actually true (i.e., the actual relationship is non-zero). In other words, the researcher claims that there is no relationship when there actually is one.

Variance explained (R^2). The proportion of variation in an outcome variable that is accounted for by the predictors in a model.

Notes

Introduction

1. George H.W. Bush, Inaugural Address, January 20, 1989.
2. Quoted in Mark Landler, "Clinton Acts as Emissary to Congress," *New York Times*, November 17, 2010.
3. Washington 1796.
4. Mark Twain, "Anti-Imperialism," *New York Herald*, October 15, 1900.
5. McCormick and Wittkopf 1990; McCormick, Wittkopf, and Danna 1997: 134.
6. Aldrich et al. 2006: 489.
7. http://foxnewsinsider.com/2012/01/17/transcript-fox-news-channel-wall-street-journal-debate-in-south-carolina/.
8. http://cnsnews.com/news/article/hillary-clinton-opposition-sea-treaty-based-mythology.
9. http://republicanpartyofhighlandscounty.com/?p=1743.
10. Kupchan 2012.
11. Friedman and Mandelbaum 2011.
12. Taiwan is not formally an independent country.
13. CNN/ORC Poll: "Opinion of Foreign Countries," May 24–26, 2011, at Roper Center.
14. The Chicago Council's mean scores tend to be about 5° warmer than ours, however, likely because they ask about feelings towards "countries and people," while we ask only about "countries."
15. ANCOVA control for seven standard demographics: age, gender, education, income, region, race, and ethnicity. All p's < .001, with the exception of England, South Korea, and Taiwan, which were p = .004, .014, and .009, respectively. Effect sizes ranged from a small η_p^2 = .014 for South Korea to a massive η_p^2 = .50 for the United Nations.
16. The Chicago Council's 2010 data revealed no statistically significant difference between liberals and conservatives on Great Britain (−2°) and South Korea (2°), our two smallest, followed by North Korea (4°), Germany (4°), and Japan (5°), our next smallest

group. And as with our data, it found the largest ideological differences on Mexico (19°), France (13°), and Israel (–14°). Each ANCOVA controlled for age, gender, education, income, and being from the South.

17. Substantial partisan differences emerged on "favorability" towards the European Union and Muslims, and small but statistically significant differences emerged on Iran, China, and Mexico. In each case, Democrats were more favorable than Republicans. E.U.: $F(1, 406) = 20.64$, $p < .001$, $\eta_p^2 = .048$; Muslims: $F(1, 420) = 18.78$, $p < .001$, $\eta_p^2 = .043$; Iran: $F(1, 448) = 4.68$, $p = .031$, $\eta_p^2 = .01$; China: $F(1, 445) = 4.26$, $p = .04$, $\eta_p^2 = .009$; Mexico: $F(1, 438) = 3.86$, $p = .05$, $\eta_p^2 = .009$. The only exception was Russia, on which no partisan differences emerged: $F(1, 428) = .036$, $p = .85$. This is likely due to greater measurement error in the Pew survey, which was conducted by telephone and used a rating scale that varied less than ours. All Pew ANCOVA controlled for age, gender, education, and income.

18. Chicago Council 2012: 41.

19. Page with Bouton 2006: 95–96; Kohut and Stokes 2006: 218.

20. Busby, Monten, and Inboden 2012.

21. Chicago Council 2012: 42.

22. Chicago Council 2012, Question 5. Wilks' Lambda: $F(9, 1114) = 45.42$, $p < .001$, $\eta_p^2 = .27$, controlling for age, gender, education, income, and being black, Hispanic, or from the U.S. South.

23. One of the nine—"*Promoting and defending human rights in other countries*"— was only marginally significant. The largest partisan differences were on the goals of "*Controlling and reducing illegal immigration*," a topic we will explore in detail in Chapter 6's discussion of Mexico, and "*Limiting climate change*," a topic we will briefly touch on in Chapter 10. Immigration: $F(1, 1148) = 135.10$, $p < .001$, $\eta_p^2 = .11$; climate change: $F(1, 1148) = 166.70$, $p < .001$, $\eta_p^2 = .13$. Both ANCOVA controlled for seven demographics listed above.

24. Chicago Council 2012, Question 7. Wilks' Lambda: $F(11, 1129) = 37.70$, $p < .001$, $\eta_p^2 = .27$, controlling for seven demographics listed above.

25. On the shocking case of Dutch social psychologist Diederik Stapel, who fabricated data, see Yudhijit Bhattacharjee, "The Mind of a Con Man," *New York Times*, April 26, 2013.

26. Lippmann 1922; Almond 1950; Converse 1964.

27. Holsti 1992, 2004; Caspary 1970; Pierce and Rose 1974.

28. E.g., Hurwitz and Peffley 1987.

29. Wittkopf 1990.

30. Holsti and Rosenau 1988.

31. Mueller 1971, 1973.

32. See Gartner and Segura 1998; Jentleson 1992; Jentleson and Britton 1998; Gelpi, Feaver, and Reifler 2005/6, 2009; Gelpi, Reifler, and Feaver 2007; Gelpi 2010.

33. Gelpi, Feaver, and Reifler 2009: 237.

34. Zaller 1992.

35. E.g., Berinsky 2009; Berinsky and Druckman 2007.

36. Berinsky 2009: 62.

37. Baum and Groeling 2010.

38. Campbell, Converse, Miller, and Stokes 1960.

39. E.g., Federico 2012: 79; Jacoby 2011: 442.

40. Leighley, ed. 2010.

41. Hetherington 2012: 115.

42. Abramowitz 2006: 114; Bafumi and Shapiro 2009: 9–10 (figure 7).

43. Coefficients for ideology and partisanship for: prayer in public schools (β = .52 and β = .04, p = .24); the death penalty (β = .39 and β = .08, p = .06); abortion (β = .50 and β = .16); gay marriage (β = .52 and β = .13); gun control (β = .24 and β = .21).

44. All regressions were hierarchical, controlling for the seven standard demographic variables in the first stage, and entering ideology and partisanship in the second stage. Culture wars scale α = .76.

45. Feelings towards fifteen foreign countries: ideology, β = −.26; partisanship, β = −.05, p = .27. Foreign policy preferences towards fifteen foreign countries: ideology, β = .21; partisanship, β = .03, p = .95.

46. Jacoby 2011: 443.

47. Hetherington 2012: 102.

48. Cialdini et al. 1976.

49. Snyder, Lassegard, and Ford 1986.

50. On ideology as a bottom-up process, see Jost, Federico, and Napier 2009.

51. Partisanship: $F(17, 11122)$ = 10.82, p < .001, η_p^2 = .02; ideology: $F(17, 7001)$ = 1.42, p = .12. Both ANCOVA controlled for age and gender.

52. E.g., Osterlind 2006; Thorndike and Thorndike-Christ 2009.

53. ANES 2010 questions C1_V1A and C1_PP012.

54. While the means don't change much in the 2010 ANES data, the standard deviation for the "very" wording (M = 4.31, SD = 1.69) is larger than with the "extremely" wording (M = 4.27, SD = 1.45). In other words, "extremely" has artificially reduced dispersion from the mean.

55. On Paul Grice's "maxim of quantity" in conversation, see Grice 1989.

56. ANES 2010 question C1_PID7 kurtosis statistic = −1.315 (SD = .14). This exceeds the absolute value of 1 recommended in the statistical literature. On kurtosis, see De-Carlo 1997.

57. For more on "sample matching" methodology, see Rivers 2005.

58. Locally, very large samples of University of Oklahoma students, faculty, and staff were gathered in the summers of 2008 and 2009. Large national samples were also gathered, using Amazon Mechanical Turk's online marketplace for employers and workers, mturk.com.

59. Cohen 1988.

60. As part of its ongoing demographic profiling, YouGov asks all of its panelists to rate themselves on a five-point "very liberal" to "very conservative" scale. In our survey, we asked participants to situate themselves on a 101-point unnumbered placement ruler also anchored by "very liberal" and "very conservative." Responses to these two items

were standardized and averaged together to form our unidimensional ideology measure ($\alpha = .93$). The top and bottom quintiles of this scale are used to compare liberals and conservatives.

61. Ziliak and McCloskey 2008: 5, 2. My thanks to Peter Katzenstein for this reference.

62. Cohen 1994.

63. Cohen 1988; Kline 2005.

64. Cohen 1988.

65. De Tocqueville 2000 [1835]: 228. Cited in Reiter and Stam 2002: 2–3.

66. Cited in Reiter and Stam 2002: 207, note 5.

67. Aldrich et al. 2006: 496.

68. Page and Shapiro 1983.

69. "A National Security Strategy for a New Century," The White House, October 1998, 15.

70. May 1991 [1961]: 159.

71. Fiorina 2009; Fiorina and Levendusky 2006.

72. Kull and Destler 1999.

73. Page with Bouton 2006: ix.

74. Page with Bouton 2006: 236.

75. Downs 1957.

76. Fiorina and Levendusky 2006: 70.

77. Abramowitz 2006: 80.

78. Bishop with Cushing 2008.

79. Nate Silver, "As Swing Districts Dwindle, Can a Divided House Stand?" FiveThirtyEight Blog, December 27, 2012.

80. Robert Draper, "The League of Dangerous Mapmakers," *The Atlantic*, October 2012, 59.

81. Jacobson 2012: 1625.

82. Andrew Goldman, "Jon Huntsman Could Do Without Bill Clinton's Kudos," *New York Times Magazine*, January 4, 2013.

83. Aldrich, Sullivan, and Borgida 1989.

84. Knecht 2010: 5. My thanks to Sandy Thatcher for this reference.

85. Preston 2012: 280.

86. Cited in Williams 2010: 245.

87. Kloppenberg 2011.

88. Kloppenberg 2011: 26.

89. Obama 2009.

90. Mann 2012: xviii.

91. Byman and Pollack 2001.

Chapter One

1. Sowell 2007: 230.

2. Hunt 2009 [1987]: 16.

3. I am indebted to Ken Jowitt for this trinity.

4. Hartz 1955.

5. Hofstadter 1948: xxxix.

6. Stephanson 1995; Hixson 2008.

7. Desch 2007/8.

8. Hunt 2009 [1987]: 2.

9. A regression with the 2010 ANES data revealed positive associations between conservative ideology and age (β = .08), income (β = .07), and being male (β = .08) or from the South (β = .10), and negative associations with education (β = –.06) and being black (β = –.17). In its sample, however, there was no association between ideology and being Hispanic, β = .001, p = .97. Its demographic variables accounted for 6 percent of the variance in their ideology measure.

10. E.g., Norrander and Wilcox 2008.

11. E.g., Jackman 1994; Kinder and Sanders 1996.

12. E.g., McCarty, Poole, and Rosenthal 2006; Van der Waal, Achterberg, and Houtman 2007.

13. Jost, Glaser, Kruglanski, and Sulloway 2003; Jost, Federico, and Napier 2009.

14. Sidanius 1985; Jost, Glaser, Kruglanski, and Sulloway 2003; Van Hiel and Mervielde 2004.

15. Eidelman, Crandall, Goodman, and Blanchar 2012.

16. Sargent 2004.

17. Van Hiel and Mervielde 2004; Gerber et al. 2010.

18. Gosling, Rentfrow, and Swann 2003.

19. Carney, Jost, Gosling, and Potter 2008.

20. Jost, Napier, et al. 2007; Jost, Banaji, and Nosek 2004. However, Emanuele Castano and Bernhard Leidner argue, following Terror Management Theory (TMT), that while death anxiety prompts greater conservatism among conservatives, it can lead liberals to embrace more liberal ideologies. See Castano et al. 2011.

21. Bonanno and Jost 2006.

22. Jost and Amodio 2012.

23. Kanai, Feilden, Firth, and Rees 2011.

24. Oxley et al. 2008.

25. Jost, Ledgerwood, and Hardin 2007; see also Hardin and Higgins 1996.

26. Feldman 2003; Caprara et al. 2006.

27. Jennings and Niemi 1981. For an update, see Jennings, Stoker, and Bowers 2009.

28. E.g., Olson, Vernon, Harris, and Jang 2001; Alford, Funk, and Hibbing 2005; Hatemi et al. 2011.

29. Lakoff 1996.

30. Of course, our measurement of each parent's ideology was indirect, relying upon the respondent's own judgment.

31. Sowell 2007 [1987]: 30; Pinker 2002.

32. Preston 2012: 178.

33. Sowell 2007 [1987]: 30.

282 NOTES TO PAGES 40–56

34. Dueck 2010: 24.
35. Pinker 2002.
36. Rathbun 2012.
37. Fiorina, Abrams, and Pope 2011: 127, 53 (title of figure 3.2).
38. Abramowitz and Saunders 2008; Abramowitz 2010.
39. See Fiorina, Abrams, and Pope 2011: 52–53, figures 3.1 and 3.2.
40. Militarism: $F(1, 419) = 218.34$, $p < .001$, $\eta_p^2 = .225$, controlling for seven standard demographics.
41. Fordham 2007: 608; Bartels 1994: 481.
42. Cited in Dueck 2010: 209.
43. Kahneman 2011: 97, 99.
44. Slovic, Finucane, Peters, and MacGregor 2002.
45. Brady and Sniderman 1991.
46. Thorndike 1920.
47. With the inclusion of the two mediators, the direct effect of ideology on North Korea policy was reduced from 3.2 percent (semipartial correlation = .18) to just 1 percent (semipartial correlation = .10).
48. See Hayes 2013.
49. E.g., Waltz 1979.
50. With the inclusion of the two mediators, the direct effect of ideology on foreign policy preferences was reduced from 4.3 percent (semipartial correlation = .21) to just 0.8 percent (semipartial correlation = .09).
51. Kahneman 2011: 103.
52. Walt 1985.

Chapter Two

1. Patrick Buchanan, Address to the Chicago Council on Foreign Relations, November 18, 1998.
2. Paul 2008: 94.
3. $F(1, 667) = 0.03$, $p = .87$, controlling for seven standard demographics.
4. Laponce 1981: 51. Cited in Jost and Amodio 2012: 56.
5. Jost 2006: 659.
6. Feldman and Johnston 2013: 17.
7. Treier and Hillygus 2009: 680, 683.
8. The standard demographic covariates account for another 8 percent, bringing the total to 57 percent.
9. Phillips-Fein 2011: 727.
10. Feldman and Johnston 2013.
11. E.g., Jost 2006; Duckitt and Sibley 2007.
12. Ronald Reagan, Speech to the National Association of Evangelicals, March 8, 1983.
13. George W. Bush, State of the Union Address, January 29, 2002.
14. Williams 2010: 2.
15. George Will, cited in Williams 2010: 245.

16. Terence Burlij, "Rick Perry's Latest TV Ad Appeals to Religious Voters," *PBS NewsHour*, December 7, 2011.

17. Mike Lillis, "Pelosi Accuses GOP of Waging 'War on Women' in Fundraising Pitch," *The Hill*, March 21, 2012.

18. Fiorina, Abrams, and Pope 2011: 87, figure 5.5, and 88.

19. 2004 GSS: $F(1, 554) = 121.48$, $p < .001$, $\eta_p^2 = 18$, controlling for age and gender. Weighted (WTSS) comparison of those, following Fiorina, Abrams, and Pope (2011: 87), who claim to attend church (ATTEND) "several times a year" or less, with those who claim to attend "nearly every week" or greater. This very large religious attendance gap on abortion persists in the 2008 GSS data, $F(1, 807) = 201.24$, $p < .001$, $\eta_p^2 = .20$.

20. Putnam and Campbell 2010: 22.

21. For the sake of comparability, YouGov borrowed item wordings from Pew.

22. Putnam and Campbell 2010: 21.

23. Abortion: $F(1, 436) = 387.22$, $p < .001$, $\eta_p^2 = .47$; gay marriage: $F(1, 436) = 292.60$, $p < .001$, $\eta_p^2 = .40$, both controlling for our seven standard demographics.

24. Prayer in public schools: $F(1, 436) = 300.05$, $p < .001$, $\eta_p^2 = .41$; gun control: $F(1, 436) = 32.95$, $p < .001$, $\eta_p^2 = .07$; death penalty: $F(1, 436) = 17.01$, $p < .001$, $\eta_p^2 = .04$. All ANCOVA control for our seven standard demographics.

25. Item wording from Pew.

26. This item was not used when examining relationships between biblical literalism and attitudes towards Israel, the Palestinians, or the Middle East.

27. We created a five-item "culture wars" scale ($\alpha = .76$) by averaging together policy preferences on abortion, gay marriage, prayer in public schools, gun control, and the death penalty. In separate regressions controlling for our seven standard demographics, biblical literalism ($R^2 = .44$) accounted for almost twice the variance in our "culture wars" scale as religiosity ($R^2 = .23$) did.

28. Kohut and Stokes 2006: 94.

29. Numbers represent the change in R^2 after entering our seven standard demographics in the first step of a two-stage hierarchical regression. Our biblical literalism scales are entered in the second stage. A four-item measure without the Israel item is used in the Israel policy regression. The other two use all five biblical literalism items.

30. $r = .33$ and $r = .22$, respectively.

31. Altemeyer 1996; Duckitt, Bizumic, Krauss, and Heled 2010.

32. In a regression controlling for the seven standard demographics, cultural traditionalism accounted for 37 percent of the variance in culture wars preferences.

33. Gries and Crowson 2010; Gries, Crowson, and Cai 2012.

34. Theodore Roosevelt, "The Strenuous Life," 1899. Cited in Hofstadter 1944: 180.

35. William Jennings Bryan, "The Paralyzing Influence of Imperialism," Democratic National Convention, Kansas City, Missouri, July 1900.

36. Hofstadter 1944: 170–71.

37. Hunt 2009 [1987]: 79.

38. Smith 1993: 549.

39. Sidanius and Pratto 1999.

40. Jost and Thompson 2000; Kugler, Cooper, and Nosek 2010; Ho et al. 2012.

41. Ho et al. 2012: 585.

42. Baldwin 1963: 111. Cited in Bellah 1992 [1975]: 78.

43. For a review, see Pratto, Sidanius, and Levin 2006.

44. This was a three item-scale ($\alpha = .79$) that averaged standardized responses to (1) an eleven-point feeling thermometer towards the "Chinese people" (reverse coded), and seven-point "strongly disagree" to "strongly agree" rating scale items; (2) "The Chinese PEOPLE are trustworthy" (reverse coded); and (3) "The Chinese PEOPLE are devious."

45. $F(1, 419) = 82.68, p < .001, \eta_p^2 = .17$, controlling for seven standard demographics.

46. Kinder and Kam 2009: 60.

47. Sidanius and Pratto 1999: 302.

48. Krugman 2007: 245.

49. Alana Semuels, "Rick Santorum: 'We Have to Be Concerned' About the Very Poor," *Los Angeles Times*, February 16, 2012.

50. Wolfe 2009: 12.

51. Nisbet 1986: 47.

52. Hunt 2009 [1987]: 124, 101.

53. Hunt 2009 [1987]: 99.

54. Hunt 2009 [1987]: 105, 123–24.

55. Cited in Krugman 2007: 61.

56. Goldin and Margo 1992.

57. Larson 1956: 9.

58. Krugman 2007.

59. Phillips-Fein 2009: 5, 57.

60. Goldwater 1960: 69, 62. Italics in original.

61. "Romney Defends Donor Comment, Says More Jobs Will Mean More Paying Taxes," foxnews.com, September 18, 2012.

62. Krugman 2007: 267.

63. $\alpha = .81$. Our lab also tried developing a "market fundamentalism" scale that would range from support for a planned or heavily regulated market on the one hand, to extreme "laissez-faire" on the other, but failed to produce scales of adequate internal reliability. The items were likely too abstract.

64. $F(1, 419) = 485.39, p < .001, \eta_p^2 = .54$, controlling for seven standard demographics.

65. 2006 WVS, question V116: $F(1, 890) = 101.88, p < .001, \eta_p^2 = .10$, controlling for age, gender, and education only.

66. Alterman 2008: 62.

67. Goldwater 1960: 13.

68. McGovern 2011: 63.

69. Rothbard 1972.

70. Duncan and Machan 2005: 6; Nozick 1974.

71. Huebert 2012: 11.

72. Duncan and Machan 2005: 4. Italics in original.

73. Arendt 1951; Brzezinski and Friedrich 1956.

74. Burns 2009: 2–3.

75. Iyer et al. 2010.

76. Kirby and Boaz 2010.

77. Bellah 1992 [1975]: 152, 18.

78. Sandel 1982; Bellah et al. 1985.

79. Etzioni 2004: 3.

80. Sandel 2012: 10–11, 203.

81. Tiffany Gabbay, "Elizabeth Warren on Class Warfare," theblaze.com, September 21, 2011.

82. Cronbach's α = .68. The last item was drawn from Mehrabian 1996: 490.

83. On cluster analysis, see Hair and Black 2000; and the Statistical Glossary at the end of this volume.

84. Cluster quality was fair, 0.4 on a silhouette measure of cohesion. Other solutions reached no more than 0.3.

85. Economic: $F(1, 1045) = 762.57, p < .001, \eta_p^2 = .42$; cultural: $F(1, 1045) = 713.14, p < .001, \eta_p^2 = .41$; social: $F(1, 1045) = 320.95, p < .001, \eta_p^2 = .24$; political: $F(1, 1045) = 6.15, p = .013, \eta_p^2 = .006$, controlling for seven standard demographics.

86. The cluster quality was again fair, 0.4 on a silhouette measure of cohesion. Other solutions reached no more than 0.3.

87. Political: $F(1, 389) = 7.58, p = .006, \eta_p^2 = .02$, controlling for seven standard demographics.

88. Social: $F(1, 389) = 238.39, p < .001, \eta_p^2 = .38$; cultural: $F(1, 389) = 153.40, p < .001, \eta_p^2 = .28$; economic: $F(1, 389) = 108.51, p < .001, \eta_p^2 = .22$, controlling for seven standard demographics.

89. The cluster quality was again fair, 0.4 on a silhouette measure of cohesion. While a two-cluster solution was of comparable quality, it was more difficult to interpret.

90. Social: $F(2, 302) = 0.80, p = .45$, controlling for seven standard demographics.

91. Political: $F(2, 302) = 215.43, p < .001, \eta_p^2 = .59$; cultural: $F(2, 302) = 153.53, p < .001, \eta_p^2 = .50$; economic: $F(2, 302) = 53.81, p < .001, \eta_p^2 = .26$, all controlling for the seven standard demographics.

92. Brody 2012.

93. $F(1, 194) = 517.01, p < .001, \eta_p^2 = .73$, controlling for seven standard demographics.

94. $F(1, 451) = 26.01, p < .001, \eta_p^2 = .06$, controlling for the seven standard demographics.

95. Biblical literalism: $F(2, 302) = 45.34, p < .001, \eta_p^2 = .23$; religiosity: $F(2, 302) = 34.75, p < .001, \eta_p^2 = .19$, controlling for seven standard demographics.

96. "Editorial: Gov. Mary Fallin overstepped with order to ban tobacco use," *The Oklahoma Daily*, February 10, 2012. oudaily.com.

97. Skocpol and Williamson 2012: 35, 36.

98. Democrats: $F(1, 389) = 87.81, p < .001, \eta_p^2 = .18$; Republicans: $F(2, 302) = 29.75, p < .001, \eta_p^2 = .17$. Both ANCOVA and all mean temperatures control for seven standard demographics.

99. Dionne 2012: 114.

Chapter Three

1. Powell Lecture Series, Texas A&M University, April 6, 1998.

2. In *The National Review*; cited in Rogak 2008: 54.

3. Deibel 2005: 67.

4. Becker 1976.

5. Piaget 1965 [1932]; Kohlberg 1969.

6. Gilligan 1982.

7. Trivers 1971.

8. Dawkins 1976.

9. Shweder 1991; Haidt 2012; Haidt and Graham 2009.

10. See also Sidanius and Kurzban 2003.

11. Graham, Haidt, and Nosek 2009.

12. Lakoff 2010: 43, 47, 60.

13. Compare Figure 3.1 to Graham, Haidt, and Nosek 2009: 1033, figure 1; or Haidt 2012: 158, figure 8.1.

14. All ideological differences were statistically significant, with effect sizes of .05, .02, .10, .13, and .22 for harm, fair, loyalty, authority, and purity, respectively. They thus range from small to very large in size.

15. Haidt 2001; Leidner and Castano 2012.

16. The libertarianism model involved a suppression effect whereby the addition of the five moral values as mediators *increased* its direct relationship with our unidimensional ideology measure, a finding that is difficult to interpret.

17. Green, Ha, and Bullock 2010: 202. My thanks to Xiaobo Lü for this reference.

18. Haidt, Koller, and Diaz 1993.

19. The direct effect was reduced from 31 percent (semipartial correlation = .56) to just 6 percent (semipartial correlation = .25) with the inclusion of the five mediators.

20. Helzer and Pizarro 2011.

21. E.g., Inbar, Pizarro, and Bloom 2009.

22. Bellah 1992 [1975]: 67.

23. Indirect effect statistics are online at SUP.org. See "Ideology to gay marriage (simultaneous)."

24. The direct effect was reduced from 10 percent (semipartial correlation = .32) to just 2 percent (semipartial correlation = .15) with the inclusion of the five mediators.

25. Dickson 2012.

26. E.g., Sidanius and Pratto 1999; Sibley, Wilson, and Duckitt 2007.

27. Regression controlled for our seven standard demographics.

28. The direct effect of ideology on spanking was reduced from 14.4 percent (semipartial correlation = .38) to just 5.3 percent (semipartial correlation = .23) with the inclusion of the two mediators. Indirect effect statistics are online at SUP.org. See "Ideology to spanking (serial)."

29. The direct effect was reduced from 36 percent (semipartial correlation = .60) to 16 percent (semipartial correlation = .40) with the inclusion of the five mediators.

30. Nicholas D. Kristof, "Scott's Story and the Election," *New York Times*, October 17, 2012.

31. McGovern 2011: 5, 231.

32. Obama 2006: 66, 67.

33. Friedman and Friedman 1979: 146.

34. http://www.ontheissues.org/George_W__Bush_Principles_and_Values.htm.

35. Napier and Jost 2008: 566.

36. Napier and Jost 2008: 566, 571.

37. Goldberg 2006: 110–12.

38. Moore 1978: 43.

39. Sowell 2007 [1987]: 138.

40. Inbar, Pizarro, Iyer, and Haidt 2012: 542.

41. The direct effect was reduced from 8 percent (semipartial correlation = −.28) to 4 percent (semipartial correlation = −.20) with the inclusion of the five mediators.

42. Janoff-Bulman 2009: 124.

43. My thanks to Matthew Sanders for this interpretation of the mediation model.

44. Tajfel 1981; Turner 1987.

45. Perdue, Davidio, Gurtman, and Tyler 1990.

46. Thomas Pettigrew (1979) first called this phenomenon the "ultimate attribution error"; Miles Hewstone (1990) later labeled it, more modestly, the "intergroup attribution bias."

47. Deibel 2005: 67–8.

48. Hunt 2009 [1987]: 146.

49. Barack Obama, "Darfur: Current Policy Not Enough Security," podcast, February 15, 2006. Available at obamaspeeches.com.

50. Coulter 2003: 1.

51. Mauldin 1945: 64.

52. Mauldin 1961.

53. Singer 1981.

54. McFarland, Webb, and Brown 2012.

55. Personal communication with Sam McFarland, shared by permission.

56. Indirect effect statistics available online at SUP.org as "Ideology to foreign policy preferences (simultaneous)."

57. The direct effect was reduced from 4.4 percent (semipartial correlation = .21) to 1.4 percent (semipartial correlation = .12) with the inclusion of the two mediators.

58. Ditto and Koleva 2011.

Chapter Four

1. Paul 2008: 19.

2. Marco Rubio, "The New American Century," Washington, D.C., June 4, 2011.

3. Isolationism, α = .78; multilateralism, α = .81; militarism, α = .74. Although the wording is ours, to promote comparison the latter four items were modeled after the Chicago Council's foreign policy goals battery (e.g., CCGA 2010, Question 7).

4. Desch 2007/8: 42.

5. Cited in Preston 2012: 279.

6. Cited in Dueck 2010: 47.

7. Cited in Dueck 2010: 61.

8. Cited in Dueck 2010: 80.

9. Cited in Rogak 2008: 90.

10. Kull and Destler 1999: 16.

11. Todorov and Mandisodza 2004.

12. Kull and Destler 1999: 47 (figure 2-3); Todorov and Mandisodza 2004: 329.

13. $F(1, 419) = 29.66$, $p < .001$, $\eta_p^2 = .07$, controlling for seven standard demographics.

14. Point estimate (PE) = .0395; lower and upper 95% confidence intervals (CI) from .0141 to .0712.

15. See Janoff-Bulman 2009.

16. The direct effect was reduced from 3 percent (semipartial correlation = .17) to just 0.3 percent (semipartial correlation = .06). Indirect effect statistics are online at SUP.org under "Ideology to isolationism (simultaneous)."

17. Cited in Berinsky 2009: 139.

18. Kohut and Stokes 2006: 180, 182.

19. Russett 1990–91: 516.

20. Cited in Rogak 2008: 53.

21. Mauldin 1945: 13–14.

22. GOP 2012: 39.

23. Preston 2012: 33, 35.

24. Cited in Mann 2004: 328, 329, 315.

25. Cited in Preston 2012: 223.

26. Altemeyer 1996; Crowson 2009.

27. Cited in Rogak 2008: 53.

28. Bush 2010: 209.

29. $\alpha = .86$, $.63$, and $.81$; and $M = 5.04$, 4.76, and 4.91 for humanitarian, political, and religious idealisms, respectively.

30. Humanitarian: $F(1, 419) = 99.58$, $p < .001$, $\eta_p^2 = .19$; political: $F(1, 419) = 11.87$, $p = .001$, $\eta_p^2 = .03$; religious: $F(1, 419) = .03$, $p = .87$, controlling for seven standard demographics.

31. Scale $\alpha = .62$; $F(1, 419) = 113.61$, $p < .001$, $\eta_p^2 = .21$, controlling for seven standard demographics.

32. 2006 USA WVS, Question V118: $F(1, 893) = 184.96$, $p < .001$, $\eta_p^2 = .17$, controlling for age, gender, and education only.

33. Mauldin 1961: 2.

34. $F(1, 419) = 221.35$, $p < .001$, $\eta_p^2 = .35$, controlling for seven standard demographics.

35. The direct effect of ideology on humanitarian idealism was reduced from 10 percent (semipartial correlation = −.32) to just 1 percent (semipartial correlation = −.12)

when the sexual education item was added as a mediator. Indirect effect via sexual education: PE = −.2967, 95% CI from −.3520 to −.2338.

36. Goldwater 1960: 95.

37. Cited in Preston 2012: 253.

38. The direct effect, β = −.10, p = .003, was reduced to statistical nonsignificance, β = −.04, p = .24, with the inclusion of compassion as a mediator. The indirect effect via compassion was statistically significant: PE = −.0861, 95% CI from −.1213 to −.0598.

39. Moderating effect of ideology on the relationship between religious and political idealism: interaction ΔR^2 = .01, $F(1, 989)$ = 11.14, p < .001, controlling for seven standard demographics.

40. The direct effect was reduced from 1.7 percent (semipartial correlation = −.13) to just .5 percent (semipartial correlation = −.07) when isolationism is entered as a mediator. The indirect effect was statistically significant: PE = −.0570, 95% CI from −.0902 to −.0338.

41. Cited in Preston 2012: 156, 226.

42. Cited in Preston 2012: 599.

43. GOP 2012: 45.

44. Preston 2012: 572.

45. Barack Obama, "A World That Stands as One," Berlin, Germany, July 24, 2008.

46. Newt Gingrich, speech to the Senate and House Republican campaign committees, Washington, D.C., June 8, 2009.

47. Charles Krauthammer, "Decline Is a Choice: The New Liberalism and the End of American Ascendancy," *The Weekly Standard* 15 (5), October 19, 2009.

48. $F(1, 419)$ = 29.26, p < .001, η_p^2 = .07, controlling for seven standard demographics.

49. Kosterman and Feshbach 1989.

50. An exploratory factor analysis of these four items also produced a single-factor solution. This finding differs from that of Huddy and Khatib (2007), who used confirmatory factor analysis on the 1996 General Social Survey (GSS) and their own 2002 and 2004 student samples to argue that national identity (our patriotism) is empirically distinct from nationalism.

51. See Brewer 1999.

52. Cited in Prochaska 2008: 96.

53. Brown, Budzek, and Tamborski 2009; Golec de Zavala, Cichocka, Eidelson, and Jayawickreme 2009.

54. Cai and Gries 2013.

55. Hunt 2009 [1987]: 41, 42.

56. Kohut and Stokes 2006: 70.

57. Patriotism: $F(1, 419)$ = 38.42, p < .001, η_p^2 = .08; nationalism: $F(1, 419)$ = 169.87, p < .001, η_p^2 = .29; national narcissism: $F(1, 419)$ = 125.25, p < .001, η_p^2 = .23, controlling for seven standard demographics.

58. In the 2006 WVS, Republicans (n = 390) scored substantially higher than Democrats (n = 502) on a four-point scale from "*Quite proud*" to "*Not at all proud*" in response to the question, "*How proud are you to be an American?*" $F(1, 897)$ = 64.34, p < .001, η_p^2 = .07, controlling for age, gender, and education only.

59. $F(1, 419) = 4.70, p = .031, \eta_p^2 = .01$, controlling for the seven standard demographics *and* nationalism.

60. Together they accounted for 70 percent of the relationship, with the direct effect of ideology on foreign policy preferences reduced from 4.3 percent (semipartial correlation = .21) to just 1.3 percent (semipartial correlation = .12) when patriotism and nationalism were added as mediators.

61. Inclusion of the four mediators reduced the direct effect from 15 percent (semipartial correlation = .39) to just 1 percent (semipartial correlation = .12). Indirect effect statistics are online at SUP.org under "Ideology to nationalism I (simultaneous)."

62. Indirect effect statistics are online at SUP.org under "Ideology to nationalism II (simultaneous)."

63. Barack Obama, "Nobel Peace Prize Acceptance Speech," Stockholm, Sweden, December 9, 2009.

64. Hillary Clinton, May 10, 2011, cited in Jeffrey Goldberg, "Hillary Clinton: Chinese System Is Doomed, Leaders on a 'Fool's Errand,'" *The Atlantic*, June 2011.

65. Mead 2001: 86–89, 220.

66. Patriotism and national narcissism were not included, as they correlated so highly with nationalism.

67. Drezner 2008: 63, 64.

68. Dueck 2010: 306, 321.

69. $F(1, 303) = .87, p = .35$, controlling for seven standard demographics.

70. Dueck 2010: 291.

71. Nationalism: $F(1, 701) = 94.82, p < .001, \eta_p^2 = .12$; military force: $F(1, 701) = 78.93, p < .001, \eta_p^2 = .10$, controlling for seven standard demographics.

72. Mann 2012: 38.

73. Mann 2012: 166.

Chapter Five

1. Lewin 1935.

2. Mesquita, Barrett, and Smith 2010.

3. David Brooks, "Social Science Palooza III," *New York Times*, December 11, 2012.

4. "Westie Side Story," *King of the Hill*, Season 1, Episode 7, first aired March 2, 1997.

5. See Pew Research Center for the People and the Press, "What the Public Knows— In Words and Pictures," November 7, 2011. Available online at people-press.org.

6. Gelpi 2010: 108, 88.

7. Berinsky 2009: 210.

8. Baum and Groeling 2010: 2.

9. $\beta = -.01, p = .88; \beta = -.05, p = .18$. Regressions controlled for the standard demographics.

10. $\beta = -.26$ vs. $\beta = -.05, p = .27$; and $\beta = .23$ vs. $\beta = .14, p = .002$, respectively.

11. Twain 1869: 650.

12. From over 5 percent (semipartial correlation = .073) to less than 1 percent (semipartial correlation = .03).

13. Allport 1954.
14. Ideology: $F(1, 419) = 1.35, p = .25$; party ID: $F(1, 701) = .11, p = .74$, controlling for seven standard demographics.
15. Pearson's $\chi^2(1, N = 791) = .25, p = .62$. Program on International Policy Attitudes, "World Public Opinion and Global Citizenship." Available at DRUM, http://hdl.handle.net/1903/10690.
16. For more on moderation, see Hayes 2013; or the Statistical Glossary at the end of the book.
17. Interaction $\Delta R^2 = .01, F(1, 989) = 13.57, p < .001$. The positive slope for cultural conservatives was statistically significant, $B = .18, p < .001$; the negative slope for cultural liberals was marginally significant, $B = -.11, p = .06$.

Chapter Six

1. From *On the Road* (1957); reproduced in Holden and Zolov 2011: 201–2.
2. Beck and Balfe 2007: 277.
3. Feelings towards Haiti: $F(1, 419) = 51.25, p < .001, \eta_p^2 = .11$; Brazil: $F(1, 419) = 94.82, p < .001, \eta_p^2 = .18$; Mexico: $F(1, 419) = 138.90, p < .001, \eta_p^2 = .25$, controlling for seven standard demographics.
4. Fiske, Cuddy, Glick, and Xu 2002; Fiske 2012.
5. Foreign policy preferences towards Haiti: $F(1, 419) = 26.67, p < .001, \eta_p^2 = .06$; Brazil: $F(1, 419) = 35.41, p < .001, \eta_p^2 = .08$; Mexico: $F(1, 419) = 141.63, p < .001, \eta_p^2 = .25$, controlling for seven standard demographics.
6. Mexican border policy: $F(1, 303) = 160.74, p < .001, \eta_p^2 = .35$; aid to Haiti: $F(1, 303) = 97.90, p < .001, \eta_p^2 = .24$. White liberals and conservatives only $(n = 310)$. ANCOVA therefore controlled for just five demographics: age, gender, education, income, and region.
7. Cited in Hunt 2009 [1987]: 127.
8. Cited in Holden and Zolov 2011: 104–5.
9. Feelings towards Mexico (three-item scale): indirect effect via social dominance orientation (SDO): PE $= -.0632$, 95% CI from $-.0918$ to $-.0361$. Feelings towards Haiti: indirect effect via SDO: PE $= -2.212$, 95% CI from -3.135 to -1.538. Direct effects reduced from $\beta = -.38$ to $-.31$, and $\beta = -.26$ to $-.20$, respectively.
10. In a regression, $\beta = -.05, p = .19$. β for the other three ideological dimensions were .01 or less, with p values all greater than .80.
11. Hunt 2009 [1987]: 59.
12. Cited in Holden and Zolov 2011: 76.
13. Cited in Holden and Zolov 2011: 134.
14. Cited in Luck 1999: 91.
15. Cited in Hunt 2009 [1987]: 166.
16. Noer 2003: 145.
17. Cited in Fuchs 1990: 1. My thanks to Jim Hollifield for this reference.
18. Cited in Shanks 2001: 44.
19. Cited in Fuchs 1990: 66.
20. "The Limbaugh Laws," April 6, 2006, at rushlimbaugh.com.

21. Fuchs 1990.

22. Cited in Michelle McIntyre, "The Abortion/Illegal Immigration Link: Not What You May Think," The Reagan Wing (blog), February 5, 2007, thereaganwing.com.

23. Scale $\alpha = .88$. $F(1, 303) = 160.74$, $p < .001$, $\eta_p^2 = .35$. Whites-only ANCOVA controlled for age, gender, education, income, and region.

24. Direct effect reduced from 20 percent (semipartial correlation = .45) to just 5 percent (semipartial correlation = .22).

25. Kia Makerechi, "'MariKKKopa': Conor Oberst Explains New Desaparecidos Track," August 1, 2012, huffingtonpost.com.

26. GOP 2012: 25–26.

27. The indirect effect through loyalty was statistically significant: PE = .1565, 95% CI from .1056 to .2264.

28. Duckitt and Sibley 2007, 2010.

29. Cited in Holden and Zolov 2011: 348.

30. Cited in Shanks 2001: 58.

31. Huntington 2004: 33.

32. John F. Kennedy, speech to the Latin American Diplomatic Corps, March 13, 1961. Cited in Holden and Zolov 2011: 222.

33. Paul 2008: 99.

34. Cited in Holden and Zolov 2011: 241–42.

35. "2012 Democratic National Platform: Moving America Forward," at democrats. org.

36. GOP 2012: 45–46.

37. $F(1, 303) = 97.90$, $p < .001$, $\eta_p^2 = .24$. Whites-only ANCOVA controlled for age, gender, education, income, and being from the South.

38. Pearson's $\chi^2(1, N = 519) = 10.36$, $p = .01$; $\chi^2(1, N = 515) = 37.37$, $p < .01$; $\chi^2(1, N = 517) = 39.28$, $p < .01$, respectively. Liberals and conservatives were defined as the bottom and top 20 percent on their ideology self-placement scale. There was no ideological difference on a fourth type of aid—"*Aid to increase U.S. influence over counties that are important to U.S. interests*"—which is about helping Americans, not about helping other countries; Pearson's $\chi^2(1, N = 515) = .021$, $p = .89$.

39. Inclusion of the four mediators reduced the direct effect from 13.7 percent (semipartial correlation = .37) to just 2.6 percent (semipartial correlation = .16).

40. E-mail correspondence, October 2, 2012. Reproduced by permission.

41. "Ron Paul: Foreign Aid Takes Money from Poor in U.S., Given to Rich," October 18, 2011, realclearpolitics.com.

42. O'Reilly 2006: 111.

43. For more on suppressor effects in mediation analyses, see Rucker, Preacher, Tormala, and Petty 2011.

44. From $\beta = .39$ to $\beta = .45$.

45. FAIR, http://www.fairus.org/about. *Italics* added.

46. Indirect effect PE = −.0873, 95% CI from −.1673 to −.0142. Direct effect *increases* from $\beta = .39$ to $\beta = .45$.

47. $F(1, 570) = 7.82$, $p = .005$, $\eta_p^2 = .01$; and $F(1, 570) = 16.15$, $p < .001$, $\eta_p^2 = .03$, controlling for age, gender, education, and income. Women and the less educated were more likely to overestimate actual foreign aid and to suggest giving more. Program on International Policy Attitudes data, http://hdl.handle.net/1903/11376.

48. 2006 World Values Survey: Pearson's $\chi^2(1, N = 850) = 30.36$, $p < .001$.

49. My thanks to Paul Kowert for this insight.

50. Hispanics only: $F(1, 133) = 3.95$, $p = .049$, $\eta_p^2 = .03$, controlling for age, gender, education, income, and region.

51. The direct effect of gender on warmth towards Brazil was reduced from $\beta = .17$ to statistical nonsignificance, $\beta = -.02$, $p = .92$. The indirect effect was statistically significant, PE = 2.68, 95% CI from .1535 to 7.735.

52. Adding traditionalism as a mediator *increases* the direct relationship between immigration generation and feelings towards Mexico from 9 percent (semipartial correlation = $-.30$) to 14 percent (semipartial correlation = $-.37$). Indirect effect statistics: PE = 2.12, 95% CI from .1934 to 4.858.

53. Cited in Rachel Weiner, "Sean Hannity: I've 'Evolved' on Immigration," *Washington Post*, November 8, 2012.

54. $F(1, 205) = 11.03$, $p = .001$, $\eta_p^2 = .05$; and $F(1, 205) = 14.59$, $p < .001$, $\eta_p^2 = .07$, controlling for seven standard demographics.

Chapter Seven

1. Kagan 2002.
2. Drezner 2012.
3. Jervis 2003: 84.
4. Chicago Council 2010: 60.
5. England: $F(1, 419) = 8.16$, $p = .004$, $\eta_p^2 = .02$; Germany: $F(1, 419) = 29.77$, $p < .001$, $\eta_p^2 = .07$; France: $F(1, 419) = 117.38$, $p < .001$, $\eta_p^2 = .22$, controlling for seven standard demographics.
6. Europeans: $F(1, 419) = 44.79$, $p < .001$, $\eta_p^2 = .10$; EU: $F(1, 419) = 292.29$, $p < .001$, $\eta_p^2 = .41$, controlling for seven standard demographics.
7. Twain 1935: 153.
8. *Tonight Show* with Jay Leno, March 5, 2003.
9. Newt Gingrich attack ad, "The French Connection," January 2012.
10. Fiske, Cuddy, Glick, and Xu 2002; Fiske 2012.
11. Chicago Council 2010: 62.
12. Cited in Rohrs 1994: 734.
13. Cited in Katz 1994: 395.
14. Ibid.
15. Three-item France measure: direct effect reduced from 15 percent (semipartial correlation = $-.39$) to 4 percent (semipartial correlation = $-.21$). Indirect effect via economic ideology was statistically significant: PE = -0927, 95% CI from .1462 to $-.0456$.
16. William H. Grimes, "A Newspaper's Philosophy," *Wall Street Journal*, January 2, 1951.

17. "French Revolution," editorial, *Wall Street Journal*, September 20, 2007, A12.

18. "Socialist France," editorial, *Wall Street Journal*, May 7, 2012; "France's Class Warrior," editorial, *Wall Street Journal*, March 3, 2012, A14.

19. Paul Krugman, "The Plot Against France," *New York Times*, November 10, 2013.

20. Alterman 2008: 63.

21. Christian Toto, "Woody Allen's 'Midnight in Paris' Flatters France, Batters U.S.," *Washington Times*, July 7, 2011, washingtontimes.com.

22. The direct effect of openness on feelings towards France (three-item measure) was reduced from 1.1 percent (semipartial correlation = .103) to just .0001 percent (semipartial correlation = .001) with the inclusion of the two mediators.

23. Cited in Dumbrell 2006: 23.

24. Cited in Preston 2012: 446.

25. Coulter 2011: 129.

26. The direct effect of ideology on foreign policy towards France was reduced from 4 percent (semipartial correlation = .20) to just 1.4 percent (semipartial correlation = .12) with the inclusion of the two mediators.

27. Cited in Metzler 2010: 24.

28. Cited in Schlesinger 1973: 834. These French actions in the 1960s are best understood in the context of the 1956 Suez crisis, in which the United States supported Egypt against France, Britain, and Israel.

29. Cited in Metzler 2010: 40.

30. Quoted in Stephen Dinan, "A Lost Appetite for 'French' Food; House Renames Fries, Toast," *Washington Times*, March 12, 2003.

31. Miller and Molesky 2004: 6–7.

32. Hoffmann 2004.

33. Mauldin 1965: 7.

34. Tina Fey, "Weekend Update," *Saturday Night Live*, March 15, 2003.

35. Abraham Lincoln, "Letter to Queen Victoria," 1861, cited in Prochaska 2008: 85.

36. From her *This I Remember* (1949); quoted in Prochaska 2008: 136.

37. http://www.archives.gov/exhibits/charters/declaration_transcript.html.

38. Cited in Prochaska 2008: xiii–xiv, 24, 1, 111.

39. Cited in Prochaska 2008: 8, 36.

40. Cited in Prochaska 2008: 169.

41. Prochaska 2008: 156, 179.

42. $F(1, 419) = 8.16$, $p = .004$, $\eta_p^2 = .02$, controlling for seven standard demographics.

43. The direct relationship *increased* from .86 percent (semipartial correlation = −.093) to 2.13 percent (semipartial correlation = −.146).

44. $F(1, 418) = 19.64$, $p < .001$, $\eta_p^2 = .05$, controlling for seven standard demographics *and* nationalism.

45. $F(1, 419) = 17.65$, $p < .001$, $\eta_p^2 = .04$, controlling for seven standard demographics.

46. Culture was only marginally significant at $p < .10$.

47. Coulter 2011: 131, 140.

48. Cited in Dumbrell 2006: 24.

49. Cited in Prochaska 2008: 96, 98.

50. When run in separate hierarchical regressions, ideology and partisanship both predict England policy at $\beta = -.09$, $p < .01$, controlling for the standard demographics in the first stage.

51. Dumbrell 2006: 26.

52. Miller and Molesky 2004: 12.

53. Cited in Dumbrell 2006: 28.

54. "Awarding a Congressional Gold Medal to Prime Minister Tony Blair," House of Representatives, June 25, 2003, http://thomas.loc.gov/cgi-bin/query/C?r108:./temp/~r108Howh5r.

55. Cited in Prochaska 2008: 119.

56. Quoted in Nicholas D. Kristof, "Romney's Economic Model," *New York Times*, October 24, 2012.

57. Cited in Mistler 2012.

58. Cited in Fuchs 1990: 11–12.

59. Cited in Moore 2010: 19.

60. Friedrich Graetz, "A Family Party," centerfold editorial cartoon for *Puck*, October 3, 1883. Library of Congress, LC-DIG-ppmsca-28430.

61. Cited in Moore 2010: 19.

62. Schurz 1913: 190.

63. Moore: 2010: 8, 6.

64. Dower 1986: 79.

65. Moore 2010: 342.

66. If economic ideology is the only mediator in the model, the direct relationship between conservatism and feelings towards Germany *increases* from $\beta = -.18$ to $\beta = -.23$.

67. "Europe's Phony Growth Debate," *Wall Street Journal*, April 25, 2012, A14.

68. Cited in Kristof, "Romney's Economic Model."

69. Paul Krugman, "Euro Austerity, Continued," *New York Times*, April 28, 2012.

70. As the sole mediator of the relationship, cultural traditionalism *reduces* the direct effect of ideology on warmth towards Germany from over 3 percent to less than 1 percent.

71. Duckitt and Sibley 2007, 2010.

72. Cited in Kirakofe 2009: 180.

73. Crawford and Martel 1997: 307.

74. E-mail correspondence, October 30, 2012. Reproduced by permission.

75. $F(1, 418) = 40.13$, $p < .001$, $\eta_p^2 = .09$.

76. Lindsey 1969: 94.

77. Hagee 2006: 115.

78. "Statement by NSC Spokesman Tommy Vietor on the Awarding of the Nobel Peace Prize to the European Union," Office of the Press Secretary, The White House, October 12, 2012.

79. "A Nobel for the Continent," *New York Times*, October 12, 2012.

80. Christian Whiton, "The EU Wins the Nobel Peace Prize—Is This a Joke?" *Fox News*, October 12, 2012.

81. http://online.wsj.com/community/groups/europes-question-day-695/topics/did-european-union-deserve-win. Accessed November 5, 2012.

82. $F(1, 416) = 19.35, p < .001, \eta_p^2 = .04$, covarying for the seven standard demographic variables *and* feelings towards the United Nations and Europeans, and belief in Satan.

83. Lindsey 1994: 156.

84. Chuck Missler, "Europa Rising: Part I," *Profiles in Prophecy Series*, June 2003, Koinonia House, khouse.org.

Chapter Eight

1. Mearsheimer and Walt 2007: 5.
2. Ross 2006: 61.
3. Friedberg 2006: 60.
4. Ben-Ami 2006: 62.
5. Oren 2006.
6. Mead 2008: 30.
7. Mead 2007.
8. Mead 2008: 30.
9. Koplow 2011: 280, 302.
10. Mead 2008: 46.
11. Chicago Council 2010: 60. Our focus on the Palestinian "people" rather than the Palestinian "Authority" likely accounts for the greater warmth we found, while the intensification of the Iran nuclear situation likely accounts for our survey's greater coolness towards Iran.
12. In the 2009 PIPA survey, Republicans felt more "sympathy" towards Israelis and less towards Palestinians than Democrats did: $F(1, 458) = 13.49, p < .001, \eta_p^2 = .03$; $F(1, 458) = 24.90, p < .001, \eta_p^2 = .05$, both controlling for age, gender, and education only. In the 2010 Chicago Council Survey, conservatives felt 14° warmer towards Israel, and 11° cooler towards the Palestinian Authority than liberals did: $F(1, 441) = 25.25, p < .001, \eta_p^2 = .05$; $F(1, 478) = 27.51, p < .001, \eta_p^2 = .05$, both controlling for age, gender, education, income, and being from the South.
13. 2011 CNN: $F(1, 415) = 33.03, p < .001, \eta_p^2 = .07$, controlling for age, gender, education, and income.
14. Fiske, Cuddy, Glick, and Xu 2002; Fiske 2012.
15. Israel: admiration: $F(1, 419) = 99.08, p < .001, \eta_p^2 = .19$; annoyed: $F(1, 419) = 76.94, p < .001, \eta_p^2 = .16$, both controlling for seven standard demographics.
16. $\alpha = .88$.
17. Israel policy (three-item scale): $F(1, 419) = 201.51, p < .001, \eta_p^2 = .33$; Iran policy (single item): $F(1, 419) = 64.17, p < .001, \eta_p^2 = .13$, both controlling for seven standard demographics.
18. 2011 CNN: Pearson's $\chi^2(2, N = 321) = 32.97, p < .001$.
19. CBS 2011: $F(1, 541) = 34.31, p < .001, \eta_p^2 = .06$, controlling for age, gender, education, and income.
20. From his *White-Jacket*, cited in Mead 2008: 35.

21. Mark Twain, "Concerning the Jews," *Harper's New Monthly Magazine*, September 1899.

22. Grose 1983: 3.

23. Cited in Grose 1983: 5.

24. Cited in Grose 1983: 36; Boyer 1999 [1992]: 186.

25. Cited in Preston 2012: 438.

26. Carenan 2012.

27. Preston 2012: 114.

28. Oren 2007: 30–32.

29. Cited in Kidd 2009: 64.

30. Cited in Jacobs 2011: 71.

31. Oren 2007: 520, 542.

32. Cited in Alexander and Nanes 1980: 482.

33. McAlister 2001: 198–234.

34. From his *Listen America*, cited in Carenen 2012: 189.

35. Ronald Reagan, telephone conversation with Thomas Dine of the American Israel Public Affairs Committee, October 1983, cited in Carenen 2012: 194.

36. Direct effect reduced from 20 percent (semipartial correlation $= -.45$) to just .08 percent (semipartial correlation $= -.09$).

37. Cited in Boyer 1999 [1992]: 189.

38. Hagee 2006: 194.

39. The direct relationship was reduced from 17 percent (semipartial correlation $= -.41$) to just .08 percent (semipartial correlation $= -.09$). The indirect effect was significant: $PE = -.31$, 95% CI from $-.3780$ to $-.2501$.

40. Hitchcock 2012: 193, 194.

41. Clark 2007: 263.

42. Cited in Kirakofe 2009: 181.

43. Cited in Ariel Levy, "Prodigal Son: Is the Wayward Republican Mike Huckabee Now His Party's Best Hope?" *New Yorker*, June 28, 2010.

44. Cited in Spector 2009: 32.

45. Hagee 2006: 64.

46. Hitchcock 2012: 193.

47. convention.texasgop.org.

48. 2.5 percent to 1.4 percent, based on semipartial correlations of .158 and .117. Three-item measure of feelings towards Israel.

49. Tom DeLay, "Be Not Afraid," July 30, 2003, nationalreview.com.

50. Mauldin 1985: 7.

51. From his *Hopes of the Church*, cited in Boyer 1999 [1992]: 200.

52. Hitchcock 2012: 18.

53. Religiosity: $F(1, 153) = 1.45$, $p = .23$; biblical literalism: $F(1, 153) = 5.62$, $p = .02$, $\eta_p^2 = .035$, controlling for six demographics (race is excluded).

54. Israel: $F(1, 153) = 14.36$, $p < .001$, $\eta_p^2 = .09$; Palestinians: $F(1, 153) = 13.38$, $p < .001$, $\eta_p^2 = .08$, controlling for six demographics (race is excluded).

55. Eleven colored countries scale $\alpha = .87$. $F_{(1, 153)} = .005$, $p = .95$, controlling for six demographics (race is excluded).

56. McAlister 2001.

57. $F_{(1, 241)} = 3.87$, $p = .05$, $\eta_p^2 = .02$, controlling for six demographics (ethnicity is excluded).

58. $F_{(1, 240)} = .22$, $p = .64$, controlling for six demographics (ethnicity is excluded).

59. Carter 2006: 216.

60. Barack Obama cell phone podcast from Tel Aviv, January 14, 2006, available at obamaspeeches.com.

61. E.g., Thomsen, Green, and Sidanius 2008.

62. Skocpol and Williamson 2012: 69.

63. Gingrich and DeSantis 2010: 303.

64. McAlister 2001: 157.

65. Mead 2008: 42–44.

66. McGovern 2011: 179, 181.

67. Carter 2009: xxii.

68. Jerry L. Van Marter, "Religious Leaders Ask Congress to Condition Israel Military Aid on Human Rights Compliance," *Presbyterian News Service*, October 5, 2012, pcusa.org.

69. Newt Gingrich, "Super Tuesday" speech, Atlanta, Georgia, March 6, 2012.

70. Harry Reid, press conference, March 6, 2012.

71. Mearsheimer and Walt 2007: 4.

72. Cited in Kirakofe 2009: 180.

73. "Reed Concerned with Romney's Overheated Iran Rhetoric," March 5, 2012, news release, reed.senate.gov.

74. "Three Oklahoma City Billboards Call for 'No War on Iran,'" July 10, 2012, news release, Americans Against the Next War, wordpress.com.

75. Inclusion of the two mediators reduced the shared variance between ideology and Iran policy from 7.5 percent (semipartial correlation = .27) to just 1.5 percent (semipartial correlation = .12).

76. Nationalism also correlated positively with preferences for tougher foreign policies towards North Korea ($r = .29$), Russia ($r = .27$), and China ($r = .27$). All of these countries represent potential threats to the nationalist belief that "*America is the best country in the world.*" The zero-order correlation $r = .38$ is greater than the $\beta = .32$ in the mediation analysis because the latter factors in the seven standard demographic covariates, not displayed in Figure 8–10, to reduce clutter.

77. Nationalism did not correlate at all with feelings towards Japan or South Korea.

78. Indirect effect statistics are online at SUP.org under "Chapter 8, Iran section: Nationalism to warmth towards Israel (simultaneous)."

79. Why support for income inequality would also contribute to American nationalism's positive relationship with warmth towards Israel is harder to interpret. Perhaps American nationalists take pride in Israel's economic success.

80. Cited in Haugen, Musser, and Lovelace 2009: 73.

81. Billy Graham, Advertisement, *New York Times*, October 28, 2012, p. 9.

82. Aldrich et al. 2006.

83. Koplow 2011: 268.

84. Thomas L. Friedman, "Israel's Best Friend," *New York Times*, March 6, 2012.

85. Chicago Council 2008: $F(1, 441) = 35.50$, $p < .001$, $\eta_p^2 = .08$, controlling for age, gender, income, and education.

86. Spector 2009: 245.

87. Mead 2007: 162.

Chapter Nine

1. Nancy Pelosi, "The Violent Response by Chinese Police Forces to Peaceful Protesters in Tibet Is Disgraceful," March 12, 2008, press release, pelosi.house.gov.

2. "Forbes' Statement on Chinese Vice President Xi Jingping's Visit to the United States," press release, February 13, 2012.

3. Christopher Smith, "Google … China … and U.S.: Moral Challenges We Face," *National Review*, April 20, 2006.

4. Page and Xie 2010: 37. See also 57, 66, and 103. For a critique, see Gries 2011.

5. $F(1, 419) = 64.97$, $p < .001$, $\eta_p^2 = .13$, controlling for the seven standard demographics.

6. Feelings towards Taiwan: $F(1, 420) = 6.94$, $p = .009$, $\eta_p^2 = .02$; South Korea: $F(1, 420) = 6.00$, $p = .015$, $\eta_p^2 = .01$; Japan: $F(1, 420) = 10.75$, $p = .001$, $\eta_p^2 = .03$, controlling for the seven standard demographics.

7. In the Chicago Council's 2010 "countries and peoples" feeling thermometer, the average American felt coolest towards North Korea (26°), followed by China (45°), South Korea (52°), and Japan (61°), the same sequence as our 2011 survey (it did not measure feelings towards Taiwan). Conservatives (39°) in its survey felt 10° cooler towards China than liberals (49°) did, a small-to-medium-sized difference statistically: $F(1, 1002) = 41.41$, $p < .001$, $\eta_p^2 = .04$, controlling for age, gender, education, income, and being from the South. Democrats had a more favorable view of China than Republicans in Pew's 2010 global attitudes telephone survey: $F(1, 1869) = 36.31$, $p < .001$, $\eta_p^2 = .02$, controlling for age, gender, education, and income. And in a September 2011 CNN telephone poll, conservatives scored higher than liberals did on a China as ally-to-enemy question: $F(1, 270) = 8.53$, $p = .004$, $\eta_p^2 = .03$. The smaller effect sizes in the CNN and Pew polls are likely due to the greater measurement error in telephone polls, as well as the more restricted response options, which limited the variation they captured.

8. $F(1, 419) = 89.47$, $p < .001$, $\eta_p^2 = .18$, controlling for the seven standard demographics. Three-item China policy scale α = .68.

9. Cited in McClellan 1971: 223.

10. Cited in Dower 1986: 81.

11. Hunt 2009 [1987]: 69.

12. Trubowitz and Seo 2012: 194–97.

13. Cited in Daniels 2004: 13–14.

14. Hunt 2009 [1987]: 70.

15. Jespersen 1996: 9, 1–2.

16. Hunt 2009 [1987]: 70.

17. Hunt 2009 [1987]: 77.

18. Cited in Dower 1986: 80.

19. Cited in Dower 1986: 91.

20. Cited in Williams 2010: 26.

21. Jespersen 1996: 172.

22. Isaacs 1957: 10, 11.

23. Madsen 1995: xi.

24. Cited in Williams 2010: 79.

25. As noted in the Introduction, the Chicago Council's feeling thermometer solicits feelings towards a list of "countries and peoples," conflating these two attitude objects.

26. Cronbach's α = .78 and .79, respectively. Together with the three-item China policy scale introduced above, these two three-item scales were used in all the mediation, path, and structural equation models in this chapter.

27. $t(999) = 34.29, p < .001$. Cohen's $d = 1.05$.

28. $F(1, 419) = 24.02, p < .001, \eta_p^2 = .05$; and $F(1, 419) = 59.44, p < .001, \eta_p^2 = .12$, controlling for the seven standard demographics.

29. $F(1, 419) = 6.40, p = .012, \eta_p^2 = .02$; and $F(1, 419) = 89.79, p < .001, \eta_p^2 = .18$, controlling for the seven standard demographics.

30. The direct effect was reduced from 10.9 percent (semipartial correlation = .33) to 2.8 percent (semipartial correlation = .17) with the inclusion of the four mediators.

31. The only crossover between the two paths was that warmth towards communist countries had a small impact ($\beta = -.12$) on prejudice, although it was overwhelmed by the impact of feelings towards Asians ($\beta = -.56$).

32. Sidanius and Pratto 1999.

33. Cited in Preston 2012: 488.

34. The direct effect was reduced from 8.8 percent (semipartial correlation = $-.296$) to just .8 percent (semipartial correlation = $-.09$).

35. Cited in Williams 2010: 21; Preston 2012: 469.

36. Williams 2010: 23.

37. Friedman 2002 [1962]: 13.

38. Bellah 1992 [1975]: 124.

39. Preston 2012: 101.

40. Cited in Preston 2012: 553.

41. Kahneman 2011: 97.

42. Indirect effect statistics are online at SUP.org under "Chapter 9, policy section. Social dominance to prejudice against Chinese."

43. Huma Khan, "Rush Limbaugh Mocks Chinese President Hu Jintao," ABC News, January 20, 2011.

44. Duckitt and Sibley 2007; Jost 2006.

45. "Rohrabacher Statement on the Threat of Chinese Satellite Technology and Export Controls," April 2, 2009, floor speech, rohrabacher.house.gov.

46. Romney 2010: 14.

47. E.g., Giddens 1987.

48. GOP 2012: 49.

49. Pew Research Center for the People and the Press, "What the Public Knows—In Pictures, Maps, Graphs and Symbols," February 5, 2013, p. 13.

50. $t(999) = -8.78$, $p < .001$; Cohen's $d = -.28$.

51. World Economic Outlook Database, imf.org.

52. Cronbach's $\alpha = .74$.

53. Allport 1954.

54. Pettigrew and Tropp 2006.

55. See Gries, Crowson, and Cai 2011.

56. Interaction $\Delta R^2 = .01$, $F(1, 415) = 4.35$, $p = .037$. The negative slope for cultural liberals (low traditionalism) was statistically significant, $B = -.22$, $p = .03$; the positive slope for cultural conservatives was not, $B = .08$, $p = .49$.

57. George W. Bush, "Address to Members of the Knesset," Jerusalem, Israel, May 15, 2008.

58. GOP 2012: 48.

59. Wu 2010.

60. Thomas Perez, "Remembering Vincent Chin," June 22, 2012, blog post, whitehouse.gov.

61. E.g., President George W. Bush, "Address at The Citadel," Charleston, South Carolina, December 11, 2001; President George W. Bush, "Remarks on the Future of Iraq," Washington, D.C., February 26, 2003.

62. President George W. Bush, "West Point Commencement," United States Military Academy, West Point, New York, June 1, 2002.

63. "Inhofe Urges Support of Taiwan," June 30, 2008, press release, inhofe.senate.gov.

64. William Lowther, "Taiwan Democracy in Peril: U.S. Senator," *Taipei Times*, September 16, 2009.

65. Cited in Kennedy 2003: 106.

66. Cited in Leuchtenburg 1991.

67. James McGregor, "The China Fix," *Time*, February 1, 2010.

Chapter Ten

1. 2012 "Democratic Party Platform: Moving America Forward," democrats.org.

2. GOP 2012: 45.

3. Jim Abrams, "Republican Opposition Downs U.N. Disability Treaty," Associated Press, December 5, 2012.

4. Michael Bowman, "US Fails to Ratify Convention on the Disabled," VOA, December 4, 2012, voanews.com.

5. Jennifer Steinhauer, "Dole Appears, but G.O.P. Rejects a Disabilities Treaty," *New York Times*, December 4, 2012.

6. Page with Bouton 2006: 154.

7. Busby and Monten 2012: 137.

8. Chicago Council 2012: 44, 4.

9. $F(1, 420) = 411.29$, $p < .001$, $\eta_p^2 = .50$, controlling for seven standard demographics.

10. $F(1, 420) = 96.87$, $p < .001$, $\eta_p^2 = .19$, controlling for seven standard demographics.

11. 2004 Chicago Council, Question 335: $F(1, 622) = 106.88$, $p < .001$, $\eta_p^2 = .15$, controlling for age, gender, income, and education.

12. Scale $\alpha = .81$. $F(1, 420) = 431.91$, $p < .001$, $\eta_p^2 = .51$, controlling for seven standard demographics.

13. 2010 Chicago Council, Question 7/2: $F(1, 1058) = 166.67$, $p < .001$, $\eta_p^2 = .14$, controlling for age, gender, education, income, and being from the South.

14. 2010 Chicago Council, Question 220/1-7: $F(1, 467) = 132.95$, $p < .001$, $\eta_p^2 = .22$, controlling for age, gender, education, income, and being from the South. Scale $\alpha = .85$.

15. $\chi^2(1, N = 588) = 57.63$, $p < .001$, Phi = .31; and $\chi^2(1, N = 537) = 28.14$, $p < .001$, Phi = .23. Gallup poll, February 25–26, 2013, downloaded from the Roper Center.

16. $F(1, 420) = 431.91$, $p < .001$, $\eta_p^2 = .51$, controlling for seven demographics. Scale $\alpha = .71$, good for just two items.

17. Rathbun 2012: 52, 2.

18. $\chi^2(1, N = 325) = 17.30$, $p < .001$, Phi = .23; $\chi^2(1, N = 333) = 11.93$, $p = .001$; and $\chi^2(1, N = 349) = 25.01$, $p < .001$, Phi = .27, respectively. November 2007 PIPA Knowledge Networks Internet survey, http://hdl.handle.net/1903/10632.

19. Woodrow Wilson, "Fourteen Points Speech," to a joint session of Congress, Washington, D.C., January 8, 1918.

20. Cited in Graebner and Bennett 2011: 72.

21. Cited in Graebner and Bennett 2011: 43.

22. Senator William E. Borah, Senate speech on the League of Nations, November 19, 1919.

23. "This Day in Politics: Senate Ratifies United Nations Charter," July 28, 1945, politico.com.

24. Helms 1996: 2, 3.

25. Cited in Ruotsila 2008: 14.

26. Cited in Ruotsila 2008: 62.

27. Ruotsila 2008: 187–88, 171.

28. The direct effect was reduced from 10.25 percent (semipartial correlation = −.32) to 2.25 percent (semipartial correlation = −.15).

29. Cited in Ruotsila 2008: 13.

30. Cited in Ruotsila 2008: 23.

31. Preston 2012: 280.

32. Cited in Preston 2012: 392.

33. Ruotsila 2008: 28.

34. Cited in Ruotsila 2008: 140.

35. Cited in Preston 2012: 402.

36. Robertson 1991: 37.

37. Cited in Williams 2010: 219.

38. Hagee 2006: 16.

39. Hitchcock 2012: 193.

40. Indirect effect statistics are online at SUP.org under "Chapter 10, Satan section. Cultural traditionalism to warmth towards the U.N. (simultaneous)."

41. Cited in Ruotsila 2008: 39, 49, 108.

42. Dueck 2010: 27.

43. Cited in Ruotsila 2008: 61, 48.

44. Cited in Ruotsila 2008: 177, 178, 179.

45. Abramson, Seligman, and Teasdale 1978.

46. Kay et al. 2008.

47. Kay et al. 2010. My thanks to Colin Barnes for bringing this remarkable series of experiments to my attention.

48. Cited in Graebner and Bennett 2011: 11.

49. Cited in Ruotsila 2008: 38, 64.

50. Cited in Ruotsila 2008: 99.

51. Cited in Preston 2012: 555.

52. The direct effect was reduced from 52 percent (semipartial correlation = .72) to 13 percent (semipartial correlation = .36).

53. Preston 2012: 556. Italics added.

54. Cited in Luck 1999: 91.

55. Cited in Luck 1999: 100.

56. Luck 1999: 89.

57. Direct effect reduced from 4.2 percent (semipartial correlation = −.21) to .81 percent (semipartial correlation = −.09).

58. Luck 1999: 90, 91. Italics added.

59. Noer 2003: 147, 153.

60. Cited in Luck 1999: 96.

61. Cited in Luck 1999: 98, 76.

62. $F(1, 1047) = 6.96$, $p = .008$, $\eta_p^2 = .007$, controlling for age, gender, education, income, and being from the South.

63. From *The Great Betrayal*, cited in Luck 1999: 70.

64. Cited in Luck 1999: 46.

65. Cited in Luck 1999: 76.

66. Bandow 1985.

67. Moynihan 1975.

68. E.g., Tim Murphy, "Old Ron Paul Video Warns of One-World Religion, UN Dictatorship," December 27, 2011, motherjones.com.

69. From their *Agenda 21*. glennbeck.com/agenda21.

70. Beck and Parke 2012: 280, 284.

71. John Birch Society, "Agenda 21: How Will It Affect You?" jbs.org.

72. Morris and McGann 2012.

73. Brett D. Schaefer, "The U.S. Should Withdraw from UNESCO," Heritage Foundation Issue Brief, no. 3760, October 19, 2012.

74. Cited in Luck 1999: 59.

75. "Alabama Senate Bill 477," legiscan.com.

76. GOP 2012: 45.

77. Direct effect reduced from 6.8 percent (semipartial correlation = −.26) to 1.7 percent (semipartial correlation = −.13).

78. Cited in Ruotsila 2008: 166.

79. Luck 1999: 84.

80. Goldwater 1960: 111–12.

81. Cited in Luck 1999: 112.

82. McGirr 2001: 178.

83. Cited in Luck 1999: 30.

84. Goldwater 1960: 113.

85. Cited in Luck 1999: 117

86. Claudia Rosett, "U.N. Bows Again to Kim Jong Il," *The Rosett Report,* December 28, 2011, pjmedia.com.

87. Luck 1999: 44.

88. Cited in McGirr 2001: 178. Italics added.

89. Cited in Luck 1999: 45. Italics added.

90. Cited in Luck 1999: 41, 66.

91. Christopher Arias, "Head of NRA Discusses 'The Global War on Your Guns' with the *Liberty Sentinel*," *Liberty Sentinel of Florida*, vol. 1, no. 2, November 2007.

92. "Letter to President Obama and Secretary Clinton," July 26, 2012, moran.senate. gov.

93. Cited in Luck 1999: 71.

94. Cited in Pinker 2011: 288.

95. Cited in Luck 1999: 41, 61.

96. $F(1, 1046) = 65.91$, $p < .001$, $\eta_p^2 = .06$, controlling for six demographics (not gender).

97. Male = 51°; female = 39°. $F(1, 1046) = 53.43$, $p < .001$, $\eta_p^2 = .05$, controlling for six demographics (not gender).

98. Malka, Krosnick, and Langer 2009; McCright and Dunlap 2011.

99. Mooney 2012: 48.

100. Indirect effect PE = −.3965, 95% CI from −1.0917 to −.0428, controlling for six demographics (not education).

101. Indirect effect PE = −.1083, 95% CI from −.7079 to .5392, controlling for six demographics (not education).

102. Cited in Nash 2008 [1976]: 416.

103. McGirr 2001: 179.

104. Fiorina 2009; Fiorina and Levendusky 2006; Kull and Destler 1999; Page with Bouton 2006; Busby and Monten 2012.

105. Peake, Krutz, and Hughes 2012: 1299.

Conclusion

1. Cited in Smith 1999: 1–2.
2. Chicago Council 2012: 41, 4.
3. Kohut and Stokes 2006: 218–19, 94, 70.
4. Page with Bouton 2006: 95–96. See also Page and Xie 2010: 37, 57, 66, 103.
5. Busby, Monten, and Inboden 2012.
6. Kupchan and Trubowitz 2007: 9.
7. Page with Bouton 2006: 96.
8. Berinsky 2009: 2.
9. Campbell, Converse, Miller, and Stokes 1960; Leighley, ed. 2010.
10. Converse 1964; Federico 2012: 90.
11. Jost, Glaser, Kruglanski, and Sulloway 2003; Jost, Federico, and Napier 2009.
12. Kanai, Feilden, Firth, and Rees 2011; Oxley et al. 2008.
13. E.g., Feldman and Johnston 2013; Treier and Hillygus 2009.
14. E.g., Fiorina, Abrams, and Pope 2011; Abramowitz and Saunders 2008; Abramowitz 2010.
15. See Aldrich et al. 2006.
16. Jacobson 2012: 1625.
17. Skocpol and Williamson 2012: 76.
18. $F(2, 302) = 37.72$, $p < .001$, $\eta_p^2 = .20$; $F(2, 302) = 12.74$, $p < .001$, $\eta_p^2 = .08$, controlling for seven standard demographics.
19. $F(1, 205) = 38.50$, $p < .001$, $\eta_p^2 = .16$; $F(1, 205) = 37.05$, $p < .001$, $\eta_p^2 = .15$; and $F(1, 205) = 21.59$, $p < .001$, $\eta_p^2 = .10$, respectively, controlling for seven standard demographics.
20. Peake, Krutz, and Hughes 2012.

References

Abramowitz, Alan I. 2006. "Comment: Disconnected or Joined at the Hip?" In *Red and Blue Nation?* edited by Pietro S. Nivola and David W. Brady, Vol. 1. Washington, DC: Brookings Institution Press.

———. 2010. *The Disappearing Center: Engaged Citizens, Polarization, and American Democracy.* New Haven, CT: Yale University Press.

——— and Kyle L. Saunders. 2008. "Is Polarization a Myth?" *Journal of Politics* 70: 542–55.

Abramson, L. Y., M.E.P. Seligman, and J. D. Teasdale. 1978. "Learned Helplessness in Humans: Critique and Reformulation." *Journal of Abnormal Psychology* 87: 49–74.

Aldrich, John H., Peter Feaver, Christopher Gelpi, Jason Reier, and Kristin Sharp. 2006. "Foreign Policy and the Electoral Connection." *Annual Review of Political Science* 9: 477–502.

——— John L. Sullivan, and Eugene Borgida. 1989. "Foreign Affairs and Issue Voting: Do Presidential Candidates Waltz Before a Blind Audience?" *American Political Science Review* 83 (1): 123–41.

Alexander, Yonah, and Allan Nanes, eds. 1980. *The United States and Iran: A Documentary History.* Frederick, MD: University Publications of America.

Alford, John R., Carolyn L. Funk, and John R. Hibbing. 2005. "Are Political Orientations Genetically Transmitted?" *American Political Science Review* 99: 153–67.

Allport, Gordon. *The Nature of Prejudice.* 1954. Reading, MA: Addison-Wesley.

Almond, Gabriel. 1950. *The American People and Foreign Policy.* New York: Harcourt, Brace.

Altemeyer, Robert. 1996. *The Authoritarian Specter.* Cambridge, MA: Harvard Univesity Press.

Alterman, Eric. 2008. *Why We're Liberals: A Political Handbook for Post-Bush America.* New York: Viking.

Arendt, Hannah. 1951. *The Origins of Totalitarianism.* New York: Harcourt, Brace.

Bafumi, Joseph, and Robert Shapiro. 2009. "A New Partisan Voter." *Journal of Politics* 71: 1–24.

Baldwin, James. 1963. *Nobody Knows My Name*. New York: Dell.

Bandow, Doug. 1985. "Totalitarian Global Management: The U.N.'s War on the Liberal International Economic Order." *Cato Institute Policy Analysis* 61 (October 24).

Bartels, Larry M. 1994. "The American Public's Defense Spending Preferences in the Post-Cold War Era." *Public Opinion Quarterly* 58 (4): 479–508.

Baum, Matthew A., and Tim J. Groeling. 2010. *War Stories: The Causes and Consequences of Public Views of War*. Princeton, NJ: Princeton University Press.

Beck, Glenn, and Kevin Balfe. 2007. *An Inconvenient Book*. New York: Simon & Schuster.

———— and Harriet Parke. 2012. *Agenda 21*. New York: Threshold Editions.

Becker, Gary S. 1976. *The Economic Approach to Human Behavior*. Chicago: University of Chicago Press.

Bellah, Robert N. 1992 [1975]. *The Broken Covenant: American Civil Religion in Time of Trial*. 2nd ed. Chicago: University of Chicago Press.

———— Richard Madsen, William M. Sullivan, Ann Swidler, and Steven M. Tipton. 1985. *Habits of the Heart: Individualism and Commitment in American Life*. Berkeley: University of California Press.

Ben-Ami, Shlomo. 2006. "The Complex Truth: Hijacking America's Middle East Policy Is Not so Easy." *Foreign Policy* 155: 62–63.

Berinsky, Adam J. 2009. *In Time of War: Understanding American Public Opinion from World War II to Iraq*. Chicago: University of Chicago Press.

———— and James Druckman. 2007. "Public Opinion Research, Presidential Rhetoric, and Support for the Iraq War." *Public Opinion Quarterly* 71 (1): 126–41.

Bishop, Bill, with Robert G. Cushing. 2008. *The Big Sort: Why the Clustering of Like-Minded America Is Tearing Us Apart*. New York: Houghton Mifflin.

Bonanno, George A., and John T. Jost. 2006. "Conservative Shift Among High-Exposure Survivors of the September 11th Terrorist Attacks." *Basic and Applied Social Psychology* 28: 311–23.

Boyer, Paul. 1999 [1992]. *When Time Shall Be No More: Prophecy Belief in Modern American Culture*. Cambridge, MA: Harvard Belknap Press.

Brady, Henry, and Paul Sniderman. 1991. "The Likability Heuristic." In *Reasoning and Choice: Explorations in Political Psychology*, edited by Paul M. Sniderman, Richard A. Brody, and Philip E. Tetlock, ch 6. New York: Cambridge University Press.

Brewer, Marilynn B. 1999. "The Psychology of Prejudice: Ingroup Love or Outgroup Hate?" *Journal of Social Issues* 55 (3): 429–44.

Brody, David. 2012. *The Teavangelicals: The Inside Story of How the Evangelicals and the Tea Party Are Taking Back America*. Grand Rapids, MI: Zondervan.

Brown, Ryan, Karolyn Budzek, and Michael Tamborski. 2009. "On the Meaning and Measure of Narcissism." *Personality and Social Psychology Bulletin* 35 (7): 951–64.

Brzezinski, Zbigniew, with Carl Friedrich. 1956. *Totalitarian Dictatorship and Autocracy*. New York: Praeger.

Burns, Jennifer. 2009. *Goddess of the Market: Ayn Rand and the American Right.* New York: Oxford University Press.

Busby, Joshua W., and Jonathan Monten. 2012. "Republican Elites and Foreign Policy Attitudes." *Political Science Quarterly* 127 (1): 105–42.

———. Jonathan Monten, and William Inboden. 2012. "American Foreign Policy Is Already Post-Partisan: Why Politics Does Stop at the Water's Edge." ForeignAffairs.com snapshot, May 30.

Bush, George W. 2010. *Decision Points.* New York: Crown.

Byman, Daniel L., and Kenneth M. Pollack. 2001. "Let Us Now Praise Great Men: Bringing the Statesman Back In." *International Security* 25 (4): 107–46.

Cai, Huajian, and Peter Gries. 2013. "National Narcissism: Internal Dimensions and International Correlates." *PsyCh Journal* 2: 122–32.

Campbell, A., P. E. Converse, W. E. Miller, and D. E. Stokes. 1960. *The American Voter.* New York: Wiley.

Caprara, Gian Vittorio, Shalom Schwartz, Cristina Capanna, Michele Vecchione, and Claudio Barbaranelli. 2006. "Personality and Politics: Values, Traits, and Political Choice." *Political Psychology* 27 (1): 1–28.

Carenen, Caitlin. 2012. *The Fervent Embrace: Liberal Protestants, Evangelicals, and Israel.* New York: New York University Press.

Carney, Dana R., John T. Jost, Samuel D. Gosling, and Jeff Potter. 2008. "The Secret Lives of Liberals and Conservatives: Personality Profiles, Interaction Styles, and the Things They Leave Behind." *Political Psychology* 29: 807–40.

Carter, Jimmy. 2002. *The Blood of Abraham: Insights into the Middle East.* Fayetteville: University of Arkansas Press.

———. 2006. *Palestine: Peace Not Apartheid.* New York: Simon & Schuster.

———. 2009. *We Can Have Peace in the Holy Land.* New York: Simon & Schuster.

Caspary, William R. 1970. "The 'Mood Theory': A Study of Public Opinion and Foreign Policy." *American Political Science Review* 64 (2): 536–47.

Castano, Emanuele, Bernhard Leidner, Alain Bonacossa, John Nikka, Rachel Perrulli, Bettina Spencer, and Nicholas Humphrey. 2011. "Ideology, Fear of Death, and Death Anxiety." *Political Psychology* 32: 601–21.

CBS. 2011. "2012 Presidential Election/Economy/Foreign Affairs" [USCBS2011-11A].

Chicago Council. 2010. "Global Views 2010—Constrained Internationalism: Adapting to New Realities." Chicago.

———. 2012. "Foreign Policy in the New Millennium." Chicago.

Cialdini, Robert B., Richard J. Borden, Avril Thorne, Marcus Randall Walker, Stephen Freeman, and Lloyd Reynolds Sloan. 1976. "Basking in Reflected Glory: Three (Football) Field Studies." *Journal of Personality and Social Psychology* 34: 366–75.

Clark, Victoria. 2007. *Allies for Armageddon: The Rise of Christian Zionism.* New Haven, CT: Yale University Press.

Cohen, Jacob. 1988. *Statistical Power Analysis for the Behavioral Sciences.* Mahwah, NJ: Lawrence Erlbaum.

———. 1994. "The Earth Is Round (*p*< .05)." *American Psychologist* 45 (12): 997–1003.

Converse, Phillip E. 1964. "The Nature of Belief Systems in Mass Publics." In *Ideology and Discontent*, edited by David E. Apter. New York: Free Press.

Coulter, Ann. 2003. *Treason: Liberal Treachery from the Cold War to the War on Terrorism*. New York: Crown Forum.

———. 2011. *Demonic: How the Liberal Mob Is Endangering America*. New York: Crown Forum.

Crandall, Christian S., and S. Eideleman. 2009. "A Psychological Advantage of the Status Quo." In *Social and Psychological Bases of Ideology and System Justification*, edited by John T. Jost, A. C. Kay, and H. Thorisdottir, 85–106. New York: Oxford University Press.

Crawford, Beverly, and James Martel. 1997. "Representations of Germans and What Germans Represent: American Film Images and Public Perceptions in the Postwar Era." In *Transatlantic Images and Perceptions: Germany and American Since 1776*, edited by David Barclay and Elisabeth Glaser-Schmidt, 285–308. New York: Cambridge University Press.

Crowson, H. Michael. 2009. "Right-Wing Authoritarianism and Social Dominance Orientation as Mediators of Worldview Beliefs on Attitudes Related to the War on Terror." *Social Psychology* 40: 93–103.

Daniels, Roger. 2004. *Guarding the Golden Door: American Immigration Policy and Immigrants Since 1882*. New York: Hill and Wang.

Dawkins, Richard. 1976. *The Selfish Gene*. New York: Oxford University Press.

De Tocqueville, Alexis. 2000 [1835]. *Democracy in America*. Chicago: University of Chicago Press.

DeCarlo, L. T. 1997. "On the Meaning and Use of Kurtosis." *Psychological Methods* 2: 292–307.

Deibel, Terry L. 2005. "Intraparty Factionalism on Key Foreign Policy Issues: Congress Versus Clinton, 1995–2000." In *Divided Power: The Presidency, Congress, and the Formation of American Foreign Policy*, edited by Donald R. Kelley. Fayetteville: Arkansas University Press.

Desch, Michael. 2007/8. "America's Liberal Illiberalism: The Ideological Origins of Overreaction in U.S. Foreign Policy." *International Security* 22 (3): 7–43.

Dickson, Caitlin. 2012. "Michele Bachmann's Attacks on Women, from Huma Abedin to Nancy Pelosi." *The Daily Beast*, July 20.

Dionne, E. J. 2012. *Our Divided Political Heart: The Battle for the American Idea in an Age of Discontent*. New York: Bloomsbury.

Ditto, Peter H., and Spassena P. Koleva. 2011. "Moral Empathy Gaps and the American Culture War." *Emotion Review* 3 (3): 331–32.

Dower, John W. 1986. *War Without Mercy: Race and Power in the Pacific War*. New York: Pantheon.

Downs, Anthony. 1957. *An Economic Theory of Democracy*. New York: HarperCollins.

Drezner, Daniel W. 2008. "The Realist Tradition in American Public Opinion." *Perspectives on Politics* 6 (1): 51–70.

————. 2012. "The Power of Economics and Public Opinion." *Policy Review* 172: 7–26.

Duckitt, John, Boris Bizumic, Stephen W. Krauss, and Edna Heled. 2010. "A Tripartite Approach to Right-Wing Authoritarianism: The Authoritarianism-Conservatism-Traditionalism Model." *Political Psychology* 31 (5): 685–715.

———— and Chris G. Sibley. 2007. "Right Wing Authoritarianism, Social Dominance Orientation and the Dimensions of Generalized Prejudice." *European Journal of Personality* 21: 113–30.

———— and Chris G. Sibley. 2010. "Right-Wing Authoritarianism and Social Dominance Orientation Differentially Moderate Intergroup Effects on Prejudice." *European Journal of Personality* 24: 583–601.

Dueck, Colin. 2010. *Hard Line: The Republican Party and U.S. Foreign Policy Since World War II*. Princeton, NJ: Princeton University Press.

Dumbrell, John. 2006. *A Special Relationship: Anglo-America Relations from the Cold War to Iraq*, 2nd ed. New York: Palgrave Macmillan.

Duncan, Craig, and Tibor R. Machan. 2005. *Libertarianism: For and Against*. Lanham, MD: Rowman & Littlefield.

Eidelman, Scott, Christian S. Crandall, J. A. Goodman, and J. C. Blanchar. 2012. "Low-effort Thought Promotes Political Conservatism." *Personality and Social Psychology Bulletin* 38: 808–20.

Etzioni, Amitai. 2004. *The Common Good*. Cambridge, UK: Polity.

Federico, Christopher M. 2012. "Ideology and Public Opinion." In *New Directions in Public Opinion*, edited by Adam Berinsky, 79–100. New York: Routledge.

Feldman, Stanley. 2003. "Enforcing Social Conformity: A Theory of Authoritarianism." *Political Psychology* 24 (1): 41–74.

———— and Christopher Johnston. 2013. "Understanding the Determinants of Political Ideology: Implications of Structural Complexity." *Political Psychology*. DOI: 10.1111/pops.12055.

Fiorina, Morris. P. 2009. *Disconnect: The Breakdown of Representation in American Politics*. Norman: University of Oklahoma Press.

———— Samuel J. Abrams, and Jeremy C. Pope. 2011. *Culture War? The Myth of a Polarized America*. 3rd ed. New York: Longman.

———— and Matthew S. Levendusky. 2006. "Disconnected: The Political Class Versus the People." In *Red and Blue Nation?* edited by Pietro S. Nivola and David W. Brady, Vol. 1. Washington, DC: Brookings Institution Press.

Fiske, Susan T. 2012. *Envy Up, Scorn Down: How Status Divides Us*. New York: Russell Sage Foundation.

———— A. J. Cuddy, P. Glick, and J. Xu. 2002. "A Model of (Often Mixed) Stereotype Content: Competence and Warmth Respectively Follow from Perceived Status and Competition." *Journal of Personality and Social Psychology* 82 (6): 878–902.

Fordham, Barry O. 2007. "The Evolution of Republican and Democratic Positions on Cold War Military Spending." *Social Science History* 31 (4): 603–36.

Friedberg, Aaron L. 2006. "An Uncivilized Argument." *Foreign Policy* 155: 59–60.

Friedman, Milton. 2002 [1962]. *Capitalism and Freedom*. Chicago: University of Chicago Press.

———— and Rose Friedman. 1979. *Free to Choose: A Personal Statement.* New York: Mariner.

Friedman, Thomas L., and Michael Mandelbaum. 2011. *That Used to Be Us: How America Fell Behind in the World It Invented and How We Can Come Back.* New York: Farrar, Straus and Giroux.

Fuchs, Lawrence H. 1990. *The American Kaleidoscope: Race, Ethnicity and Civic Culture.* Hanover, NH: University Press of New England.

Gartner, Scott S., and Gary M. Segura. 1998. "War, Casualties and Public Opinion." *Journal of Conflict Resolution* 42 (3): 278–300.

Gelpi, Christopher. 2010. "Performing on Cue? The Formation of Public Opinion Towards War." *Journal of Conflict Resolution* 54 (1): 88–116.

———— Peter Feaver, and Jason Reifler. 2005/6. "Success Matters: Casualty Sensitivity and the War in Iraq." *International Security* 30 (3): 7–46.

———— Peter Feaver, and Jason Reifler. 2009. *Paying the Human Costs of War: American Public Opinion and Casualties in Military Conflicts.* Princeton, NJ: Princeton University Press.

———— Jason Reifler, and Peter Feaver. 2007. "Iraq the Vote: Retrospective and Prospective Foreign Policy Judgments on Candidate Choice and Casualty Tolerance." *Political Behavior* 29 (2): 151–74.

Gerber, Alan S., Gregory A. Huber, David Doherty, Conor M. Dowling, and Shang E. Ha. 2010. "Personality and Political Attitudes: Relationships Across Issue Domains and Political Contexts." *American Political Science Review* 104 (1): 111–33.

Giddens, Anthony. 1987. *The Nation State and Violence.* Berkeley: University of California Press.

Gilligan, Carol. 1982. *In a Different Voice: Psychological Theory and Women's Development.* Cambridge, MA: Harvard University Press.

Gingrich, Newt, and Joe DeSantis. 2010. *To Save America: Stopping Obama's Secular-Socialist Machine.* Washington, DC: Regnery.

Goldberg, Michelle. 2006. *Kingdom Coming: The Rise of Christian Nationalism.* New York: Norton.

Goldin, Claudia, and Robert A. Margo. 1992. "The Great Compression: The U.S. Wage Structure at Mid-Century." *Quarterly Journal of Economics* 107: 1–34.

Goldwater, Barry. 1960. *The Conscience of a Conservative.* Sheperdsville, KY: Victor.

Golec de Zavala, Agnieszka, Aleksandra Cichocka, Roy Eidelson, and Nuwan Jayawickreme. 2009. "Collective Narcissism and Its Social Consequences." *Journal of Personality and Social Psychology* 97 (6): 1074–96.

GOP. 2012. "2012 Republican Platform: We Believe in America."

Gosling, Samuel D., Peter J. Rentfrow, and William B. Swann Jr. 2003. "A Very Brief Measure of the Big Five Personality Domains." *Journal of Research in Personality* 37: 504–28.

Graebner, Norman, and Edward Bennett. 2011. *The Versailles Treaty and Its Legacy.* Cambridge, UK: Cambridge University Press.

Graham, Jesse, Jonathan Haidt, and Brian Nosek. 2009. "Liberals and Conservatives Use

Different Sets of Moral Foundations." *Journal of Personality and Social Psychology* 96: 1029–46.

Green, Donald P., Shang E. Ha, and John G. Bullock. 2010. "Enough Already About 'Black Box' Experiments: Studying Mediation Is More Difficult than Most Scholars Suppose." *Annals of the American Academy of Political and Social Science* 628: 200–208.

Grice, H. Paul. 1989. *Studies in the Way of Words*. Boston: Harvard University Press.

Gries, Peter H. 2011. "Review of *Living with the Dragon: How the American Public Views the Rise of China*, by Benjamin I. Page and Tao Xie." *Public Opinion Quarterly* 75 (2): 399–404.

———— and H. Michael Crowson. 2010. "Political Orientation, Party Affiliation, and American Attitudes Towards China." *Journal of Chinese Political Science* 15 (3): 219–44.

———— H. Michael Crowson, and Huajian Cai. 2011. "When Knowledge Is a Double Edged Sword: Contact, Media Exposure, and American Attitudes Towards China." *Journal of Social Issues* 67 (4): 787–805.

———— H. Michael Crowson, and Huajian Cai. 2012. "God, Guns, and . . . China? How Ideology Impacts American Attitudes and Policy Preferences Toward China." *International Relations of the Asia-Pacific* 12 (1): 1–40.

Grose, Peter. 1983. *Israel in the Mind of America*. New York: Alfred Knopf.

Hagee, John. 2006. *Jerusalem Countdown: A Warning to the World*. Lake Mary, FL: Front-Line.

Haidt, Jonathan. 2001. "The Emotional Dog and Its Rational Tail: A Social Intuitionist Approach to Moral Judgment." *Psychological Review* 108: 814–34.

————. 2012. *The Righteous Mind: Why Good People Are Divided by Politics and Religion*. New York: Pantheon.

———— and Jesse Graham. 2009. "Planet of the Durkheimians: Where Community, Authority, and Sacredness Are Foundations of Morality." In *Social and Psychological Bases of Ideology and System Justification*, edited by John Jost, Aaron C. Kay, and Hulda Thorisdottir, 371–401. New York: Oxford University Press.

———— Silvia Koller, and Maria Dias. 1993. "Affect, Culture, and Morality, Or Is It Wrong to Eat Your Dog?" *Journal of Personality and Social Psychology* 65: 613–28.

Hair, J. F., Jr., and W. C. Black. 2000. "Cluster Analysis." In *Reading and Understanding More Multivariate Statistics*, edited by L. G. Grimm and P. R. Yarnold, 147–205. Washington, DC: American Psychological Association.

Hardin, C. D., and E. T. Higgins. 1996. "Shared Reality: How Social Verification Makes the Subjective Objective." In *Handbook of Motivation and Cognition: The Interpersonal Context*, edited by E. T. Higgins and R. M. Sorrentino, Vol. 3. New York: Guilford Press.

Hartz, Louis. 1955. *The Liberal Tradition in America: An Interpretation of American Political Thought Since the Revolution*. New York: Harcourt, Brace.

Hatemi, P., N. A. Gillespie, L. J. Eaves, B. S. Maher, B. T. Webb, A. C. Heath, S. E. Medland, D. C. Smyth, H. N. Beeby, S. D. Gordon, G. W. Montgomery, G. Zhu, E. M. Byrne, and N. G. Martin. 2011. "A Genome-Wide Analysis of Liberal and Conservative Political Attitudes." *Journal of Politics* 73: 271–85.

Haugen, David, Susan Musser, and Kacy Lovelace. 2009. *The Middle East*. Farmington Hills, MI: Greenhaven Press.

Hayek, Friedrich. 1976. *Law, Legislation and Liberty, Vol. 2: The Mirage of Social Justice*. Chicago: University of Chicago Press.

Hayes, Andrew F. 2013. *Introduction to Mediation, Moderation, and Conditional Process Analysis: A Regression-Based Approach*. New York: Guilford Press.

Helms, Jesse. 1996. "Saving the U.N.: A Challenge to the Next Secretary-General." *Foreign Affairs* 75 (5): 2–7.

Helzer, Erik G., and David A. Pizarro. 2011. "Dirty Liberals! Reminders of Physical Cleanliness Influence Moral and Political Attitudes." *Psychological Science* 22: 517–22.

Hetherington, Marc. 2012. "Partisanship and Polarization." In *New Direction in Public Opinion*, edited by Adam J. Berinsky. New York: Routledge.

Hewstone, Miles. 1990. "The 'Ultimate Attribution Error'? A Review of the Literature on Intergroup Causal Attribution." *European Journal of Social Psychology* 20 (4): 311–35.

Hitchcock, Mark. 2012. *Middle East Burning*. Eugene, OR: Harvest House.

Hixson, Walter L. 2008. *The Myth of American Diplomacy: National Identity and U.S. Foreign Policy*. New Haven, CT: Yale University Press.

Ho, Arnold K., Jim Sidanius, Felicia Pratto, Shana Levin, Lotte Thomsen, Nour Kteily, and Jennifer Sheehy-Skeffington. 2012. "Social Dominance Orientation: Revisiting the Structure and Function of a Variable Predicting Social and Political Attitudes." *Personality and Social Psychology Bulletin* 38 (5): 583–606.

Hoffmann, Stanley. 2004. "Review of *Our Oldest Enemy*." *Foreign Affairs* 83 (6) (November/ December): 153.

Hofstadter, Richard. 1944. *Social Darwinism in American Thought*. Boston: Beacon.

———. 1948. *The American Political Tradition, and the Men Who Made It*. New York: Vintage.

Holden, Robert H., and Eric Zolov, eds. 2011. *Latin America and the United States: A Documentary History*. New York: Oxford University Press.

Holsti, Ole R. 1992. "Public Opinion and Foreign Policy: Challenges to the Almond-Lippmann Consensus." *International Studies Quarterly* 36 (4): 439–66.

———. 2004. *Public Opinion and American Foreign Policy*. Ann Arbor: University of Michigan Press.

——— and James N. Rosenau. 1988. "The Domestic and Foreign Policy Beliefs of American Leaders." *Journal of Conflict Resolution* 32 (4): 248–94.

Huddy, Leonie, and Nadia Khatib. 2007. "American Patriotism, National Identity, and Political Involvement." *American Journal of Political Science* 51 (1): 63–77.

Huebert, Jacob. H. 2012. *Libertarianism Today*. Westport, CT: Praeger.

Hunt, Michael H. 2009 [1987]. *Ideology and U.S. Foreign Policy*. New Haven, CT: Yale University Press.

Huntington, Samuel P. 2004. *Who Are We? The Challenges to America's National Identity*. New York: Simon & Schuster.

Hurwitz, Jon, and Mark Peffley. 1987. "How Are Foreign Policy Attitudes Structured? A Hierarchical Model." *American Political Science Review* 81 (4): 1099–120.

Inbar, Yoel, David A. Pizarro, and Paul Bloom. 2009. "Conservatives Are More Easily Disgusted than Liberals." *Cognition and Emotion* 23: 714–25.

—— David A. Pizarro, Ravi Iyer, and Jonathan Haidt. 2012. "Disgust Sensitivity, Political Conservatism, and Voting." *Social Psychological and Personality Science* 5: 537–44.

Isaacs, Harold R. 1957. "How We 'See' the Chinese Communists." *New Republic* 136 (8) (February 25): 7–13.

Iyer, Ravi, Sena Koleva, Jesse Graham, Peter H. Ditto, and Jonathan Haidt. 2010. "Understanding Libertarian Morality: The Psychological Roots of an Individualist Ideology." *PLoS ONE* 7 (8): e42366. DOI:10.1371/journal.pone.0042366.

Jackman, Mary. 1994. *The Velvet Glove: Paternalism and Conflict in Gender, Class, and Race Relations.* Berkeley: University of California Press.

Jacobs, Matthew F. 2011. *Imagining the Middle East: The Building of an American Foreign Policy, 1918–1967.* Chapel Hill: University of North Carolina Press.

Jacobson, Gary C. 2012. "The Electoral Origins of Polarized Politics: Evidence from the 2010 Cooperative Congressional Election Study." *American Behavioral Scientist* 56 (12): 1612–30.

Jacoby, William G. 2011. "Attitude Organization in the Mass Public." In *The Oxford Handbook of American Public Opinion and the Media*, edited by Lawrence R. Jacobs and Robert Y. Shapiro. New York: Oxford University Press.

Janoff-Bulman, Ronnie. 2009. "To Provide or Protect: Motivational Bases of Political Liberalism and Conservatism." *Psychological Inquiry* 20: 120–28.

Jennings, M. Kent, and Richard G. Niemi. 1981. *Generations and Politics.* Princeton, NJ: Princeton University Press.

—— Laura Stoker, and Jake Bowers. 2009. "Politics Across Generations: Family Transmission Reexamined." *Journal of Politics* 71 (3): 782–99.

Jentleson, Bruce W. 1992. "The Pretty Prudent Public: Post Post-Vietnam American Opinion on the Use of Military Force." *International Studies Quarterly* 36 (1): 49–73.

—— and Rebecca Britton. 1998. "Still Pretty Prudent: Post-Cold War American Public Opinion on the Use of Military Force." *Journal of Conflict Resolution* 42 (4): 395–417.

Jervis, Robert. 2003. "The Compulsive Empire." *Foreign Policy* 137: 82–87.

Jespersen, T. Christopher. 1996. *American Images of China, 1931–1949.* Stanford, CA: Stanford University Press.

Jost, John T. 2006. "The End of the End of Ideology." *American Psychologist* 61: 651–70.

——. 2009. "'Elective Affinities': On the Psychological Bases of Left-Right Ideological Differences." *Psychological Inquiry* 20: 129–41.

—— and D. M. Amodio. 2012. "Political Ideology as Motivated Social Cognition: Behavioral and Neuroscientific Evidence." *Motivation and Emotion* 36: 55–64.

—— M. R. Banaji, and B. A. Nosek. 2004. "A Decade of System Justification Theory: Accumulated Evidence of Conscious and Unconscious Bolstering of the Status Quo." *Political Psychology* 25: 881–919.

—— C. M. Federico, and J. L. Napier. 2009. "Political Ideology: Its Structure, Functions, and Elective Affinities." *Annual Review of Psychology* 60: 307–33.

———— J. Glaser, A. W. Kruglanski, and F. Sulloway. 2003. "Political Conservatism as Motivated Social Cognition." *Psychological Bulletin* 129: 339–75.

———— A. Ledgerwood, and C. D. Hardin. 2007. "Shared Reality, System Justification, and the Relational Basis of Ideological Beliefs." *Social and Personality Psychology Compass* 2: 171–86.

———— J. L. Napier, H. Thorisdottir, S. D. Gosling, T. P. Palfai, and B. Ostafin. 2007. "Are Needs to Manage Uncertainty and Threat Associated with Political Conservatism or Ideological Extremity?" *Personality and Social Psychology Bulletin* 33: 989–1007.

———— and E. P. Thompson. 2000. "Group-Based Dominance and Opposition to Equality as Independent Predictors of Self-Esteem, Ethnocentrism, and Social Policy Attitudes Among African Americans and European Americans." *Journal of Experimental Social Psychology,* 36, 209–32.

Kagan, Robert. 2002. "Power and Weakness." *Policy Review* 113: 3–28.

Kahneman, Daniel. 2011. *Thinking Fast and Slow.* New York: Allen Lane.

Kanai, Ryota, Tom Feilden, Colin Firth, and Geraint Rees. 2011. "Political Orientations Are Correlated with Brain Structure in Young Adults." *Current Biology* 21: 677–80.

Katz, Philip M. 1994. "Lessons from Paris: The American Clergy Responds to the Paris Commune." *Church History* 63 (3) (September): 393–406.

Kay, Aaron C., D. Gaucher, J. L. Napier, M. J. Callan, and K. Laurin. 2008. "God and the Government: Testing a Compensatory Control Mechanism for the Support of External Systems." *Journal of Personality and Social Psychology* 95: 18–35.

———— Steven Shepherd, Craig W. Blatz, Sook Ning Chua, and Adam D. Galinsky. 2010. "For God (or) Country: The Hydraulic Relation Between Government Instability and Belief in Religious Sources of Control." *Journal of Personality and Social Psychology* 99 (5): 725–39.

Kennedy, Scott. 2003. *China Cross Talk: The American Debate over China Policy Since Normalization, A Reader.* Lanham, MD: Rowman & Littlefield.

Kidd, Thomas S. 2009. *American Christians and Islam: Evangelical Culture and Muslims from the Colonial Period to the Age of Terrorism.* Princeton, NJ: Princeton University Press.

Kinder, Donald R., and Cindy D. Kam. 2009. *Us Against Them: Ethnocentric Foundations of American Opinion.* Chicago: University of Chicago Press.

———— and Lynn M. Sanders. 1996. *Divided by Color: Racial Politics and Democratic Ideals.* Chicago: University of Chicago Press.

Kirakofe, Clifford A. 2009. *Dark Crusade: Christian Zionism and U.S. Foreign Policy.* New York: Tauris.

Kirby, David, and David Boaz. 2010. "The Libertarian Vote in the Age of Obama." *Policy Analysis* 658 (January 21).

Kline, Rex B. 2005. *Principles and Practice of Structural Equation Modeling.* 2nd ed. New York: Guilford Press.

Kloppenberg, James T. 2011. *Reading Obama: Dreams, Hope, and the American Political Tradition.* Princeton, NJ: Princeton University Press.

Knecht, Thomas. 2010. *Paying Attention to Foreign Affairs. How Public Opinion Affects Presidential Decision Making*. College Park: Pennsylvania State University Press.

Kohlberg, Lawrence. 1969. "Stage and Sequence." In *Handbook of Socialization Theory and Research*. New York: McGraw-Hill.

Kohut, Andrew, and Bruce Stokes. 2006. *America Against the World: How We Are Different and Why We Are Disliked*. New York: Times Books.

Koplow, Michael J. 2011. "Value Judgment: Why Do Americans Support Israel?" *Security Studies* 20 (2): 266–302.

Kosterman, Rick, and Seymour Feshbach. 1989. "Towards a Measure of Patriotic and Nationalistic Attitudes." *Political Psychology* 10 (2): 257–74.

Krugman, Paul. 2007. *The Conscience of a Liberal*. New York: Norton.

Kugler, Mathew B., Joel Cooper, and Brian A. Nosek. 2010. "Group-Based Dominance and Opposition to Equality Correspond to Different Psychological Motives." *Social Justice Research* 23: 117–55.

Kull, Steven, and I. M. Destler. 1999. *Misreading the Public: The Myth of a New Isolationism*. Washington, DC: Brookings Institution Press.

Kupchan, Charles A. 2012. *No One's World: The West, the Rising Rest, and the Coming Global Turn*. New York: Oxford University Press.

——— and Peter L. Trubowitz. 2007. "Dead Center: The Demise of Liberal Internationalism in the United States," *International Security* 32 (2): 7–44.

Lakoff, George. 1996. *Moral Politics: What Conservatives Know That Liberals Don't*. Chicago: University of Chicago Press.

———. 2010. *The Political Mind: Why You Can't Understand 21st-Century American Politics with an 18th-Century Brain*. New York: Viking.

Laponce, Jean. 1981. *Left and Right: The Topography of Political Perceptions*. Toronto: University of Toronto Press.

Larson, Arthur. 1956. *A Republican Looks at His Party*. New York: Harper & Brothers.

Leidner, Bernhard, and Emanuele Castano. 2012. "Morality Shifting in the Context of Intergroup Violence." *European Journal of Social Psychology* 42 (1): 82–91.

Leighley, Jan, ed. 2010. *The Oxford Handbook of American Elections and Political Behavior*. Oxford, UK: Oxford University Press.

Leuchtenburg, William E. 1991. "The Conversion of Harry Truman." *American Heritage* 42 (7) (November): 55–68.

Lewin, Kurt. 1935. *A Dynamic Theory of Personality*. New York: McGraw-Hill.

Lindsey, Hal. 1970. *The Late, Great Planet Earth*. Grand Rapids, MI: Zondervan.

———. 1994. *Planet Earth—2000 A.D.: Will Mankind Survive?* Palos Verdes, CA: Western Front Ltd.

Lippmann, Walter. 1922. *Public Opinion*. New York: Harcourt, Brace.

Luck, Edward C. 1999. *Mixed Messages: American Politics and International Organization, 1919–1999*. Washington, DC: Brookings Institution Press.

Madsen, Richard. 1995. *China and the American Dream*. Berkeley: University of California Press.

Malka, Ariel, Jon A. Krosnick, and Gary Langer. 2009. "The Association of Knowledge with Concern About Global Warming: Trusted Information Sources Shape Public Thinking." *Risk Analysis* 29: 633–47.

Mann, James. 2004. *The Rise of the Vulcans: Bush's War Cabinet*. New York: Viking.

——. 2012. *The Obamians: The Struggle Inside the White House to Redefine American Power*. New York: Viking.

Mauldin, Bill. 1945. *Up Front*. New York: Henry Holt.

——. 1961. *What's Got Your Back Up?* New York: Harper & Brothers.

——. 1965. *I've Decided I Want My Seat Back*. New York: Harper & Brothers.

——. 1985. *Let's Declare Ourselves Winners . . . and Get the Hell Out*. Novato, CA: Presidio.

May, Ernest R. 1991 [1961]. *Imperial Democracy: The Emergence of America as a Great Power*. New York: Harcourt, Brace, and World.

McAlister, Melani. 2001. *Epic Encounters: Culture, Media, and U.S. Interests in the Middle East, 1945–2000*. Berkeley: University of California Press.

McCarty, Nolan, Keith T. Poole, and Howard Rosenthal. 2006. *Polarized America: The Dance of Ideology and Unequal Riches*. Cambridge, MA: MIT University Press.

McClellan, Robert. 1971. *The Heathen Chinee: A Study of American Attitudes Toward China, 1890–1905*. Columbus: Ohio State University Press.

McCormick, James M., and Eugene R. Wittkopf. 1990. *Bipartisanship, Partisanship, and Ideology*. New York: Routledge.

—— Eugene R. Wittkopf, and D. M. Danna. 1997. "Politics and Bipartisanship at the Water's Edge: A Note on Bush and Clinton." *Polity* 30 (1): 133–49.

McCright, Aaron M., and Riley E. Dunlap. 2011. "The Politicization of Climate Change and Polarization in the American Public's Views of Global Warming, 2001–2010." *Sociological Quarterly* 52 (2): 155–94.

McFarland, Sam, Matthew Webb, and Derek Brown. 2012. "All Humanity Is My Ingroup: A Measure and Studies of Identification with All Humanity." *Journal of Personality and Social Psychology* 103 (5): 830–53.

McGirr, Lisa. 2001. *Suburban Warriors: The Origins of the New American Right*. Princeton, NJ: Princeton University Press.

McGovern, George. 2011. *What It Means to Be a Democrat*. New York: Blue Rider Press.

Mead, Walter Russell. 2001. *Special Providence: American Foreign Policy and How It Changed the World*. New York: Knopf.

——. 2007. "Jerusalem Syndrome: Decoding the Israel Lobby" *Foreign Affairs* 86 (6): 160–68.

——. 2008. "The New Israel and the Old." *Foreign Affairs* 87 (4) (July/August): 28–46.

Mearsheimer, John J., and Stephen M. Walt. 2007. *The Israel Lobby and US Foreign Policy*. New York: Farrar, Straus and Giroux.

Mehrabian, Albert. 1996. "Relations Among Political Attitudes, Personality, and Psychopathology Assessed with New Measures of Libertarianism and Conservatism." *Basic and Applied Social Psychology* 18: 469–91.

Mesquita, Batja, Lisa Feldman Barrett, and Eliot R. Smith, eds. 2010. *The Mind in Context*. New York: Guilford Press.

Metzler, John J. 2010. *Trans-Atlantic Divide: The USA—Euroland Rift?* New York: University Press of America.

Miller, John J., and Mark Molesky. 2004. *Our Oldest Enemy: A History of America's Disastrous Relationship with France.* New York: Doubleday.

Mistler, Steve. 2012. "LePage Calls IRS the 'New Gestapo.'" *Portland Press Herald,* July 8.

Mooney, Chris. 2012. *The Republican Brain: The Science of Why They Deny Science.* New York: Wiley.

Moore, Barrington, Jr. 1978. *Injustice: The Social Bases of Obedience and Revolt.* White Plains, NY: Sharpe.

Moore, Michaela Hoenicke. 2010. *Know Your Enemy: The American Debate on Nazism, 1933–1945.* New York: Cambridge University Press.

Morris, Dick, and Eileen McGann. 2012. *Here Come the Black Helicopters! U.N. Global Governance and the Loss of Freedom.* New York: HarperCollins (Broadside Books).

Moynihan, Daniel P. 1975. "The United States in Opposition." *Commentary* 59 (March).

Mueller, John E. 1971. "Trends in Popular Support for the Wars in Korea and Vietnam." *American Political Science Review* 65: 358–76.

———. 1973. *War, Presidents, and Public Opinion.* New York: Wiley.

Napier, Jaime L., and John T. Jost. 2008. "Why Are Conservatives Happier than Liberals?" *Psychological Science* 19 (6): 565–72.

Nash, George H. 2008 [1976]. *The Conservative Intellectual Movement in America Since 1945.* Wilmington, DE: ISI Books.

Nisbet, Robert. 1986. *Conservatism: Dream and Reality.* Buckingham, UK: Open University Press.

Noer, Thomas. 2003. "Segregationists and the World: The Foreign Policy of the White Resistance." In *Windows on Freedom: Race, Civil Rights, and Foreign Affairs, 1945–1988,* edited by Brenda Gayle Plummer, 141–62. Chapel Hill: University of North Carolina Press.

Norrander, Barbara, and Clyde Wilcox. 2008. "The Gender Gap in Ideology." *Political Behavior* 30: 503–23.

Nozick, Robert. 1974. *Anarchy, State, and Utopia.* New York: Basic Books.

O'Reilly, Bill. 2006. *Culture Warrior.* New York: Broadway Books.

Obama, Barack. 2006. *The Audacity of Hope: Thoughts on Reclaiming the American Dream.* New York: Crown.

———. 2009. "Nobel Lecture: A Just and Lasting Peace." Oslo, December 10. nobelprize. org.

Olson, J. M., P. A. Vernon, J. A. Harris, and K. L. Jang. 2001. "The Heritability of Attitudes: A Study of Twins." *Journal of Personality and Social Psychology* 80: 845–60.

Oren, Michael B. 2006. "Quiet Riot: Tinfoil Hats in Harvard Yard." *The New Republic.* April 10.

———. 2007. *Power, Faith, and Fantasy: America in the Middle East, 1776 to the Present.* New York: Norton.

Osterlind, Steven J. 2006. *Modern Measurement: Theory, Principles and Applications of Mental Appraisal.* New York: Pearson.

Oxley, Douglas R., Kevin B. Smith, John R. Alford, Matthew V. Hibbing, Jennifer L. Miller, Mario Scalora, Peter K. Hatemi, and John R. Hibbing. 2008. "Political Attitudes Vary with Physiological Traits." *Science* 321 (5896): 1667–70.

Page, Benjamin I., with Marshall Bouton. 2006. *The Foreign Policy Disconnect: What Americans Want from Our Leaders But Don't Get.* Chicago: University of Chicago Press.

——— and Robert Y. Shapiro. 1983. "Effects of Public Opinion on Policy." *American Political Science Review* 77: 175–90.

——— and Tao Xie. 2010. *Living with the Dragon: How the American Public Views the Rise of China.* New York: Columbia University Press.

Patrick, Stewart M. 2009. *The Best Laid Plans: The Origins of American Multilateralism and the Dawn of the Cold War.* Lanham, MD: Rowman & Littlefield.

Paul, Ron. 2008. *The Revolution: A Manifesto.* New York: Grand Central.

Peake, Jeffrey S., Glen S. Krutz, and Tyler Hughes. 2012. "President Obama, the Senate, and the Polarized Politics of Treaty Making." *Social Science Quarterly* 93 (5): 1295–315.

Perdue, Charles, J. F. Dovidio, M. B. Gurtman, and R. B. Tyler. 1990. "Us and Them: Social Categorization and the Process of Intergroup Bias." *Journal of Personality and Social Psychology* 59 (3): 475–86.

Pettigrew, Thomas F. 1979. "The Ultimate Attribution Error: Extending Allport's Cognitive Analysis of Prejudice." *Personality and Social Psychology Bulletin* 5 (4): 461–76.

——— and Linda R. Tropp. 2006. "A Meta-Analytic Test of Intergroup Contact Theory." *Journal of Personality and Social Psychology* 90 (5): 751–83.

Phillips-Fein, Kim. 2009. *Invisible Hands: The Making of the Conservative Movement from the New Deal to Reagan.* New York: Norton.

———. 2011. "Conservatism: A State of the Field." *Journal of American History* 98 (3): 723–43.

Piaget, Jean. 1965 [1932]. *The Moral Judgment of the Child.* New York: Free Press.

Pierce, John C., and Douglas D. Rose. 1974. "Nonattitudes and American Public Opinion: The Examination of a Thesis." *American Political Science Review* 68 (2): 626–49.

Pinker, Steven. 2002. *The Blank Slate: The Modern Denial of Human Nature.* New York: Penguin.

———. 2011. *The Better Angels of Our Nature: Why Violence Has Declined.* New York: Viking.

Pratto, Felicia, Jim Sidanius, and Shana Levin. 2006. "Social Dominance Theory and the Dynamics of Intergroup Relations: Taking Stock and Looking Forward." *European Review of Social Psychology* 17: 271–320.

Preston, Andrew. 2012. *Sword of the Spirit, Shield of Faith: Religion in American War and Diplomacy.* New York: Knopf.

Prochaska, Frank. 2008. *The Eagle and the Crown: Americans and the British Monarchy.* New Haven, CT: Yale University Press.

Putnam, Robert D., and David E. Campbell. 2010. *American Grace: How Religion Divides and Unites Us.* New York: Simon & Schuster.

Rathbun, Brian C. 2012. *Trust in International Cooperation: The Creation of International*

Security Institutions and the Domestic Politics of American Multilateralism. Cambridge, UK: Cambridge University Press.

Reiter, Dan, and Allan C. Stam. 2002. *Democracies at War.* Princeton, NJ: Princeton University Press.

Rivers, Douglas. 2005. "Matched Sampling." Unpublished paper presented at the annual meeting of the American Association for Public Opinion Research.

Robertson, Pat. 1991. *The New World Order.* Nashville, TN: Thomas Nelson.

Rogak, Lisa, ed. 2008. *Barack Obama in His Own Words.* New York: PublicAffairs.

Rohrs, Richard C. 1994. "American Critics of the French Revolution of 1848." *Journal of the Early Republic* 14 (3): 359–77.

Romney, Mitt. 2010. *No Apology: The Case for American Greatness.* New York: St. Martin's Press.

Ross, Dennis. 2006. "The Mindset Matters: Foreign Policy Is Shaped by Leaders and Events, Not Lobbies." *Foreign Policy* 155: 60–61.

Rothbard, Murray. 1972. "Interview." *The New Banner: A Fortnightly Libertarian Journal* 25 (February).

Rucker, Derek D., Kristopher J. Preacher, Zakary L. Tormala, and Richard E. Petty. 2011. "Mediation Analysis in Social Psychology: Current Practices and New Recommendations." *Social and Personality Psychology Compass* 5/6: 359–71.

Ruotsila, Markku. 2008. *The Origins of Christian Anti-Internationalism: Conservative Evangelicals and the League of Nations.* Washington, DC: Georgetown University Press.

Russett, Bruce M. 1990–91. "Doves, Hawks, and U.S. Public Opinion." *Political Science Quarterly* 105: 515–38.

Sandel, Michael J. 1982. *Liberalism and the Limits of Justice.* Cambridge, UK: Cambridge University Press.

———. 2012. *What Money Can't Buy: The Moral Limits of Markets.* New York: Farrar, Straus and Giroux.

Sargent, Michael. 2004. "Less Thought, More Punishment: Need for Cognition Predicts Support for Punitive Responses to Crime." *Personality and Social Psychology Bulletin* 30: 1485–93.

Schlesinger, Arthur M., ed. 1973. *The Dynamics of World Power.* New York: McGraw-Hill.

Schurz, Carl. 1913. *Speeches, Correspondence and Political Papers of Carl Schurz, Volume 5: 1889–1898.* New York: G. P. Putnam's Sons, Knickerbocker Press.

Shanks, Cheryl. 2001. *Immigration and the Politics of American Sovereignty 1890–1990.* Ann Arbor: University of Michigan Press.

Shweder, Richard A. 1991. *Thinking Through Cultures: Expeditions in Cultural Psychology.* Cambridge, MA: Harvard University Press.

Sibley, Chris G., Marc S. Wilson, and John Duckitt. 2007. "Antecedents of Men's Hostile and Benevolent Sexism: The Dual Roles of Social Dominance Orientation and Right-Wing Authoritarianism." *Personality and Social Psychology Bulletin* 33 (2): 160–72.

Sidanius, Jim. 1985. "Cognitive Functioning and Socio-Political Ideology Revisited." *Political Psychology* 6: 637–61.

———— and Robert Kurzban. 2003. "Evolutionary Approaches to Political Psychology." In *Handbook of Political Psychology*, edited by D. O. Sears, L. Huddy, and R. Jervis, 146–81. Oxford, UK: Oxford University Press.

———— and Felicia Pratto. 1999. *Social Dominance: An Intergroup Theory of Social Hierarchy and Oppression*. New York: Cambridge University Press.

Singer, Peter. 1981. *The Expanding Circle: Ethics and Sociobiology*. New York: Oxford University Press.

Skocpol, Theda, and Vanessa Williamson. 2012. *The Tea Party and the Remaking of Republican Conservatism*. New York: Oxford University Press.

Slovic, Paul, Melissa Finucane, Ellen Peters, and Donald G. MacGregor. 2002. "The Affect Heuristic." In *Heuristics and Biases: The Psychology of Intuitive Judgment*, edited by Thomas Gilovich, Dale Griffin, and Daniel Kahneman, 397–420. Cambridge, UK: Cambridge University Press.

Smith, E. Timothy. 1999. *Opposition Beyond Water's Edge: Liberal Internationalists, Pacifists and Containment, 1945–1953*. Westport, CT: Greenwood Press.

Smith, Rogers. 1993. "Beyond Tocqueville, Myrdal, and Hartz: The Multiple Traditions in America." *American Political Science Review* 87: 549–66.

Snyder, C. R., MaryAnne Lassegard, and Carol E. Ford. 1986. "Distancing After Group Success and Failure: Basking in Reflected Glory and Cutting Off Reflected Failure." *Journal of Personality and Social Psychology* 51: 382–88.

Sowell, Thomas. 2007 [1987]. *A Contest of Visions: Ideological Origins of Political Struggles*. Rev. ed. New York: Basic Books.

Spector, Stephen. 2009. *Evangelicals and Israel: The Story of American Christian Zionism*. New York: Oxford University Press.

Stephanson, Anders. 1995. *Manifest Destiny: American Expansion and the Empire of Right*. New York: Hill & Wang.

Tajfel, Henri. 1981. *Human Groups and Social Categories*. Cambridge, UK: Cambridge University Press.

Thomsen, Lotte, Eva G.T. Green, and Jim Sidanius. 2008. "We Will Hunt Them Down: How Social Dominance Orientation and Right-Wing Authoritarianism Fuel Ethnic Persecution of Immigrants in Fundamentally Different Ways." *Journal of Experimental Social Psychology* 44 (6): 1455–64.

Thorndike, Edward L. 1920. "A Constant Error in Psychological Ratings." *Journal of Applied Psychology* 4 (1): 25–29.

Thorndike, Robert M., and Tracy M. Thorndike-Christ. 2009. *Measurement and Evaluation in Psychology and Education*. 8th ed. Upper Saddle River, NJ: Prentice Hall.

Todorov, Alexander, and Anesu N. Mandisodza. 2004. "Public Opinion on Foreign Policy: The Multilateral Public That Perceives Itself as Unilateral." *Public Opinion Quarterly* 68: 323–48.

Treier, Shawn, and D. Sunshine Hillygus. 2009. "The Nature of Political Ideology in the Contemporary Electorate." *Public Opinion Quarterly* 73 (4): 679–703.

Trivers, Robert L. 1971. "The Evolution of Reciprocal Altruism." *Quarterly Review of Biology* 46 (1): 35–57.

Trubowitz, Peter, and Jungkun Seo. 2012. "The China Card: Playing Politics with Sino-American Relations." *Political Science Quarterly* 127 (2): 189–211.

Turner, John. 1987. *Rediscovering the Social Group: A Self-Categorization Theory.* Oxford, UK: Blackwell.

Twain, Mark. 1869. *The Innocents Abroad.* Hartford, CT: American Publishing Company.

———. 1935. *Mark Twain's Notebook.* New York: Harper & Brothers.

Van der Waal, Jeroen, Peter Achterberg, and Dick Houtman. 2007. "Class Is Not Dead—It Has Been Buried Alive: Class Voting and Cultural Voting in Postwar Western Societies (1956–1990)." *Politics and Society* 35 (3): 403–26.

Van Hiel, Alain, and Ivan Mervielde. 2004. "Openness to Experience and Boundaries in the Mind: Relationships with Cultural and Economic Conservatism." *Journal of Personality* 72: 659–86.

Walt, Stephen M. 1985. "Alliance Formation and the Balance of World Power." *International Security* 9 (4): 3–43.

Waltz, Kenneth. 1979. *Theory of International Politics.* New York: McGraw-Hill.

Washington, George. 1796. "Farewell Address." September 17. Washington, DC: Library of Congress, Manuscript Division.

Williams, Daniel K. 2010. *God's Own Party: The Making of the Christian Right.* New York: Oxford University Press.

Wittkopf, Eugene R. 1990. *Faces of Internationalism: Public Opinion and American Foreign Policy.* Durham, NC: Duke University Press.

Wolfe, Alan. 2009. *The Future of Liberalism.* New York: Knopf.

Wu, Frank H. 2010. "Embracing Mistaken Identity: How the Vincent Chin Case Unified Asian Americans." *Asian-American Policy Review* 19: 17–22.

Zaller, John. 1992. *The Nature and Origins of Mass Opinion.* New York: Cambridge University Press.

Ziliak, Stephen T., and Dierdre N. McCloskey. 2008. *The Cult of Statistical Significance: How the Standard Error Costs Us Jobs, Justice, and Lives.* Ann Arbor: University of Michigan Press.

Index

Abortion, 17, 57–58, 60, 223, 266
Abramowitz, Alan I., 25, 57, 266
Acheson, Dean, 22, 23, 213–14
Adam, Thomas, 179
Adams, Ansel, 214, 215 (fig.)
Adams, John, 65, 161, 170
Adams, William, 86
Adelson, Sheldon, 203
Affect heuristics, 43–48, 44 (fig.), 131, 220
Afghanistan, U.S. military presence,
    130–31
Africa: independence movements, 142,
    251; slaves from, 143
African Americans: Baptists, 199; civil
    rights after Civil War, 84–85, 85
    (fig.); civil rights movement, 54, 251;
    intergroup contacts, 133; political
    ideologies, 36, 37, 72; views of Latin
    America, 154–55; warmth feelings
    toward Middle East, 199; warmth
    feelings toward United Nations, 251.
    See also Race relations
Agenda 21, 253, 254, 261
Agnostics, 197–98
Aid, see Foreign aid
AIPAC, see American Israel Public Affairs
    Committee
Aldrich, John H., 22, 27
Allen, Woody, 163–64
Alliance for Progress, 142, 149

Allport, Gordon, 133, 229
Almond, Gabriel, 15
Altemeyer, Robert, 60
Alterman, Eric, 69, 163
Altruism, reciprocal, 78
AmCham China, 209, 233
American exceptionalism, 116
American Israel Public Affairs Committee
    (AIPAC), 183, 184, 193, 203, 204–5, 206,
    207, 208
American National Election Surveys
    (ANES), 17, 18, 19, 21, 36, 42, 53, 55, 88
American Revolution, 169, 173
"Americans Against the Next War"
    billboards, 203, 204 (fig.)
Americans with Disabilities Act, 235
Amerika miniseries, 253–54
Anarchist libertarians, 69
ANES, see American National Election
    Surveys
Anglophiles, 158, 169–70, 173–74. See also
    Britain
Anglophobes, 169, 170–71
Antichrist: European Union as, 159,
    181–82; Pope as, 249; United Nations
    as, 244–45, 247, 267
Anticommunism, 54, 56, 70, 215, 219,
    255–56
Anti-Imperialist League, 2 (fig.)
Anti-Semitism, 187–88, 193

Applied political psychology, 14–15, 16
Arab-Israeli conflict: ideological
    differences in attitudes toward, 186,
    199–202, 207–8; Israel as David or
    Goliath, 186, 195–96, 199–202, 205–6;
    Six-Day War (1967), 189, 192–93,
    195–96, 200–201. *See also* Israel;
    Palestinians
Arabs, 190, 198. *See also* Muslims;
    Palestinians
Arab Spring, 199
Arpaio, Joe, 146
Arthur, Chester, 213
Asay, Chuck, 162, 163 (fig.)
Asia: history of U.S. attitudes, 211–16;
    immigration from, 143, 212–13, 221–22;
    racial stereotypes of, 177, 212–13;
    warmth feelings toward, 210, 217–18,
    299n7; World War II, 176–77, 214–15.
    See also individual countries
Asian Americans, *see* Chinese Americans;
    Japanese Americans
Atheists, 197–98, 219
Attribution errors, 91, 97
The Audacity of Hope (Obama), 87
Authoritarian governments, 23, 94, 215,
    224, 226
Authority: foreign policy toughness and,
    95 (fig.), 95–97; immigration policy
    and, 145 (fig.), 147; militarism and,
    108; as moral value, 78; of parents, 86;
    valued by conservatives, 84, 85–86,
    95–96. *See also* Social dominance
    orientation

Bachmann, Michele, 85–86, 88
Baldwin, James, 63
Bandow, Doug, 252
Baptists, 78–79, 199, 246
Barbary pirates, 189
Batchelder, Nathaniel, 203
Baum, Matthew A., 16, 130
Bauman, Louis, 247
Beard, Charles, 35
Beck, Glenn, 116, 137, 253
Bellah, Robert N., 70, 71, 82–83, 220
Ben-Ami, Shlomo, 183

Bentley, Robert, 254
Berinsky, Adam J., 16, 130, 265
Berryman, Clifford, 2, 2 (fig.), 33, 34 (fig.),
    238–39, 239 (fig.), 240, 240 (fig.)
Bible: New Testament, 106; Old
    Testament, 187, 194
Bible Belt, 59, 59 (fig.), 86
Biblical literalism: foreign policy
    preferences and, 58–59, 186, 191–93;
    parental discipline methods and,
    86; regional differences, 59, 59 (fig.);
    survey questions on, 58, 191; views of
    Middle East and, 59, 187–88, 191–95,
    192 (fig.), 196–99, 197 (fig.), 267; views
    of United Nations and, 243, 243 (fig.),
    244–46, 247, 248
"Big L" liberalism, 33–36, 69–70
Binding values, *see* Authority; Loyalty;
    Purity
Bin Laden, Osama, 127
Bipartisanship, 101. *See also* Partisanship
Birth control, *see* Family planning
Black helicopters, 253, 261. *See also* United
    Nations
Blackstone, William E., 187–88
Blair, Tony, 173–74
Block, Herbert ("Herblock"), 34, 35 (fig.),
    42, 42 (fig.), 88, 89 (fig.), 93, 94 (fig.),
    201, 202 (fig.)
Blue helmets, 257, 261. *See also* United
    Nations
Bolton, John, 236, 241
Borah, William E., 240
Boren, David, 18, 269–70
Bouton, Marshall, 25
Brady, Henry, 43
Brains, 38
Brazil: racial composition of population,
    139–40, 154–55; warmth feelings
    toward, 137, 154–55
Breen, Steve, 151, 151 (fig.)
Brezhnev, Leonid, 34
Britain: American attitudes toward, 118,
    169–74; Anglophiles, 158, 169–70, 173–
    74; Anglophobes, 169, 170–71; cultural
    commonalities with Americans,
    170, 172–74; ideological differences

in attitudes toward, 158, 171–74; monarchy, 118, 169–70, 173; "Special Relationship" with United States, 158, 172; treaties with United States, 238; warmth feelings toward, 157–58, 171–74
Brody, David, 74
Brooks, David, 128, 261–62
Brotherhood of the Kingdom, 243
Bryan, William Jennings: anti-imperialism, 1–3, 60, 61, 106, 114, 140; cultural traditionalism, 56; political cartoons, 2 (fig.), 2–3, 3 (fig.); presidential campaigns, 1–3, 55, 176; Scopes Trial, 56, 242–43; as secretary of state, 55
Buchanan, Pat, 49, 50, 69, 251, 252
Bullock, John G., 81
Burnham, James, 260
Burns, Jennifer, 70
Busby, Joshua W., 236
Bush, George H. W., 1, 126, 235
Bush, George W.: "axis of evil" speech, 55, 56; compassionate conservatism, 76, 87–88; "The Duty of Hope," 76; foreign policy preferences, 106; idealism in foreign policy, 109, 112, 113–14; Iraq war, 160, 167, 173; in Israel, 245; on Japan, 230, 231–32; religious beliefs, 28, 56; traditional values, 77; on United Nations, 245; use of military force, 106; war on terror, 157
Business conservatives, 209, 224, 233, 234. *See also* Economic conservatives
Byman, Daniel L., 29

Cai, Huajian, 118
California, Proposition 187, 148
Campbell, David E., 14, 58
Capitalism: anarchist libertarian view, 69; critiques of, 71; laissez-faire economics, 54, 65, 67
Caras, Harvey, 205
Care, *see* Compassion
Caribbean countries, *see* Cuba; Haiti
Carnegie, Andrew, 140
Carney, Dana R., 38
Carson, Johnny, 169

Carter, Jimmy, 152, 190, 199, 201
Catholic Charities, 152
Catholics: distrust of, 248–49; foreign aid support, 152; foreign policy preferences, 122; immigrants, 142–43; Popes, 249; prejudice against, 56, 142–43; views of Middle East, 199. *See also* Christianity
Cato Institute, 252
Cautious idealists, 124, 124 (fig.), 268–69
CBS, 186
Certainty, needs for, 37
Chandler, Walter, 148
Charitable giving, 152
Chastity, *see* Purity
Chiang Ching-kuo, 215
Chiang Kai-shek, 214, 215
Chicago Council for Global Affairs, 6, 7–8, 15, 21, 22, 25, 41, 150, 157–58, 160, 184–85, 210, 236, 263
Chicago Sun-Times, 68
Children: hunger, 111; spanking, 86, 105. *See also* Parents
Chin, Vincent, 231
China: Boxer Rebellion, 96–97, 214, 224–25; Christian missionaries, 212, 213–14, 218–19, 224; economic policies, 216, 224, 234; economic power, 227–28; foreign business community, 234; ideological differences in attitudes toward, 60, 210–11, 217 (fig.), 217–26, 221 (fig.); immigration from, 212–13, 221–22; imperial, 212; Korean War, 215–16; one-child policy, 60; seen as threat, 223; survey questions on, 210, 216–17; Tiananmen Square massacre, 216, 226; trade policies, 209; trade with, 224, 228, 238; UN membership, 255–56; U.S. foreign policy toward, 209–11, 220–21, 221 (fig.), 223, 225–26, 298n76; warmth feelings toward, 210, 299n7. *See also* Chinese government; Chinese people
China Knowledge Quiz, 227, 227 (table)
Chinese Americans, 223, 231
Chinese Exclusion Act, 213, 214
Chinese government: communist regime,

215–16, 226; Confucius Institutes, 226, 229; survey questions on, 216; warmth feelings toward, 216–18, 223–24, 226, 229, 230

Chinese people: foreign contacts, 226, 228 (fig.), 228–30; prejudice against, 212–13, 214, 217, 218, 221–23, 228–29, 230; survey questions on, 217; warmth feelings toward, 216–18, 226

Chirac, Jacques, 167

Christian conservatives: anticommunism, 219; fundamentalists, 56, 242–43; opposition to family planning funding, 111–12; views of China, 209–10; views of human nature, 40; views of international organizations, 242–43, 246–49; warmth feelings toward Israel, 189, 193–95, 194 (fig.), 198, 245, 267. See also Christian Zionists; Cultural conservatives; Teavangelical Republicans

Christianity: Catholics, 56, 122, 142–43, 152, 199, 248–49; charity, 152; in China, 209–10, 212, 213–14, 223; civilizing mission, 82; fears of Islam, 189–90; feelings about and foreign policy preferences, 166; imperialism and, 114; Israel policy and, 189; Kingdom Theology, 243; missionaries, 212, 213–14, 218–19, 224; mixing with pagans, 248–49; moral values in sermons, 78–79; pacifism, 106; progressive, 28, 40, 243–44; Puritans, 106, 143, 173, 189; Social Gospel, 28–29, 40, 242, 243, 244, 248. See also Biblical literalism; Protestant ethic; Protestantism

Christian nationalists, 88

Christian realism, 28–29

Christians United for Israel (CUFI), 203, 207, 208

Christian Zionists, 159, 179, 181–82, 187–88, 189, 192–93, 205

Chu, Judy, 223

Churchill, Winston, 167, 241

Civil rights movement, 54, 251

Civil War, 61, 84

Clark, Victoria, 193

Clarke, William Newton, 243

Cleveland, Grover, 51, 213

Climate change, see Global warming

Clinton, Bill, 23, 126

Clinton, Hillary Rodham: liberalism, 49; on partisanship in foreign policy, 1, 4, 270; on realism and idealism, 121, 127; as secretary of state, 1, 4, 85–86, 126 (fig.), 127, 270

Clinton administration, 51

CNN, 6, 185, 186, 210

Cohen, Jacob, 21

Cold War, 70, 114, 149, 179, 215, 255

Communism, 219. See also Anticommunism; Cold War

Communist countries: ideological differences in attitudes toward, 218 (fig.), 219–20, 224; UN members, 255–56; warmth feelings toward, 218, 218 (fig.), 219–20. See also China; North Korea; Soviet Union

Communitarianism: China policy preferences and, 224; critique of libertarianism, 70–71; of cultural Republicans, 74–75, 76; of liberals, 54; views of foreign aid, 152; views of government roles, 257; views of international organizations, 258; warmth feelings toward communist countries and, 220

Compassion: aversion to war and, 92–93; of conservatives, 76, 87–88, 94; economic inequality attitudes and, 86–88, 87 (fig.); foreign aid views and, 151, 151 (fig.); humanitarian idealism support and, 110; for humankind, 94–95, 251; immigration policy and, 145–46, 147, 221–22; international engagement and, 102; as liberal value, 42, 84, 86–87, 88, 91–93, 94–95; as moral value, 78; political idealism support and, 113; social dominance orientation and, 84; toward Palestinians, 201; toward Mexico, 138, 138 (fig.); warmth feelings and, 90, 91 (fig.), 91–92, 95

Compassionate conservatism, 76, 87–88

Compensatory control, 247–48

Confucius Institutes, 226, 229

Congress: bipartisanship on foreign policy, 101; Freedom Fries, 167–68, 169; gerrymandering, 26, 207, 269; gridlock, 269; hyperpartisan districts, 26, 269; lobbyists, 233; NAFTA passage, 51; polarization, 25, 262; War Powers Resolution, 4. *See also* Electoral politics; Senate

Consensus history, 35–36, 65

Conservatives: anticommunism, 54; compassion, 76, 87–88, 94; foreign aid views, 151–53; hawks, 48; immigration policy views, 143–44, 146–49; isolationism, 101–2, 103; moral values prioritized by, 78–83, 84, 85–86, 89–90, 94, 266; nationalism, 99; opposition to equality, 55; patriotism, 91; political, 49, 54; protect orientation of, 90; psychological characteristics, 37–38, 266; resistance to change, 55; social dominance orientation, 64, 95–96, 166. *See also* Christian conservatives; Cultural conservatives; Economic conservatives; Ideological differences; Republican Party

Contact hypothesis, 133, 229. *See also* Foreign contacts

Contamination disgust, 89–90. *See also* Purity

Contraceptives, *see* Family planning

Control: external sources, 247–48; loss of, 257; personal, 247–48

Converse, Phillip, 15, 265

Conwell, Russell H., 248

Coolidge, Calvin, 142, 144, 238

Cooperative internationalism, 15

Coulter, Ann, 92, 166, 173

Crawford, Beverly, 179

Crawford, Michael, 165 (fig.)

Creel, George, 176

Cruz, Ted, 156

Cuba: American military government, 82; paternalistic attitude toward, 140, 141 (fig.); Spanish-American War, 1–3, 23–24, 61; Spanish rule, 112–13

CUFI, *see* Christians United for Israel

Cultural conservatives: China policy toughness, 60, 223; immigration policy views, 153; Middle East policy preferences, 186; moral values prioritized by, 81–83, 82 (fig.), 267; political idealism support, 113–14; reactions to foreign contacts, 132–33, 133 (fig.), 134, 229; in Tea Party, 75; views of China, 223; views of France, 158, 160, 165; views of Germany, 158, 178, 179; views of international organizations, 237, 244–49; views of United Nations, 242–43. *See also* Christian conservatives; Cultural traditionalism

Cultural ideology, 54–55, 55–60; foreign policy preferences and, 56, 58–59, 60, 266–67; survey questions on, 58, 60

Cultural liberals: libertarians as, 70; Middle East policy preferences, 186; moral values prioritized by, 54, 267; reactions to foreign contacts, 132–33, 133 (fig.), 134, 229; views of China, 223; views of France, 158, 160, 164–65; views of international organizations, 237, 243–44; views of United Nations, 242–44

Cultural Republicans: communitarianism, 74–75, 76; feelings toward Tea Party, 75; ideological profile, 74–75, 268; warmth feelings toward Germany, 158, 180

Cultural traditionalism: biblical literalism and, 191; of conservatives, 54; fairness and purity values and, 81–83, 82 (fig.); foreign aid views and, 150 (fig.), 152; foreign policy preferences and, 60, 108, 172 (fig.); of Hispanics, 155–56; immigration policy and, 145, 145 (fig.), 147, 223; political idealism support and, 113; scale, 60; survey questions on, 60; views of Middle East and, 191–92, 192 (fig.); views of United Nations and, 242–44, 243 (fig.); warmth feelings toward communist countries and, 219; warmth feelings toward France and, 164, 164 (fig.), 165–66; warmth feelings toward Germany and, 179

Cultural values, secular or modern, 60, 75. *See also* Cultural traditionalism

Culture wars, 17, 40–41, 55, 56–58, 82–83, 266–67

Czechoslovakia, Prague Spring, 34

Dalrymple, Louis, 49–50, 51 (fig.)

Darby, John, 196, 198

Darrow, Clarence, 56

Darwin, Charles, 61

Dawkins, Richard, 78

Death anxiety, 281n20

Death penalty, public opinion on, 17

Declaration of Independence, 70, 169

Defense spending, 41 (fig.), 41–42, 42 (fig.)

De Gaulle, Charles, 166–67, 168–69. *See also* Gaullism

Deibel, Terry L., 77, 91

DeLay, Tom, 195, 205

Democracies: Chinese exposure to, 226; in East Asia, 230–32; pragmatic view, 28; public opinion impact on foreign policy, 9, 22–25, 27, 206–8; religious freedom, 114, 187; support for foreign, 109, 112, 114, 231–32. *See also* Electoral politics

Democratic Party: China policies, 209, 233; compassion as priority, 91–92; economic policies, 65–66; foreign policy profiles, 122, 123 (fig.), 125 (fig.), 125–27, 268, 269; Hispanic voters, 156; ideological profiles, 73, 73 (fig.), 268; liberals, 17, 73, 87, 268; Middle East policy, 183–84, 189, 207–8; moderates, 26–27, 73, 268; platforms, 149, 235; primary voters, 26–27; trade policies, 51

Deng Xiaoping, 216

Desaparecidos, 145–46

Desch, Michael, 36, 101

Destler, I. M., 25, 102

De Tocqueville, Alexis, 22, 23, 65

Devil, believers in, 159, 181–82, 191, 244–48

Dewey, John, 28

Dickson, Caitlin, 86

Diplomacy: bilateral treaties, 238; juxtaposed to military force, 100–101, 105–8; survey questions on, 100. *See also* Multilateralism

Disability rights treaty, 235–36, 257, 261–62, 270

Ditto, Peter H., 97

Dole, Elizabeth, 173

Dole, Robert J., 235, 257

Domestic policy: ideological differences, 17, 41–42, 265; public opinion on, 17, 41–42; welfare spending, 41, 41 (fig.), 42 (fig.)

Doves: idealistic, 122, 123, 123 (fig.); in Israel, 195–96; perceptions of military strength of adversaries, 48. *See also* Pacifism

Dower, John W., 176–77, 214–15

Drezner, Daniel W., 122–23, 157

Duckitt, John, 55, 60, 147

Dueck, Colin, 40, 123, 125, 246–47

Dulles, John Foster, 28–29, 244

Du Pont, Irénée, 66

East Asia, *see* Asia; *and individual countries*

Ebens, Ronald, 231

Ecological fallacy, 45

Economic conservatives: compassion toward poor, 87–88; foreign policy preferences, 67–68, 69, 267–68; free trade views, 49, 51 (fig.); libertarians as, 70; opposition to government role in economy, 66; policies, 54, 66–67; views of China, 209, 224; views of France, 158, 160, 161–62; views of Germany, 158, 178, 180; views of international organizations, 237, 251–53; warmth feelings toward communist countries, 219

Economic ideology, 54–55, 64–69; foreign policy preferences and, 65, 67–69, 267–68; survey questions on, 67. *See also* Communism; Inequality

Economic inequality, *see* Inequality

Economic interests, 4–5, 271. *See also* Business conservatives

Economic liberals: foreign policy preferences, 68, 267, 268; policies, 54, 65–66; views of China, 224; views of France, 158, 160, 162–63; views of Germany, 178; warmth feelings toward communist countries, 219

Economic power, perceived, 227–28

Economics, laissez-faire, 54, 65, 67

Economic systems, *see* Capitalism; Communism

Education levels: correlation with ideology, 37; global warming attitudes and, 259–60; views of United Nations and, 259, 259 (fig.)

Edward VII, King, 174

Ehrhart, Samuel, 118–19, 119 (fig.), 140–41, 141 (fig.)

Eighteenth Amendment, 56

Einstein, Albert, 258

Eisenhower, Dwight D., 66, 149, 166, 244

Eisenhower, Milton, 149

Electoral politics: campaign contributors, 233; congressional districts, 26, 207, 269; influence of extremes, 25–27, 207, 261–62, 270–71; influence of public's foreign policy attitudes, 22–23, 269; influence on foreign policy decisions, 9, 22–25, 27, 206–8; median voters, 25, 269, 270; presidential campaigns, 1–4, 27, 55, 207; primary elections, 25, 26–27, 156, 207, 208, 261–62, 269, 270–71; scholarship on, 16. *See also* Democracies

Elites: foreign policy preferences, 15; ideological influences on foreign policy attitudes, 27–28; influence on public's foreign policy attitudes, 15–16, 130; partisan differences, 263, 264, 265; partisan rhetoric, 15–16; polarization, 25; responsiveness to public opinion, 25

Emerson, Ralph Waldo, 170

Emotion, *see* Affect heuristics; Warmth toward foreign countries

Empathy, *see* Compassion

England, *see* Britain

English language, 148–49, 174

Equality: economic, 66–68; opposition, 54, 55, 62, 64, 66–68, 89–90, 161, 252; racial, 62, 63 (fig.), 84–85, 140. *See also* Inequality

Ethnic groups, *see* Chinese Americans; Hispanics; Immigration; Japanese Americans

Ethnocentrism, 64

Etzioni, Amitai, 71

Europe: divisions from United States, 157; social welfare states, 69, 163, 178; warmth feelings toward, 157–59. *See also individual countries*

European Union: fiscal crisis, 178; ideological differences in attitudes toward, 159, 180–82, 181 (fig.); Nobel Peace Prize, 180; seen as Antichrist, 159, 181–82; warmth feelings toward, 103–4, 158, 159

Evangelical Christians: Bush as, 28; foreign policy profiles, 122; Reagan supporters, 56; views of international organizations, 242–43; warmth feelings toward Israel, 189, 193–95, 194 (fig.), 198, 245, 267; warmth feelings toward Palestinians, 198. *See also* Biblical literalism; Christian conservatives; Christian Zionists; Teavangelical Republicans

Evolution, 56, 242–43. *See also* Social Darwinism

Extremes, political influence, 25–27, 207, 261–62, 270–71

FAIR, *see* Federation for American Immigration Reform

Fairness: cultural traditionalism relationship, 81, 82 (fig.), 83; economic inequality attitudes and, 87 (fig.), 88–89; immigration policy and, 146–47; as liberal value, 83, 84–85, 88–89, 147; in Middle East policy, 201; as moral value, 78; social dominance orientation and, 84–85; violence and, 88–89

Fallin, Mary, 74–75
Falwell, Jerry, 191, 192–93
Families, *see* Parents
Family planning, 111
Feaver, Peter, 15
Federal Council of Churches, 244
Federation for American Immigration
    Reform (FAIR), 147, 152–53
Feelings, *see* Affect heuristics; Warmth
    toward foreign countries
Feldman, Stanley, 53, 55
Fey, Tina, 169
Fiorina, Morris P., 9, 25, 40–41, 57–58, 266
Fish, Hamilton, 106–7, 238
Fiske, Susan T., 137–38, 159, 185
Flohri, Emil, 188 (fig.), 188–89
Forbes, Randy, 209
Force, *see* Militarism
Forceful idealists, 125 (fig.), 125–27, 268,
    269
Foreign Affairs, 8, 168, 184, 241, 263, 264
Foreign aid: amounts, 153–54; debates,
    149; to Haiti, 138–39, 149–54, 150 (fig.);
    ideological differences on, 149–51,
    150 (fig.); immigration reduction
    and, 152–53; to Israel, 201–2; to Latin
    America, 149; opposition, 112, 152;
    survey questions on, 149–50
Foreign contacts: with Chinese, 226,
    228 (fig.), 228–30; foreign policy
    preferences and, 228 (fig.), 228–30;
    increased, 226; by party, 133; prejudice
    reduction and, 229; reactions of
    cultural conservatives and liberals,
    132–33, 133 (fig.), 134, 229; survey
    questions on, 131, 228
Foreign countries, *see* Warmth toward
    foreign countries
Foreign Missions Conference of North
    America, 218–19
Foreign Policy Leadership Project, 15
Foreign policy orientations, *see* Idealisms;
    Internationalism; Realism
Foreign policy preferences: elite cues,
    130; media influences, 16, 130. *See also*
    Foreign policy toughness; Ideology,
    impact on foreign policy preferences

Foreign policy profiles: cautious idealists,
    124, 124 (fig.), 268–69; cluster analysis,
    122–24, 123 (fig.); in Democratic Party,
    122, 123 (fig.), 125 (fig.), 125–27, 268,
    269; forceful idealists, 125 (fig.), 125–27,
    268, 269; global citizens, 125 (fig.),
    125–26, 127, 268; idealistic doves, 122,
    123, 123 (fig.); idealistic hawks, 122,
    123, 123 (fig.); isolationist skeptics,
    124, 124 (fig.), 268; religious beliefs
    and, 122, 123 (fig.); in Republican
    Party, 122, 123 (fig.), 124 (fig.), 124–25,
    268–69; skeptics, 125 (fig.), 126, 268;
    unilateralist hawks, 122, 123 (fig.),
    123–24
Foreign policy toughness: cultural
    conservatism and, 59, 60; foreign
    contacts and, 134; moral values and, 95
    (fig.), 95–97; nationalism and, 119–20,
    121 (fig.), 298n76; social dominance
    orientation and, 95 (fig.), 95–97, 166,
    167 (fig), 221; toward China, 209–11,
    217, 217 (fig.), 220–21, 221 (fig.), 223,
    225–26, 228–30, 298n76; toward
    France, 158, 166, 167 (fig); toward Iran,
    120, 184, 203–6, 205 (fig.); toward
    Israel, 120, 185–86, 191–93, 192 (fig.);
    toward North Korea, 120, 298n76
Fox News, 130, 131, 180, 260
France: culture, 158, 160, 163–66;
    Gaullism, 158, 160–61, 166–69;
    ideological differences in attitudes
    toward, 158, 159–69, 160 (fig.);
    relations with United States, 166–69;
    revolution of 1848, 161; secularism,
    165–66; socialist policies, 158, 160,
    161–63; U.S. foreign policy toward, 158,
    166, 167 (fig), 167–68; warmth feelings
    toward, 157–58, 159, 164 (fig.), 164–65.
    See also French Revolution
Frank Leslie's *Illustrated Newspaper*,
    84–85, 85 (fig.)
Franklin, Benjamin, 173, 174–75, 187,
    195
Freedom: "Big L" liberalism, 33–34,
    69–70; communist threat to, 220;
    communitarian view, 258; individual,

257; Israel as symbol of, 195, 205–6; as libertarian priority, 70, 195; threats seen from international organizations, 253–58. *See also* Libertarianism; Religious freedom
Free trade, differences among conservatives on, 49–51, 50 (fig.)
French Revolution, 53, 65, 161, 166
Friedberg, Aaron L., 183
Friedman, Milton, 67, 87, 219
Friedman, Rose, 87
Friedman, Thomas L., 5, 207
Friends, foreign, *see* Foreign contacts
Fuchs, Lawrence H., 143
Fundamentalist Christians, *see* Biblical literalism; Christian conservatives; Evangelical Christians

Gaddafi, Muammar, 29
Gaebelein, Arno, 247, 248
Gallup polls, 236–37
Garfield, James, 212–13
Gates, Robert, 127
Gaullism, 158, 160–61, 166–69
Gays, *see* Homosexuality
Gelpi, Christopher, 15, 130
Gender differences: among Hispanics, 155; in attitudes toward United Nations, 258; in ideology, 37, 72; sexism, 86. *See also* Women
General Social Survey (GSS), 19, 21, 41, 57–58
Generational transmission of ideology, 38–39, 39 (fig.)
George III, King, 169, 170, 187
German-American Bund, 177, 177 (fig.)
German Americans, 174–76, 176 (fig.), 177, 222
Germany: culture, 158; economic policies, 158, 178, 180; ideological differences in attitudes toward, 158, 177–80, 178 (fig.); immigrants from, 174–75; Nazi regime, 24, 176, 179, 193; secularism, 179; warmth feelings toward, 157–58, 177–80
Gerrymandering, 26, 207, 269
Gilbert and Sullivan, *H.M.S. Pinafore*, 118

Gillam, F. Victor, 3, 3 (fig.), 112–13, 117 (fig.), 117–18, 143, 144 (fig.)
Gilligan, Carol, 78
Gingrich, Newt: compassionate conservatism, 88; on Iran, 202, 203; on Muslims as enemy, 200; nationalism, 115, 116; presidential campaigns, 4, 159; view of war, 4, 92
Global citizens, 125 (fig.), 125–26, 127, 268
Globalization, increased foreign contacts, 226
Global warming, 259–60
Goldberg, Michelle, 88
Goldin, Claudia, 66
Goldwater, Barry, 66–67, 69, 255–56
Good Neighbor Policy, 141, 149
Graham, Billy, 206, 216, 219
Grandiosity, national, 118–19
Grant, Ulysses S., 84, 85, 106–7, 238
Great Britain, *see* Britain
Greeley, Horace, 84, 85
Green, Donald P., 81
Gries, Peter, 118
Grimes, William H., 162
Groeling, Tim J., 16, 130
Group-based dominance, 62–63. *See also* Social dominance orientation
GSS, *see* General Social Survey
Gun control, 17, 254–55, 256–58
Gut feelings, *see* Warmth toward foreign countries

Ha, Shang E., 81
Habitat for Humanity, 152
Hagee, John, 159, 179, 180, 181–82, 193, 203, 245
Haidt, Jonathan, 78, 79, 81
Haiti: aid to, 138–39, 149–54, 150 (fig.); earthquake (2010), 149–50, 151; immigrants from, 153; racial composition of population, 139; racial stereotypes of, 142; warmth feelings toward, 137, 154
Halo effect, 43, 44, 44 (fig.)
Hamilton, Grant E., 50, 52 (fig.), 147, 148 (fig.)
Hamiltonians, 121

Hancock, Winfield, 212
Hannity, Sean, 156
Happiness, ideological differences, 88
Harding, Warren, 245
Hargis, Billy James, 220
Harm, *see* Compassion
Harper's Weekly, 62, 63 (fig.), 106, 107
    (fig.), 108 (fig.), 221–22, 222 (fig.),
    224–25, 225 (fig.)
Harrison, Benjamin, 50–51, 188
Hartz, Louis, 33
Hatcher, M. G., 245
Hawks: humanitarian, 125–26; idealistic,
    122, 123, 123 (fig.); perceptions of
    military strength of adversaries, 48;
    unilateralist, 122, 123 (fig.), 123–24; in
    War of 1812, 5
Helms, Jesse, 236, 241
Helzer, Erik G., 81–82
Herblock, *see* Block, Herbert
Hetherington, Marc, 16, 17
Heuristics, *see* Affect heuristics
Hewitt, Abraham, 117–18
Hierarchy, *see* Authority; Social
    dominance orientation
High culture, French, 164–66
Hill, Jayne, 255
Hill, Joseph, 258
Hillygus, D. Sunshine, 53
Hispanics: Democratic voters, 156;
    immigrants, 145–46, 148, 155;
    liberalism, 36; views of Latin America,
    154–56; views of Middle East, 199
Hiss, Alger, 255
Hitchcock, Mark, 193, 194, 199, 245
Hitler, Adolf, 24, 176, 179, 189
H.M.S. Pinafore (Gilbert and Sullivan),
    118
Ho, Arnold K., 62
Hobbes, Thomas, 40
Hoffmann, Stanley, 168
Hofstadter, Richard, 35, 61
Hollande, Francois, 162
Holsti, Ole R., 15
Homosexuality: conservative views of,
    82–83; liberal views of, 83; marriage
    issue, 17, 58, 60, 83

Hoover, Herbert, 143, 144
House of Representatives, *see* Congress
Huckabee, Mike, 193, 195
Huebert, Jacob H., 70
Hu Jintao, 222–23
Humanitarian idealism, 99, 109–12, 110
    (fig.), 115, 265
Human nature, views of, 39–40, 246–47
Human rights protection, 109, 113, 201–2,
    209
Hunt, Michael H., 33, 35–36, 61, 65, 119,
    140, 212, 214, 229, 232
Huntington, Samuel P., 148
Huntsman, Jon, 27
Hutchins, Frank, 170, 171 (fig.)

Idealisms: compared to realism, 108–9;
    European, 157; foreign policy goals,
    109; humanitarian, 99, 109–12, 110
    (fig.), 115, 265; political, 99, 109, 112–14;
    public support, 109; religious, 28, 99,
    109, 114–15; supporters, 122, 123–24;
    survey questions on, 109; Wilsonian,
    121–22, 127
Idealistic doves, 122, 123, 123 (fig.)
Idealistic hawks, 122, 123, 123 (fig.)
"Identification with all humanity"
    (IWAH), 94–95. *See also* Compassion
Identity: national, 115–16; social, 17–18,
    90–91
Ideological differences: on domestic
    policy, 17, 41–42, 265; in happiness,
    88; on human nature, 39–40;
    moral empathy gap, 97; in moral
    priorities, 78–81, 80 (fig.); origins,
    36–40; partisanship and, 263, 265–66;
    patriotism and nationalism, 91, 99,
    120–21; physiological differences, 38,
    266; policy differences as consequence,
    40–42; psychological differences,
    37–38, 266; in warmth toward foreign
    countries, 6–7, 7 (fig.), 90, 264–65. *See
    also* Conservatives; Liberals
Ideological profiles: cluster analysis,
    72–76; of Democrats, 73, 73 (fig.), 268;
    of Republicans, 73 (fig.), 73–76, 268
Ideology: definition, 33; demographic

correlates, 36 (fig.), 36–37; in
domestic policy, 17, 265; generational
transmission, 38–39, 39 (fig.);
geographical self-sorting by, 26, 269;
influence compared to partisanship,
16–17; measures, 19; multidimensional
model, 52–55, 54 (fig.), 266;
relationship to partisanship, 17;
scholarship on, 265; shared, 35–36;
stability, 18; unidimensional model,
53–54, 266
Ideology, impact on foreign policy
preferences: of cultural ideology,
56, 58–59, 60, 266–67; of economic
ideology, 65, 67–69, 267–68; of elites,
27–28; future research directions, 260,
269; ideology dimensions and, 52–53;
influence of extremes, 25–27, 207,
261–62, 270–71; limited effects seen,
7–8, 41, 263–64; mediated by affect
heuristic, 43–48, 46 (fig.), 47 (fig.);
mediated by moral values, 90–97; of
political ideology, 55, 72, 102–3, 268;
situational factors and, 16, 128, 131–34,
233; of social ideology, 55, 61, 64, 102–3,
267; surveys on, 5, 6, 20–21, 263, 264;
warmth feelings and, 6–7, 265. See also
Partisanship in foreign policy; specific
issues and countries
Ideology dimensions, 52–55, 54 (fig.), 266;
correlations among, 72; foreign policy
preferences and, 52–53; moral values
as mediators, 81–90; profiles, 72–73,
73 (fig.). See also Cultural ideology;
Economic ideology; Political ideology;
Social ideology
Immigration: from Asia, 143, 212–13, 214,
221–22; assimilation, 143–44, 174; from
China, 212–13, 221–22; fear of, 61–62,
62 (fig.), 65, 142–43, 147–49, 250–51;
generations, 155–56; from Germany,
174–75; from Haiti, 153; illegal, 143,
145–46, 148, 156; from Ireland, 170,
222; from Japan, 214; Jewish, 187; of
labor, 143; from Latin America, 143,
154; nationalism and, 117 (fig.), 117–18;
in nineteenth century, 65, 142–43,

147; restrictions, 212, 213, 214; survey
questions on, 144
Immigration debates: African American
views, 154; among Republicans, 156;
Hispanic views, 154; "Massachusetts
idea," 143–44, 147; moral values in, 145
(fig.), 145–47; opposition, 52 (fig.),
142–43, 147–49, 152–53; "Pennsylvania
idea," 143, 145; "Virginia idea," 143, 144
(fig.)
Imperialism: American, 1–3, 61, 82, 106,
114, 118–19, 140; opposition, 60, 106,
114, 140
Income inequality, see Inequality
Incomes: correlation with ideology, 36, 37;
poverty, 87–88
India, warmth feelings toward, 232
Individualism: foreign policy preferences
and, 104–5; libertarian, 54, 70–71,
75–76
Individualizing values, see Compassion;
Fairness
Inequality: China policy preferences
and, 223–24; economic, 66–67, 86–90;
foreign aid views and, 150 (fig.), 151–
52; global, 88; humanitarian idealism
support and, 110; liberal opposition,
64, 87, 88, 161, 267; moral values and
attitudes toward, 86–90, 87 (fig.);
support, 55, 64, 66–68, 89–90, 161,
252; survey questions on support, 67;
warmth feelings toward communist
countries and, 219. See also Equality
Inferior groups, see Social dominance
orientation
In-group, see Loyalty
Inhofe, Jim, 4, 232, 235
Interest groups, 4–5. See also Lobbyists
Intergroup relations, see Foreign contacts;
Social dominance orientation
International engagement/activism:
juxtaposed to isolationism, 100, 101–3;
public support, 102; survey questions
on, 100; U.S. policies, 101
Internationalism: cooperative, 15;
ideological differences, 100–108; of
liberals, 100–101, 102, 265; meanings,

99–100; militant, 15; survey questions
on, 100
International law, 106. *See also*
Diplomacy; Treaties
International organizations: ideological
differences in attitudes toward, 7, 7
(fig.), 236–37; religious differences in
views, 242–49, 261; survey questions
on, 236, 237; warmth feelings toward,
6 (fig.), 6–7, 7 (fig.), 103–4, 180–82, 181
(fig.), 236. *See also* European Union;
League of Nations; Multilateralism;
United Nations
Iran: hostage crisis, 190, 200; ideological
differences in attitudes toward,
202–6, 205 (fig.); nuclear weapons
program, 202–6; revolution, 190; U.S.
foreign policy toward, 120, 184, 203–6,
205 (fig.); warmth feelings toward,
184
Iraq war, 160, 167, 173
Irish Americans, 170, 171, 222
Isaacs, Harold R., 215–16
Islam, *see* Muslims
Isolationism: of conservatives, 101–2,
103; Jeffersonian, 122; juxtaposed to
international engagement, 100, 101–3;
pre-World War II, 3; public views, 102;
of unilateralist hawks, 122; in United
States, 101–2
Isolationist skeptics, 124, 124 (fig.), 268
Israel: feelings of U.S. public, 7, 184;
founding, 189; ideological differences
in attitudes toward, 184, 185–86,
191–97, 192 (fig.), 200–202; military
strength, 200–201; pacifists, 195–96;
survey questions on, 185–86; U.S.
foreign policy toward, 120, 183–84,
185–86, 201–2, 206–8; West Bank
settlements, 193, 201. *See also* Arab-
Israeli conflict
Israel, warmth feelings toward:
attitudes toward United Nations
and, 245–46; biblical literalism and,
196–99, 197 (fig.), 267; of Christian
conservatives, 189, 193–95, 194 (fig.),
198, 245, 267; ideological differences,

184–85, 185 (fig.); of libertarians, 195,
205; as mediator of foreign policy
preferences, 192, 192 (fig.); as mediator
of Iran policy preferences, 204–6, 205
(fig.); nationalism and, 205–6
Israel lobby, 183, 184, 206–7, 208
Italian Americans, 143
Italy, in World War II, 92

Jackson, Andrew, 4, 92
Jackson, Henry "Scoop," 114, 189
Jacksonians, 122
Jacobson, Gary C., 26, 269
Jacoby, William G., 17
James, William, 28
Janoff-Bulman, Ronnie, 90
Janssen, Weert, 249
Japan: democracy, 231–32; ideological
differences in attitudes toward,
230–32, 231 (fig.); immigration from,
214; Russo-Japanese War, 238–39;
war in China, 214; warmth feelings
toward, 210, 230–32, 231 (fig.), 299n7;
Westernization, 214; World War II, 177
Japanese Americans: internment, 214, 215
(fig.); prejudice against, 231
Jay, John, 189
Jefferson, Thomas, 1, 65, 161, 169
Jeffersonians, 122
Jenkins, Jerry, 245
Jennings, M. Kent, 38–39
Jervis, Robert, 157
Jespersen, T. Christopher, 213, 214, 215
Jews: anti-Semitism, 187–88, 193;
evangelical Christians and, 193–95;
Holocaust, 193; homeland for, 188, 189,
193, 246; in Russia, 188–89; in Soviet
Union, 114, 189; in United States, 187–
88, 197, 204–5, 208; warmth feelings
toward Middle East and, 197. *See also*
Israel
John Birch Society, 252, 253, 270
Johnson, Lyndon B., 66, 167
Johnston, Chris, 53, 55
Jones, Terry, 199
Jones, Walter B., 167–68
Jost, John T., 37, 38, 53, 55, 62, 88, 260

Judge magazine, 2–3, 3 (fig.), 50, 52 (fig.),
    82, 83 (fig.), 112–13, 117 (fig.), 117–18,
    143, 144 (fig.), 188 (fig.), 188–89
Justice, *see* Fairness

Kagan, Robert, 157, 182
Kahneman, Daniel, 43, 48, 220
Kam, Cindy D., 64
Kay, Aaron C., 247–48
Kennedy, John F., 56, 142, 149, 251, 258
Keppler, Udo I., 96 (fig.), 96–97, 140, 141
    (fig.), 175, 176 (fig.)
Kerby, R. A., 249
Kerouac, Jack, 137
Kerry, John, 114, 235
Keyes, Alan, 254
Keynes, John Maynard, 65
Kim Jong-il, 256
Kinder, Donald R., 64
King, Martin Luther, Jr., 28
King, Pete, 173–74
King, Steve, 178
Kingdom Theology, 243
King of the Hill, 129
Kirkpatrick, Jeane, 254, 256
Kissinger, Henry, 114, 127, 189
Kloppenberg, James T., 28, 127
Knecht, Thomas, 27
Knowledge: about China, 226–28, 227
    (table), 228 (fig.); prejudice reduction
    and, 229; of world politics, 43, 129–30,
    226–28. *See also* Foreign contacts
Knowledge Networks, 19, 67, 110
Know-Nothing Party, 142–43, 144, 222
Kohlberg, Lawrence, 78
Kohut, Andrew, 8, 58–59, 104, 119, 263
Koleva, Spassena P., 97
Koplow, Michael J., 184, 207
Korea, *see* North Korea; South Korea
Korean War, 101, 215–16
Krauthammer, Charles, 116
Kristof, Nicholas, 86–87
Krugman, Paul, 64, 66, 67, 162, 178
Kucinich, Dennis, 49
Kugler, Mathew B., 62
Kull, Steven, 25, 102
Kupchan, Charles A., 5, 265

LaGuardia, Fiorello, 143
LaHaye, Tim, 245
Laissez-faire economics, 54, 65, 67. *See
    also* Free trade
Lakoff, George, 39, 79
Lamont, Ned, 27
LaPierre, Wayne, 257
Laponce, Jean, 53
Larson, Arthur, 66
Latin America: foreign aid to, 149;
    foreign policy preferences toward,
    138–39; Hispanic views, 154–56;
    ideological differences in attitudes
    toward, 139; immigration from,
    143, 154; miscegenation, 140;
    paternalistic attitude toward,
    140–41; racial differences in
    attitudes toward, 154–55; U.S.
    relations with, 140–42, 149; warmth
    feelings toward, 137, 154–56. *See also
    individual countries*
Law of the sea treaty, *see* UN Convention
    on the Law of the Sea
League of Nations: Christian opposition,
    242–43, 246, 247, 248–49; Senate
    debate on, 101, 103, 141–42, 239–40,
    245, 250–51; supporters, 248; as threat
    to liberty, 255
Lee, Mike, 235
Left-right divisions, 53. *See also*
    Ideological differences
Leighton, Alexander, 106
Leno, Jay, 159
LePage, Paul, 174
Lewin, Kurt, 128
Liberalism ("Big L"), 33–36, 69–70
Liberals: aversion to war, 92–93, 105;
    compassion, 42, 84, 86–87, 88, 91–93,
    94–95; in Democratic Party, 17, 73, 87,
    268; foreign aid views, 151, 151 (fig.),
    152, 153 (fig.), 154; immigration policy
    views, 145–47, 146 (fig.); moral values
    prioritized by, 78–81, 83, 84–85, 88, 90,
    266; political, 54; provide orientation
    of, 90; psychological characteristics,
    37–38, 266; "small l," 34–35; social, 54.
    See also Cultural liberals; Democratic

Party; Economic liberals; Ideological differences

Libertarianism: anarchist, 69; anticommunism, 255–56; China policy preferences and, 224–26; communitarian critique of, 70–71; foreign policy preferences and, 172, 172 (fig.), 268; free trade, 49, 51 (fig.); individualism, 54, 70–71, 75–76; intellectual roots, 69–70; isolationism, 103; laissez-faire economics, 65, 67; political idealism support and, 113, 114

Libertarians: cultural liberals, 70; foreign aid views, 112, 150 (fig.), 152; psychological characteristics, 70; secular, 75; in Tea Party, 75; views of East Asian democracies, 231 (fig.), 231–32; views of government roles, 69; views of international organizations, 237, 253, 254–58, 255 (fig.); warmth feelings toward communist countries, 220; warmth feelings toward Israel, 195, 205. *See also* Paul, Ron; Teavangelical Republicans

Liberty, *see* Freedom

Libya, U.S. military attacks, 29, 127

Lieberman, Joe, 26–27, 204–5

Limbaugh, Rush, 143, 144, 222–23

Lincoln, Abraham, 169

Lindsey, Hal, 159, 180, 181, 247

Lippmann, Walter, 15

Literary Digest, 82, 83 (fig.)

Lobbyists, 233. *See also* Israel lobby

Locke, John, 69–70

Lodge, Henry Cabot, 142, 239–40, 250–51

Lorenz, Lee, 56, 57 (fig.)

Low, Seth, 173

Loyalty: of German Americans, 175–76; to in-group, 90–91, 92; to humankind, 90; immigration policy and, 147; as moral value, 78; warmth feelings and, 90–91, 91 (fig.)

Luck, Edward C., 249–50, 255, 257

Lugar, Richard, 26

Luther, Martin, 193

Madison, James, 1, 189

Madsen, Richard, 216

Maine, USS, 23–24

Mandelbaum, Michael, 5

Mann, James, 29, 127

Mann, Thomas C., 142

Manzanar "War Relocation Center," 214, 215 (fig.)

Margo, Robert A., 66

Martel, James, 179

"Massachusetts idea," 143–44, 147

Massee, J. C., 246

Mauldin, Bill, 68, 68 (fig.), 92–93, 93 (fig.), 105, 111 (fig.), 111–12, 153 (fig.), 154, 168 (fig.), 168–69, 195–96, 196 (fig.)

May, Ernest R., 23–24

McAlister, Melani, 190, 199, 201

McCarthyism, 255

McCaul, Michael, 232

McCloskey, Dierdre N., 21

McConnell, Mitch, 5

McCutcheon, John, 25

McFarland, Sam, 94–95

McGirr, Lisa, 256, 261

McGovern, George, 4, 69, 87, 126

McGregor, James, 234

McKinley, William: assassination, 61; Boxer Rebellion and, 224–25; election campaign (1900), 1–3, 55; foreign policy, 118–19; German American supporters, 176; Philippines colony and, 2–3, 82, 114; political cartoons, 2 (fig.), 3 (fig.), 23 (fig.), 83 (fig.); Spanish-American War, 1–3, 23–24

McKinley Tariff, 51

Mead, Walter Russell, 121–22, 184, 201, 206

Mearsheimer, John J., 183, 184, 206, 208

Media: elite cues transmitted, 130; entertainment, 179; influence on public's foreign policy attitudes, 16, 130; Iran hostage crisis coverage, 190; partisanship, 130, 131, 260

Media exposure: influence on foreign policy preferences, 130–31, 230; survey questions on, 130; views of United Nations and, 260

Median voters, 25, 269, 270

Melville, Herman, 187
Men, *see* Gender differences
Merkel, Angela, 69, 158, 178, 180
Mexico: border policy, 138–39, 144–49, 154; ideological differences in feelings toward, 137, 138, 138 (fig.); immigrants from, 143, 154; racial composition of population, 139; warmth feelings toward, 137, 154, 155–56
Middle East: Arab Spring, 199; history of U.S. engagement, 187–90; ideological differences in attitudes toward, 185–86, 199–202; racial differences in attitudes toward, 199; religious differences in attitudes toward, 196–99, 201–2; U.S. foreign policy toward, 183–84, 206–8; warmth feelings toward countries, 184–85, 185 (fig.). *See also* Arab-Israeli conflict; Iran; Israel
Midnight in Paris, 163–64
Militant internationalism, 15
Militarism: defense spending, 41 (fig.), 41–42, 42 (fig.); ideological differences, 41, 100–101, 105–6, 108; juxtaposed to diplomacy, 100–101, 105–8; political idealism and, 112–13; survey questions on, 100. *See also* War
Military strength: as guarantee of peace, 107–8; of Israel, 200–201; perceived, 45–47, 46 (fig.), 48
Miller, John J., 168, 173
Miniarchists, 69
Missionaries, in China, 212, 213–14, 218–19, 224
Missler, Chuck and Nancy, 182
Moderates: Democrats, 26–27, 73, 268; Republicans, 26, 27, 156, 261–62, 268, 270
Molesky, Mark, 168, 173
Monten, Jonathan, 236
Moodey, Joshua, 106
Mooney, Chris, 259–60
Moore, Barrington, 88–89
Moore, Michaela Hoenicke., 176
Moral empathy gap, 97
Moral values: binding, 78–79, 266; evolution of, 78; foreign policy

preferences and, 77, 90–97, 108, 266–67; ideological differences in priorities, 78–81, 80 (fig.), 266–67; individualizing, 78–79, 266; as mediators of ideology dimensions, 81–90; as mediators of social dominance orientation, 84–86, 95 (fig.), 250 (fig.), 250–51; as mediators of warmth toward foreign countries, 90–95; nationalism and, 120–21; survey questions on, 79. *See also* Authority; Compassion; Fairness; Loyalty; Purity
Moran, Jerry, 257–58
Morris, Dick, 253
Morrison, A. Cressy, 252
Mourdock, Richard, 26
Moyers, Bill, 88
Moynihan, Daniel Patrick, 252
MSNBC, 130, 131, 260
Mueller, John E., 15
Muldaur, Maria, 190
Multidimensional model of ideology, 52–55, 54 (fig.), 266. *See also* Ideology dimensions
Multilateralism: history, 239–41; ideological differences in support, 100, 104–5, 236–37; juxtaposed to unilateralism, 100, 103–5; liberal support, 100, 105, 258; public support, 103–4; survey questions on, 100. *See also* International organizations; League of Nations; Treaties; United Nations
Munich, 24
Muslims: seen as threat, 85–86, 189–90, 198–99, 200; warmth feelings toward, 184, 185 (fig.), 191, 192 (fig.), 200. *See also* Arabs
Myers, Cortland, 246

NAFTA, *see* North American Free Trade Agreement
Napier, Jaime L., 88
Narcissism, national, 118–20
Nast, Thomas, 62, 63 (fig.), 106–8, 107 (fig.), 108 (fig.), 221–22, 222 (fig.)
The Nation, 175

National Association of Evangelicals, 56
National identity: American, 115–16; ideological differences, 115–16; survey questions on, 116
Nationalism: Christian, 88; of conservatives, 99; of Democrats, 126; distinction from patriotism, 116, 204; foreign policy preferences and, 119–20, 121 (fig.), 166, 167 (fig), 203–4, 205 (fig.), 205–6, 298n76; of idealistic hawks, 122; ideological differences, 120–21; Middle East policy preferences and, 186; reactions to foreign contacts, 132–33, 133 (fig.), 229; relationship to patriotism, 116–18; of Republicans, 124–25, 126; social dominance orientation and, 166; superiority feelings in, 116, 117–18, 120, 172, 204; survey questions on, 116; warmth feelings toward England and, 171–72; warmth feelings toward Israel and, 205–6. See also Loyalty; Patriotism
National narcissism, 118–20
National Rifle Association (NRA), 257
National security, 41–42, 203, 237. See also Defense spending; Military strength
Nativists, 117–18, 142–44
Nature and nurture, 38–39, 266
Nazi Germany, 24, 176, 179, 193
Nelson, Knute, 114
New Deal, 65–66
News media, see Media
New Yorker, 56, 165, 165 (fig.), 198, 198 (fig.)
New York Times, 86–87, 178, 180
Niemi, Richard G., 38–39
9/11 attacks, 38, 102, 157
Nisbet, Robert, 64
Nitz, Michael, 231
Nixon, Richard M., 3–4
Nixon administration, détente with Soviet Union, 114, 189
Noer, Thomas, 251
North American Free Trade Agreement (NAFTA), 51
North Korea: feelings of U.S. public toward, 44, 44 (fig.), 299n7; Kim Jong-il's death, 256; U.S. foreign policy toward, 120, 298n76
NRA, see National Rifle Association

Obama, Barack: on American exceptionalism, 116; The Audacity of Hope, 87; Berlin speech, 115; communitarian rhetoric, 71, 76; compassion as priority, 92, 201; on equality, 77; foreign policy, 108, 112, 127, 262; foreign policy team, 126 (fig.), 127; idealism, 108, 112, 121, 127; international engagement, 102, 244; military force used, 29, 127; Nobel Peace Prize acceptance speech, 28; on Palestinians, 200, 201; pragmatism, 127; presidential campaign (2012), 27, 71, 207; on realism and idealism, 121, 127; religious beliefs, 28–29, 244; Republican opponents in Congress, 5; support for diplomacy, 105
Obedience, see Authority
Oberst, Conor, 146
O'Brien, Conan, 169
Oklahoma: "Americans Against the Next War" billboards, 203, 204 (fig.); no-smoking law, 74–75; senators, 4, 232, 235
The Oklahoma Daily, 74–75
Openness to new experience, 37–38, 164–65, 230
O'Reilly, Bill, 152, 168
Oren, Michael B., 183, 189–90
Orientalism, 190
Oxford Handbook of American Elections and Political Behavior, 16

Pacifism: of Christians, 106; in Israel, 195–96; during World War I, 24 (fig.), 24–25
Pagans, mixing with, 248–49
Page, Benjamin L., 8, 22, 25, 210, 236, 263, 265
Palestinians: ideological differences in attitudes toward, 186, 193, 195–96, 200; racial differences in attitudes toward, 199; U.S. foreign policy toward, 186;

warmth feelings toward, 184–85, 185 (fig.), 191, 192 (fig.), 196–99, 197 (fig.). *See also* Arab-Israeli conflict

Parents: family planning, 111; generational transmission of ideology, 38–39, 39 (fig.); spanking children, 86, 105

Paris Commune, 161

Parke, Harriet, 253

Partisan differences: among elites, 263, 264, 265; on foreign aid, 149; in foreign policy, 263–64, 265; ideological roots, 263, 265–66. *See also* Democratic Party; Republican Party

Partisan media exposure, 130, 131, 260

Partisan polarization: in Congress, 25, 262; denied, 40–41; on domestic policy, 41; of elites, 25; increased, 17

Partisanship: fluidity, 17–18; influence compared to ideology, 16–17; measures, 8, 19; parental socialization, 39, 39 (fig.); relationship to ideology, 17

Partisanship in foreign policy: consequences, 269–70, 271; criticism of, 1, 4, 270; of elites, 265; explanations, 4–5; history, 1–5; public opinion surveys, 8, 263; studies denying, 8, 263–64

Paternalism, 82, 140, 239

Paterno, Joe, 80

Patriotism: of conservatives, 91; distinction from nationalism, 116, 204; foreign policy preferences and, 119–20, 121 (fig.); ideological differences, 120–21; pure, 120; relationship to nationalism, 116–18; survey questions on, 116. *See also* Loyalty

Patton, George, 93

Paul, Rand, 103

Paul, Ron: German heritage, 103; isolationism, 99, 102, 103; opposition to foreign aid, 149, 152; opposition to wars, 4, 203; presidential campaigns, 4, 69; support of free trade, 49; on United Nations, 252–53; views of government roles, 69

Pelosi, Nancy, 57, 209

Pennsylvania Germans, 174–75

"Pennsylvania idea," 143, 145

Pennsylvania State University, child abuse scandal, 80–81

People's Republic of China (PRC), 215. *See also* China

Perez, Thomas E., 231

Perry, Matthew, 214

Perry, Rick, 56–57

Personal control, feelings of, 247–48

Personality traits: ideology and, 37–38; openness to new experience, 37–38, 164–65, 230; survey questions on, 38

Pettigrew, Thomas F., 229

Pew Research Center, 21, 104, 227, 263; Global Attitudes Project, 7, 8; News IQ quiz, 43, 129–30

Philippines, 1–3, 82, 83 (fig.), 106, 114

Phillips-Fein, Kim, 54, 66

Physiological differences, between liberals and conservatives, 38, 266

Piaget, Jean, 78

Pinker, Steven, 40

Pizarro, David A., 81–82

Polarization, *see* Partisan polarization

Political conservatives, 49, 54. *See also* Conservatives

Political idealism, 99, 109, 112–14. *See also* Idealisms

Political ideology, 54, 69–72; foreign policy preferences and, 55, 72, 102–3, 268; gender and, 37, 72; survey questions on, 72. *See also* Communitarianism; Libertarianism

Political liberals, 54. *See also* Liberals

Political psychology: applied, 14–15, 16; survey design, 18, 20–21

Polk, James, 161

Pollack, Kenneth M., 29

Polls, *see* Surveys

Popes, 249. *See also* Catholics

Populism, 122, 170

Poverty, 87–88. *See also* Foreign aid; Inequality

Power, economic, 227–28. *See also* Military strength

Pragmatism, 28

Pratto, Felicia, 62, 64
Prayer in public schools, 17, 60
PRC, see People's Republic of China
Prejudice: anti-Semitism, 187–88, 193;
against Asians, 218; against Catholics,
56, 142–43; against Chinese people,
217, 218, 221–23, 228–29, 230; contact
hypothesis, 133, 229; ideological
differences, 233; survey questions on,
63. See also Racism
Premillennial dispensationalism, 13,
244–45. See also Antichrist; Christian
Zionists
Presbyterian Church, 201–2, 243, 244, 247
Presbyterian of the South magazine, 241
Presidential election campaigns: foreign
policy issues, 1–4, 27, 55, 207; primary
voters, 27. See also Electoral politics
Preston, Andrew, 28, 40, 115, 189, 220, 243,
249
Primary elections: importance, 25, 207,
269; presidential, 27; voters, 25, 26–27,
156, 208, 261–62, 269, 270–71
Prince, Derek, 193
Prochaska, Frank, 169, 170–71
Profiles, see Foreign policy profiles;
Ideological profiles
Program on International Policy
Attitudes, 21, 133, 154, 184–85, 237
Progressive Christianity, 28, 40, 243–44.
See also Social Gospel
Prohibition, 56
Property: attitudes toward, 65; defense,
161–62; redistribution, 10, 64, 90, 152,
161, 162, 163, 219, 252
Protectionism, 50–51
Protestant ethic: foreign aid views and,
152; humanitarian idealism support
and, 110–12; survey questions on,
109–10; views of international
organizations and, 254, 255 (fig.),
256–57
Protestantism: Baptists, 78–79, 199,
246; foreign policy preferences, 122;
mainline, 28, 122, 152, 189, 194 (fig.),
195, 201–3, 218–19; Puritans, 106, 143,
173, 189; sermons, 78–79. See also

Christianity; Evangelical Christians;
WASPs
Psychological predispositions: ideology
and, 37–38, 266; in racism, 62–64. See
also Social dominance orientation
Psychology, 16, 43–44. See also Political
psychology
Public opinion: on domestic policy,
17; influence on foreign policy, 9,
22–25, 27, 206–8; influences on, 15–16;
partisanship, 8; stability, 15. See also
Surveys
Public Opinion Quarterly, 102
Puck magazine, 49–50, 51 (fig.), 96, 96
(fig.), 118–19, 119 (fig.), 140–41, 141
(fig.), 170, 171 (fig.), 175, 176 (fig.),
212–13, 213 (fig.)
Puerto Rico, 149
Punch Magazine, 103, 104 (fig.)
Puritans, 106, 143, 173, 189
Purity: Christian, 248–49; Christian
civilizing mission and, 82; as
conservative value, 81–82; cultural
traditionalism relationship, 81–83, 82
(fig.); in culture wars debates, 82–83;
economic inequality attitudes and, 87
(fig.), 89–90; foreign aid views and,
153; as moral value, 78; racial, 140,
250–51; views of United Nations and,
243, 243 (fig.), 250
Putnam, Robert D., 14, 58

Race relations: equality, 62, 63 (fig.),
84–85, 140; ideological differences
in views, 61–62, 84–85, 140;
miscegenation, 140. See also African
Americans; Whites
Racial differences: in attitudes toward
United Nations, 251; in views of Latin
America, 154–55; in views of Middle
East, 199
Racial purity, 140, 250–51
Racial thinking: feelings toward other
countries and, 139–40; in foreign
policy, 61, 141–42, 250–51; immigration
and, 61–62, 62 (fig.); stereotypes, 142;
in World War II, 176–77

Racism: against Asians, 212, 214, 218, 221–23; contact hypothesis, 133, 229; in foreign policy, 61; in immigration policy, 212, 214; moral values and, 218, 221–23; persistence, 233; psychological factors, 62–64; views of international organizations and, 249–51; violence, 231

Rand, Ayn, 70, 103

Rankin, John, 211, 214

Rarick, John R., 251, 257

Rathbun, Brian C., 40, 237

Rational choice theory, 77–78

Rationalist approach, 15–16

Rauschenbusch, Walter, 243

Reagan, Ronald: anticommunism, 219; Christian Zionism and, 191; conservative ideology, 71; defense spending, 42; "Evil Empire" speech, 55, 56, 219; "Global Gag Rule," 111–12; on Soviet Jews, 114; supporters, 62, 66; view of United Nations, 254

Realism: of American public, 122–23, 157; Christian, 28–29; compared to idealism, 108–9; in foreign policy, 45, 127; Hamiltonian, 121; of unilateralist hawks, 122; in U.S. foreign policy, 183

Reciprocal altruism, 78

Redistribution, income and property, 10, 64, 90, 152, 161, 162, 163, 219, 252

Reed, Jack, 203

Reed, James, 141–42, 249, 250

Reid, Harry, 4, 202, 203, 235–36

Reid, Whitelaw, 170

Reifler, Jason, 15

Religiosity: survey questions on, 49; warmth feelings toward Israel and, 194 (fig.), 194–95

Religious beliefs: foreign policy preferences and, 58–59; foreign policy profiles, 122, 123 (fig.); role in politics, 56–57. See also Biblical literalism; Christianity; Cultural ideology; Culture wars; Jews; Muslims

Religious freedom: in China, 209–10; in democracies, 114; protecting, 109,

114–15; in Russia, 188–89; in United States, 187

Religious idealism, 28, 99, 109, 114–15

Religious right, see Christian conservatives

Republican Party: China policies, 209–10, 226, 233; economic policies, 66–67; foreign policy preferences, 101–2, 105; foreign policy profiles, 122, 123 (fig.), 124 (fig.), 124–25, 268–69; Hispanic vote, 156; ideological profiles, 73 (fig.), 73–76, 268; immigration policies, 147, 154, 156; Middle East policies, 183–84, 194, 207, 245–46; moderates, 26, 27, 156, 261–62, 268, 270; platform (2012), 105, 114, 116, 147, 149, 154, 226, 230, 235, 245–46, 254; in post-Civil War era, 84–85; primary voters, 26, 27, 156, 261–62, 269, 270–71; in Southern states, 18; Taiwan policy, 230; trade policies, 51

Republic of China, see Taiwan

Respect, see Authority

Revolutions, 65, 88–89, 112–13, 161. See also American Revolution; French Revolution

Rice, Condoleezza, 106

Robertson, Pat, 245

Rockefeller, John D., 101

Rogers, William Allen, 224–25, 225 (fig.)

Rohrabacher, Dana, 226

Rommel, Erwin, 179

Romney, Mitt, 27, 67, 156, 202–3, 207, 226

Roosevelt, Eleanor, 169

Roosevelt, Franklin D.: economic policies, 65–66; New Deal, 65–66; relations with Latin America, 141, 149; United Nations and, 240–41; World War I experience, 92; Yalta Conference, 167, 241

Roosevelt, Theodore: foreign policy, 60, 61, 174; Nobel Peace Prize, 238–39, 239 (fig.); racial views, 139, 140; Russian Jews and, 189; in Spanish-American War, 1, 61; as vice president, 61, 176

Rosenau, James N., 15

Ross, Dennis, 183

Rothbard, Murray, 69

Rothman, Steve, 206
Rousseau, Jean-Jacques, 40
Rubio, Marco, 100, 102
Rumsfeld, Donald, 106, 165
Ruotsila, Markku, 242–43, 244
Rural backgrounds, 131–32, 132 (fig.)
Rushdoony, Rousas John, 247
Rusk, Dean, 251, 258
Russett, Bruce M., 104–5
Russia: Jews in, 188–89; U.S. foreign
    policy toward, 298n76. See also Soviet
    Union
Russo-Japanese War, 238–39
Ryan, Paul, 75–76

Sanctity, see Purity
Sandel, Michael J., 70–71
Sandusky, Jerry, 80
Santorum, Rick, 64, 67, 149, 203
Sarkozy, Nicolas, 162, 167
Satan, see Devil
Scheirman, Katherine, 203
Schurz, Carl, 175
SCM, see Stereotype content model
Scofield, C. I., 173
Scopes Trial, 56, 242–43
Scowcroft, Brent, 127
SDO, see Social dominance orientation
Secular humanism, 237, 244–45, 247
Secular libertarians, 75
Secular values, 60
Security, needs for, 37, 38. See also
    National security
Self-defense, 256–57
Self-help, see Protestant ethic
Senate: disability rights treaty debate,
    235–36, 257, 261–62, 270; Law of
    the Sea treaty debate, 4, 5, 270, 271;
    League of Nations debate, 101, 103,
    141–42, 239–40, 245, 250–51; McCarthy
    hearings, 255; primary voters, 26–27;
    ratification of UN Treaty, 241; Taiwan
    Caucus, 232. See also Congress
September 11 attacks, 38, 102, 157
Sermons, 78–79
Sexism, social dominance orientation
    and, 86

Sexuality: debates, 112; family planning,
    111; seen as impure, 82–83; traditional
    values, 54, 60. See also Homosexuality
Shapiro, Robert Y., 22
Sheffield, D. Z., 211
Shields, Mark, 261–62
Shweder, Richard A., 78
Sibley, Chris G., 147
Sidanius, Jim, 62, 64
Silver, Nate, 26
Singer, Andy, 145, 146 (fig.)
Situational factors, 16, 128, 131–34, 233. See
    also Foreign contacts; Media exposure
Six-Day War (1967), 189, 192–93, 195–96,
    200–201
Skocpol, Theda, 75, 200, 270
Slavery, 61, 84, 143
Slovic, Paul, 43
Smith, Arthur, 212
Smith, Christopher, 209–10, 223
Smith, Rogers, 61
Smith, Wilbur, 247
Sniderman, Paul, 43
Soccer, 116
Social conservatives: free trade views, 49,
    50, 52 (fig.); support of inequality, 54;
    in Tea Party, 75. See also Conservatives
Social Darwinism, 50, 56, 61
Social dominance orientation (SDO): of
    conservatives, 95–96; of Democrats,
    73; foreign aid views and, 150 (fig.),
    151; foreign policy preferences and,
    108, 139–40, 156, 267; foreign policy
    toughness and, 95 (fig.), 95–97, 166,
    167 (fig), 221; group-based dominance,
    62–63; humanitarian idealism support
    and, 110; ideological differences, 64;
    immigration policy and, 145, 145
    (fig.), 147, 156; isolationism and, 103;
    Middle East policy preferences and,
    186, 192 (fig.), 200; moral values as
    mediators, 84–86, 95 (fig.), 95–96, 250
    (fig.), 250–51; nationalism and, 166;
    opposition to equality, 64, 66–68, 89–
    90, 161, 252; racist views of Chinese,
    221; of Republicans, 73–74; survey
    questions on, 63; views of East Asian

democracies and, 230–31, 231 (fig.); views of United Nations and, 242 (fig.), 249–50, 250 (fig.)

Social Gospel, 28–29, 40, 242, 243, 244, 248

Social identities, 17, 90–91

Social ideology, 54, 60–64; foreign policy preferences and, 55, 61, 64, 102–3, 267; survey questions on, 63. *See also* Social dominance orientation

Socialism, 66. *See also* Communism; Welfare states

Social issues, *see* Culture wars

Social liberals, 54. *See also* Liberals

Solarz, Stephen, 232

Solidarity, needs for, 37, 38

Sorge, Friedrich, 161

South Africa, apartheid, 142

South America, *see* Brazil; Latin America

South Asia, *see* India

Southern states: biblical literalism, 59, 59 (fig.); Republican Party, 18

South Korea: ideological differences in attitudes toward, 230–32, 231 (fig.); warmth feelings toward, 210, 230–32, 231 (fig.), 299n7

Sovereignty, multilateralism as threat, 239–40, 241, 253, 254, 256–58, 261

Soviet Union: communist regime, 70, 219; Czech invasion, 34; détente, 114, 189; Jews, 114, 189; Reagan's view as evil empire, 56, 219

Sowell, Thomas, 33, 40, 89

Spanish-American War, 1–3, 23 (fig.), 23–24, 61

Spanking children, 86, 105

Stalin, Joseph, 167, 241

Stars and Stripes, 92, 93 (fig.)

Stereotype content model (SCM), 138, 159, 185

Stevenson, Adlai, I, 51

Stevenson, Adlai, III, 249, 251

Strategic bias theory, 16

Stuyvesant, Peter, 187

Sullivan, Mark, 175

Sumner, Charles, 84–85, 212

Surveys: Gallup, 236–37; on ideology and

foreign policy preferences, 5, 6, 20–21, 263, 264; methodology and design, 18–21, 264; on partisanship in foreign policy, 8, 263; statistical analysis of results, 21–22; on warmth toward foreign countries and international organizations, 6 (fig.), 6–7. *See also* American National Election Surveys; Chicago Council for Global Affairs; CNN; Pew Research Center

Taft, Robert, 101–2, 256

Taiwan: democracy, 232; ideological differences in attitudes toward, 230–32, 231 (fig.); Nationalist government, 215; UN membership, 255–56; warmth feelings toward, 210, 230–32, 231 (fig.)

Tancredo, Tom, 143

Tanner, John, 26

Tea Party: fear of Islam, 200; feelings toward, 75; members, 75, 270; opposition to UN Agenda 21, 253, 261

Teavangelical Republicans: antipathy toward United Nations, 253, 261, 270, 271; characteristics, 270; ideological profile, 74, 268; primary voters, 26, 27, 156, 261–62, 269, 270–71; warmth feelings toward Germany, 158, 180; warmth feelings toward Mexico, 156

Ten-Item Personality Inventory, 38

Terrorism: 9/11 attacks, 38, 102, 157; Palestinian, 201; war on terror, 157

"Texas GOP Platform," 194, 254

Thatcher, Margaret, 69, 71

Thompson, Bill, 170

Thwing, Eugene, 246

Time magazine, 190, 216, 234

Tocqueville, Alexis de, *see* De Tocqueville, Alexis

Toughness, *see* Foreign policy toughness

Tower, John, 251

Trade: with China, 209, 224, 228, 238; protectionism, 50–51. *See also* Free trade

Traditional cultural values, 60. *See also* Cultural traditionalism

Travel, *see* Foreign contacts

Treaties: bilateral, 238; disability rights, 235–36, 257, 261–62, 270; Law of the Sea, 4, 5, 270, 271; survey questions on, 237. *See also* International organizations; Multilateralism
Treier, Shawn, 53
Trivers, Robert L., 78
Tropp, Linda R., 229
Trubowitz, Peter L., 265
Truman, Harry S., 189, 233, 241, 263, 270
Trust: in Chinese government, 216–17; ideological differences, 40
Twain, Mark, 1–2, 61, 132, 159, 187

UN, *see* United Nations
UN Convention on the Law of the Sea (UNCLOS), 4, 5, 270, 271
Unilateralism: of Bush administration, 157; conservative support, 104–5; juxtaposed to multilateralism, 100, 103–5
Unilateralist hawks, 122, 123 (fig.), 123–24
United Kingdom, *see* Britain
United Nations (UN): Agenda 21, 253, 254, 261; Arms Trade Treaty, 257–58; communist member states, 255–56; disability rights treaty, 235–36, 257, 261–62, 270; dues, 241; former colonies as members, 249, 251, 252; founding, 240–41, 244, 255; gender differences in attitudes toward, 258; ideological differences in attitudes toward, 236–37, 241–50, 242 (fig.), 251–53, 254–61, 258, 267; law of the sea treaty, 4, 5, 270, 271; racial differences in attitudes toward, 251; seen as Antichrist, 244–45, 247, 267; seen as world government, 252, 253–54, 257; U.S. ambassadors, 241, 251, 252, 254; warmth feelings toward, 103–4, 236, 241–42, 242 (fig.), 254–55, 255 (fig.), 258–59
U.S.-China Business Council, 209, 233
U.S. Congress, *see* Congress
University of Oklahoma, Norman, 74, 75 (fig.)
Urban backgrounds, 131–32, 132 (fig.)
Utt, James B., 251, 257

Values, *see* Cultural values; Moral values
Vandenberg, Arthur, 3, 101, 270
Victoria, Queen, 118, 173
Vietnam War, 3–4, 15, 93, 94 (fig.), 126, 201
Villepin, Dominique de, 167
Violence, *see* Militarism; War
"Virginia idea," 143, 144 (fig.)
Voters, *see* Electoral politics

Wales, James Albert, 212–13, 213 (fig.), 218
Wallace, George, 142
Wall Street Journal, 161–62, 178, 180, 224
Walt, Stephen M., 48, 183, 184, 206, 208
Waltz, Kenneth, 45
War: avoiding through diplomacy, 106–7; conservative views, 92, 93; liberal aversion to, 92–93, 105; loyalty and, 92, 93; preemptive, 106. *See also individual wars*
Warmth feelings: toward international organizations, 6 (fig.), 6–7, 7 (fig.), 103–4, 180–82, 181 (fig.), 236; toward Tea Party, 75
Warmth toward foreign countries: communist countries, 34, 44; dictatorships, 34; foreign contacts and, 131–32, 132 (fig.); ideological differences, 6–7, 7 (fig.), 90, 158; Latin America, 137, 154–56; media influences, 130–31; moral values as mediators, 90–95; as predictor of foreign policy preferences, 43–48, 46 (fig.); survey results, 6, 6 (fig.), 264–65. *See also individual countries*
War of 1812, 1, 4–5
War on terror, 157
Warren, Elizabeth, 71
Washington, George, 1, 142, 143, 187, 238
Washington Post, 2, 33–34, 42, 88, 93, 238–39
Washington Times, 163–64
WASPs: cultural values, 60, 148–49, 153; English culture and, 170; Know-Nothing Party, 142–43, 144, 222. *See also* Whites
Weber, Robert, 198, 198 (fig.)
Webster, Daniel, 161

Weldon, Curt, 173
Welfare programs, 41, 41 (fig.), 42 (fig.), 66
Welfare states: in Europe, 69, 163, 178; in former colonies, 252
Wherry, E. M., 190
Whites: Baptists, 199; conservatives, 66; foreign aid views, 150 (fig.), 150–54; ideological differences in foreign policy preferences, 138–39; immigration policy views, 144–49, 145 (fig.); intergroup contacts and racism, 133; racial attitudes and feelings toward other countries, 139–40; warmth feelings toward Middle East, 199. See also Race relations; WASPs
Whiton, Christopher, 180
Wilhelm II, Kaiser, 175
Will, George, 28
Williams, Daniel K., 56, 219
Williamson, Vanessa, 75, 200
Wilson, Joe, 174
Wilson, Woodrow: Bryan and, 55; "Fourteen Points" speech, 238, 239; internationalism, 248; Nobel Peace Prize, 239; political cartoons, 240, 240 (fig.); progressive Christianity, 28, 241, 243; relations with Latin America, 139, 141; World War I, 113. See also League of Nations
Wilson-Gorman Tariff, 51
Wilsonians, 121–22, 127
Wittkopf, Eugene R., 15
Wolfe, Alan, 64
Women: equal pay, 86; "war on," 57. See also Gender differences

Wood, Leonard, 82, 83 (fig.)
World Bank, 103–4, 236. See also International organizations
World Christian Fundamentals Association, 245
World Cup, 116
World government, see International organizations; United Nations
World Knowledge Quiz, 129 (table), 129–30
World politics knowledge, 43, 129–30, 226–28
World Values Survey (WVS), 67, 88, 110, 120, 154
World War I: FDR's experiences, 92; images of Germans, 176; pacifism, 24 (fig.), 24–25; Treaty of Versailles, 103, 239, 246; U.S. entry, 101, 113
World War II: anti-Japanese attitudes, 214–15; cartoons, 92–93, 93 (fig.); ethnicity and support for U.S. intervention, 103; images of Germans, 176; in Italy, 92; in Pacific, 176–77, 214–15; Pearl Harbor, 101, 102; propaganda, 176–77, 214; racial thinking, 176–77
WVS, see World Values Survey

Xie, Tao, 210

Yoke fellowship, 248–49, 256
YouGov, 20, 36–37
YourMorals.org, 78

Zaller, John, 15
Ziliak, Stephen T., 21
Zionism, 245. See also Christian Zionists